PUBLICATIONS OF THE UNIVERSITY OF GEORGIA

THE DIPLOMATIC HISTORY OF GEORGIA

Sir Benjamin Keene

THE DIPLOMATIC HISTORY OF GEORGIA

A Study of the Epoch of
Jenkins' Ear

By

John Tate Lanning

Chapel Hill
The University of North Carolina Press
1936

COPYRIGHT, 1936, BY
THE UNIVERSITY OF NORTH CAROLINA PRESS

MANUFACTURED IN THE UNITED STATES OF AMERICA

The University of North Carolina Press, Chapel Hill, N. C.; The Baker and Taylor Company, New York; Oxford University Press, London; Maruzen-Kabushiki-Kaisha, Tokyo; Edward Evans & Sons, Ltd., Shanghai; D. B. Centen's Wetenschappelijke Boekhandel, Amsterdam.

THIS BOOK WAS DIGITALLY PRINTED.

To
FRANCES J. LEARY

FOREWORD

THE SPANISH period of Georgia's history began when Menéndez sailed up the coast in 1566 and left a garrison on St. Catherines Island as a defense against the French and a protection to a mission which he was soon to plant. Thereafter until 1763 this region south and west of Charles Town was claimed with varying insistence by Spain. The missions grew in number and in strength for a hundred years, but ultimately British aggressions caused them to recede and the last mission to disappear from Georgia in 1689. A definitive account of the religious activities of the Spanish in this region has recently appeared, written by Professor John Tate Lanning, of Duke University, and entitled *The Spanish Missions of Georgia.*

An even more important side of Spanish activities was concerned with the diplomatic struggle. There developed in this southeastern corner of North America a contest for supremacy among Spain, England, and France, which kept the diplomats of those nations busy for almost two hundred years. The chief antagonists were Spain and England, and although the struggle was carried on for the most part through the devious ways of the diplomats, these countries resorted to sterner methods in Queen Anne's War, the War of Jenkins' Ear, and in the French and Indian War. As a companion volume, rounding out the period of Spain in Georgia, Professor Lanning has here told the story of this other side. As in his first book, he has used the results of his research in the archives of the countries concerned, and has produced a work which untangles that little-known and complicated part of American colonial history.

This volume appears as the second of the *University of Georgia Publications*, a series planned and begun by Mr. Hughes Spalding while he was chairman of the Board of Regents of the University System of Georgia, and by Dr. Stedman V. Sanford, then President of the University of Georgia. Though this series is intended to be primarily the productions of members of the University faculty, Professor Lanning was invited to contribute these two volumes on account of the thorough study he has made in this field.

         E. MERTON COULTER
          For the Committee on Publications
           University of Georgia

PREFACE

THE ENGLISH frontier advanced southward from Virginia in three well-timed movements, each of which aroused the indignation and evoked the protests of the Spanish government. The first, extending from the efforts of Sir Walter Raleigh to those of John Smith, is best known. So acute was the situation in 1670, with the beginning of the second contest at Charles Town, that England and Spain guaranteed to each other all the possessions then held. In 1721, however, the English began to build forts in localities which had known the Spaniards for more than a hundred years. Thus, they ushered in the third epoch of diplomatic wrangling. It is the purpose of this work to chronicle this latter important phase of the story.

The Georgia diplomatic controversy raged until 1763, and was inextricably connected with the dispute about navigation in the West Indies. In 1739 the imperialists and disgruntled public forced the hand of the pacific but office-loving Walpole, and plunged England and Spain into the desultory War of Jenkins' Ear. For a brief period after the Treaty of Aix-la-Chapelle, 1748, the diplomatic cudgel was again taken up, but was permanently abandoned after the Treaty of Paris, 1763.

In this international conflict the Atlantic coast was definitely attached to England on Oglethorpe's cardinal principle that ultimately the only valid right was the ability to occupy, to dissemble, and to hold. Moreover, the monopolist ideals of men like Gerónimo Uztáriz, which were coming into vogue again in Spain, were thoroughly destroyed with the abandonment of the fleet system in 1748. As a study of English expansion, imperial affairs, and the practical reversal of the mercantile concept, this work makes only limited pretensions; yet it is a sketch of American diplomatic history in the first part of the eighteenth century. Over this period historians have hurried to the more glamorous events of the subsequent half century.

It is a well known fact that a book can no longer be the work of any one man. To record the names of contributors merely involves them in responsibility for a product the demerits of which are entirely divorced from their part in it. There are some, however, whose contribution to this undertaking has been so specific, or whose influence has been so vital, that not to mention their names would involve one in the risk of misunderstanding. Many important concrete obligations like that to Professor Bolton in the insert on the map entitled the "Crossing Lines of Anglo-Spanish Expansion," or that to Professor Crane in the early chapters, deserve a better fate; but they have been consigned to footnotes. Professor E. Merton Coulter of the University of Georgia published my first short studies on Georgia in 1927. Since then his confidence and interest have had no small part in the consummation of my work. My colleagues, Professor J. Fred Rippy and Professor Earl J. Hamilton, since the beginning of our acquaintance in the British Museum and the Archivo General de Indias in 1926-1927, have assumed a personal interest far beyond the casual requirements that men with similar concerns have a right to expect of each other. My indebtedness to Professor Herbert Eugene Bolton of the University of California could rightfully be confined to the preface of a single book only if another were never contemplated. Señor Juan Tamayo y Francisco, Director of the Archivo General de Indias, and José de la Peña y Cámara, secretary of the same institution, have been equally steadfast in the demands of research and the pleasure of friendship. Miss Helen Chandler of Gastonia has generously given me the advantage of her keen critical faculties. The map on the Cartagena expedition and another on the conflict of Anglo-Spanish expansion were drawn by Dr. Ben F. Lemert who, in the capacity of cartographer, is frequently taxed by his colleagues. He aways gives bountifully and cheerfully of his time and talents.

JOHN TATE LANNING

Washington, D. C.
June 17, 1934

CONTENTS

	Page
FOREWORD, by Professor E. Merton Coulter	vii
PREFACE	ix

Chapter

I. THE ISSUE	1
II. FIRST DIPLOMATIC JOUSTS	7
III. FOUNDING A COLONY: CONFERENCES IN GEORGIA AND FLORIDA	34
IV. DON MIGUEL WALL AND THE SPANISH ATTEMPT AGAINST THE EXISTENCE OF GEORGIA	55
V. SPANISH ALARUMS AND ENGLISH EXCURSIONS IN EUROPEAN DIPLOMACY	85
VI. GEORGIA IN THE CONVENTION OF PARDO: THE FIRST PHASE	124
VII. GEORGIA AND THE FAILURE OF THE CONVENTION OF PARDO: THE DIPLOMATIC COLLAPSE OF 1739	154
VIII. FORCING THE HAND OF WALPOLE: THE DRAMA OF 1739 IN AMERICA	174
IX. AMERICA AND JENKINS' EAR	204
X. THE SEAL OF OGLETHORPE'S DIPLOMACY	220
XI. THE END OF A HALF-CENTURY OF NEGOTIATIONS	230
BIBLIOGRAPHY	237
INDEX	257

THE DIPLOMATIC HISTORY OF GEORGIA

CHAPTER I

THE ISSUE

> Has Heaven reserved, in pity to the poor,
> No pathless waste, or undiscovered shore?
> No secret island in the boundless main?
> No peaceful desert, yet unclaimed by Spain?
> JOHNSON's *London* (1738)

THE SPANISH EMPIRE in America was not built while the rest of Europe slumbered; that empire was created and sustained in the face of natural obstacles in the New World and international opposition from the Old. Yet so great was the ascendency which a few years leeway gave Spain, that for almost a century determination openly to compete for dominion in America was not proclaimed in England. Her efforts were confined to the lucrative practice of semi-official buccaneering. And almost two hundred years elapsed before Spain admitted the right of England in America. Spain, however, was aware of the unheralded contest. When Georgia in the eighteenth century assumed a paramount place in European diplomacy and threatened to break the peace of Europe, interested persons in both countries turned their eyes to the vague but grim panorama through which England and Spain had tacitly passed into the then *status quo*. As if gazing at an illuminated prism from distinct perspectives each nation espied different colors—their national ones.

There was no express stipulation relating to America in any of the treaties concluded between the crowns of England and Spain before 1667. The eighth article of the Treaty of Peace and Commerce, concluded in that year, granted to the English in both the Indies all that was granted to the States General by the Treaty of Münster in 1648. To each party all possessions then held in America were thereby confirmed.[1] This

---

[1] Earl of Marchmont, *A State of the Rise and Progress of Our Disputes with Spain*, p. 2.

was the same vexatious problem which had been passed over silently in 1604, just on the heels of Governor Gonzalo Méndez Canzo's disclosure of English designs on the coast, and again in 1630 when English colonization was no longer a matter of dread conjecture to Madrid. In America, however, the Elizabethan tradition had it that Spaniards and Englishmen might commit depredations or even make war against each other without disturbing the tranquil relations of the two countries in Europe. Doubts arose, therefore, as to whether this treaty of 1667 referred to America. These doubts were obliterated in the next pact. The American Treaty of 1670 expressly stipulated in Article VII that the British should keep forever all they then possessed in the New World.[2]

In the fury of debate, and in complete ignorance of the activities of the Spanish on the Atlantic coast, it occurred to imperialistic merchants in 1739 that the concessions of this treaty were too great; because, ran the argument, England placed herself under obligation not to trade with the American subjects of the crown of Spain, a right Spain would hardly have been able to assert. But England neither hearkened to nor obeyed that part of the treaty which limited her trade—only that which extended her domain.[3]

By the Treaty of Utrecht of 1713, a document ever memorable in the commercial history of Spanish America, the English, instead of emphasizing what they then held, took care to provide that "neither the Catholic King, nor any of his heirs or successors whatsoever shall sell, yield, pawn, transfer, or by any means, or under any name alienate from them and the Crown of Spain to the French or to any other nations whatever, any Lands or Dominions, or Territories, or any part thereof belonging to Spain in America." The government even agreed to give assistance to the Spaniards in restoring their ancient limits and possessions if they appeared to have been broken into or lessened since the death of Charles II of Spain

---

[2] *Loc. cit.;* State Papers Foreign (hereafter cited as S. P. F.), Spain, Treaty Papers, 67, Additional Manuscripts in the British Museum (hereafter cited as Add. MSS), 33005. Lewis Hertslet, *A Complete Collection of Treaties and Conventions*, II, 197.

[3] *Great Britain's Complaint against Spain*, pp. 3-4; J. T. Lanning, "The American Colonies in the Preliminaries of the War of Jenkins' Ear," *Georgia Historical Quarterly*, XI (June, 1927), 129-55.

in 1700. The agreement was ratified and renewed in the treaty of 1721.[4]

Thus sovereignty in the disputed territory was to be determined by the extent of the limits in 1700; but were those limits determined by the original discovery, royal grants, or actual occupation? The British attempted to sustain their case on all three counts. They were indefatigable in emphasizing the alleged discoveries made by Sebastian Cabot along the American coast from the fifty-sixth to twenty-eighth degree of northern latitude under the auspices of King Henry VII in 1497. This they said was two decades before any European visited the North American continent. The names of Peter Martyr, Oviedo, Herrera, Gómara, and Ramusio were conjured up to lend credibility to an uncertain story.[5] Once more, many years after Spanish conquistadores had traversed the South with the diaries of their predecessors in their hands, it was urged that under the patronage of some gentlemen merchants in Cromwell's time a group of men "discovered all the coast of Florida from the Bay of Apalachy on the West Side of the Peninsula of Florida for about two hundred miles and within twenty leagues of the River Majchebee."[6]

Many tomes, original and authoritative, have been devoted to Spanish discoveries in the "Continent of Florida" in the century and a quarter before Cromwell. In laying a structural foundation for the claim by right of discovery, the Spaniards recited the details of the founding of St. Augustine and of the expeditions of Juan Ponce de León and Hernando de Soto. By right of discovery England's claims could rest only on the rather obscure voyage of Sebastian Cabot.[7]

The problem of right in the new world, when devoid of all dissimulation and metaphysics, reduced itself to the ability of the contestants to seize and to hold by force if necessary. Reasonably enough, especially in the light of the concessions of the Spanish in 1667 and 1670, the universal right to all America

---

[4] Add. MSS, 33005, Diplomatic Papers, I, 220, 227, 271.

[5] Daniel Coxe, *A description of the English Province of Carolana, by the Spaniards call'd Florida, and by the French la Luisiane, as also of the Great and Famous River Meschacebe or Missisipi*, p. 114.

[6] Add. MSS, 15903, p. 117.

[7] M. Serrano y Sanz (ed.), *Documentos Históricos de la Florida y la Luisiana*, pp. 20-88; *Old England Forever, or Spanish Cruelty Displayed*, p. 25.

could not belong to the Spaniards merely because of their being the first Europeans to get sight of the unknown land. Pointing out this fact, a contemporary English writer continued: "It must then follow, that they ground their *Claim* upon their actual *Possession;* and, if so, such *Claim* cannot extend to any Parts whereof they never were possessed."[8]

With astounding lack of knowledge of the string of actual settlements which Spain maintained from her Florida base to Port Royal Harbor between 1566 and 1670, Oglethorpe and his supporters based their arguments to substantiate their supposed rights by previous occupation on the raid of Sir Francis Drake at St. Augustine, the charters of King Charles II, the submission of the Indians, and the occupation of a small fortress for a period which no Englishman appeared willing to define. Detachments from the English garrison on the Altamaha during this indefinite time were reputed to have occupied the coast as far south as 30° 2'. The only question which Oglethorpe would admit was whether or not the twenty-ninth degree belonged to England or Spain.[9]

Almost as singular as the raid of Sir Francis Drake on St. Augustine were the grants of Charles I as bases for the claim to the Old Southwest. A large grant of this land was made to the Earl of Arundel, and was afterward assigned to Dr. Daniel Coxe, who called the country Carolana. In 1629 he sent two hundred people there to make settlements, intending to dispatch more settlers later and to make Sir William Welles governor, an undertaking which the hostility of the French caused to be suspended and the territory to be neglected.[10] In 1630 Charles I gave to Sir Robert Heath a patent of all America from the River St. Mathias in thirtieth degree north latitude to another river in the thirty-sixth degree, in longitude extending from the Atlantic to the Pacific, territory said not to be "in actual Possession of any Christian Prince or State." No claim to the Bay of San Marcos or to New Mexico therein included was seriously expressed.[11]

---

[8] *Old England Forever*, p. 39.

[9] Colonial Office Papers (hereafter cited as C. O.) 5/654, Oglethorpe's Memorandum on Georgia, August 18, 1737.

[10] C. O. 5/384, Papers of Governor Bull to the Secretary of State; Coxe, *op. cit., passim.*

[11] *Ibid.*, p. 116.

THE ISSUE

In 1663 and again in 1665 King Charles II of England by letters patent made grants to some of his subjects who established a colony and laid the permanent foundations of Carolina. The grant in 1663 to eight patentees extended from Virginia to the River St. Johns. In 1665 a new grant pushed the boundary to the 29° below St. Augustine. These grants superceded the grant to Sir Robert Heath, but within their boundaries were to fall the lands assigned to the Georgia Company. It appears that to a Britisher, granting and actual occupation were synonymous. The Spaniards alleged the Georgia charter was diametrically opposed to the seventh article of the Treaty of Utrecht; but, said the English, by the eighth article of the same treaty it could have no farther retrospect than the decease of King Charles II of Spain in 1700, thirty-five years after the last Carolina grant. That argument could not be admitted by a contestant who recognized the incompatibility of granting what one did not have, a vulnerable position which no interested Spaniard failed to assail.[12] The Catholic King's ministers would never recognize any *status quo* except that of 1670, the year of the American Treaty. They took note of the English legal sophistry that sustained the usurpations made before the end of the seventeenth century and ironically asked by what specious reasoning England could attempt to justify so many seizures since 1700.[13]

---

[12] *Great Britain's Complaint against Spain*, pp. 65-66; Don Iñigo Abad y Lasiera, *Relación del Descubrimiento, Conquista y Poplación de las Provincias y Costas de la Florida*, 1785, in M. Serrano y Sanz, *op. cit.*, pp. 89-93, summarizes the sound claims of Spain which she even then advanced on the ground of actual possession: "A expensas de mucha sangre, de inmensos gastos y trabajos estaban los españoles poblados y en pacífica posesión (como se ha visto en los capítulos antecedentes) del país comprendido desde la altura de Polo septentrional de 33° hasta los 25, en que por la parte oriental se termina el continente de la Florida, firme, hasta 150 leguas en lo interior de las provincias de Guale, Coabe, Orista, Timucua, Santa Fe, San Martín, San Pedro, Acile, Vitachuco, Apalache, Cabeta, Apalachicola, Atalapuses y otras y que las los ingleses se hicieron indebidamente dueños desde el cabo y bahía de Santa María hasta la Carolina ó Charlestown del Sur cuando Carlos II, rey de la Gran Bretaña, y el Señor Carlos II, rey de España, accordaron solemnemente un tratado y amigable composición para restaurar y conciliar en las Indias occidentales la paz y buena correspondencia interrumpida por varias y mutuas injurias y depredaciones que se experimentaban." Would England, he continues, have conceded to the Court of Spain absolute dominion over all the West Indies if the concession were against her real right? At this late date Spain was urged to reclaim the Georgia country from 33° to 30° and 26'.

[13] Archivo General de Simancas (hereafter cited as A. G. S.), Sec. de Estado,

In the last resort international comity was cast aside. The issue was first seriously joined in 1721 by Don Jacinto Pozobueno, maintained by Don Tomás Geraldino with pacific but troublesome persistency until the debacle of 1739, and finally solved by domination.

---

legajo 7633 (antiguo), Conde de Montijo to the King, San Lorenzo, 9 November, 1737, puntos 10-15; Marqués de la Regalia to the King, Madrid, 30 November 1738, puntos 32-37; Joseph de Layssequilla to the King, Madrid, 4 December, 1738, puntos 6-8; Joseph de Quintana to the King, Madrid, 5 December, 1738, puntos, 3-9; Andrés González de Barcía to Conde de Montijo, Madrid, 21 February, 1739, puntos 3-6. Further powerful testimony that Spain never acquiesced in English southward thrusts after 1670 can be seen in the royal cedula of June 20, 1671, and another in 1675, generally for the expulsion of the English in the defence of Florida, and specifically for the preservation of St. George. *Ibid.*, Montijo to the King, San Lorenzo, 9 November, 1737, puntos 3, 5; Layssequilla to the King, 5 December, 1738, punto 3.

CHAPTER II

FIRST DIPLOMATIC JOUSTS

THE PAWN in international decisions in Georgia was the Indian tribe; the object, supremacy, and the enemy, Spaniards or Englishmen. Ambassador Don Pedro de Zúñiga had tried in vain to impress upon his sovereign, Philip III, the fact that one successful English settlement, which Philip III refused to think Jamestown would be, meant a process of development which would ultimately put the Spanish on the defensive.[1] A half century of conflict with the English traders in the Florida territory, however, had aroused the thorough antagonism of the Spaniards. The Yamasee War of 1714-1716 had jeopardized the very existence of Carolina. The resulting feeling of insecurity led the English to a tacit but open avowal of policy. Twenty-five years before the founding of Georgia a fantastic project for a buffer colony, Azilia, had found its way to the pigeon hole,[2] but when in 1721 Governor Francis Nicholson sent Colonel John Barnwell to build a fort at the mouth of the Altamaha, a point the Spaniards had occupied as well as claimed, a diplomatic battle was joined which ceased only when Spain was displaced in the old South by the Treaty of Paris. The curtain on the pungent truth which Zúñiga had sought to impress upon Spain was thereby rung up. Although even the Spanish officials could discern the new dilemma, Governor Antonio de Benavides y Bazán of Florida was the first to face the new problem. Meanwhile the English danger was clearly revealed in the Azilia project.[3]

---

[1] A. G. S., Secretaría de Estado, leg. 844, fols. 44, 50; I. A. Wright," Spanish Policy towards Virginia, 1606-1612," *American Historical Review*, XXV (April, 1920), 452.

[2] H. E. Bolton and Mary Ross, *The Debatable Land*, p. 69; C. C. Jones, *History of Georgia*, I, 70-75; *South Carolina Historical Society Collections*, II, 232-33.

[3] The best succinct treatment of the Azilia scheme is Verner W. Crane, *The Southern Frontier*, pp. 210-14, upon which this account is based. The purely Eng-

The Margravate of Azilia, the best known of the pre-Georgia schemes, was designed to solve the problem of southern defense in almost a feudal manner, even after the failure of the Carolina proprietors. It embraced exactly the region which fifteen years later became Georgia. Sir Robert Montgomery, the projector, was a Scotch baronet, and his interest in colonization was a family one. His father backed Lord Cardross in bringing Scottish settlers to South Carolina and in the founding of Stuart's Town. The very environment—its stories and descriptions—then lured him into colonial affairs and inspired him with an affection for the southern marches.[4] Fellow-projectors were Amos Kettleby, discharged agent of South Carolina, and Aaron Hill, the poet.[5] This was probably the first literary enlistment of Georgia which became so famous for flamboyant descriptions. The very name "Azilia" was eloquent of decadent feudalism.

The petitions of the projectors for deeds of lease were promptly met, conveying to Montgomery and his heirs "All that Tract of Land which lies between the Rivers Altamaha and the Savanna."[6] The right to distribute all unoccupied lands beyond the Altamaha was reserved, and in accordance with lessons already learned in America, there were to be no taxes or obstructions to the navigation of Azilian rivers. In 1717 Montgomery published his well-known *Discourse* concerning this most delightful country of the universe. "Paradise with all her Virgin beauties may be modestly supposed at most but equal to its native Excellencies," declared the lavish advocate in a Goldsmith strain. Yet the plan for peopling this paradise was as artificial and unreal as its description was rapturous; it consisted of four-square tracts for gentlemen-tenants and concentric zones for towns and in the center the Margravate's palace. Many were the exotic and bizarre commodities to abound—wine, silk, and spices.

That this paradise was to be thrust up against the very mouths of Spanish guns was not emphasized. Its buffer nature

---

lish citations and data concerning Fort King George, John Barnwell, Charlesworth Glover, and Tobias Fitch come from the same authority.

[4] *Dictionary of National Biography*, XXXVIII, 321.

[5] C. O. 5/387, fol. 8; Dorothy Brewster, *Aaron Hill: Poet, Dramatist, Projector* (New York, 1913), pp. 50-59.

[6] C. O. 5/1265, Q 144, 145.

would not attract colonists. Aware of Cardross's disaster, Montgomery hoped his colony would not only stand firm but would protect others, for "a British Colony shou'd, like the Roman, carry with it always something of the Mother's Glory." The projectors, moreover, planned to surround each settlement with fortifications. Montgomery hoped to be governor for life. In July, 1717, the Proprietors recommended the project to the Privy Council.[7]

The petitions and appeals to the colonial authorities placed great emphasis on Azilia's strategic value, Anglo-Spanish and Anglo-French rivalry. It might ultimately cut through to the Gulf of Mexico and check the encircling movement and designs of the French. Acting on the warnings of the Carolinians and Governor Alexander Spotswood of Virginia, the Board of Trade received the scheme with favor, but the insistence of the Lords of Trade that the Proprietors surrender their powers of government brought the scheme to rest until 1720.[8] Hill tried to grasp the falling banner from Montgomery's hands, and appealed to noble patronage and projected a lottery in Scotland, but in this era of bubbles Azilia had many rivals for the favor of the speculative public. William Paterson, another Scotchman, and his Darién scheme had left many credulous and greedy Englishmen gaping. The collapse of the South Sea Stock was not an unheeded lesson. Transformed into a bubble, it burst as the current of speculation ebbed and suddenly disappeared,[9] but not before Azilia had gained a place on the maps and in the current pamphlets. This was the proprietor's only show of appreciation of the strategic needs of the Carolina colony and the possible profit of peopling the Golden Isles.[10]

It was Fort King George and not Azilia, which foreshadowed the establishment of the buffer colony of Georgia and the most bitter international problems. The vigilant leader of the southern frontier was the famous Carolinian John Barnwell. In England in 1719 it was the second purpose of Barnwell to convert the authorities there to a vigorous program of defense on the southern march. No one was better qualified to play this rôle

---

[7] C. O. 5/1265. Journals of the Board of Trade, 20 February, 1718.
[8] *Ibid.*, Q 146.
[9] Historical MSS, Commission Report, pt. IV, 256.
[10] *An Account of the Foundation and Establishment of a Design now on Foot for a settlement on the Golden Islands, to the South of Port Royal in Carolina* (London, 1720).

since the death of Captain Nairne, trader, geographer, diplomat. Barnwell's suggestions, based on the Carolina Indian system, were conceived on a truly continental scale. There is little doubt that the anti-French strategy of Governor Spotswood was taken from this Beaufort planter. Advice on the matter was sought from those lately interested in Azilia. Fortunately Barnwell in this interval frequented the lodge of General Francis Nicholson, soon to be sent out as governor. It was Barnwell who for all practical purposes wrote the governor's instructions for 1720.

The idea of French encirclement was a very alarming item in the late report of the assembly. The "French particularly pretend a Right to the River May," suggested the report. Nor was the ever-present menace of St. Augustine forgotten. These were the necessities urged for occupation of the mouth of the Altamaha.[11] Savannah Town, Pensacola, and the Altamaha, speedily fortified and garrisoned, would serve the purpose.

Still more unfortunate for Anglo-Spanish relations, Barnwell expected these outposts to become the nuclei of settlements, and the garrisons to support themselves from the adjacent land. A conference, presaging the Albany Congress of 1754, was suggested. Great interest was evinced by the celerity with which the Board of Trade endorsed the suggestions. This was an open imitation of the French plan of fortified frontier posts, and perhaps commended itself to the British government for that reason. Four battalions were to be sent to each location, but at Barnwell's insistence the Carolina outpost was to be established immediately. An emergency report was submitted along with Nicholson's instructions. It appears certain that the origins of that policy which was to run the gauntlet of Anglo-Spanish diplomacy for more than a quarter of a century were colonial. The resolution "not to suffer any other Nation to take possession of any Part of the said River, or of the Sea Coasts from Port Royal to St. Augustine" was one whose history was to be that of trouble.[12]

In this manner began the occupation of Guale, the Spanish name for the Indian province of Georgia, in the discussions of which no allusions were made to Spanish rights. It was at the behests of the Carolinians that the occupation of the country

---
[11] Journals of the Board of Trade, 16 August, 1720; C. O., 5/358, A 7, 8.
[12] C. O. 5/358, A 11.

which after a decade was to become Georgia began in 1721. The assembly at Charles Town, at the expense of a thousand pounds, prepared for the occupation, and there was genuine anxiety to hold the Altamaha. To desert the place at the mouth of this river would mean that "the Spanish or French would take immediate possession."[13] Although Fort King George was primarily designed against the French, it was a flagrant intrusion into Spanish territory. Not a half century had gone by since Spanish mission bells from Santo Domingo and Tolomato had sounded over the Bocas de Talaje, and in that interval Spain had not relinquished her title. Evidence that Barnwell expected the enmity of the Spanish is revealed in his selection of the more sheltered mainland, rather than St. Simons Island, where Spaniards before and Oglethorpe afterwards built their defenses, as a site for his fort.

In 1720 King George I ordered the governor of South Carolina to secure the Altamaha with a contingent of a hundred men and to build a fort designed to control the navigation of that stream and to insure British domination in the region. The fort which was consequently constructed at the mouth of the Altamaha on an "unsound site" was accidentally destroyed by fire and rebuilt by South Carolina, but in a very unsubstantial manner. The lonely fortress was manned by soldiers too lazy to fish and hunt or even to build corrals for the cattle sent them by Governor Nicholson. Needless to say, wholesome water and vegetable gardens were not arranged and unhealthiness was soon added to indolence. Unfortunately for the English diplomats, the post was abandoned within a few years and although memorialized to reëstablish the fort, the English never did so. In urging the English claims, however, this post was never forgotten. Naturally Governor Benavides of Florida took umbrage at this aggressiveness.[14]

Notwithstanding that a general peace was already published, Governor Benavides had already been compelled to complain to the court at Madrid in 1720 against the constant hostilities and excesses of the English and Indians along the Florida-Carolina boundary, which old issue embittered the delicate

---

[13] *Journals of the Commons House of Assembly*, June 15, 1722.

[14] Jones, *op. cit.*, I, 70; B. R. Carroll (ed.), *Historical Collections of South Carolina*, I, 236, 240, 254, 257-59, 278, 280, 281, 282-92; Edward McCrady, *The History of South Carolina under the Royal Government*, pp. 32, 25, 54-55.

boundary question. The Spanish minister Marqués de Grimaldo took up the cue in an energetic fashion. To the Spanish ambassador at London he dispatched the orders of his king to pass a vigorous memorial to the court at London, demanding a repetition of the orders suspending arms as a result of the general truce. At the same time he called upon the English Ambassador at Madrid, William Stanhope, to transmit the same instance to his court.[15]

The memorial was obediently presented. The Floridians, Pozobueno complained, "could not stir out of their houses to cultivate their lands, nor turn out their cattle without apparent danger from the said Indians." England complied with the Spanish wishes. John Lord Carteret wrote promptly to the governor of South Carolina, enclosing a copy of the official note handed to him by Pozobueno, and with this communication went the king's command to permit no act of violence either by Indian or Carolinian. Every effort was to be made to secure and to preserve a good correspondence with the subjects of Spain in Florida.[16]

A second protest and duplicate of the order of September 6 was forwarded to Nicholson on November 28.[17] The observance of these instructions was, in America at least, nothing more than a hollow truce, and in Europe scarcely more than diplomatic dallying. At this juncture of diplomatic maneuvering and military recuperation, the construction of Fort King George at the mouth of the Altamaha was spark enough to relight the torch.

The building of the Fort King George had cost the English almost as much trouble as it later caused the Spanish in attempting its removal. Barnwell arrived from London on H.M.S. *Enterprise*, May 2, 1721, with Governor Francis Nicholson—both imperialists. His expansionist scheme was almost defeated by official lethargy in England. Instead of the battalion needed and requested, came a company—invalids instead of hardy

---

[15] Archivo Histórico Nacional (hereafter cited as A. H. N.), sec. IX, Papeles de Estado, leg. 1705, Benavides to the king, St. Augustine, 30 September, 1720; Grimaldo to Pozobueno, Madrid, 24 March, 1721.

[16] *Ibid.*, sec. IX, leg. 1705, Pozobueno's memorial, London, 28 April, 1721; *ibid.*, legajo 1720, Carteret to Nicholson, Whitehall, 6 September, 1721. C. O, 5/387, fol. 64. This letter, written in French, was enclosed in Pozobueno's dispatches to Madrid.

[17] C. O. 5/387, fol. 64.

soldiers and young skilled craftsmen, engineers, carpenters and smiths. As a makeshift, it was proposed that some scouts should take possession with a "palissado Fort and a few Huts."[18] After the concurrence of the governor and council, Barnwell was given command of the southern coasts, to take possession in the name of the king "for the use of the crown of Great Britain." If attacked either by Indians or Europeans he was to "repel force by force." But the scouts on whom this undertaking so largely depended had lost in his absence all semblance of discipline and were "continually sotting if thay can get any rum for Trust or Money." With twenty-six of these characters, "all drunk as beasts," one carpenter and his Indian slaves Barnwell made rendezvous in the embouchure of the Altamaha. After exploring the region he selected a site on the northern branch formerly occupied by the Huspaw Indian people which was, except for the depots of traders, the first English settlement in Georgia.

The erection of the fort was a Herculean task. Cypress timber for the purpose was dragged from the swamp by wading waist deep. By such slavery, the horrors of which were augmented by the swarms of vigorous mosquitoes, was built a gabled block house twenty-six feet square with fascines, palisades and a moat, and grandly named Fort King George—a frontier improvisation ridiculed by the king's own officers.[19]

Governor Benavides protested to Governor Nicholson.[20] At the same time he represented to the court at Madrid the jeopardy in which he conceived the Spanish dominions to be standing. Fresh on the heels of Indian massacres, the erection of this fort augured an English policy of relentless expansion. Each day, charged the governor of St. Augustine, the English augmented their settlements and assured their domination. In letters of April 19 and 21 these general surmises were dispatched to Madrid with the more specific information that the fort erected was within less than a hundred miles of St. Augustine itself, was manned by fifty soldiers, but as yet was inadequately fortified since its mounted guns numbered only five.

---

[18] C. O. 5/328, A 34, "Letters and Papers relating to Landing His Majesty's Independent Company now in South Carolina . . . and likewise concerning Coll. Barnwell's going to Altamaha River in order to build a Fort there."

[19] C. O. Maps, Georgia, 1, 2, 4, 5, 7, 8.

[20] Carroll, *op. cit.*, I, 270; McCrady, *op. cit.*, pp. 53-54.

At the instigation of Benavides, a Spanish officer went to reconnoitre and to ascertain additional facts. The commandant sullenly refused him admission. In a final attempt to secure an agreement, Don Francisco Menéndez Marqués, auditor at St. Augustine, headed a diplomatic mission to Carolina. He proposed to settle by treaty all matters at issue. To the first point of his instructions—a suspension of arms—Menéndez obtained expressions of good faith since this would constitute a guarantee against the excesses of the Indians and the English and had already been voiced by both the governor of Florida and Pozobueno. Aside from instructions to secure regulation of partisan warfare, Menéndez was directed to demand the return of certain Negro and Spanish prisoners. To enforce this argument, he hinted at retaliation. At the same time he asked the motive for the construction of the disagreeable Fort King George. The response was that the governor and assembly of South Carolina had an order from the King of England to expand his fortifications and settlements, "for the better securing his Majesty's dominions," which order would be maintained so long as he saw fit.

The crowning stroke was Nicholson's declaration that he had no powers to make a treaty. He took occasion, however, warmly to resent charges of ill usage of Spanish prisoners and to make a counter claim for runaway slaves and prize vessels taken since the peace. He then very shrewdly invited the Spaniards to define those tribes claimed as subjects of Spain. To all overtures Nicholson steadfastly refused to issue a formal response.[21]

At last the boundary question was squarely raised. Benavides, upon the return of his agent, Menéndez, lost no time in reporting the situation to the Council of the Indies, accusing Nicholson of aiming to capture St. Augustine and to command the Bahama Channel.

In view of the grave injuries which seemed likely to result to Spanish rights by virtue of sufferance, the Marqués de Grimaldo, Spanish Secretary of State, instructed Pozobueno, the ambassador in London, to make the most efficacious offices possible; to lodge a firm complaint against erecting a fort in

---

[21] C. O. 5/358, A 103, A 104.

Spanish territory, and to demand the demolition of Fort King George on the Altamaha.[22]

Meanwhile the Florida commissaries continuously pestered South Carolina. With every new overture the suspicions that the missions were designs against the fort became more settled convictions. In August, 1722, Governor Benavides had sent a captain and friar, the usual Spanish exploring duo, with a bodyguard by an inland passage to demand the restitution of ships and merchandise according to the stipulations of the Convention of the Hague and the return of all Spanish Indians held as slaves. Governor Nicholson, after consulting the assembly, consented to return Indians only in exchange for fugitive Negro slaves, and in return demanded English vessels and prisoners captured since the termination of the war. Since it was on the shoulders of the governor alone that the burden of hospitality rested, the assembly openly protested the uninvited guests. Nicholson insisted that agents in the future come directly to Charles Town by sea without stopping at any point en route.[23] For one embassy of seventeen Spaniards, Nicholson's safe conduct required their return to St. Augustine by direct route within sixteen days, without entering any harbors except in emergency.[24] Nevertheless, an officer from the presidio at St. Augustine called at Fort King George and with his entourage was dispatched to Charles Town. The real feelings of the Carolinians are evinced in this note from Nicholson to Carteret: "We are apprehensive that the Governor of St. Augustine sent them as spyes to see what condition Fort King George was in and what other things they could inform themselves in." This old animosity was again inflamed in December, 1722, when a report was received by the assembly from the

---

[22] "... ni permita construir fortalezas algunas en Dominios de su Mag. y haza se demuela el fuerte construido en el sitio nombrado la Jamaha y bocas de Talaje. ..." This is evidently the Altamaha site. A. H. N., sec. IX, Papeles de Estado, leg. 1701, Grimaldo to Pozobueno, Balsain, 27 October, 1722; Archivo General de Indias, 58-1-31, Benavides to the king, St. Augustine, 19, 21 April, 1722. In the letter of 21 April was enclosed a letter from Benavides to the governor of South Carolina, 11 February, 1722. *Ibid.* See Bolton and Ross, *op. cit.*, p. 71. A. G. S., Sec. de Estado, leg. 7633 (antiguo), Joseph de Layssequilla to the King, Madrid, 4 December, 1738, puntos 7-9.

[23] C. O. 5/358, A 58.   [24] C. O. 5/382, no. 34.

Creek agent to the effect that the Spanish were arousing and spurring the Indians to attack the new English fort.[25]

South Carolina was further agitated by the rumor that the surrender of Gibraltar and Port Mahon, the capital and principal seaport of Minorca, was imminent. The assembly thereupon declared that Spanish St. Augustine was a ruinous potentiality to South Carolina and proposed that in place of West Indian colonies the eastern half of the continent from the Mississippi, including St. Augustine, be substituted and annexed. It was this Carolinian mistrust of Florida which led the Carolinians and Governor Nicholson, likewise sharing the antipathy for the Spaniards, to hope and believe that, upon the resumption of hostilities, Fort King George, which the Floridians were so zealous to destroy, would protect the flank of Carolina and serve as a base to harass and ultimately reduce Florida.

Pozobueno's vigorous office began with a reiteration—a dignified request that the governor of South Carolina be required to observe the stipulations of the suspension of arms with the last exactitude. The information that the English had built a fort on the Altamaha, conveyed to Spain by the governor of St. Augustine, and considered by the Council of the Indies, was received with bitterness. The principal facts as embodied in Grimaldo's letter of instructions were now repeated. The memorial embraced a demand that England dispatch orders at once, in order to forestall prejudicing and overawing the Indians of the neutral jurisdiction, that the fort located so contrary to the rights of His Catholic Majesty and his subjects be demolished and the ground forever relinquished.[26]

Aided by Walter Chetwynd, Thomas Pelham-Holles, Paul Docminique, and Martin Bladen, who had only vague notions, seemingly, of the merits of the dispute, Carteret, with this peremptory demand, referred the question to the Board of Trade.[27] The personnel of that body knew little more of the foundations of the argument, although in the expansionist re-

---

[25] C. O. 5/387, fol. 60.

[26] A. H. N., sec. IX, Papeles de Estado, leg. 1720, Pozobueno to Carteret, London, 6/17 November, 1722; Pozobueno to Grimaldo, London, 19 November, 1722, and another 26 November, 1733.

[27] C. O. 5/358, Carteret to Board of Trade, 8 December, 1722.

ports of 1720 they had made the most sweeping claims. Succinctly on December 20, 1722, the Board reviewed the origin of the recent project to suppress disorders. Moreover, it emphatically laid claim to the bank of the Altamaha, where stood Fort King George, as in the province of Carolina. The fort in dispute, it averred, was on the southern boundary of South Carolina where both the safety of the British territory in America and the navigation of the Altamaha demanded its erection. The council was surprised, it said, that the Catholic King should even offer a complaint.[28] In case of necessity the Board promised with nonchalant assurance to produce sufficient proofs "of the incontestable right of the English."[29]

That the Board of Trade enjoyed undisturbed ignorance of the matter appeared later in a communication to Carteret. Addressing themselves primarily to the Spaniards they then reminded Carteret of the conditions:

. . . whereby we have reserved to Ourselves an opportunity of applying such particular Proofs arising from Charters and otherwise as we are already masters of, as well as those we may further discover.

The charters ever constituted a nebulous legal argument, but there was another, which Oglethorpe finally used to the utmost, of an absolute, undeniable, and imponderable, although unethical, countenance and authorization—a challenge the Spaniards tacitly accepted.

We were the rather induced to take this Method because His Majesty being in Possession it will certainly be incumbent on the Spaniards to produce Proofs of their Title before His Majesty can be under any necessity of justifying his own Right.[30]

This second protest of the Marqués de Pozobueno was partially efficacious, notwithstanding the Board of Trade. Carteret sent a letter to the governor of South Carolina reviewing the devious movement of the information concerning the dire straits to which the policy of the border province had brought Anglo-Spanish diplomacy. The orders required by the Spanish

---

[28] A. H. N., sec. IX, Papeles de Estado, leg. 1724, London, n.d.
[29] C. O. 5/382, fol. 35.
[30] *Idem.*

ambassador were promptly dispatched, and a punctual report on the possibility of their execution demanded.[31]

The reviews of the Spanish offices which Pozobueno sent to Madrid were favorably received by the king. And Carteret had responded favorably to the protest concerning the excesses of the Indians of English allegiance.[32]

To the mind of Pozobueno the pliability of Carteret was extremely gratifying, but he had not reckoned the importance of Georgia in domestic British politics. The English were procrastinating either to gain time or because the full weight of American interests had not yet been felt in the government.

In reply to Carteret's demand for information, a committee of the South Carolina legislature drew up, May, 1723, the famous and imperialistic "Observations" from which outline the English argument never deviated subsequently in the almost perpetual dispute. This fact Arredondo appreciated when he noted and attacked the "Observations" in his *Historical Proof of Spain's Title to Georgia*.[33] The essence of this South Carolina document was that the charter conceded to Carolina not only the Altamaha, but a great swath to the southward. In the original draft St. Augustine was held to be within the Proprietors' Charter, but this provision was later struck through. Never since the charter, went the reasoning, had the Spanish possessed any lands on the Altamaha, which assertion revealed an appalling but helpful ignorance of Spanish establishments from St. Catherine to Cumberland Island less than forty years before. Forgetting the American Treaty of 1670, whereby Spain and England guaranteed the then *status quo*, the South Carolinians asserted that the Spaniards could claim Charles Town with as much validity as they could claim the Altamaha, but they overlooked the possibility that by the same token England had as good a right to St. Augustine as to the Altamaha. Although the argument was weak and fallible, both legally and historically, the assembly found a firmer foundation in

---

[31] A. H. N., sec. IX, Papeles de Estado, leg. 1720, Carteret to Governor Nicholson, Whitehall, 28 November, 1722; Carteret to Pozobueno, Whitehall, 28 November, 1722.

[32] *Ibid.*, sec. IX, Papeles de Estado, leg. 1720; Grimaldo to Pozobueno, Pardo, 14 December, 1722; *ibid.*, 10 January, 1723; *ibid.*, leg. 1724, Madrid, 8 March, 1723.

[33] H. E. Bolton (ed.), *Arredondo's Historical Proof of Spain's Title to Georgia*.

Barnwell's argument that Fort King George had been built to secure His Majesty's dominions against the usurpations of the French and Spanish. The river which was the pathway to the heart of the continent, once in the power of France or Spain, would paralyze that now historical commerce of the interior and menace the existence of the colony itself.[34]

Scarcely less dogmatic than the position of the Board of Trade was the information conveyed by Carteret to Pozobueno. That the fort to which this ambassador and his government objected was in South Carolina, on the evidence of the aforementioned Board, was incontestable. The king, besides, ordered his minister to send to Pozobueno a copy of the confirmatory letter of the council.[35] The situation was evidently becoming serious, and the South Carolinians sinister. Grimaldo was notified of the new turn which the negotiations had taken as a result of the vigorous and dogmatic stand taken by the Board of Trade.[36]

Inopportunely for the English, who prior to their arrival could not always be expected to be conversant with the state of the Spanish settlements on the seaboard, there was sufficient documentary and admitted evidence to prove that the English did not hold by actual occupation a single foot of territory south of Charles Town in 1670. Yet in this year, by the American Treaty, Spain and England adopted the principle of actual possession. Now the problem had reached a crisis. England was pushing southward from Charles Town and was by royal order threatening to knock at the doors of St. Augustine itself—not only with the wares of traders and settlers but with muskets.

So in the maze of official reports and letters that passed between the officials of the courts the two positions on this point were sharply defined. The earnestness of Spain's officials and the preponderant emphasis they placed on the Altamaha section were both unexpected and embarrassing to the English. England made no attempt to justify herself by international agreement, but passed silently by the subsequent American Treaty and stood firmly upon the Carolina grant of 1665. In

---

[34] *Journals of the Commons House of Assembly*, 10 May, 1723.

[35] A. H. N., sec. IX, Papeles de Estado, leg. 1724, Carteret to Pozobueno, Whitehall, 28 January, 1722/3.

[36] *Ibid.*, sec. IX, Papeles de Estado, leg. 1724, Pozobueno to Grimaldo, London, 27 February, 1723.

this grant Charles II, probably unwittingly, included a number of Spanish possessions—even St. Augustine itself. The English agreed that to assert their claim to St. Augustine on the basis of the English royal grant of 1665 would have been ludicrous, but the logic would inevitably have remained the same. This step would have thrown a far from impregnable position into bold relief. If the sacking of St. Augustine by Sir Francis Drake could be used as a foundation for an English claim, so could this charter!

To destroy the logic of this reasoning was a simple process. Spain could have but one reply. England did not possess the territory to 29°, the southern limit of the charter, and therefore could not dispose of it. Neither could she erect forts in Spanish territory to the occupation of which Spain had not given her assent and which England herself had renounced in 1670, in order to clear her title to any of America.[37]

From the measures of the Council of the Indies and Governor Benavides, the importance of the affair to the Spanish can be discerned. In 1724 Benavides received orders to negotiate with the governor at Charles Town and to entertain no motion for a discussion of any substitute or equivalent for the Altamaha fort.[38] But American diplomacy was impeded by the slow course of diplomacy in London and Madrid.

In the heat of the negotiations the court at London admitted, probably inadvertently, that the crown of Spain possessed Guale and Santa Elena. An admission to that effect, it has been claimed, was made by the Duke of Newcastle to Pozobueno.[39]

From Madrid to Spain's envoy came instructions to arrange for an amicable settlement of the problem of limits. The Spaniards tinted the proposal with an alternative of force to back

---

[37] A. H. N., sec. IX, Papeles de Estado, leg. 1726, Pozobueno to Grimaldo, accompanying the former's memorials on the subject of the fort, London, 2 June, 1723.

[38] Bolton, *op. cit.*, pp. 173-75.

[39] Serano y Sanz, *Documentos Históricos de la Florida y la Luisiana*, pp. 106-8. *Ibid.*, pp. 243, *et seq.*, "Testimonio de los autos y demas diligencias fechas sobre la division de los términos de este jurisdicción, y la de Carolina, en virtud de las dos reales zedulas que ellos se contienen, sus fechas 10 de Juno y 18 de Agosto de 1724. Año de 1725. Archivo de Indias, Audiencia de Santo Domingo. Provincia de la Florida. Cartas y expedientes; años 1728 á 1733. Est. 58, caj. 1°, leg. 31."

up their offers. If Fort King George should be found in the dominions of His Catholic Majesty, England would be bound by her own agreement to order the governor of South Carolina to destroy that fortification immediately. In the office which was presented at London there was a clear sign that the home government was pressing its representative to renew his attempts with vigor. He importuned the English to send to the governor of South Carolina with all diligence and dispatch orders for an exact determination of the boundary. He expected that line to be determined by the terms of the treaty of 1670 and fortified by a guarantee of the Spanish possessions existing at that time.[40] In case no order was given to the Carolinians to demolish Fort King George, the demolition was to be undertaken by the governor of Florida and the action accompanied by a formal justification. Everything depended upon whether or not the English would agree to a conference to regulate those limits—a concession which would render futile the martial steps contemplated.[41]

Contingent upon this instruction from Spain, a letter was promptly sent to the Duke of Newcastle calling for the destruction of Fort King George and the prompt dispatching of plenary powers to the two governors in America to call a conference for the purpose of determining on the spot the boundaries of the disputed area. In the absence of Governor Nicholson of South Carolina, the negotiations might be impeded. But impediments Spain wished at this time to avoid, for she would suffer loss with every delay. The Spaniards hinted that the government of South Carolina ought to be charged to carry on the negotiation in the absence of the governor in order to terminate with expedition an affair which had jeopardized the peace of the area.[42]

Newcastle announced the king's consent to a conference of governors; but he gently evaded the now perfectly rehearsed Spanish demand for the destruction of the obnoxious fortress, agreeing to raze it only if it were located in Spanish territory

---

[40] For the Spanish view of their possessions at that time see Bolton, *op. cit.*, p. 176.

[41] A. H. N., sec. IX, Papeles de Estado, leg. 1726, a letter with no date and signature, but apparently a notice of Pozobueno to Grimaldo from London about June, 1724.

[42] *Ibid.*, Pozobueno to Newcastle, London, 4 June, 1724.

(a concession he deliberately avoided making). However, this authorization was not officially sanctioned until a year later.[43]

In December, 1724, Newcastle handed Pozobueno the "Observations" drawn up in 1723 by the Assembly of South Carolina. His delay in acting about the fort, the ambassador was informed, turned upon the expectation of the momentary arrival of Governor Nicholson in London. The magnanimous king, naturally, would be gracious enough to withold his final judgment until Nicholson's evidence was in. Spain was beguiled into believing that instructions had been sent to the Council of South Carolina to search out the facts and appraise the evidence—an order which awaited signature until June 2, 1725. Even so it sanctioned only a joint inquiry which could be abandoned the moment the Carolinians found it going against them on the pretext that they were not empowered to act. The ultimate voice, then, remained that of the king. Still another delay was occasioned in conveying the letter which was probably suppressed by President Middleton of the council. Certainly it only appeared in the journal of the council in November, 1725. By that time another half-militant, half-pompous Spanish diplomatic troop had wrought another fiasco in South Carolina. The English were beating the Spaniards with the extensive use of the Spanish weapons—shirking and delaying.[44]

Since the accession of Anne, October 12, 1714, scarcely a moment's security had been felt in the southern colony. The Yamasee War was probably the result of Spanish efforts to debauch Carolina's neighbors, yet such efforts were the common practice in that dark and bloody ground. Memorial after memorial in protest against the excesses of the Indians of English leaning was presented at the court of London. The information was always gleaned from the copious correspondence of the governor of Florida.[45]

---

[43] Serrano y Sanz, *op. cit.*, p. 248.

[44] C. O. 5/382, fol. 35; *ibid.*, Middleton to Newcastle, Charles Town, 20 December, 1725; Council Journals of South Carolina (hereafter cited as Council Journals), 2 November, 1725.

[45] A. H. N., sec. IX, Papeles de Estado, legajos 1724, 1726, *passim;* Carroll, *op. cit.*, I, 187-223. "For either peace or war the very situation impelled the Europeans to court the favor of the Indians. They were not ignorant that the subjects of both England and Spain always endeavoured, for the sake of peace, to court the friendship of Indian nations, who were such powerful and dangerous enemies.

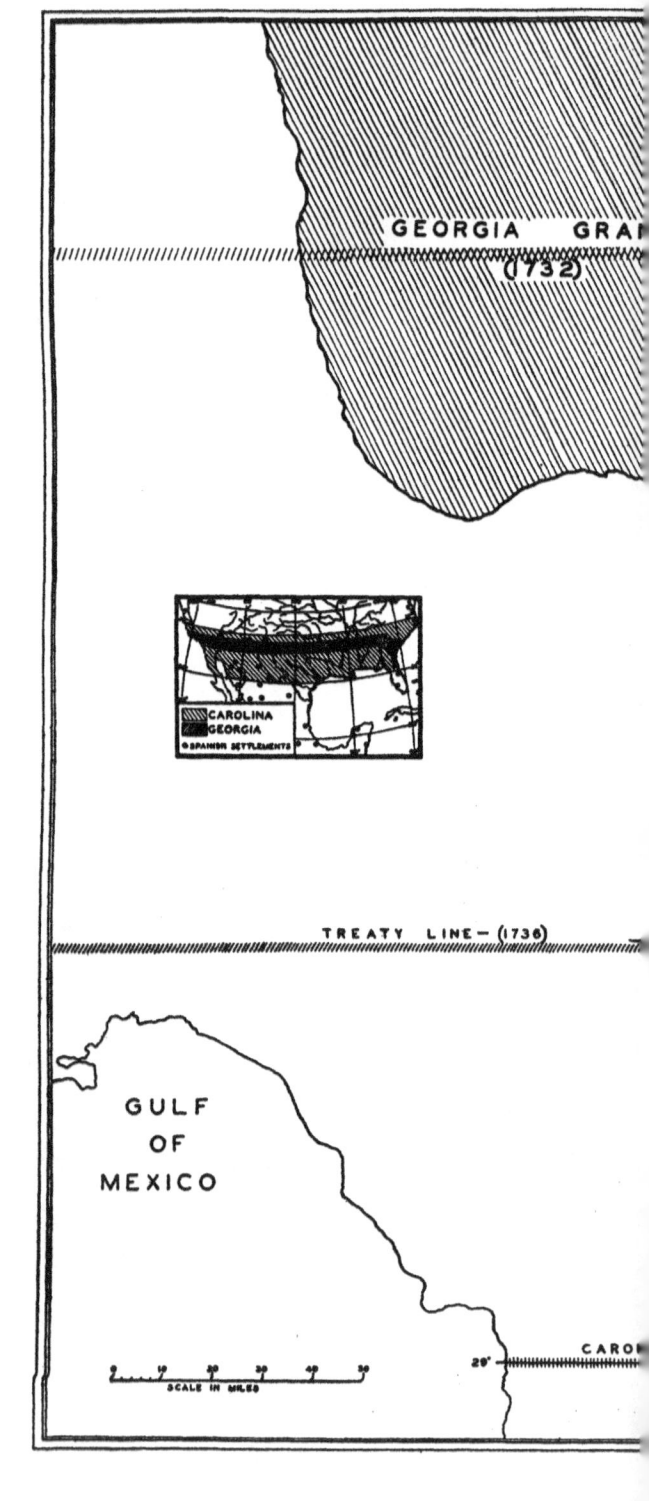

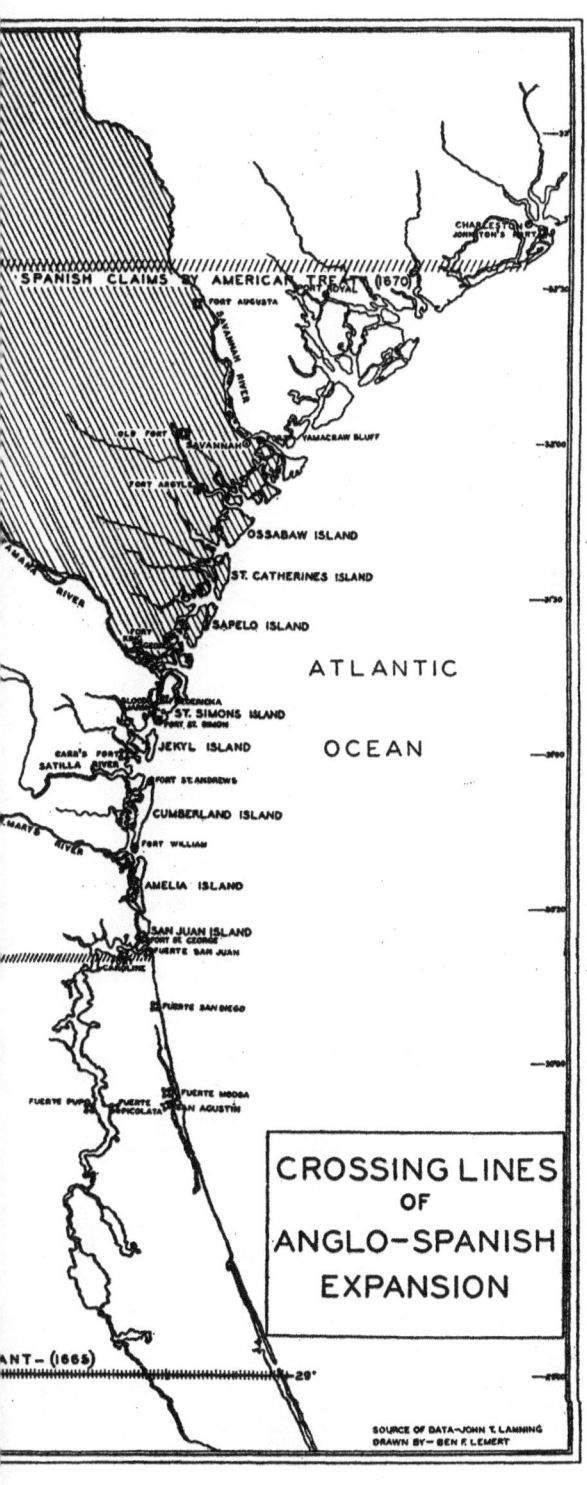

The memorial of 1725, based on letters of complaint, dated August 18 and October 15, from Governor Benavides was even more strained than ever. The Spanish lieutenant at Fort San Marcos learned that the English were alienating the Indians in his jurisdiction, that preparations were being made to destroy two Indian posts in the province of Apalache, and that ten other recent converts to the Catholic religion had been scalped.[46] This new declaration by order was attached to a memorial against the fort near the mouth of the Altamaha. The office concluded in a strong strain—one seemingly conscious of both strength and justice—calling for a cessation of the attempts to alienate the spirit of the Indians, an immediate halt to all hostile preparations and an answer to the instance for the information of the Spanish king. At about the same time in a letter to Madrid, the memorial in the above tenor was laid before the Duke of Newcastle. The Marqués de Grimaldo was informed that upon the dissolution of Parliament an answer to all pending offices could be expected.[47]

Throughout the year 1725 the Spanish government never forgot to ply its agent in London to press the case against this obnoxious fort and by all means to secure a satisfactory answer from the Duke of Newcastle concerning a fortification erected in Florida without the royal consent.[48] The following year the crown of Spain had received only a noncommital reply from the Duke of Newcastle. The king, therefore, in a personal order commanded his minister to complain both against the fort and the alienation of the Indians and to require a prompt answer to all points in the original memorial.[49]

Not content with these precautions, further steps were taken to insure entire satisfaction. Newcastle was continually waiting

---

Each competitor knew their passion for war, and how heavy their vengeance, wherever it pointed, generally fell, and therefore good policy dictated the necessity of turning the edge of their fierce and bloody temper against their neighbors, in order to save themselves." *Ibid.*, p. 192.

[46] A. H. N., sec. IX, Papeles de Estado, leg. 1726, Pozobueno to Newcastle, London, 4/24 June/May, 1725. "Vulgairement appellés Tamazas qui se trouvent palacés dans la Province d'Apalaché deplar dix autres qui ont nouvellement embrassés la Religion Catholique, et qui sont situés aux environs de ce Fort."

[47] *Ibid.*, Pozobueno to Grimaldo, London, 18 June, 1725.

[48] *Ibid.*, Grimaldo to Pozobueno, Madrid, 5 February, 22 October, 10 December, 1725.

[49] *Ibid.*, royal order of 2 June, 1726; Serano y Sanz, *op. cit.*, p. 111.

for the arrival of the governor of South Carolina, who was more versed in the affairs of Carolina. This very reasonable pretext did not prevent the officials in Madrid from sending an order to the governor of Florida, along with a copy of Newcastle's response, requiring an investigation into the affair. His Britannic Majesty's principal Secretary of State, however, promised to demolish the fort if it was found to be in Spanish territory. At the same time he spoke of issuing orders to the governor of South Carolina to prevent any excesses by Indians, and formally expressed himself as willing to settle the question of limits through commissaries.[50]

Governor Benavides made studied plans for the dramatic diplomatic comedy of 1725. From officers grown old in the Castle of St. Augustine and the service of Spain wordy depositions were taken to prove what nearly everyone knew—that the Fort was in Florida and that these very soldiers had served in Santa Catalina, Zápala, Guadalquini, Santa María, and San Juan at least ten years after the treaty of 1670 which confirmed Spain's right to all territory then held.[51] The commissaries appointed were Don Francisco Menéndez Marqués, who had already been a commissary to South Carolina, and the commanding officer of the St. Augustine Presidio, José Primo de Rivera. Repeatedly enjoined by the Council of the Indies to consider no substitute for the troublesome fort, they were now required not only to demand its extirpation but to watch the gratifying ceremony and to satisfy themselves that no inhabitants—either Indian or English—were suffered to stay. The concrete limits they were expected to uphold reached northward to venerable but hectic old Santa Elena and westwardly to Apalachicola. If by any chance the English should object, the delegates were authorized to present their papers and require a written acknowledgment for His Catholic Majesty's government. Then there was a rather wily instruction. Formerly the English had successfully befuddled the negotiations by harping on runaway slaves, but to prevent this invariable stall, they were to declare that only seven slaves were held at the presidio in St. Augustine who, according to former royal

---

[50] Archivo General de Indias (hereafter cited as A. G. I.), Audiencia de Santo Domingo, 87-1-1, Doc. No. 6, dated 2 June, 1726.

[51] Bolton, *op. cit.*, p. 176.

orders, could not be returned, but compensation to their owners could be expected.[52]

The thirty gaily-bedecked Spanish delegates were received in Charles Town with great éclat and formality matched only by the wary circumspection of the occasion. For generations Englishmen had sung their deep-seated mistrust of Spaniards. The Carolinians knew them to be incorrigible and conscienceless Negro-harborers. The council, therefore, ordered special vigilance in order to forestall plots. With the exception of the two diplomats, the beat of the seven o'clock tattoo was the deadline for visitors, upon pain of being arrested by the marshal, to retire to their quarters. Arrayed in their flashing old-world uniforms, the Spaniards presented their credentials. Then came the fiasco. The necessary full powers, the Floridians were assured, had not been received from England, pending which receipt it would be necessary to maintain the fort. The Spaniards, when failure of their mission became apparent (as was the case from the moment they presented their papers), tried to buy a sloop to carry them home, but, fearing that this attempt covered a design against Fort King George, the Council refused. Then the Carolinians resumed the diplomatic offensive by protesting in the invariable strain against the sequestering of Carolina slaves at St. Augustine, but the righteous and indignant retort that the English were making a scrap of paper of the Treaty of 1670 should have more than offset this allegation.[53]

The long-delayed instruction for an investigation was at last inserted in the journal of the Council of South Carolina, and by a rather revealing coincidence, Arthur Middleton wrote of the utmost importance of the fort to South Carolina and the colonial policy as a whole. He had already stressed the same point to Nicholson and Newcastle. The fort, he said, could be given up only as a tacit admission of the dependence of all the

---

[52] A. G. I., Audiencia de Santo Domingo, 87-1-1, Doc. No. 43A, including letters of President Middleton, Governor Benavides, and affidavits of St. Augustine signed by Juan Solano, notary public. Serrano y Sanz, *op. cit.*, pp. 243-52.

[53] A.G.I., Audiencia de Santo Domingo, 87-1-1, Doc. No. 43; Bolton and Ross, *op. cit.*, p. 70; Council Journals, 6-13 September, 1725; C.O. 5/387, fol. 80; Serrano y Sanz, *op. cit.*, pp. 255-58; N. D. Mereness (ed.), *Travels in the American Colonies*, p. 159.

Creeks on Spain, whereas Creek policy demanded that another fort should be constructed at the junction of the Altamaha and South Altamaha.[54] No one knew better than Middleton the significance of the instruction, which he was now forced to enter in the journal, requiring a settlement of the boundary by the Treaty of 1670, "at which time the English were in possession of no more land than in and about Charles Towne, so that with submission I think that the Spaniards may as well claime all the lands within a few miles adjacent, as those lying on the Altamahaw River."[55] The Spaniards observed the same logic and thought it not so ridiculous. On November 4, 1725, the conference suspended negotiations until the weather, at least, was warmer and more auspicious.[56] Significant it is that there were no further attempts on the part of Carolina to open up the discussion. Newcastle suddenly lost interest now that he was informed of the consequences of admitting the validity of the Spanish legal position. Even the Spaniards themselves made no great attempt to resuscitate the perishing negotiations. In Europe war between England and Spain was a foregone conclusion. Besides, the accidental burning of Fort King George in the winter of 1725-26 was taken, at least outwardly, as deliberate, and as a token of diplomatic triumph. The question then was whether (as the Spaniards pretended) the disaster was a mere compliance with Spanish wishes or an accident (as the English believed), for the miserable garrison was not above this decisive means of relief.

In spite of the sporadic outbreaks on the border in America in 1725, the Spaniards accusing the English of stealing land and the English accusing the Spaniards of stealing slaves, the Georgia question assumed a lesser place between the receipt of the news that the fort against which the Spaniards complained so bitterly had been destroyed and the signing of the charter for the establishment of a colony including all the land between the Savannah and the Altamaha.[57] Questions more remote—Parma and Placentia, Tuscany, the captured ship *Woolball*—went to make up a sufficient catalogue of controversial

---

[54] C. O. 5/387, fol. 80.
[55] *Ibid.*, fol. 79.
[56] Council Journals, November 4, 1725.
[57] Sloane MSS (British Museum), 3986, p. 38.

questions.[58] Anglo-Spanish contact in the Carolina-Florida region had reached the breaking point several times before the erection of Fort King George. Aside from occasional incursions in the seventeenth century, Governor Moore in 1702 undertook a project against the Spanish which ended in disgrace. In 1706 the French and Spanish under La Fibaer attacked Charles Town, but without success; however, some ten years later Don Juan de Ayola y Escobar procured a general combination of natives, including the Yamasees, against the English.[59]

Late in the third decade of the eighteenth century it seemed that England and Spain would come to an agreement. The Marqués de la Paz considered that Fort King George had been abandoned deliberately out of deference to his government,[60] but was such the case? The report of Captain Edward Massey, who had been sent to investigate the burning of the fort, did not reveal an incendiary origin. The hardships of the place and the indolence of the garrison, which refused to exert itself to supply clean water or to build corrals for the cattle sent by the governor, were strikingly revived and the officials apprised of the situation of the fort.[61] After much haggling at Charles Town between Nicholson and the Assembly, the latter finally consented to an order advancing two thousand pounds currency as a loan for rebuilding the post awaiting a permanent royal establishment. Such generosity is not hard to understand. "As possession gives a right in this case, so the abandoning of what we have held so many years is tacitly giving that right away."[62] So much turned on the point that Governor Johnson of South Carolina was extended two thousand pounds and instructed to rebuild the fort,[63] which was accordingly done. The garrison, however, was withdrawn in the fall of 1727. Border policy and not Spanish pressure probably dictated the step. Mean-

---

[58] Add. MSS, 32777, Newcastle Papers (hereafter cited as N. P.), XCII, 224; *ibid.*, 32779, XCIV, *passim*.

[59] W. W. Dewhurst, *The History of St. Augustine*, pp. 83-85.

[60] Add. MSS, 32752, N. P., LXVII, 150-52, Newcastle to Walpole, London, 3 October, 1727.

[61] C. O. 5/360, C8; C. O. 5/387, fol. 73.

[62] C. O. 5/233, Instructions to Governor Johnson.

[63] Add. MSS, 32752, N. P., LXVII, 316, Keene to Walpole, Madrid, 3 November, 1727.

while the two countries were drifting into the desultory War of Hanover in which the English attacked Porto Bello and attempted to take the silver fleet. In Madrid, the English minister, Benjamin Keene, had been doing his best to maintain the armistice which had been agreed upon, but the baleful influence of the Queen, who often fell into a violent rage against the English, was hardly capable of being underestimated. At one juncture it became necessary to avoid efforts at conciliating her, as such attempts would only drive her into the arms of Austria.[64] The immortal DeFoe, succumbing to the "hireling" tendencies then common among literary people, lent his facile pen to the opposition polemics. Forthright he suggested that gain from a war with France was problematical but that England could never lose in a contest of arms with Spain.[65] Great though the odds were, representatives at Seville succeeded in framing and signing a treaty for the appointment of commissaries to adjust the maritime difficulties and the limits in America.[66]

In 1728 the negotiations looking to the Treaty of Seville began to brew.[67] Preliminary to this conference, the Duke of Newcastle, as was his custom, solicited information from the Board of Trade regarding territory in America disputed with Spain, naming particularly Fort King George, the Bahamas, and Campeche. The answer of the Board of Trade placed special emphasis on the testimonials of people in England who had lived in America or made special studies of border problems.[68] The secretary to the Carolina Proprietors, Richard Shelton, thought that the St. Marys was the southern boundary, but he was a little bewildered upon reading the ancient maps, especially Nairne's, to find that St. Augustine was included.

---

[64] Add. MSS, 32756, N. P., LXXI, 10, Newcastle to Keene, London, 17 May, 1728.

[65] *Evident Advantages to Great Britain and its Allies from the Approaching War: Especially in Matters of Trade* . . . (London, 1727), p. 15.

[66] Add. MSS, 32765, N. P., LXXX, 181-83, Newcastle to Keene, 20 January, 1729/30; Add. MSS, 33006, Diplomatic Papers of the Duke of Newcastle, II, 111, Article VI of the Treaty of Seville.

[67] A. G. S., Secretaria de Estado, 396.7.634, "que es el tomo 1° de las memorias, manuscritas de D. Joseph de la Quintana, sobre la Junta de comisarios españoles y engleses en Sevilla. . . ; 397.7.635, otro: *idem.*, tomo 2° de dichas memorias; 398.7636, otro: *idem.*, tomo 3° de dichas memorias."

[68] C. O. 5/360, C 21, C 22, C 23, C 24, C 25.

All those testifying took the occupation of the River Altamaha, dating from the third decade of the eighteenth century, as ground for title fifty years earlier. Those consulted held with one accord, often in conflict with the Spanish testimony,[69] that Spain had not enjoyed any control north of the Altamaha for many years. They also declared in unison that a well fortified southern march was required by the menace of France as well as Spain. Most of these papers reiterated the familiar thesis of Dr. Coxe and the "Observations" prepared by the Assembly in 1723. The Duke of Newcastle, arguing that the occupation of one point preëmpted the whole province, declared that on no other ground could Spain object to foreign settlements and claims outside St. Augustine. The good Duke overlooked the farmers, soldiers, and missionaries sent scurrying by English raids.

The Board of Trade also overlooked the Spanish missions in the Georgia country and perverted the historical meaning of the Treaty of 1670, thereby endeavoring to establish title not only to the actual possessions of 1670 but also to the charter concessions such as those of Coxe, Heath, and the Lords Proprietors which by no stretch of the imagination could have been "held" in 1670. The Spaniards, the argument ran, had never recognized the opposition to them. Neither did the English proclaim their opposition to Virginia or London, but, by such reasoning they proceeded to turn the tables on the Spaniards. If Spain would not subscribe to the theory that "planting one part of a Province secures the Title to the whole, any Nation," the Board reasoned, "is at liberty and may settle the remaining part of Florida," with the exception of St. Augustine, over which Spain had even at one time been sovereign. After the Treaty of Seville the American boundary problems still dangled. They were left for later and unwitting diplomats.

The British commissioners named in 1730 for the settlement of the Carolina boundary question were Benjamin Keene, John Goddard, and Arthur Stert. To them was entrusted the thankless task of persuading the Spanish plenipotentiaries that the sole basis and source of information for adjusting international boundaries was the British Board of Trade. Thereupon the

---

[69] *Idem.*

Board dutifully submitted copies of its labor in the year 1728. Not even Florida would Newcastle concede to the King of Spain. On the same occasion the Spanish delegates were required by their government to negotiate on the terms of the Treaty of 1670 and by an interpretation which would admit only a plain, strict reading of that document.[70]

Nothing developed from this proposed negotiation, but it served to draw out from the Board of Trade another irreconcilable claim of the English to ancient Guale which was only another step in the program already evolved for the effective occupation of the disputed region between the Savannah and the Altamaha. After the disastrous experience of the Yamasee wars, rangers were substituted for the stationary forts. It was here that three empires—English, French, and Spanish—clashed. Coupled with the unstable conditions of reconstruction this clash rendered a reorientation of Creek policy vitally necessary, for with the red man were connected the designs and undertakings of Montgomery, Barnwell, Purry, and Oglethorpe.

A problem that was to test the prowess and diplomacy of Oglethorpe now faced the Carolinians. The rivalry between the Spanish and English for control of Coweta developed to a fever pitch. The wily old Creek, Brims, wisely took a neutral stand. Meanwhile the Spanish were not idle. They had had Seepeycoffee, the son of Brims, and the chief Indian warrior, down to St. Augustine, a fact which did not augur well for English diplomatic assets.[71] Lieutenant Don Diego Peña, escorting the returning visitors with twelve soldiers, headed a diplomatic mission from St. Augustine. The English were planning to build a fort in Apalachicola. Coweta was divided and Brims was evading the censure and "harsh words" of Peña and yet not coöperating with him too fully in his efforts to buy horses. Finally, after some heated debates and sinister plots, Peña withdrew to St. Augustine. Later Primo de Rivera, of the same presidio, erected a post to maintain the prestige of Spain among the important Lower Creeks. Hastings and Musgrove, however, managed to arrange a treaty of questionable validity and utility with the Creeks, in spite of Spanish opposition. Old Brims was turning his advantage to account. His ascendency

---

[70] Diplomatic Papers of the Duke of Newcastle, II, 111 *et seq.*; Add. MSS, 33006, fols. 298-303.

[71] C. O. 5/1265, Q 121, 126, 131.

was not overlooked by the Carolinians, one of whom declared that Brims was "as great a politician as any governor in America."[72]

But the skein of international intrigue was frequently tangled with the lesser one of inter-tribal politics. The Carolinians needed every possible auxiliary, and their plots and intrigues between 1725 and 1728 in order to turn the Creek-Cherokee feud to their advantage were worthy of the best French-Indian diplomacy. The agent Chicken was dispatched to the Cherokees[73] and another, Fitch, to the Creeks.[74] While one agent was exercising the wiles of aboriginal oratory in the frequent confabulations, the companion was inciting his group against the other. This policy of duplicity was justly rewarded by the Indian statesman, Brims. In 1726 Brims and his son Seepeycoffee were reported on their way to St. Augustine to make a peace— a sign of their intention to ignore the untrustworthy English.[75] Only a peace between the Cherokees and Creeks would now restore English prestige, and to that end solemn ceremonies were held in the Province House at Charles Town where the governor told the natives the French only hoped to make slaves of them. The agent Glover was working to arrange the peace. His mission in 1727 was one of the utmost significance and it required the most consummate tact.[76] Since the southern Indians were seriously disaffected, it was the news of Palmer's successful raid against the Yamasees that brought this mission to a successful fruition. That great concern of the Carolinians —the western trade—was at last opened up, while Brims was plied with presents. Ten years of watchful waiting and three years of precipitate uneasiness were at last crowned with the assurance of Creek loyalty and dependability—as nearly as these qualities can be approximated among Indians. By this achievement Glover and Fitch smoothed the rough edges of the frontier and laid the foundation for the half-flaunting, half-Quixotic Indian diplomacy of the master—Oglethorpe. The surrender of the charter by the Carolina Proprietors was an important step in the advancement of the English frontier, for

---

[72] *Ibid.*, Q 121.
[73] C. O. 5/12, fols. 14-34.
[74] *Ibid.*, fols. 55, 35-55.
[75] C. O. 5/383, Middleton to Nicholson, Charles Town, 24 May, 1726.
[76] C. O. 5/387, fol. 171.

it opened the gates to the region which the English imperialists had already repeatedly designed for English colonization.

However scant the right to the debatable land may have been, it appears the English had never relinquished it. Indeed Fort King George had been abandoned, but under circumstances which left open the possibility of reassertion in the near future. After Palmer's raid, English prestige was sufficiently restored, but even then the garrison was not to be withdrawn until such action would not "be any Injury to His Majesty's claim to the River Altamaha."[77] The Spanish contention that the fort was abandoned at the instance of the Madrid government was a diplomatic maneuver. The Board of Trade was already completely committed to the retention of the Altamaha boundary. Nicholson, now growing old, consulted with the board and urged that an engineer should be sent to select a site for a fort "to answer His late Majesty's intention of securing the property and Trade of the Said River from the French and Spaniards."[78] The Board endorsed the plan, stating that the reasons at that juncture were "rather stronger for maintaining this fort than they were at first for erecting it."[79] The project was carried no farther until 1730, when occupation of the site and the colonization of the Savannah were a part of the instructions issued to Governor Johnson. The building of Frederica on St. Simons Island in 1736 was the logical fruition of the ideas of Barnwell and Nicholson.

The anti-Spanish feeling added to the imperialism of the Carolinians foretold the impending thrust to the south. Sanctioned by the colonial officials and long urged by the Carolinians, the basic project of international rivalry was carried out under the guise of philanthropy—ecclesiastical imperialism.[80] Although the unwearying leader of the movement was for many years Dr. Thomas Bray, James Oglethorpe was the chairman of the committee from the House of Commons "to enquire into the state of the Goals of the Kingdom."[81] It was Oglethorpe, "a young man of public spirit," whose vigorous personality rather than philanthropic impulses propelled this religio-imperialistic project.[82] Oglethorpe frequently defied the political

---

[77] C. O. 5/387, fol. 167.   [78] C. O. 5/360, C 8.   [79] C. O. 5/383, fol. 30.
[80] *Idem.*   [81] Journals of the House of Commons, 25 February, 1728-1729.
[82] E. B. Greene, 'The Anglican Outlook on the American Colonies in the Early Eighteenth Century," *American Historical Review*, XX (October, 1914), 64-85.

current with his challenging speeches against the reign of Walpole. His leanings also drew him into the Society for the Propagation of the Gospel in Foreign Parts, and ever a versatile mortal, they later drew him as deputy-governor into the Royal African Company—one to traffic in souls and the other in slaves. Under Oglethorpe's leadership Georgia as a religious and philanthropic undertaking took second place to Georgia, the imperialistic colony. Oglethorpe's aims were worldly.[83] Many were the times that opposition members of Parliament with worldly aims were to goad the Walpole ministry almost into desperation with Spain—a situation which kept alive the Anglo-Spanish diplomatic feud for nearly half a century.

Spain implicitly agreed not to molest the English "so long as they keep in their proper distances, and are not concerned in any illicit trade"—two almost impossible conditions. Little wonder that Horace Walpole in Paris wrote his colleague at Madrid that the English ministry was in a violent dilemma and threatened by a coalition that was more than a chimera with the first news of a *pacte de famille* in 1732:

> If they take the King of Spain's word, well and good; if He does not, they will be blamed and censured for not using the means put into the King's hands, for obtaining satisfaction. Surely there never was a greater ferment than the present in Europe. This Court hitherto looks on quietly, if not encourages yours.

The Creek problem in America continued to be a vexing one, and it became a settled conviction that Carolina must take St. Augustine or St. Augustine would take Carolina.[84] Complaints against the violation of the armistice continued to roll in, but the Treaty of Seville was destined to become the basis for much good stalling material for Oglethorpe's diplomacy. Once its pacific tendencies almost got beyond the control of the Georgia faction, to whose interest it was to keep up the dispute in the Convention of Pardo, and came near to settling the Anglo-Spanish feud of centuries standing—in a manner which would have been a catastrophe for the Georgia enterprisers.

---

[83] "Coram, to be sure, belonged to a religious-minded faction of the Trustees, who soon came to reprobate the more worldly aims of the 'Oglethorpians'." See Stevens, *Castle Builders*, p. 66.

[84] C. O. 5/4, fol. 36.

CHAPTER III

FOUNDING A COLONY:
CONFERENCES IN GEORGIA AND FLORIDA

By 1732, the Carolinian demand that the southern rivers be protected from the danger of permanent Spanish occupation and a French fur trade monopoly found concrete expression in the plans of Governor Nicholson and the Board of Trade, and governmental sanction in the ill-fated Fort King George. Among the opposition in Parliament was often heard the voice of a young imperialist, James Oglethorpe. How could Walpole silence this growing faction? Curiously enough most of the Trustees of Georgia were not philanthropists, but mere opposition members.

It is little surprising, therefore, that men "of compassion and public spirit" formed a plan for transporting to America, particularly to the south of Carolina, the poor and indigent people of Great Britain and Ireland. In response to their application, the project was rewarded with a charter dated June 9, 1732. To wheedle the king, they called the new province Georgia. A corporation of twenty-one trustees was constituted to settle and establish it. It was probably no mere coincidence that the projected colony should embrace the territory between the rivers Altamaha and the Savannah, and that its western confines should be the Pacific. This wide swath, so deftly cut by King George, more fantastic than Ferdinand and Isabella's grant of all in the "Ocean Sea," or as inexplicable as Charles II's donation of St. Augustine, embraced great areas of Florida, Louisiana, and Texas, and ripped off the top of the Spanish Empire itself—New Mexico. Savannah at Yamacraw Bluff, Frederica on St. Simons Island, and Darien on the Altamaha arose to present a solid front to the Spaniards.

An incident of this nature could not go unnoticed; Spain made that mistake with Jamestown. In 1734 Friar Joseph Ramón Escudero had hastened to dispatch an historical appraisal to the Marqués de Monteleón, Spanish ambassador in London. A combination of French, Spaniards, and Indians was suggested to expel the English. From Florida, where the danger was immediate, a barrage of protests was kept up by quaking governors, yet the diplomatic silence maintained by Spain was inexplicable.[1]

Many times had the Spanish bull winced under the stabs from the English picador. Three times he had been violently goaded. In 1607 those Spaniards gifted with prescience saw in a successful Jamestown the beginning of a great contest. In 1670 an English settlement at Charles Town confirmed their suspicions and enhanced their incredulity about English purposes. Georgia must not have been a great surprise, but the decision to fortify the banks of the Altamaha had created an international alarm. Inadvertently, Fort King George had been destroyed, the Spaniards pretending that diplomatic pressure had had results while the English were uncertain of the fort's utility, and laboring under no illusions about Spanish diplomatic reports. Inadvertently or deliberately, the peace that reigned after the construction of the fort in 1721 was precarious.

With even more vigor than characterized the protests of Pozobueno, Geraldino, through the blustering nature of his remonstrances, showed the desperation to which the Spaniards had been brought by the extreme aggressiveness of the English in Georgia. Calm assurance was no longer his chief attribute. As in the case of Fort King George, not only London and Mad-

---

[1] The Spaniards ultimately learned that it was unwise to settle boundaries with the English in terms of degrees. The instructions to the Spanish plenipotentiaries in 1739 referred to this method as "measuring ground by the sky." While advising caution with the English, the same writer observed: "Although a degree is but 17½ leagues in width, it is well nigh infinite in length," A. G. S., Sec. de Estado, leg. 7633, Barcía to Conde de Montijo, Madrid, 21 February, 1739, punto 6. The following documents illustrate the one-sided correspondence of the governors of Florida from 1733 to 1735. A. G. I., Audiencia de Santo Domingo, 87-1-1, Doc. No. 8, Governor Antonio de Benavides to Joseph Patiño, St. Augustine, 3 February, 1733; Doc. No. 9, same to same, 27 July, 1733; Doc. No. 10, Dionisio Martínez de la Vega to Patiño, Havana, 14 October, 1733; Doc. No. 11, Benavides to Patiño, St. Augustine, 6 April, 1734; Doc. No. 12, same to same, St. Augustine, 12 April, 1734; Doc. No. 14, the Crown to Moral Sánchez, Madrid, 18 January, 1735; Doc. No. 15, Moral Sánchez to the Crown, 5 March, 1735; Doc. No. 16, same to same, St. Augustine, 2 April, 1735; Doc. No. 17, Montijo to Patiño, St. Augustine, 15 April, 1735; Doc. No. 18, Moral Sánchez to the Crown, St. Augustine, 23 May, 1735.

rid, but Georgia and Florida took an active part in the anxious parleys and negotiations which followed. With the Altamaha, which the Spanish refused to relinquish, as the southern boundary, Oglethorpe might have expected a successful, if tacit, solution of his problem; but Oglethorpe in many respects never appeared to have a direct interest in Georgia beyond the play it gave to his buccaneering spirit and the field which it offered for his military inclinations. He was more than a Georgian; he was an Englishman—perhaps first of all an Englishman.

Upon his return from England in 1735, Oglethorpe determined to colonize effectively all land to the Altamaha and to fortify the seaboard islands beyond St. Simons. The Spaniards had been bitter because of the deliberate intrusion to this point fifteen years before. That ancient resentment was again properly aroused. Yet Oglethorpe, martial and imperialistic rather than humble and philanthropic, was a wily entrepreneur. Before leaving London he obtained from the Spanish minister a sanction of the appointment of a commissioner to act as an internuncio between himself and the governor of St. Augustine. For this purpose Charles Dempsey returned to America with Oglethorpe in the ship *Symond*.

The conciliation of the Spanish authorities in Florida, the pacification of slumbering disagreements, was entrusted to Dempsey.[2] Unfortunately for the harmony of those negotiations, it was now certain that Oglethorpe intended strenuously to insist on the St. Johns as the boundary between the colonies. "I cannot deliver up a foot of ground belonging to his Majesty," he tersely informed the Duke of Newcastle, "to a foreign Power without the breach of my allegiance to his Majesty. I will alive or dead keep possession of it till I have his Majesty's orders." In this decision he was encouraged and persuaded that the Spaniards might be inclined thereto.[3] A fort was already being erected on St. George Island.

General Oglethorpe instructed Major William Richards of Purrysburgh to procure a suitable boat and to proceed with Dempsey to St. Augustine. On February 19, 1736, Dempsey

---

[2] C. O. 5/638, Samuel Eveleigh to Herman Verelst, South Carolina, 24 March, 1735; Bolton and Ross, *The Debatable Land*, p. 73; W. B. Stevens, *A History of Georgia*, I, 145-46; Jones, *History of Georgia*, I, 239.

[3] C. O. 5/638, Oglethorpe to Thomas Towers, Frederica, 17 April, 1736; C. O. 5/654, fols. 60-61, Oglethorpe to Newcastle, Frederica, 17 April, 1736.

started for St. Augustine with a conciliatory letter from Oglethorpe to Governor Don Francisco Moral Sánchez of Florida. This letter related principally to the Scotch settlement on the Altamaha, but in addition Dempsey carried several dispatches from his home government.[4] The governor of Florida was assured of the friendly disposition of Oglethorpe and his desire to preserve the existing tranquillity and to promote friendly relations. Before reaching its destination, the yawl of the English commissary capsized and the whole party was forced to scramble through the breakers to the shore, dragging the boat behind. After walking several leagues through the sand, they were sighted by a Spanish captain of horse, Don Pedro Lamberto, who conducted them to the Spanish governor.

Uncertain of the fate of Dempsey, and solicitous of his welfare, Oglethorpe, a month after the beginning of the mission, left upon his southern reconnoissance. Other motives might have been to inquire into the defenses of the Spaniards and to forestall a premature attack upon Florida by the Indians of the English allegiance, an attack which would thwart all the good offices of Dempsey. Landing at the Spanish fort at the mouth of the San Juan to inform himself concerning the movements and success of his commissioner, the general was perplexed to find the post vacated. The opportune encounter with Major Richards returning from St. Augustine relieved his anxieties.

In St. Augustine, Dempsey was received with great civility.[5] To Don Francisco Moral Sánchez this courtesy had another significance. In the first place he was a Spaniard and could not suffer himself to be overshadowed in the Latin art of kindness and suavity, especially when so much was at stake. The commissioner's urbane and affable manner mingled with a lesser degree of haughtiness was no little surprising in Florida. "I disposses him of his advantage and confuse him with kindness and sincerity, but I look upon his strange proceedings with suspicion."[6]

Three times was this gracious emissary bandied back and

---

[4] C. O. 5/690, Dempsey to the Trustees, London, 6 April, 1737; "A Voyage to Georgia," *Collections of the Georgia Historical Society*, I, 127-28.

[5] Jones, *op. cit.*, I, 240.

[6] A. G. I., Audiencia de Santo Domingo, 87-1-1, Doc. No. 56, Moral Sánchez to Güemez y Horcasitas, St. Augustine, 26 October, 1736.

forth between St. Augustine and St. Simons; three times in his nine months of service was he cast ashore by the waves.[7] The first reply of the Spaniard was courteous but cautious, and by implication plainly evinced the irritation which the encroachments of Oglethorpe upon the Catholic King's lands had occasioned. The letters which passed contained on the one hand complaints of the savage incursions and trespassing on Spanish land; and on the other, attempted vindications of the right of occupation, a thrashing over of the old arguments, and assurances of redress for unwarranted incursions. Since the Spaniards in Havana were fully advised of what was happening on the coast, and the Florida border was threatened by a Creek Indian attack, Major Richards felt constrained to promise to return to St. Augustine in three weeks with Oglethorpe's response. Mingled compliments and crimination were the reply.

So tense was the situation now that the general backed his claim to the St. Johns with arms. He soon learned from other sources that the governor of St. Augustine was buying arms for the Florida Indians, and that in conjunction with the Yamasees and reinforcements from Havana he hoped to desolate St. Simons. Upon receipt of this information, Oglethorpe dispatched a piragua and scout boat to the St. Johns to prevent a crossing, placed two vessels in the river to protect Frederica, and pressed Fort St. George on St. George Island to a rapid completion.

In reply to the messages of Major Richards, Oglethorpe on April 13 sent Major Richards and Major William Horton to smooth over these harassing difficulties. His preparations, his letter indicated, were to prevent lawlessness. He now extended his thanks to the governor for his former civilities and commended Richards and his companions to his favorable consideration. Majors Richards and Horton were surprised upon their arrival at the St. Johns not to find the stipulated signal indicating that horsemen waited to escort them to St. Augustine.

A few days later the signal was espied, and the Spaniards appeared in great force. Reluctantly Major Richards joined them for the contemplated journey. The only news from him for some time was a scribbled note in German to Captain

---

[7] *Idem;* C. O. 5/690, Dempsey to the Georgia Trustees, London, 6 April, 1737.

Hermsdorf indicating only his safe arrival at the headquarters of the Spanish captain of horse. Hermsdorf was on the verge of retreat when he was joined by Oglethorpe. Thereupon they passed over to the Spanish side under a flag of truce, only to find the post deserted. When almost ready to depart, one of Oglethorpe's men returned driving a Spaniard armed with a musket, two pistols, a long and a short sword. "Here, sir," he said, "I have caught a Spaniard for you." Treated with wine and victuals, the captive disclosed that both Richards and Horton had been placed under arrest. Oglethorpe's expectations of an early attack were soon reinforced by the discovery of concealed Spanish horsemen and launches in the vicinity. If the Spaniards actually planned an attack upon Frederica, however, knowledge of the numbers of the English and new fortifications forestalled it.

The return of Horton to Frederica on June 14 was the occasion of general rejoicing.[8] His story was a dramatic one. Dempsey was already in St. Augustine, and after firing his gun frantically, Horton was at last picked up and conveyed to the governor. After a most civil reception, he was carried to Dempsey's quarters and the next day, at Dempsey's instance, a detachment of cavalry was sent to bring over Major Richards. Evidently the terror which had grasped the Georgians had seized the inhabitants of Florida also, for together the new agents were received "with the greatest joy by the people, who looked upon them as the messengers of their deliverance for bringing them the news that the English boat patrol upon the river was to hinder the barbarous Indians from passing and molesting them."[9]

But the strain was too much for easy diplomatic intercourse. The governor had not yet prepared his answer to Oglethorpe's communication. Meanwhile, the weary emissaries gladly accepted an invitation to a general dance at the house of the governor's interpreter, where they remained until three o'clock in the morning. At this hour they returned to Dempsey's house. They were, they reported, startled to find a dozen musketeers and a sergeant lined up before the door early the next morn-

---

[8] W. B. Stevens, *op. cit.*, I, 140; "A Voyage to Georgia," *Collections of the Georgia Historical Society*, I, 146-47; *The Colonial Records of the State of Georgia* (edited by Allan D. Candler), XXI, 150.

[9] "A Voyage to Georgia," *Collections of the Georgia Historical Society*, I, 147.

ing. Diego Paulo, town major, soon came from the governor to acquaint Dempsey with news that Horton, Richards, and their servants were wanted for taking "a plan of the town and castle" that very morning. The English at least feigned astonishment. They had been abed since three o'clock! Diego Paulo then calmly informed Don Carlos Dempsey that he need fear nothing and that he might come and go as he chose. At the foot of the stairs the sergeant placed one sentry, and at the top another. The air was thick.[10]

Suddenly, two hours later, Governor Moral Sánchez appeared with some gayly dressed officers and the town scribe. Seating himself, he launched promptly into a summary examination of Major Richards. Evidently the governor feared an attack. He desired to know the object of Richards' visit, and Richards replied that his journey was undertaken pursuant to his promise to return with letters from Oglethorpe. Seizing the opening, the governor anxiously inquired as to Oglethorpe's whereabouts. Major Richards could only answer that he had left him at Frederica. Thereupon the Spaniard wished an exact account of the men and fortifications at that point. Here the major feigned ignorance, as he did in response to similar inquiries about Jeykl Sound, Cumberland Island, Amelia Island, and St. Johns. The governor retired in a huff.

Stronger methods were to be employed. Richards and Horton were summoned to the governor's house. Horton was now examined, and he likewise refused to answer. The threat to send him to the mines elicited the response that as a citizen of Great Britain he suspected his sovereign was strong enough to afford him protection. Some time the next day the guards were removed from the house when Dempsey promised upon his honor that they would not go about without the governor's permission. Determined to secure information and in a fever heat of excitement and fear, Don Ignacio Rosso, Lieutenant Colonel of the garrison, began a reconnoitring expedition. In about five days, his launch put in at St. Augustine. He was extremely fatigued, and his men had rowed the skin from their hands. From the sight of numerous scouting parties and the few mounted guns the English had, they conjectured in their fear that all the islands were fortified and full of armed men

---
[10] *Idem;* W. B. Stevens, *op. cit.*, I, 146.

and boats. At the art of bluff Oglethorpe was coming into his own.[11]

From the Spanish governor Dempsey had brought forth the cognomen, "suave."[12] While the Spaniards through their magnifying glass of fear had seen many men and guns, and before they had time to decrease the potency of that vision, the scouting officer justified the governor's opinion. Speaking to the governor, bishop, and the rest of the officers in rapid succession, he brought about a council of war.[13] The council immediately resolved to send back Richards and Horton with letters of civility to Oglethorpe. With them went Charles Dempsey, Captain Don Pedro Lamberto, and Don Manuel D'Arcy, adjutant of the garrison of St. Augustine—all instructed to express a desire for friendship with the English. Warned of the approach of the Spaniards, Oglethorpe ordered Captain Gascoigne to receive them on board his vessel, the *Hawk*. Thus the general would be free to continue his voyage of inspection to Fort St. George without a breach of the rules of hospitality, and at the same time the Spaniards would be precluded from taking plans or securing information about the strength and location of Frederica. By reloading the cannon on shore and lining his men at double distances, Oglethorpe impressed the Spaniards on Jekyl Island with his strength.[14]

---

[11] "A Voyage to Georgia," *Collections of the Georgia Historical Society*, I, 147-48.

[12] A. G. I., Audiencia de Santo Domingo, 87-1-1, Doc. No. 56, Moral Sánchez to Güemez y Horcasitas, St. Augustine, 26 October, 1736.

[13] The Spanish launch apparently encountered every craft on the Georgia coast and "made the best of her way to St. Augustine with a dismal account that ye whole Coast was covered with Men, boats & Cannon. I also made use of some small Strategems on the Frontiers at Fort St. George to make them believe we were numerous, and treating some Spaniards who came with messages to us with great kindness God was pleased to prosper our endeavors. The Spanish Govr was obliged to call a Council upon the terrors spread abroad, in which the Bishop, the Officers and the people declared unanimously that they were for preserving a good harmony with the King of Great Britain's Subjects, and desired the Gobernour to release ye messengers I had sent down, and sent up an Officer with them to excuse the having violated the Laws of a Nation and Hospitality." *The Colonial Records of the State of Georgia*, XXI, 154, 160.

[14] "A Voyage to Georgia," *Collections of the Georgia Historical Society*, I, 150; R. Wright, *A Memoir of General James Oglethorpe*, p. 159; Jones, *op. cit.*, I, 247; "I sent a boat to escort them to St. Simon's & found Major Richard and all our Gentlemen sent by me on ye message had been dismissed in a very honorable manner, though when they thought us weak they had threatened Major Richard to send him to the Mines at least, if he wo^d not sign some Interrogatories which

When the Spanish commissaries were finally received, a detachment of the independent company in their regimentals lined one side of the ship, and the Highlanders under Ensign Mackay with their drawn swords and plaid the other. At the cabin door stood sentries with drawn cutlasses. In addition, the general "ordered two handsome tents lined with Chinese, with Marquises and walls of canvas, to be sent down and pitched upon Jekyl Island."[15]

Within a few days the English had turned the diplomatic, but none the less real, contempt of the Spanish governor into a respect which was bidding fair to meet success. Part of the new diplomatic advantage was due no doubt to the great energy of Oglethorpe in creating false impressions. Yet it must be remembered that Dempsey was not only master of Oglethorpe's technique, but while in St. Augustine he was handsomely supported by the Trustees. Such suavity and urbanity in an English frontiersman surprised his rivals, and in a Latin effort not to be disarmed by graciousness the Spaniards made it possible for Dempsey to pacify them in more than one crisis.

After dinner on June 19 the Spanish commissaries presented their messages in writing. This was the signal for toasts to the royal health, Oglethorpe drinking to that of the king and queen of Spain and the Spaniards to the king of Great Britain and the royal family. On the twenty-first the answer to the messages was delivered. Simultaneously presents—snuff, chocolate, and similar commodities—changed hands. All the time, the colonists were attempting to impress the Spaniards with the opulence of the colony and the strong foothold which the English had already secured by sending them an abundance of sheep, hogs, poultry, garden stuff, butter, cheese, and wine.[16]

Indian troubles had often been a source of friction between the two peoples and the two courts and at this point they threatened to disrupt the negotiations. Being given the first opening, the Indians appeared in tribal costume and war paint. Don Pedro, the Spanish commissary, knew some of the facts. Before

---

they presented to him. The Spanish officers are now at ye Garrison where the Independent Company lies, I shall see them too morrow and shall by Dymond send you an acco^t of their message." Oglethorpe to the Trustees, Frederica, 18 May, 1736, *The Colonial Records of the State of Georgia*, XXI, 160-61.

[15] *Idem.*

[16] "A Voyage to Georgia," *Collections of the Georgia Historical Society*, I, 151.

him Tomochichi, who had travelled with Oglethorpe to London, carried the news that a party of forty Spaniards and Indians, violating, he said, the agreement then existing with the Spaniards, had taken some Indians of the English allegiance by surprise and had killed part of them. A second, Hyllispilli, demanded justice for this affair. The Spaniard was struck with horror at the stories which the natives told concerning the exploits of the raiders who, it was reported, dashed out the brains of the prisoners, the wounded, and the boys. The native testimony tended to weave a skein around the affair and to dangle it before the eyes of the commissaries as a Spanish intrigue. An Indian boy was produced who had lurked and observed the whole affair. Another had bragged at St. Marks that he was a member of the party which was sent from St. Augustine "which was so known a thing it could not be denied."[17]

No doubt both factions had been guilty of the same practice. Realizing that larger aims might be thwarted, Oglethorpe requested Don Pedro to represent to the governor of St. Augustine that since these Indians were subjects of Great Britain, satisfaction must be forthcoming. Here the general was interrupted, and Chief Hyllispilli represented that the outrage was effected during his absence in Europe with the general. He now desired the general's company for the revenge which he planned to take. Thereupon Don Pedro Lamberto admitted knowledge of a group of Indians not of the Spanish allegiance who went from the vicinity of St. Augustine. He agreed to arrest Pohoia, king of the Floridas, who commanded the party, should he enter St. Augustine. If he did not enter, the governor and council would outlaw him. To this Hyllispilli replied: "We hear what you say; when we see it done, we will believe you." Only the temporizing influence of Tomochichi saved a violent outbreak. The incredulity of another Indian was pertinent. He supposed that notice would be given to Pohoia not to come into St. Augustine, but staying out would be just as well since there was no other place in Florida where he would be safe! During the night, a group of English Indians landed on Jekyl Island where the Spanish emissaries were encamped and attempted to begin a quarrel through all kinds of annoy-

---

[17] A. G. I., Audiencia de Santo Domingo, 87-1-1, Doc. No. 40; "A Voyage to Georgia," *Collections of the Georgia Historical Society*, I, 151; Wright, *op. cit.*, pp. 160 *et seq.*

ances. In each instance the Spaniards retired quietly from it. On the twenty-second, the Spaniards set out for Florida. A peace had been secured, which, in spite of frequent rumors, was to prevent bloodshed for about two years. It was the unfortunate governor who ratified the treaty who suffered. But the time which it took to execute justice from a seat three thousand miles distant was precious to Oglethorpe. This time he planned to make use of it to push his frontiers southward.

Many an interesting light upon the question of Georgia is reflected, more often indirectly than directly, in Oglethorpe's letter to the Trustees:

After dinner we drank to the King of Britain's and the king of Spain's health under a discharge of cannon from the ship; which was answered with fifteen pieces of cannon from Delegal's fort at the Sea-point. That again was followed by cannon from the fort of St. Andrew's, and by those of Frederica and Darien, as I had before ordered. The Spaniards seemed extremely surprised that there should be so many forts, and all within hearing of one another. Don Pedro smiled and said, "No wonder Don Ignacio made more haste home than out." After the healths were done, a great number of Indians came on board, naked, painted, and their heads dressed with feathers. They demanded of me justice against the Spaniards for killing some of their men in time of peace. . . .[18]

The Indian matters being thus settled, we had a conference with the Spanish commissioners. They thanked me first for my restraining the Indians who were in my power, and hoped I would extend that care to the upper Indians. They, then, after having produced their credentials, presented a paper the contents whereof were to know by what title I settled upon St. Simon's, being lands belonging to the king of Spain. I took the paper, promising an answer the next day. The substance was that the lands belonged to the king of England by undoubted right: that I had proceeded with the utmost caution, having taken with me Indians, the natives and possessors of those lands; that I had examined every place to see if there were any Spanish possessions, and went forward until I found an outguard of theirs, over against which I settled the English without committing any hostilities or dislodging any. Therefore I did not extend the king's dominions, but only settled with regular garrisons that part of them which was before a shelter for Indians, pirates, and such sort of disorderly men.

The rest of the evening we spent in conversation, which chiefly

---

[18] "A Voyage to Georgia," *Collections of the Georgia Historical Society*, I, 150.

turned upon the convenience it would be both to the Spaniards and English, to have regular garrisons in sight of each other. Don Pedro smiled and said he readily agreed to that, and should like very well to have their Spanish guard upon the south side of the Helena River,[19] which is within five miles of Charlestown, and where the Spaniards had a garrison in King Charles the First's time. I replied I thought it was better as it was; for there were a great many people living between who could never be persuaded to come in to his sentiments. At last Don Pedro acquainted us that he thought the Spaniards would refer the settling of the limits to the Courts of Europe, for which purpose he should write to their Court, and in the meantime desired no hostilities might be committed, and that I would send up a commissary to sign with the government an agreement to this purpose. I thereupon appointed Mr. Dempsey to be my commissary and to return with them. Don Pedro is the ruling man in Augustine and has more interest with the council of war than the Governor. As he passed by George's point, he sent a whole ox as a present to the garrison. He gave me some sweetmeats and chocolate. I gave him a gold watch, a gun, and fresh provisions. To Don Manuel I gave a silver watch, and sent back a boat to escort them. If the Spaniards had committed any hostilities, I could, by the help of the Indians, have destroyed Augustine with great facility. But God be praised, by His blessing, the diligence of Dempsey, and the prudence of Don Pedro, all bloodshed was avoided.[20]

The witty and urbane Don Pedro returned home; and with him went the diplomatic Dempsey and instructions to negotiate a treaty with the governor of St. Augustine.[21] Georgia and Florida were on the verge of war before the conference in which the prudence of Don Pedro Lamberto Rotinello saved the day. Sinister shadows were again cast over the colonists, who bore the brunt of two empires. News of the arrival of men, ammunition, and money in St. Augustine augured ill for the negotiations, and struck Dempsey, then at that town, with a sense of fear.[22] In the midst of the consequent confusion came the news that the governor of Havana had abruptly sent the engineer, Don Antonio Arredondo, to St. Augustine. He came with in-

---

[19] This quip evidently fell on immune faculties; Don Pedro must have been a clear thinker and an insatiable wit.

[20] Wright, *op. cit.*, p. 160 *et seq.*

[21] *Idem;* Jones, *op. cit.*, I, 251.

[22] C. O. 5/690, Dempsey to the Trustees, London, 6 April, 1737; *Colonial Records of the State of Georgia*, XXI, 179.

structions to make demands and propositions to Oglethorpe.[23]

Arredondo immediately dispatched a letter to the English general and repeated it in English, but all to no avail. The new Spanish commissioner was somewhat appeased by the probability that Oglethorpe was occupied with his assembly or with the Carolinians, for the trouble with Carolina about trading rights came near assuming the ascendency over the extension or limitation of the southern boundary.[24] In spite of much embarrassment at the incident, Arredondo wrote to his governor expressing his firm resolution to start for Frederica. That projects were on foot to demolish Georgia seems clear from the extensive report over the condition of the contiguous provinces.[25]

Don Antonio's reception rivaled that of his predecessors in entertainment and provisioning.[26] He demanded of Oglethorpe that the English should evacuate all they stood possessed of as far as St. Helena Sound.[27] There the Spaniards had had forts almost before the English came to America, Arredondo emphasized.[28] The Spaniards were originally much disturbed over the building of Fort St. George at the mouth of the St. Johns River[29] and the memorials to Oglethorpe became bitter on the injury which this fort caused to Spanish trade, aside from the indignity inflicted by its location in Spanish territory.[30] For the demand which the Spanish envoy made, he supplied historical and logical evidence.[31]

---

[23] C. O. 5/638, an enclosure dated Frederica, 30 August, 1736; *Colonial Records of the State of Georgia*, XXI, 225, 363. Oglethorpe's response, A. G. I., Audiencia de Santo Domingo, 87-1-1, Doc. No. 46.

[24] A. G. I., Audiencia de Santo Domingo, 86-1-1, Docs. Nos. 48 and 58, Arredondo to Güemez y Horcasitas, St. Augustine, 31 August, 1736; *Colonial Records of the State of Georgia*, XXI, 206.

[25] A. G. I., Audiencia de Santo Domingo, 87-1-1, Doc. No. 49, Arredondo to Güemez y Horcasitas, Saint Simon, 8 September, 1736.

[26] *Colonial Records of the State of Georgia*, XXI, 225; C. O. 5/638, enclosure to the Trustees, Frederica, 30 August, 1736.

[27] C. O. 5/638, enclosure, Frederica, 20 September, 1736.

[28] A. G. I., Audiencia de Santo Domingo, 87-1-1, Doc. No. 49, Arredondo to Güemez y Horcasitas, aboard the *Nuestra Señora*, 8 September, 1736.

[29] *Colonial Records of the State of Georgia*, XXI, 179; see Chap. IV.

[30] See A. Arredondo, *Demonstración del derecho que tiene el Rey Catholico al territorio de Nueva Georgia* . . . Chap. VI. This work, copies of which are in the British Museum, the Archivo General de Simancas, and the Archivo General de Indias, and the Bancroft Library, has been carefully and ably edited and translated by Professor H. E. Bolton.

[31] Arredondo, *op. cit.*, Chap. VI.

Counter demands were the most efficacious method at the disposal of the English, and they employed them. The Spanish were called upon to evacuate all lands to the twenty-ninth degree, since Sir Francis Drake had occupied the country that far south by raiding and capturing St. Augustine! After a series of conferences, an agreement was reached stipulating that upon the withdrawal of the garrison from St. George, that island should be depopulated, the fortifications dismantled, and all remain unpossessed; and that no hostilities should be committed until the will of the two courts should be known. Disputes referring to the boundaries were referred to Europe. All other matters would be deferred pending the action of the governments. On September 3, the representatives of Spain sailed southward after making profuse acknowledgments of the civilities with which they had met during the negotiations. This agreement was subsequently ratified by the Council of War and the Governor of St. Augustine.[32]

The accord reached between Arredondo, Oglethorpe, and Dempsey was soon published in one of the Carolina newspapers. Those in a position to appreciate the gravity of the situation were jubilant over the removal of the danger of which they had been so apprehensive.[33] The troublesome boundary question was again passed back to Europe; the courts were now expected to deal with it. The English general was himself very happy over the treaty, and gleefully reported: "All matters with the Spaniards are regulated, and the governor of Augustine contented. Therefore all being safe I shall set out immediately for Europe."[34] When the treaty was rejected or violated, he realized that he would need more soldiers, more funds, and more power—and he resolved to get them all.[35]

The arrangement made by Dempsey met with the hearty approval of the Georgia Trustees and the English government.

---

[32] C. O. 5/638, p. 142; Add. MSS, 32794, N. P., CIX, 255-59; John Harris. *Navigantium atque Itinerantium Bibliotheca*, II, 331-32. W. B. Stevens, *op. cit.*, I, 148, See in appendix copy of the treaty signed by Oglethorpe and the governor of St. Augustine, 11/27 October, 1736.

[33] C. O. 5/638, Eveleigh to Verelst, Charles Town, 13 October, 1736; *Colonial Records of the State of Georgia*, XXI, 212.

[34] *Ibid.*, p. 236.

[35] *Ibid.*, I, 323-24; IV, 140-51; V, 18-19; W. B. Stevens, *op. cit.*, I, 150-52; Jones, *op. cit.*, I, 256-75; Earl of Egmont, *Diary*, II, 339, 368, 383, 401, 414-17, 427-31, 433-38, 457, 469, 494, 501.

Immediately upon his return, Oglethorpe read before the Board of Trustees an account of his proceedings in Georgia, of the state of that colony, and also laid before the Trustees two treaties of peace concluded between the Georgians and the Spaniards. One of these treaties was concluded and ratified by Dempsey and the Council of War in St. Augustine; the other by Dempsey and Governor Don Francisco de Moral Sánchez. The general was congratulated upon his return to England, and voted the thanks of the Trustees for the service rendered the colony of Georgia.[36]

If the English were satisfied with the treaty arrangements, the Spaniards thought that they had a right to be. Madrid immediately denied the authority of the governor of St. Augustine to make the treaty and informed England that the treaty was neither made by the Spanish government nor acceptable to it; the governor had exceeded his instructions. Evidently the government was not merely dissembling, for Sánchez was recalled to Spain by the court at Madrid, probably at the instigation of the Spanish king. It was rumored that Sánchez had not only been sent home in chains for signing the Treaty of Neutrality with Oglethorpe but that he had been hanged. The report also got abroad that Captain Dempsey's brother, an officer in the Spanish service, had been cashiered because the captain assisted Oglethorpe in concluding the treaty.[37]

Meanwhile Don Antonio Arredondo, in his leisure, proceeded to render a lengthy account of his stewardship to Governor Güemez y Horcasitas in a document of more than fifty pages.[38] It included the most minute details of the defense of Georgia and Florida.[39] "It occasions me profound grief," wrote Arredondo, "that the king has lost such beautiful possessions." However arduous the occupation may have been, he thought recovery would now be difficult.[40]

---

[36] *Colonial Records of the State of Georgia*, V, 267.

[37] John Campbell, *A Concise History of Spanish America* (London, 1741), p. 101; W. B. Stevens, *op. cit.*, I, 148; *Colonial Records of the State of Georgia*, V, 351; Egmont, *op. cit.*, II, 326, 410; Bolton and Ross, *op. cit.*, p. 74.

[38] A. G. I., Audiencia de Santo Domingo, 87-1-1, Doc. No. 59, Arredondo to Güemez y Horcasitas, St. Augustine, 22 November, 1736.

[39] *Ibid.*, 86-6-5, "Copia del papel reserbado que escrivio al Govr de Havana el Ingeniero Ordinario Dn. Antonio de Arredondo desde el Presidio de la Florida." *Passim.*

[40] *Idem.*

A resolution probably already fixed in Oglethorpe's mind was more than ever impressed there. The recall of the governor of Florida, the increase of the garrison at St. Augustine, and the augmenting of the naval force of that colony served as a pretext for Oglethorpe's trip to England and bolstered up his attempt to secure the passage of active measures for the defense of the colony.[41] With this resolution he arrived in London and the following day presented himself before the queen at St. James's before reporting to the Trustees. His activities became a thorn in the flesh of the Walpole ministry and the almost exclusive subject of conversation in Anglo-Spanish diplomatic circles.[42]

So precipitate was the departure of the English general that letters dispatched from St. Augustine arrived too late.[43] The Spaniards, who themselves were contemplating a military expedition of a secret nature, were occasioned no little uneasiness. Such a step interpreted by Manuel de Montiano, the new governor of St. Augustine, placed the colony in the direst jeopardy. In a letter to the king he voiced his sentiment in fewer words than the Spaniard is wont to use, reporting for a second time that Oglethorpe, "Commander of the English Colonies," had said openly that although he should receive orders from his king and court to fix the boundary limits, he would delay the execution "so that there should never be a sign of these limits." He never even answered the letters sent him from Florida.[44] In judging this attitude as of basic importance, and in recommending that it would be well to relieve the colonies "of a gentleman whom it would be exceedingly troublesome to manage," Montiano was eminently right. But what Spanish mouse would trap this English cat?

---

[41] W. B. Stevens, *op. cit.*, I, 149; *Colonial Records of the State of Georgia*, XXI, 377; Chap. III.

[42] A. G. I., Audiencia de Santo Domingo, 87-1-2, Doc. No. 5, Geraldino to Torrenueva, London, 31 January, 1737; Egmont, *op. cit.*, *passim*. These activities in Europe constitute a part of European diplomacy and are not considered at length in connection with the Georgia-Florida diplomacy.

[43] *Colonial Records of the State of Georgia*, XXI, 284.

[44] A. M. Brooks, *The Unwritten History of Old St. Augustine*, p. 175. There is abundant evidence that the Spaniards understood this game of delaying and holding. A. G. S., Sec. de Estado, leg. 7633 (antiguo), Joseph de Layssequilla to the King, Madrid, 4 December, 1738, punto 6; Conde de Montijo to the King, San Lorenzo, 9 November, 1737, puntos 15-16.

Already the lines of communication between the Spanish embassy and Whitehall were hot with the angry and, as Keene said, "blustering memorials" of the Spanish minister, Tomás Geraldino.[45] Simultaneously a great and somewhat quixotic campaign was on foot to "reannex all that formerly belonged to the Spanish monarchy."[46] Contingents were assembling at Havana, and the news had leaked out that seven thousand men and seven warships were made ready there.[47] The hurried order for the suspension of the campaign came suddenly to Governor Güemez y Horcasitas, March 21. Deliberation over the boundaries would be a question for the European courts. At St. Augustine, this peaceful news was jubilantly received and joyously proclaimed through the streets by the staccato rattle of kettledrums. In London, Geraldino was thoroughly convinced that by a judicious play of opposition politics he could thwart Oglethorpe, ruin the Trustees, and force the abandonment of Georgia. The political strength of the Georgia group was all Walpole and his cohorts were interested in. Both Geraldino and the Floridians had misplaced their confidence. The Spaniard had not reckoned on the shrewdness of his antagonist for favor, Don Diego Oglethorpe. Moving silently and swiftly, and using the war scare which was reported and stressed in tones of great tenseness from every angle and by nearly every prominent official in the Caribbean and southern colonies, the general gained the ear of the king. Geraldino learned that a regiment was to be sent to Georgia and inferred from the news that Oglethorpe was to be made commander-in-chief of the southern forces. He doubted that this was a measure of pacification.[48]

The return of the new commander-in-chief from Europe be-

---

[45] A. G. I., Audiencia de Santo Domingo, 87-1-1, Doc. No. 69, Geraldino to Torrenueva, London, 4 July, 1737. These papers are to be found in the Archives at Seville, and also at Simancas in the Spanish state papers. See chap. IV. Documents accessible in this country are *Collections of the Georgia Historical Society*, VII, pt. III, 16-18; Egmont, *op. cit.*, II, 300-304, 426-38; W. Coxe, *Memoirs of the Life and Administration of Sir Robert Walpole*, IV, 9; W. B. Stevens, I, 148-49; Wright, *op. cit.*, chap. X; Arredondo, *op. cit.*, chap. VI; H. W. V. Temperley, "Causes of the War of Jenkins' Ear, 1739," *Royal Historical Society Transactions*, 3rd ser., III, 197-236.

[46] For a bibliography of war preparations at this juncture see Bolton and Ross, *op. cit.*, p. 72, and chap. IV below.

[47] *Idem.*   [48] A. G. I., Audiencia de Santo Domingo, 87-1-1, Doc. No. 69.

gan another period of anxious communications between governors and courts. By agreement, there existed an armed truce.[49] To Florida the natural outcome of the efforts on foot in London would be the augmentation of the settlements and fortifications to the north.[50] So anxious were they that Governor Don Manuel Montiano dispatched messengers to reconnoitre and to return with information relative to the fortifications under way in the contiguous provinces.[51] The movements of the potential enemy had been vigorously protested at London, but the ministry showed its susceptibility to parliamentary necessity and ended by appointing the person least desired by Spain.[52] This did not occur, however, before a promise was secured from a docile government that nothing against Florida was intended, and that Geraldino would be given prompt notice on all points relative to Georgia.[53]

In June the governor, council of war, and Don Antonio de Arredondo, captain, engineer and special commissary, sent a memorial to Oglethorpe stipulating that abandonment of St. Johns Island would restore good correspondence between the colonies.[54] That it was vital to St. Augustine is obvious from the consideration that it commanded the only passage to the Spanish fortresses at Picolata, San Francisco de Popa, and San Marcos de Apalache. Never refusing a challenge to match wits in the hide-and-seek diplomacy of this southern frontier, Oglethorpe met the Spanish suggestion for a parley by sending a sloop to St. Augustine to bring the engineer-diplomat and empire defender, Don Antonio de Arredondo, to St. Simons. No more succinct statement of the positions of both contestants was ever made than in this conference. Arredondo, destined to make himself the classical defender of the Spanish title, peremptorily demanded the withdrawal of the English behind the

---

[49] Add. MSS, 32794, N. P. CIX, 255; A. G. I., Audiencia de Santo Domingo, 87-1-2, Geraldino to the Crown, London, 2 May, 1737; *ibid.*, 87-1-3, the Crown to Güemez y Horcasitas, 23 May, 1737.

[50] A. G. I., Audiencia de Santo Domingo, 86-6-5, Noticias, 29 October, 1737.

[51] A. G. I., Audiencia de Santo Domingo, 86-6-5, Montiano to the King, St. Augustine, 19 December, 1737. An opinion of the motives of Oglethorpe and the state of St. Augustine is given in this letter.

[52] A. G. I., Audiencia de Santo Domingo, 87-1-2, Doc. No. 69, Geraldino to Torrenueva, London, 4 July, 1737.

[53] *Ibid.*, 31 January, 1737.

[54] C. O. 5/283, deposition of Charles Dempsey, 13 April, 1739.

Edisto River and St. Helena Sound. Oglethorpe, never to be outdone where temerity was expedient, called upon the Spaniard to his face to remain south of the twenty-ninth degree! Between the Edisto and the twenty-ninth degree lay "the debatable land." But most of all the soldier and engineer in Arredondo looked with more than alarm upon Fort St. George which commanded the St. Johns. It must be evacuated and dismantled. An agreement to this effect was signed between Arredondo and Oglethorpe, August 30, 1736. The proposal to remove the garrison and to demolish the fortification was only a gesture of Oglethorpe's. In the same month of the following year, Governor Güemez y. Horcasitas extended his gratitude to Oglethorpe for the kind reception of Arredondo. This, however, was a ruse; his real message was a veiled demand for compliance with the stipulation of an agreement signed between Arredondo and the English, August 30, 1736, requiring the immediate evacuation of the island of San Juan and demolition of its fortification. By way of emphasis, Güemez y Horcasitas, trusting his message to an Irish pilot, expressed his inability to understand the non-compliance in the face of an act so formal and so solemn, given with every profession of good faith and correspondence to the accredited commissary of Spain, Don Antonio Arredondo.[55]

In his report to the Spanish minister, Matheo Pablo Marqués de Torrenueva, a sadder strain accompanied a recitation of the default of the English at San Juan; they had received information of the Spanish preparations to remove the diplomatic difficulty of Georgia by force. The English knew of the arrival of the four hundred troops at St. Augustine. Meanwhile, Güemez y Horcasitas knew the English were assembling forces. He then laid before Torrenueva a bold plan of a surprise attack by both water and land which would, by the use of a superior force in front and river transports to pierce the interior and cut off retreat, trap the subjects of His Britannic

[55] A. G. I., Audiencia de Santo Domingo, 87-1-1, Doc. No. 87, Güemez y Horcasitas to Oglethorpe, Havana, 13 August, 1735. Oglethorpe called the island in question Fort St. George. See also A. G. I., Audiencia de Santo Domingo, 87-1-2, Doc. No. 45B, Oglethorpe to Arredondo, Savannah, 29 July, 1736; same to same, Frederica, 9 August, 1736; Doc. No. 45, Oglethorpe to Arredondo, Georgia, 30 August, 1736; Doc. No. 46, Oglethorpe to Güemez y Horcasitas, Georgia, 30 August, 1736; *ibid.*, 87-1-3, Doc. No. 1, Arredondo to Güemez y Horcasitas, St. Augustine, 31 August, 1736.

Majesty who would not be treated as belligerent subjects of the king of England, but as usurpers to be captured and expelled at the discretion of their just lords, the Spaniards. It was time to strike—Charles Town, St. Simons Sound—before the English were given time to arrange their settlers and place their positions in a posture of defense. Don Miguel Wall, being found unsuited to the expedition, was allowed to return to Spain under the pretext of conferring with the ministry. As to referring any question of limits to Carolina or Georgia, some definite proof beyond attestation of their good faith would be absolutely prerequisite.[56] At any rate he still held to the conviction that the Spanish could hardly with safety occupy the disputed area beyond the St. Johns. The fact that the English protested their right to the twenty-ninth parallel bore witness to the validity of that assumption.[57]

As late as November, 1737, the troops and command issued so blandly to the same buccaneering governor were being vigorously protested in America and in Europe.[58] Oglethorpe's instructions the following year did not evince a supine deference to Spanish wishes, as both Geraldino and the enemies of the reign of Walpole so fervidly preached. Every possible investigation of the designs of the Spaniards on the frontiers, at Havana, and at St. Augustine was begun immediately. Although no umbrage was to be given and the maintenance of good correspondence was ardently to be sought by holding the Indians in check and by other means, forces were to be arranged and forts strengthened. In case the Spaniards attacked, which eventuality was not expected, any forts within the grants of 1663, 1666, or within the Charter of Georgia, notice to the ships should be given upon first signs, and the main attack met in the most effectual manner possible.[59]

Into this restless, disturbed, and expectant state came news of the intention of the two courts amicably to adjust both their maritime and boundary troubles through a convention of commissaries. This resolve entailed a very exacting armistice on

---

[56] A. G. I., Audiencia de Santo Domingo, 87-1-2, Doc. No. 77, Güemez y Horcasitas to Torrenueva, Havana, 26 August, 1737.

[57] *Ibid.*, 87-1-3, Doc. No. 31.

[58] S. P. F., Spain, Supplementary, 246, Torrenueva to Geraldino, 28 November, 1737.

[59] C. O. 5/654, pp. 133-35, Oglethorpe's instructions, 8 May, 1738.

the Georgia-Florida boundary. And in this state things stood while those who wished peace awaited the adjustment of the boundary question. Thus it happened that Oglethorpe's plan of dissimulation coupled with activity prevented a settlement of the essential issue and enhanced his opportunities for achieving glory. Since his spirit was essentially buccaneering, it is no wonder that the Spaniards saw in him and his every fomentation an eye adjusted solely to the plaudits contingent upon successful conquest.[60] But they could not deny that he had laid down the policy of his master—a policy which baffled all efforts at settlement. His was an irreconcilable and unreasonable policy. And, indeed, this much mooted question was brought to a termination only when Florida was ceded to England. Nothing else could have solved it on the foundations laid by Oglethorpe. Debarring the element of force as a justification or right of occupation, the English had as good a claim to St. Augustine as to the St. Johns River, and even Oglethorpe himself did not have the temerity to claim the former.

[60] A. G. I., Audiencia de Santo Domingo, 86-6-5, Montiano to the king, St. Augustine, 19 December, 1737.

CHAPTER IV

DON MIGUEL WALL AND THE SPANISH ATTEMPT AGAINST THE EXISTENCE OF GEORGIA

A CLASH in Georgia appeared inevitable, and Spain's chances of making good her claims to the South Atlantic regions meager. Only a bold, unexpected, and decisive stroke could clear the ground for her. In Don Joseph Patiño, Secretary of State for Marine and Indies, Spain had a minister whose mind responded, perhaps too readily, to this class of diplomacy. When in October, 1735, the colony of Georgia seemed not only thoroughly established, but a new menace to Florida, one John Savy, alias Don Miguel Wall, an English officer, appeared in Paris with alleged information of the highest importance to Spain. His plan was as bold as his story is fascinating.

Don Miguel Wall was a Londoner and erstwhile resident of Charles Town. There he had married a daughter of Captain Daniel Greene, an honored man in his community, but having run too far into debt, and according to his less friendly critics, having committed murder there, Wall was obliged to go to Georgia. From this colony, in June, 1735, he escaped in the brigantine *Two Brothers*, Captain William Thomson, the first loaded vessel ever to come from Georgia.[1] By agreement he was landed at Dieppe in a French fishing boat, August 19, 1735. In a very destitute condition, John Savy, alias Don Miguel Wall, began unwinding a skein of intrigue which he himself would hardly have been able to stop.

Savy appeared with the Irish Major of the Guard of Halberdiers before the Spanish Secretary, Don Fernando Treviño. He began with an account of himself as a Catholic of long residence in America and a Lieutenant of "Infantry in South Carolina in Florida." He came to France, he said, as the result of a dispute with Oglethorpe over religion. Oglethorpe's

---

[1] C. O. 5/654; Add. MSS, 32796, N. P., CXI, 46.

colony, he remarked ominously, was beginning to be settled by Protestants expelled by the Archbishop of Salsburg. His intention, Treviño was graciously informed, was to disclose "to our king what the English of the two aforementioned colonies[2] are making every day in the territory of Spain, and their intention of proceeding with them until they find themselves in possession of the fortress of St. Augustine which is of the greatest strategic importance through proximity to Cuba and the port of Havana."[3]

The essence of Savy's offer was his promise to rout the English with a few troops under the command of a Spaniard, to destroy all establishments, and to reduce Carolina and Georgia to the limits of the Treaty of Utrecht. Treviño questioned his adventurous and aspiring candidate for martial honors, but was fully satisfied. Thereupon Savy was asked to supply a formal memorial, which was sent to Patiño to ascertain his views on the expediency of the project under the circumstances. The wily Savy urged the utmost secrecy, as the very mention of his name would arouse suspicion, jealousy, and excitement! He was well known in the colonies! To demonstrate his sincerity, Savy offered to go to Madrid at his own expense if allowed to put his project into practice. Further to establish his identity, he showed his half-tattooed and powder-burnt body, markings of his captivity among the "brave Indians of Florida" during the Yamasee War in South Carolina and Georgia.[4]

Patiño responded with alacrity that he wished Savy to come to Madrid to consider his project, with all the caution desired, for expelling the English from Georgia.[5] Meantime, Savy had apparently been taken with a malignant fever, but Treviño reported him ready for his projected trip to Madrid. Savy's subsequent delay soon took the Spaniard to the intermediary, the major of the Halberdiers. Here he found the real reason for the delay. The trip could not be undertaken at the Englishman's expense. He averred that his payments had been completely cut off. Admission was even made that judicial proceedings

---

[2] South Carolina and Georgia.

[3] A. G. I., Audiencia de Santo Domingo, 87-1-1, Doc. No. 24, Treviño to Patiño, Paris, 17 October, 1735.

[4] *Loc. cit.*

[5] A. G. I., Audiencia de Santo Domingo, 87-1-1, Doc. No. 28, Patiño to Trevino, 7 November, 1735; Treviño to Patiño, 30 January, 1736.

were being instituted against him in England. The Spanish agent was inquisitive about the reason for his having written differently before. To this questioning the Irish major, whom Treviño trusted, replied that he was maintaining the English officer at his own expense. A request was made for six hundred pounds, which would enable Savy to make the trip to the Spanish court.

The Spanish minister responded with a royal order and six hundred pounds (French livres) to be allotted to "extraordinary expenses." He did not wish such a trifle to prevent the immediate beginning of the trip.[6] Savy was forthwith handed two hundred pounds and a sight bill of exchange to be collected in Bayonne. The Spaniards did not deem it appropriate to send a sailor in the more elegant coach. He was supplied with Treviño's passport under the assumed name, Captain Don Miguel Wall, native of Ireland, because of the great importance of keeping his name and mission from the ministers and officials of England.[7]

The plans of Captain Don Miguel Wall were already well known in Madrid. At the request of Treviño, Don Miguel had addressed a long letter in French to the Spanish minister, setting forth his experience, the situation of Georgia, and his plans for extirpating that colony, concluding with a skillful and curiosity-provoking step, a reservation of vital information. He depicted himself as thirty years of age, Catholic, of the city of London, a man versed in the navigation of the Carolina coast and with some knowledge of military affairs, having served on a warship there and also having been a lieutenant in a company of Colonel Palmer's South Carolina regiment. Likewise he pretended to know all the rivers, habitations, and fortresses between St. Augustine and Georgia as well as the language of the Indians, this knowledge acquired during his captivity among the Yamasees. Patiño was assured that Wall possessed perfect information of all the establishments in Georgia since the project was undertaken "by Oglethorpe in lands belonging to his Catholic Majesty"—settlements which would be pushed until the English were masters of St. Augustine itself! A recommendation for the demolition of these outposts, so audaciously

---

[6] *Ibid.*, royal order to Treviño, Aranjuez, 9 April, 1736.

[7] A. G. I., Audiencia de Santo Domingo, 87-1-1, Doc. No. 30, Treviño to Patiño, 23 April, 1736.

constructed in territory which did not belong to the English and claimed by them only through the greatest temerity, heartily followed. A seemingly most unselfish offer to direct this destruction accompanied the exposition. With four or five hundred well armed Spanish soldiers, experienced officers to enforce discipline, and six large boats to convoy the troops, he promised to destroy Georgia. All this was to be done for no other reason than that he, Savy, was now converted to the justice of his Catholic Majesty's cause. This daring letter hinted at the writer's more extensive acquaintance with South Carolina affairs, knowledge which was reserved against an examination and interrogation at the court of Spain in order further to clarify the affairs of Florida.[8]

In the following summer Benjamin Keene, British ambassador at the Spanish court, had news about Treviño's recommendation of Wall as a soldier and as a man very skillful in marine affairs and of great knowledge and practice in the navigation of the Indies. Patiño's order of six hundred pounds for his expenses to Spain and his promise to employ Savy also were reported. A French officer purporting to be in the English service reported to Keene on July 4, 1736, all the above particulars with the additional information that Wall was a talkative, blustering fellow who, so far as he could find, intended to attack some part of Jamaica; that Wall was to be supplied with three ships, one of sixty guns, and that Wall had addressed himself to this officer and some associates whom he promised both commissions and fortunes.

The French officer was then sent upon his inquiries with a promise that he would be rewarded in accordance with the importance of his advices. Keene expressed his intention of keeping the consul at Cádiz on the watch, but he refused to believe there was any real design to attack the British dominions in America. On the contrary, he imagined, and so informed Newcastle, that the probability was that Wall pretended to know of some secret manner of carrying on contraband traffic between the English colonies and the Spanish West Indies and was employed by Patiño to stop the vessels.[9]

---

[8] A. G. I., Audiencia de Santo Domingo, 87-1-1, Savy to Patiño (in French), Paris, 12 October, 1735.

[9] Public Record Office, S. P. F., Spain, General Correspondence, 126. Keene to Newcastle, Madrid, 5 July, 1736.

On July 23 the first intimations that there was actually a design against Georgia were dispatched to Newcastle by the English consul general in Madrid. Consul William Cayley at Cádiz was requested to watch Wall's proceedings there.[10] And on the thirtieth of the same month the British ambassador informed Walpole that Wall had enlisted in his service one Galloway, once commander of a ship belonging to the Pretender. They inquired of those whom they endeavored to get into their service whether or not they could bear the fatigues of long marches through woods and uninhabited places. The plan was clearly leaking through and becoming more than a mere rumor.[11]

Don Miguel Wall was sent to Cuba early in the summer of 1736, in accordance with plans arranged between him and Patiño, and in August the governor of Cuba was given complete command over Wall to make use of his experience in any manner deemed wise.[12]

The Spanish government now began to prepare in earnest for the expulsion of the English from Spanish territory. Don Juan Francisco de Güemez y Horcasitas, governor of Cuba, was charged with looking after the needs of the governor of Florida. He was called upon to remit arms, goods, and men necessary to sustain the fortress of St. Augustine, and at the same time to impede English settlements in the vicinity of St. Augustine, San Marcos de Apalache, and the Gulf of Mexico. As an aid in this important undertaking he was supplied with the correspondence of the former governor of Florida. He was told that Don Miguel Wall had been ordered to Havana, and that the latter's knowledge of the people, the territory, and coasts of South Carolina, Georgia, and Florida was treasured by the Spaniards. Wall was to communicate to the Cuban governor the plan divulged in Madrid. Roughly, the Spanish ministry informed Governor Güemez y Horcasitas, the plan was for the governor to send to St. Augustine three hundred men with the proper accoutrement under the command of

---

[10] *Ibid.*, Castres to Newcastle, Madrid, 23 July, 1736.

[11] S. P. F., Spain, General Correspondence, 126, Keene to Walpole, Segovia, 30 July, 1736.

[12] A. G. I., Audiencia de Santo Domingo, 87-1-1, Doc. No. 42, Spanish Ministry to Governor Güemez y Horcasitas, San Ildefonso, 18 August, 1736; C. O. 5/654, Savy to Newcastle, Falmouth, 17 November, 1737.

trusted and experienced officers. With the addition of such men as the governor of Florida could supply, they were to march overland to attack Georgia, for which purpose notes on the physiography, methods of fighting, as well as tactics and arms to be employed, were enclosed.

The great importance of the expedition—an expedition to prevent the injurious consequences of foreign settlements in Spanish territory—was duly emphasized. The governor of Cuba was accordingly exhorted to take up the affair with the zeal, activity, and maturity of judgment which a project so grave required.

To secure information on the tactics best adapted to harass and defeat the English and destroy their settlements, the governor was ordered to send Don Miguel Wall to confer with the governor of Florida. Four hundred rifles and a store of powder were simultaneously sent from Spain to Florida. Another warning was added that the commander of the expedition should be experienced and versatile, and, what is a greater sign of wisdom, caution against the treachery of John Savy in this expedition, as well as in future commissions, was urged.[13]

The movements of the Spaniards were soon foreshadowed. In the first week of 1736, Captain Wyatt returned from Havana and St. Augustine with ominous information, which was promptly dispatched to Oglethorpe. The newspapers mentioned a Spanish man-of-war which had sailed from Coruña with soldiers and ammunition. In St. Augustine the people were agog over the pending arrival of a man-of-war with five hundred soldiers for whom the governor had already built barracks. It was also common discourse that this ship of fifty guns was to cruise off the Florida coast.

Oglethorpe's old dictum that the land belonged to the country with the best army now recoiled upon him to send shivers up and down his spine. From May to July, 1736, he made tense and anxious overtures to the mainland colonies seeking reinforcements for his now skeletonized forces. Lieutenant Governor George Clark of New York responded with reassurances and, like the governor of South Carolina, appealed to Newcastle and posted a proclamation indicative of the wave of alarm which swept the coast upon every day that Spaniards

---

[13] A. G. I., Audiencia de Santo Domingo, 87-1-1, Patiño to Güemez y Horcasitas, Madrid, 25 July, 19 October, 1735; 24 June, 1736.

were abroad. The Council of Virginia also stood ready with militia to sail for the fighting on the marshes of Glyn.

In South Carolina there was apprehension as to the safety of the trade carried on by vessels supposedly coming from Jamaica, Honduras, and Providence. The news that the governor at St. Augustine was cavalierly receiving visiting Indians, and supplying each with a gun, powder and shot, and a blanket; that three sail of men-of-war were fitting out in Havana and that the Spaniards had instructions to build eleven more ships of sixty-six to eighty-four guns each was the distant rumble of the approaching storm. Had not M. Bienville demanded five thousand men from France?[14]

At this juncture the Spanish advice boat bearing John Savy arrived at El Puerto Príncipe and Santiago de Cuba, with a recommendation and letters of credit from Patiño. Hence he was forced to travel two hundred and eighty leagues by land.[15]

The Spanish attempt was quixotic and pusillanimous from the outset. The arrival of Captain Don Miguel Wall at Havana aroused Latin enthusiasm and was promptly reported to Patiño by the governor with repeated assurances that he would strive with all the spirit, fortitude, and caution possible to further the plan for dislodging the English from their southern settlements.[16] Immediately the fuliginous character of the guiding star of the expedition became visible to Güemez y Horcasitas. In the following month news that it would not be possible to put into practice the idea of Don Miguel Wall was remitted to the Spanish minister along with maps of the English-American coast. Nothing was possible, the governor finally pleaded, with the English factors present in Havana.[17] In May of the same year, after thorough and opportune observations, Güemez y Horcasitas wrote that he did not believe the officer Wall had the capacity for any office of trust. It was then that

---

[14] C. O. 5/639, Eveleigh to Oglethorpe, Charles Town, 3 June, 1736; C. O. 5/1093, fols. 408-411; *Documents relative to the Colonial History of the State of New York* (edited by E. B. O'Callaghan), VI, 70-71; *Executive Journals of the Council of Colonial Virginia* (edited by H. R. McIlwaine), IV, 376.

[15] C. O. 5/654, Savy to the Trustees of Georgia, Falmouth, 17 November, 1737.

[16] A. G. I., Audiencia de Santo Domingo, 87-1-1, Doc. No. 63, Güemez y Horcasitas to Patiño, Havana, 14 December, 1736.

[17] *Ibid.*, 87-1-2, Doc. No. 4, Güemez y Horcasitas to Patiño, Havana, 22 January, 1737; *ibid.*, 87-1-3, Doc. No. 411, Güemez y Horcasitas to Torrenueva, Havana, 1738 (no month).

he abandoned the original plan for an overland expedition in favor of a joint attack in which West Indian Negroes (all good swimmers) with broad swords in hand, would be landed up the rivers by means of flat-bottomed boats.[18]

Leonard Cocke, Royal Asiento Factor at Santiago, made all haste to report Wall's arrival to the English commander, Digby Dent, at Jamaica.

> The material Point [he wrote] that I thought necessary of advising you is this, that in this Advice Boat came a Gentleman Passenger, he goes here by the Name of D^n. Miguel Wall; he pretends he is an Irish Man & has, he says, a commission for a Lt. Colonel of Dragoons & for a Captain of a Man of War, which he says is now ready for him in the Havana. He has Letters of Credit & recommendation from Patiño; He is very gay and brisk & our Governor here made very much of him, & gave a Charge to all the Alcaldes of his District to see the said Gentleman should want for nothing in his way to Havana; The Bustle and Stir they made here of this Man's Arrival made me a little inquisitive & curious to know what Errand he was sent upon by the King of Spain; Accordingly invited him to the Factory to Dinner & finding him a free facetious Gentleman & that loved his Glass, I plied him Home, & as oftentimes Men over their cups drop words strangely that they don't think of, so by this came to the Knowledge he was no Irishman, nor was his Name Wall, but if I am right his Name was Peter Jac de Tombe, formerly a Lieutenant in the English Service, but am not certain of it, but as to his Errand he came upon, I think I pretty well sifted him & it seems he is to make a Descent on the new Settlements of Georgia; he is to be supplied with both Money and Men at the Havana & to go with his Man of War and other Craft . . . to St. Augustine in Florida & there to join another Party with some Indians to march to Georgia; He seems to me to have a notion, as far as I can learn, to have a Proclamation published in the King of Spain's Name, that all Slaves that will come into them shall have their Freedom and Reward.

Factor Cocke could only wish disappointment for Wall and urge that advice be sent to the governor of Carolina.[19]

[18] *Ibid.*, 87-1-2, Doc. No. 52, Güemez y Horcasitas to Torrenueva, Havana, 2 May, 1737; Doc. No. 4, Güemez y Horcasitas to Patiño, Havana, 22 January, 1737; Doc. No. 77, Horcasitas to Torrenueva, Havana, 25 August, 1737; Doc. No. 78, Viceroy of Mexico to Torrenueva, Mexico, 28 August, 1737; Docs. Nos. 26, 27, 28, 29, 30A, 30B, 30C, Güemez y Horcasitas' instructions to naval officers and communications with Governor Montiano of Florida.

[19] Add. MSS, 32994, N. P., CIX; C. O. 5/388, 639, Leonard Cocke to Digby

From the anxious letters of the governor of South Carolina, acting minister Tomás Geraldino gathered the disagreeable tidings that the English had discovered the Spanish aims. Suspicion immediately fell on Wall, whose frivolous conversation had already been marked by the Spanish. A strong warning from the government in Madrid was accordingly dispatched to the governor of Havana.[20]

The bad effects of the Spanish emissary were made clear to Geraldino through the ministry of England. Accordingly in March he began to acquaint his government with the movements of this extraordinary individual. Two months later he recommended the immediate expulsion of Nicholson and Tassel, South Sea Company Factors, from Cuba and urged that John Savy, under the assumed name of Miguel Wall, be sent to Spain upon the first occasion. Copies of these letters were sent at once to the governor of Havana.[21]

A formal order that Wall, having given ever-increasing evidence of his fickleness and propensity for drink, should not be trusted and that he could be used in the projected expedition against Georgia and South Carolina only as a guide under strict supervision, was now issued.[22] Don Sebastián de la Quadra, the new Spanish Secretary of State, requested the governor

---

Dent, Santiago de Cuba, 3 November, 1736.

Add. MSS, 32797. Later a letter from Cartagena, 10 February, 1737/8, gave a résumé of the fears held. "We are much alarmed here by a Expedition of the Spaniards at the Havana an Account of which take as follows in the Words of Capt. McCulloch, Commander of a Sloop in the Asiento Service, who is actually detained at St. Iago de Cuba by Order of the Captain General of the Havana upon that Account; He writes there are three thousand regular Troops in the Havana, besides the Garrison, and that their Transports are all ready and flat bottom'd Boats to go up the Rivers, and they have four Men of War of the Line, two of which are just come from Spain; and that they are to be joined with five thousand Troops from Mexico and 4 Men of War which they have lying at La Vera Cruz; this Expedition is designed against Georgia and Carolina, and very probably they are now employed in the Transportation of the Troops; This Account agrees with all the Accounts I have been able to learn from the Spaniards."

[20] A. G. I., Audiencia de Santo Domingo, 87-1-3, Doc. No. 17, Torrenueva to Güemez y Horcasitas, Madrid, 23 May, 1737.

[21] *Ibid.*, 87-1-2, Doc. No. 77, Geraldino to Torrenueva, 10 March, 1737; Doc. No. 15, Torrenueva to Güemez y Horcasitas, Madrid, 19 May, 1737; Doc. No. 15, Torrenueva to Güemez y Horcasitas, Madrid, 28 May, 1737.

[22] A. G. I., Audiencia de Santo Domingo, 87-1-2, Doc. No. 52; Marquis de Virrens to Güemez y Horcasitas, Madrid, 12 October, 1737; Doc. No. 77, Torrenueva to Güemez y Horcasitas, Madrid, 25 August, 1737.

of Havana to send Wall in the vessel *San Luis* as he was, despite his dissimulation, more prejudicial than beneficial to the expedition.[23]

Immediately upon receipt of the packets from Commodore Dent through the hands of Commander Fox of the *Drake*, seven weeks after they were dispatched, Thomas Broughton, governor of South Carolina, began a furious correspondence. The commander of Georgia was warned against surprise and solicited not to disclose the name of the Englishman at Havana who revealed the Spanish designs in order to prevent the utmost ill consequence to his person and business. Finally the commander, warned about a probable errand of Wall's to determine the posture of defense in Georgia, was urged to take advantage of this probability to bring the adventurer "to justice for his Villany." All commanders of ships on the Georgia coast were likewise warned.[24] He called upon Thomas Causton, the machinating bailiff of Savannah, for advice as to the state of defense in Georgia, and for suggestions for concerted movements. Captain Windham, commodore in South Carolina, sent word to Virginia in order that the ships there might repair to the southern coasts. Runners were dispatched to the Creeks and Cherokees to engage their adherence to both colonies. Others were sent to warn the frontier commanders. Vigilance was the order of the day.[25]

Meanwhile the activities of Captain Don Miguel Wall were being followed in Havana and reports duly made to General James Oglethorpe. The Spanish governor continued to treat Don Miguel with respect but to follow him with suspicion. He was forbidden to converse with any Englishmen except some English pilots who were solicited to join the Spanish service on the pretense of bringing back from the Bahamas a worthless load of salt. Oglethorpe's informants did not pass unnoticed the construction of a man-of-war and some troops which, added to the armaments of the Armada de Barlovento, would constitute a formidable array. The Havana garrison, as well as that at St. Augustine, might easily spare five or six hundred men in case of a descent. Wall enjoined Welton, who knew him as

---

[23] *Ibid.*, Doc. No. 90, La Quadra to Güemez y Horcasitas, Madrid, 25 October, 1737.

[24] C. O. 5/639, Broughton to governor of Georgia, Port Royal, 6 January, 1736.

[25] C. O. 5/639, Broughton to Causton, Charles Town, 4 February, 1736/7.

Savy in the Bailey in South Carolina, not to evince his acquaintance, a step which would mean Wall's incarceration in the Castle Morro.[26]

Certainly all doubts were expelled by the depositions made out at Nassau, New Providence, February 17, 1736. Thomas Linch, having been in Havana, confirmed Welton's information, spoke of the naval preparations there, and gathered from Wall and the Spanish officers that Wall, who had been an Indian trader in South Carolina, was to be the guide of the expedition against Georgia which was to be ready the subsequent month. John Darkins, who was then a prisoner of a Spanish *guarda costa*, uncovered Wall's attempt to enlist him and other Englishmen in the King of Spain's service with the five blank commissions which he held. Several other depositions clearly demonstrated this bustling activity and incessant plotting at Havana.[27] The affair now entered the more complex theatre of international diplomacy.

The rumor of Wall's appearance spread with astounding thoroughness and rapidity. When the lieutenant governor of South Carolina received information from Commodore Dent that a considerable Spanish force was preparing to attack Georgia, genuine alarm seized the province. A committee of assembly appealed to the agent of the province, Peregrine Fury. Fury was asked to wait upon the ministers of the crown with the assurance that the province would exert its utmost strength in the defense of Georgia. The weak and defenseless condition of the colony was, however, the indispensable corollary and refrain of this information. The currency was in a hopeless situation unless the king consented to the new act. The Spanish vessels were of seventy guns; the English twenty. And the Spanish at Havana were much stronger than Georgia and South Carolina could possibly hope to be. The loss of Georgia would jeopardize the northern colonies. "It must be left to His Majesty's Wisdom," wrote the committee, "to determine how far they ought to contribute to our Defense."[28]

---

[26] C. O. 5/639, Henry Welton to Oglethorpe, 17 January, 1737, N. S.; Welton to Oglethorpe, Havana, 6 February, 1737.

[27] C. O. 5/388, depositions of Thomas Linch, John Darkins, James Wilson, John Salter, Nassau, New Providence, 17 February, 1736.

[28] C. O. 5/388, Committee of Assembly to Fury, Charles Town, 20 February, 1736/7; Broughton to Newcastle, Charles Town, 20 February, 1736/7.

Lieutenant Governor Broughton of South Carolina hastily informed the Duke of Newcastle of the "Designs of the Spaniards to invade and unsettle Georgia, and to incite an Insurrection in this Province." The prospect that the barrier might be removed between the English colonies and Florida and the possible Negro riots in South Carolina were neither a peaceful nor a secure outlook. South Carolina hurried to give more presents to the Indians than the Spanish and French were giving; to raise additional men of arms; to muster the militia; to rrest all suspects, and to convene a conference between South Carolina and Georgia for concerting measures of mutual defense.[29]

To the Trustees of the colony of Georgia Broughton merely wrote a letter signifying to them his intention to coöperate in thwarting the Spanish design, the details of which he had already reported to the Duke of Newcastle in a letter dated the preceding day, and informing them of his reinforcements and of the ship which he was fitting out to cruise off the coast of Georgia and Florida.[30]

Newcastle hoped to countermand the Spanish expedition through the instances of Ambassador Keene at Madrid, which would show the Spaniards that their undertaking was discovered. He expressed his approval of the precautionary measures taken in South Carolina, urged that the Indians be kept in alliance, and that every attempt be made to defend the colonies if attacked, but he did not wish anything done in violation of existing treaties.[31]

It was rumored incessantly in London that ships had left Havana for St. Augustine to begin the campaign for the extirpation of Georgia. On March 24, 1737, Newcastle commanded Keene to make the strongest representations to the Spanish court. In case of success Keene was required to transmit an account to such English officials and officers in the West Indies as the matter concerned, but in case he should have had reason to suspect that the reported design was on foot, he was

---

[29] *Ibid.*, Broughton to Newcastle, Charles Town, 6 February, 1736/7.

[30] C. O. 5/639, Broughton to the Trustees of the Colony of Georgia, Charles Town, 7 February, 1736/7.

[31] C. O. 5/388, Newcastle to Broughton, London, 6 April, 1737.

THOMAS DUKE OF NEWCASTLE

to warn them and to dispatch the most authentic information obtainable in Madrid.[32]

Secretary La Quadra pretended complete ignorance of the occasion of such reports concerning armaments as Keene brought him. In order to keep the Spanish from carrying out their project, Keene entered upon a complete account of the Spanish plans, even mentioning the observations on Wall's conduct both in Madrid and America. All this La Quadra vehemently denied and began to recriminate. He had observed both from St. Gil's letters and from the newspapers that the English were fitting out some twenty ships to be sent to Georgia, which facts had occasioned him no anxiety. The only occasion for his mentioning it at all, he said, was furnished by Newcastle and Keene themselves.

The English ambassador next turned the discourse upon the limits of Georgia and Florida. La Quadra cut the point short by saying that Geraldino, the Spanish minister in England, had passed offices to the Duke of Newcastle which had not been answered, in spite of the fact that Oglethorpe had returned to England. Although he had not seen the treaty between Oglethorpe and the governor of St. Augustine, La Quadra, having heard probably from Torrenueva that the treaty was very prejudicial to the interests of Spain, said enough to let it be known that the treaty was really disapproved, although he did not formally declare it so. Upon the whole, this minister indicated that he knew of no orders being sent to proceed against English subjects or possessions. He did not believe the Spanish king would give such orders with precipitation, and was of the opinion that if any armaments were making in America, it was by virtue of general powers given to all officers in America to preserve the king's rights against intrusions and encroachments in times of emergency.

Keene replied that the English government had never given any authority or encouragement to disturb Spanish possessions. La Quadra inopportunely let drop an expression which made it appear that he regarded Georgia as a private grant to a company of adventurers which, consequently, could not im-

---

[32] Add. MSS, 32794, N. P., CIX, Newcastle to Keene, 24 March, 7 April, 1737.

mediately interest the two crowns. Upon this point he was disillusioned. It was a public and national concern, said Keene, encouraged and protected by the whole English legislature.

In spite of the temperate course prescribed by Newcastle and pursued by Keene, the Spanish secretary appeared slightly peevish and anxious to know whether he should accept this office as formal and present it to his king as such. In order to avoid any semblance of a justification for the measures which were rumored merely by keeping silent (the Spanish government expected an answer to Geraldino's memorial), Keene represented himself as speaking for himself, and said that he would be content to send an account that a man of La Quadra's probity knew nothing of sending any hostile orders to the Indies, and that it was his belief that his Catholic Majesty would not do so in any manner but the one customary between the two friendly nations.

From this minister the British representative went immediately to the Marqués de Torrenueva, president of the Council of the Indies, who seemed to have been coached by La Quadra. He denied any knowledge of Oglethorpe's treaty with the governor of Florida and pointed out that every one was to stay in his own house. To him the limits appeared sufficiently delineated, but in case they were not, he thought neither party should occupy any lands until the dispute was finished. Like La Quadra, Torrenueva assured his English interrogator that he knew of no orders being sent to Havana for arming there; that he expected letters from the Indies every day, particularly from Florida, which would inform him of the state of affairs there.

The answer to Geraldino's memorial, which had been delayed in England because information was necessary from Oglethorpe and the Trustees of Georgia, who in turn diverted the issue to America, seemed to overshadow everything at the Spanish court. This point Torrenueva also mentioned. It was Keene's opinion that in case the English government thought it proper to answer the representation, which he took every occasion to impress upon Newcastle's mind, the Trustees might enlarge their answer on Geraldino's important point concerning demarcations.

The situation again appeared portentous. London, too, was impatient. Keene, whose reports were always the essence of reality and never given over to groundless and phantasmal fears, and whose entire fortune was at stake in Spain (he was both the English minister and the agent of the South Sea Company in Madrid), could now write:

These people are certainly not content with what passes in America, neither are they in a condition to support an expensive engagement; but considerations of this sort do not always hinder them from precipitating themselves into it; and notions of injustices done them will make stronger impressions upon minds like these than the bad state of their finances.[33]

Meanwhile Geraldino had not been sleeping in London. On April 11 he reported to Torrenueva that it had been rumored for a week or more that Captain Wall had left Havana for St. Augustine with troops, there to be joined by others to throw the English out of Georgia. The Georgia directors were alarmed and appealed to the ministry who at this date had not conferred with Geraldino. To the numerous inquiries as to the veracity of the report, the Spanish minister replied that he had no news concerning it, but that it seemed natural that the king would place at the disposal of the governor of Florida means to make himself respected and peaceably to prevent the English from extending their territory beyond the demarcations established by treaty, a possibility which seemed likely in the light of the twenty thousand pounds just voted to Georgia by Parliament.

On April 10 Oglethorpe had an interview with the Duke of Newcastle by which it was privately reported to the Spanish that beyond doubt the Walpole ministry entirely disapproved the development of the colony of Georgia. Walpole and Newcastle could not, however, openly evince their displeasure with the Georgia project. Its directors were all members of the House of Commons and the ministry could not afford to antagonize these members whose support was needed for other ends. It was the concern of the Spanish minister to find some method which would bring the English government into open hostility to the directors of Georgia. His solution was to send enough troops to Florida to make Georgia appear so dangerous as to seem unprofitable. He thought the government would then peaceably relinquish the colony. The Spanish government could

---

[33] Add. MSS, 32794, N. P., CIX, Keene to Newcastle, Madrid, 22 April, 1737.

not supply Geraldino with exact information as to rumors of an attack on Georgia, but only knew that reinforcements had been requested. His idea of putting up such a strong show in Florida as to force the English ministry into hostility with Georgia was entirely approved in Madrid.[34]

Keene's conduct in his interviews with La Quadra and Torrenueva met with hearty sanction, but the government was extremely dissatisfied with the answer given by La Quadra. It was almost identical with the answer given by Patiño relating to Nova Colonia, after which it was discovered that positive orders had been sent for attacking that settlement. Keene was therefore ordered by Newcastle to be explicit—to demand to know whether any orders had been sent to the West Indies for making an attack on any settlements of English subjects and if the governors in America could make any such attack by virtue of any general orders. Newcastle here inserted orders to acquaint La Quadra with the doings of Wall and to demand a satisfactory answer concerning which an account had already been sent. By the Treaty of Seville the limits of Georgia were to have been settled by commissaries. Newcastle pointed out that, consequently, an attack against an English settlement would be decidedly unjust, especially as he held it the fault of the court of Spain that the commissaries did not proceed in the execution of their commission.

The ill consequences that would follow an attack upon Georgia were to be pictured through the strongest expostulations. News that Don Miguel Wall was giving out that his project had been suspended for four months, indicating that he might await fresh orders from Spain, offered the English an urgent occasion to insist that effectual orders be sent. Although it appeared that the court of Spain would disapprove the terms of the agreement made between Oglethorpe and the governor of St. Augustine, it could not take any measures contrary to that treaty until the Spanish government had formally declared its opposition thereto.[35]

The Spanish ambassador learned from the Duke of New-

---

[34] A. G. I., Audiencia de Santo Domingo, 87-1-1, Doc. No. 19, Geraldino to Torrenueva, London, 11 April, 1737; 87-1-2, Doc. No. 21, La Quadra to Geraldino, Madrid, 13 May, 1737.

[35] Add. MSS, 32795, N. P., CX; S. P. F., Spain, General Correspondence, 129. Newcastle to Keene, London, 5 May, 1737.

castle that the answer of the Spanish government to Keene's offices had met with a categorical response. Geraldino pressed his point and urged his superior, La Quadra, to emphasize the answer which had not been forthcoming to his memorial of October 2, 1736, concerning the excesses of the English in the Georgia country. By the time of this report an answer had been promised. Geraldino was also a little taken aback at not having been informed as to the steps taken by Keene at Madrid. Although the Spanish in England were vigilant, they could discover only an uneasiness on the part of the directors of the colony of Georgia and could learn of no armaments, except the six war vessels stationed at Jamaica, which might be used without the knowledge of the Spaniards.

In Spain Keene was still in the dark and using every method to get at the bottom of the reports concerning an attack on Georgia, but he struggled in vain to get any information other than that already transmitted to the court at London. Thus far the responses of the Spanish had been categorical, but Don Joseph Patiño, who sponsored the attack on Georgia, had died, leaving the question open again. Don Miguel Wall at Havana had talked without restraint concerning every phase of the proposed descent. He talked almost as freely away from the bottle as over it and before Englishmen as in the seclusion of the Spanish offices. The Spanish government now decided to deny emphatically the rumors of martial designs on England's southern colonies. Geraldino was accordingly ordered to say in the name of his government that there was no foundation for the reports about an attack on Georgia. His preliminary offices were also approved.[36] In addition to obeying this instruction he branded as malicious falsehoods the rumors from South Carolina and Georgia which had so disturbed London. He had already alluded to the repugnance of the ministry in England to the development of Georgia. He now recommended that the Spanish court commit no overt act in America which would force the hand of the pacific Walpole faction.[37]

After instructions for a denial of the affair had been sent to

---

[36] Add. MSS, 32795, N. P., CX, Keene to Newcastle, Madrid, 13 May, 1737; A. G. I., Audiencia de Santo Domingo, 87-1-2, Geraldino to Torrenueva, London, 30 May, 1737.

[37] A. G. I., Audiencia de Santo Domingo, 87-1-2, Geraldino to Torrenueva, London, 13 June, 1737.

England, a formal declaration was made to the English ambassador. La Quadra formally replied on June 4 that his government had no knowledge of Wall,

> . . . nor had he authorized either Wall, or any other person under any name whatsoever or the Governor of Havana to make any military preparations in order to attack any of his Majesty's Possessions, neither was it his Intention to disturb his Neighbours; but on the contrary if any disputes should happen to arise between the Governors of the respective Countries about the Limits of their Jurisdictions, the King's mind was that, instead of proceeding *a des voyes de fait*, such disputes should be amicably settled and adjusted between the two Courts.
>
> So formal a Declaration, My Lord, delivered and repeated to me in two different Conversations by a Minister who places his pride and merit in his probity, leaves me, I must confess, no room to suspect that there is any *Supercherie* couched under it. But as it is evident that Wall could not go to the Havana but by authority, one may look upon this voyage of his as a single Instance of the many I have seen of the genius of the late Minister,[38] who seldom, or never, refused to encourage a Projector, let his Schemes be never so impracticable; though afterwards he let the author of them starve in waiting for further orders and Succours he promised him; It is probably this is at present the State of Wall, when he says his Expedition is put off four months longer.[39]

Although La Quadra again mentioned the answer to Geraldino's memorial, he was informed that Newcastle had the king's orders to prepare it and that the occasion was ripe for the adjustment of the points in dispute. There was the customary Spanish delay, pride, and refusal to do anything to which it might seem they were forced, but on the other hand, concluded the ambassadorial report, "I do not perceive that there is half that prejudice and violence in their Counsels and Proceedings, which reigned but too visibly for several years last past."[40]

The English government expressed its great satisfaction to the ambassador at Madrid that La Quadra had asserted emphatically that no armaments had been making nor any person commissioned to attack the English settlements in America and

---

[38] Don Joseph Patiño.
[39] Add. MSS, 32795, N. P., CX, Keene to Newcastle, Casa del Monte, 10 June, 1737.
[40] *Idem.*

that in case of disputes over the subject of limits, such should be adjusted amicably. In spite of the notices concerning Wall, this declaration made and repeated by La Quadra removed all suspicion. The answer to Geraldino's memorial had already been prepared when the English government received word of the more clear and satisfactory answer given by the Spanish government to its instances, but this circumstance occasioned some alteration in the tenor of that document which was accordingly delayed for such revision.[41]

The month of June saw the Spanish openly declare against hostilities; but the presence of Oglethorpe in London, incessantly pushing the interests of Georgia, was a thorn in the side of the Spanish ambassador. This official reported that Oglethorpe was having less success than ever in advancing "the pretensions of the Directors of Georgia" until it was reported that a contingent of six hundred Spaniards had been defeated by the Georgians in an attempt to enter their province, a circumstance which Oglethorpe turned to his advantage with his customary astuteness. This affair Oglethorpe used in his petition for some troops located in Jamaica. In addition, he was successful in securing for himself the chief command of the regiment which was to be stationed in Georgia and to render such signal service to the English.

On June 18 Geraldino went to Sir Robert Walpole and lamented the success of the military efforts of Oglethorpe, especially in the light of the declaration of the Spanish government that the rumors concerning the jeopardy of Georgia lacked foundation. Walpole told him that he had been correctly informed, but that no action had been taken concerning Oglethorpe, and that if given command he would serve under the English government and that of Georgia and that he would have authority to use any troops which might be sent only for defensive purposes.

This Geraldino correctly discerned was an admission that Walpole planned to sanction Don Diego's (Oglethorpe's) plans. The king could not look with indifference, said the Spanish minister, at the authorization to permit a man to pass to Georgia whose last residence there had fomented so much unrest, especially since Spain had given no orders which ought to cause

---

[41] *Ibid.*, Newcastle to Keene, London, 23 June, 1737.

uneasiness. Walpole declared thereupon that it was not the intention of his government to cause unrest and that he would inform Geraldino of the step taken and communicate Oglethorpe's instructions to him.

The Duke of Newcastle was not so pliant, and his answer was less satisfactory than Walpole's. He appeared to Geraldino less ready to preserve harmony than before and would not communicate with the minister until he had talked with Walpole. The repugnance of Newcastle for Georgia was still, however, visible to Geraldino, but the latter felt that the political pressure of the directors of the colony of Georgia, as a part of the party platform, would force the government to take the resolutions for sending men as requested by Oglethorpe. Geraldino in a letter to Torrenueva pledged himself to make the English ministers understand that Spain could not tolerate the menace that a strong Georgia would constitute.[42] The report which Newcastle sent to Madrid spoke of the representations of Geraldino in a milder strain. When the command of the king's forces in Georgia and South Carolina was given to Oglethorpe, Geraldino in a friendly manner expressed his belief that his court might possibly take umbrage at the incident. Against such an event the British ambassador was instructed to say to La Quadra, in case he was questioned, that Oglethorpe had the strictest orders to do nothing contrary to the treaties or to the union and good correspondence existing between the two crowns. The very step itself, it was pointed out, was taken with a view to preventing dispute between the two nations, for hitherto Oglethorpe had acted in America by authority of the Trustees of Georgia and under their direction whereas he was henceforth to be in the king's immediate service, acting by his orders, and answerable to him for his behavior. Was not this a better situation than if Oglethorpe returned to America with the same power from the Trustees (which he certainly would have done)? The English government trusted that this explanation would remove all jealousy and suspicion and expressed its willingness in case of further trouble in the West Indies to have the matter adjusted amicably either in London

---

[42] A. G. I., Audiencia de Santo Domingo, 87-1-2, Geraldino to Torrenueva, London, 20 June, 1737. Oglethorpe naturally availed himself of the crisis to pass a bristling memorandum on preparedness in Georgia. C. O. 5/654, fols. 101-02.

or in Madrid, agreeable to the declaration of La Quadra.[43]

The Spanish government finally responded to the repeated recommendations of Geraldino and ordered that Nicholson and Tassel, who made the disclosures concerning Don Miguel Wall at Havana, be expelled at once. In addition Don Miguel was ordered to come to Spain at the first opportunity.[44] During the spring of 1737 South Carolina and Georgia, as was very natural with sparsely populated tidewater regions, were again going through a fever of anxiety at the slightest international quake, but by July 15 Governor Thomas Broughton of South Carolina reported the scare of the spring well over and the colonies in a reasonable posture of defense.[45]

For a period of almost two years the Spaniards continued their preparations for an attack on "Georgia of South Carolina." The death of Patiño, the instability and irresponsibility of the English guide, Savy, and the inability of the viceroy of New Spain to furnish sufficient troops and money finally spelled the doom of the enterprise. Governor Güemez y Horcasitas could not even find a suitable commander. The interval of strained waiting allowed the Spanish to collect evidence and to call upon the leading officials to prepare a statement of Spain's claims. By order of the minister La Quadra, ten long papers were prepared, among them those of the Marqués de la Regalia, Don Joseph de Laysequilla, the Conde Montijo, Andrés González de Barcía, and Don Joseph de la Quintana, later a plenipotentiary of Spain through the arrangements of the Convention of Pardo. In addition there were papers of La Quadra himself, *cédulas* of viceroys, *consultas* of the Council of the Indies, and incidental papers, comprising altogether four *legajos*.[46]

Meanwhile the governor of Havana, the viceroy of New Spain, and the governor of St. Augustine continued to circulate reports and orders. Numerous were the discussions of money, men, and equipment. Güemez y Horcasitas, true even

---

[43] Add. MSS, 32795, N. P., CX, Newcastle to Keene, London, 23 June, 1737.

[44] A. G. I., Audiencia de Santo Domingo, 87-1-1, Geraldino to La Quadra, London, 28 May, 1737.

[45] C. O. 5/639, Broughton to Newcastle, Charleston, 15 July, 1737.

[46] A. G. S., 7633 antiguo, papeles de 1737, 1738, 1739, Conde de Montijo to the King, San Lorenzo, 9 November, 1737, puntos 17-45.

now to the Spanish traditions of empire building, planned to hold the Georgia country by planting Spanish families. It was necessary for the governor of Havana to secure the coöperation of the archbishop and viceroy of Mexico, Juan de Bizarrón y Eguiarreta, and the commander of the Armada de Barlovento. The viceroy gave excuses for not sending men, but agreed to supply the 150,000 pesos required. The desperately aggressive, but distraught, commander made a final call upon Oglethorpe for a peaceful solution. Tropical calms landlocked Vera Cruz. The undertaking was discovered, and time gave it a chill from which it never recovered. "Don Miguel de Valle," dispatched from Havana in the *San Luis* to reconnoitre, learned from an English surgeon that coast guard vessels from Jamaica and Carolina were cruising the Florida coast for the reception of the flat-bottomed boats and the aquatic mulatto soldiers expected in them. On November 28, 1737, the Spanish government issued the order to the governor of Havana in which it had promised England to suspend the expedition. It arrived just in time to stay the movement. This appeared the inevitable end, since the temporary suspension of the project upon the death of the minister Patiño. Thus was rung down the curtain on one of the unknown dramas of American history. Alarums and excursions were the rule of the day in the South, as well as in the valleys and villages next to the French and Indians in the North.[47]

The machinery of diplomacy, which had been considerably lubricated by the few months respite resulting from the death of Patiño and the abandoning of his plans, was jarred out of order again by the appearance of Patiño's agent, Don Miguel Wall, at Cádiz, where he went before the English Consul Cayley and told an unusual story. He had been too blustering and talkative for the Spaniards and had been required to return to Spain in a Spanish man-of-war. He was now between the Spaniards and the Englishmen. After addressing himself to Consul William Cayley, not mentioning anything concerning the manner of his discharge from the Spanish service or the method used to quit it, Wall dispatched a letter, October 22, 1737, to the Trustees of Georgia, beginning "My Lords and

---

[47] A. G. I., Audiencia de Santo Domingo, 87-1-2, Doc. No. 100, and *passim;* 87-1-3, Docs. Nos. 9, 10, 30, 31, 32, 33, 36, 37, 38, and *passim*. The military papers of the War of Jenkins' Ear are included in this *legajo*.

Gentlemen." To Keene there was something extraordinary in the circumstances that a man so much in the secret of the Georgia affair should be so much left at his liberty to discover it. This ambassador was opposed to paying constant attention to the bogus colonel.[48]

Wall's letter, he said, was to inform the Trustees of all that was being done to destroy Georgia. In order to extricate himself from a precarious position, he recounted a long story which tended to show his perfect sincerity and at the same time to picture himself in possession of information concerning the Spanish designs which would make it foolhardy to dispose of its possessor. His residence and marriage in South Carolina, his report to the Spanish in Paris, and his invitation to Madrid by Patiño were told with truth and candor. Wall, however, was too wary to make a simple confession of treachery. He tinctured it with information concerning the expedition against Georgia from which he had been dropped.

Wall reported to the Trustees that four hundred Spanish soldiers were sent to St. Augustine in August, 1737, and that there was still outstanding an order for the viceroy of New Spain to send a thousand more. In addition, artillery and all provisions had been sent for an attack in the following May. It would not be amiss, he entreated, to send out scouts by both land and water to keep a sharp lookout; moreover, he spoke of Don Antonio Arredondo, the engineer at St. Augustine, and lauded Oglethorpe as the best acquainted with the affairs of America.

Don Miguel's plans for keeping himself valuable were the same as the ones he employed with the Spaniards:

Now, My Lords and Gentlemen, I hope to be in London and put myself at your feet as soon as Ships can carry me: But for fear I should miscarry, I give you this rough notice which is sincere and truth and hope your Charitys will, when it pleases God, that I arrive at London, pardon me, if you think proper, for as for my own part, I think myself unworthy of it, having offended my God, My King and my Country; but shall be satisfied with that Chastisement your Lordships think proper for me. I have surrendered myself to the Cap^n. of the *Granpus*, who will carry me to the com-

---

[48] Add. MSS, 32796, N. P., CXI, Keene to Walpole, Escorial, 4 November, 1737; S. P. F., Spain, General Correspondence, 128, Keene to Newcastle, 4 November, 1737.

mander of Gibraltar, from whence I shall proceed to London; and then shall acquaint your Lordships more at large; and as I have made the Sore, if its possible you'll pardon me, I shall soon heal it: and what I offer now, is out of pure inclination to my King and Country; and humbly beg that you'll believe that what Informations I gave the Spaniards, in regard to those Colonies, was out of necessity, and not out of good will; for now if your Lordships pardon me, which I can't pardon myself, I shall see my family fight with Courage for Georgia, and let you into all their affairs. I go here by the name of Miguel Wall, but my name is John Savy; nephew of John Lewis Paulhan in Token House, Road Exchange Broker. I hope your Lordships will pardon the bad writing, bad style, but you may assure yourselves of truth; and when it pleases God that I can be at your Office to give you an Account at Large of all I know in these affairs; and I shall die satysfied when I can be once more in the British Government. I hope to sail from hence in ten days; But nevertheless reinforce once more your Land and Water Scouts by the first Ships that sail for those Parts; and am with due respect, once more begging Pardon of your Lordships your most humble and dutyfull servent to command.[49]

Savy's plans for coming directly to London were thwarted. The consul at Cádiz, after promising to secure passage, refused to harbor a Spanish officer for fear of punishment; and Savy was in hourly jeopardy of coming into the custody of the Intendant of Marines or the governor of Cádiz. He could not, therefore, appear among the masters of ships. Abandoning all clue to his identity, even his clothes, Savy in disguise boarded a vessel for Lisbon.

Torrenueva was determined not to let Wall gain another lap in his race with fortune. He ordered Governor Varas y Valdés to watch his "steps and conversations" and to prevent his leaving Cádiz. There Wall had no friends in whom he could confide, but he accosted foreigners in the streets or at the wharves and pretended to have been in Spain on affairs of great moment. Here he represented himself as a native of Carolina; of no particular nation or legality, but versed in the customs of the Indians. He even amused the spectators by demonstrating the ways of the American native in eating meat and navigating a boat.[50]

---

[49] C. O. 5/654, John Savy to the Trustees of Georgia, Cádiz, 22 October, 1737.

[50] A. G. I., Audiencia de Santo Domingo, 87-1-2, Doc. No. 101, Francisco de Varas y Valdés to Torrenueva, Cádiz, 25 November, 1737. For caring for Savy

Governor Don Francisco de Varas was unable to locate the stopping place of Don Miguel in Cádiz in spite of his constant vigil subsequent to the orders of November 28 suspending operations against South Carolina and Georgia. The news that Wall, in disguise, had escaped in a foreign vessel threw the Spanish foreign service into consternation, but the campaign had already been suspended. The pliability of Walpole and the diligence of Geraldino soon bridged the danger gap.[51] From Lisbon, Savy was sent to England as a prisoner by Lord Tyrawly, who also sent to the Duke of Newcastle an account of Savy's extraordinary visit. Savy's report to the Trustees of Georgia when he landed at Falmouth embodied another sly request for pardon and an avowal that his relations with the Spaniards were only to know their secrets and to disclose them as shown by his attempt to leave in the preceding May on a South Sea Company ship.

Aside from the tantalizing information of October 22 concerning the Spaniards, the late Don Miguel Wall recounted the voyage of two extra engineers to Havana, the capture of several English and Dutch ships, and the orders for four more ships to join the squadron in the West Indies and either to alarm the Carolina coast or to attack Port Royal to prevent the sending of succor to Georgia before the following May. More romantic and true to the old Don Miguel was his offer to acquaint the Trustees of Georgia with a method of capturing St. Augustine or Havana in event of war, a project to which he purported to have devoted his whole attention and study while an officer in those places![52]

On the same day Savy addressed a lengthy letter to the Duke of Newcastle similar to the one written to the directors of Georgia on October 22 and forwarded to London by Ambassador Keene. His letter included a complete survey of the Spanish preparations, his movements in obtaining a commission from the Spanish government to direct the attack on the English colonies, and also many discreet requests for pardon mingled

---

Varas was to receive fifteen reales a day. A. G. S., Sec. de Estado, leg. 7633, Conde de Montijo to the King, San Lorenzo, 9 November, 1737, punto 45.

[51] *Ibid.*, Varas y Valdés to Torrenueva, Cádiz, 8 December, 1737.

[52] C. O. 5/654, Savy to the Directors of the Colony of Georgia, Falmouth, 17 November, 1737; Add. MSS, 32796, N. P., CXI, Newcastle to Keene, London, 17 December, 1737.

with austere resolutions to die like an Englishman. His whole intention, he declared, in returning to Europe in the Spanish man-of-war, the *San Luis,* was to disclose the Spanish plans, and his pretext was to discuss with the Secretary of State the things wanting to carry out the enterprise in America in May.[53] In reality Thomas Geraldino had to bear the brunt of many questions concerning this man. The news of Wall's presence in Havana and the Spanish intention of attacking Georgia had leaked out through the South Sea Company factors. After becoming suspicious of Wall, the Spanish government complied with Geraldino's request by ordering Wall to Spain and expelling the troublesome factors.[54]

The report that an officer had arrived at Falmouth via Lisbon to make important disclosures was being noised about in London early in December. The public credited the news more especially because the packet boat did not bring any letters for private people. The attention of the Spanish ambassador was drawn to the report. His investigations very nearly revealed the truth except that he arrived at the conclusion that Savy was a Frenchman. Geraldino in his inquiries found that the returned officer was the person called Wall, who, according to report, had left Havana regretting his acceptance of a commission from the Spanish king.

This account to the Spanish court included the intelligence that the British government thought that Spain's delay in replying to Newcastle's answer to Geraldino's memorial was due to an inability to verify the article quoted concerning the limits between Georgia and Florida. Nothing, however, was altered with regard to Oglethorpe's proposed commission, notwithstanding the stories in the newspapers concerning the nine hundred men sent to St. Augustine by the Spaniards.[55] Torre-

---

[53] C. O. 5/654, Savy to Newcastle, Falmouth, 17 November, 1737; A. G. I., Audiencia de Santo Domingo, 87-1-3, Doc. No. 11, La Quadra to Güemez y Horcasitas, Madrid, 10 April, 1737. In the move to hoodwink the governor of Havana as to the reason for his departure, Wall was apparently successful.

[54] A. G. I., Audiencia de Santo Domingo, 87-1-2, Geraldino to La Quadra, London, 9 May, 1737; *ibid.,* 87-1-3, La Quadra to Geraldino, Madrid, 28 May, 1737.

[55] S. P. F., Spain, Supplementary, 246, Geraldino to Torrenueva, London, 12 December, 1737.

nueva replied that he had nothing for Geraldino's direction in the matter of Georgia, an attitude which was prompted probably through negligence or a deliberate effort to keep the American question obscured even at the price of Geraldino's enlightenment on Spanish affairs.[56]

That minister, however, was thoroughly aroused over the step taken by the Trustees of Georgia in making use of the information provided by Wall in order to strengthen their pretensions and to claim the support of the government, a position from which even a reluctant government could now hardly extricate itself, under the circumstances. Upon this question the Spaniards managed to interview Sir Robert Walpole, who was always considerably clearer than his colleagues. Walpole told them candidly of Wall's activities at Havana and how he had come back to England; and in response to Geraldino's suggestion that Wall was an impostor, Walpole replied that Wall had offered to produce papers signed by Patiño. At this juncture the conversation was interrupted, but the Spanish minister, in his anxiety, procured a new interview for the very next day.[57]

In this conference Walpole told the complete story of Wall, not omitting his apparent repentance and offer to flee from Havana with Nicholson and Tassel who, in fear of the consequences, would not consent. Upon Wall's arrival at Falmouth the British government ordered him arrested and brought up to London, which instructions had not been carried out at the time of the conference. The Spanish endeavored to counter the bad effect which Wall's report might create by pointing out that no credence ought to be lent to a man of such bad repute. Notwithstanding his bad name, answered Sir Robert, it would be absolutely necessary on account of public pressure to look into the documents referred to. If they were false, then the man would be considered an impostor. The reply was that even though it should be proved that Wall had been sent to Havana upon an urgent errand, it could now be considered no more than a prudent and necessary precaution at the late juncture of affairs in the West Indies. To this defense of underhand

[56] *Ibid.*, Torrenueva to Geraldino, 30 December, 1737.
[57] S. P. F., Spain, Supplementary, 246, Geraldino to Torrenueva, London, 19 December, 1737.

methods Walpole consented without a qualm, and promised not to conceal anything essential from the Spanish ambassador.[58] Torrenueva rather tardily replied to the letters concerning the mysterious proceedings of Wall who, he averred, was not known in Madrid as a colonel.[59]

The English were still unaware of the counter orders of November 28, 1737, which had been sent to the governor of Havana and the governor of St. Augustine to suspend the expedition. Hence every movement presaged to them a continuation of the old design. Consul Cayley, writing in cipher from Cádiz, hoped that the high mortality in New Spain and the melancholy situation in the Old would "allay, in some degree, that restless Spirit, with which they have been so long inspired." This letter was soon followed by another reporting that the Spaniards had in readiness a great number of flat-bottomed boats (for going up the rivers) and men-of-war and that it was expected daily that some two thousand men would be sent from Vera Cruz. It was probable, he said, that Georgia would be attacked during the following spring.[60]

These renewed rumors occasioned a request from the British foreign office for an account of the affair. Keene's response, based on information secured through a spy in the English service, explained the original plan of Patiño, which was to attack Georgia with fifteen hundred or two thousand men, part of whom were to be sent by the viceroy of New Spain and part by the governor of Havana. It was certain that the plans had been halted upon the death of Patiño and that Governor Güemez y Horcasitas had acknowledged receipt of orders to stay the expedition, which, he hinted without foundation or certainty, might have been the result of his instances to La Quadra in the matter. The facility afforded Savy to make his escape, the agreement of Spain to refer the settlement of the boundaries to commissaries, seemed to confirm the issuance

---

[58] *Ibid.*, Geraldino to Torrenueva, London, 26 December, 1737; C. O. 5/654, Benjamin Martyn to Newcastle, London, 23 November, 1737.

[59] S. P. F., Spain, Supplementary, 246, Madrid, 20 January, 1738.

[60] A. G. I., Audiencia de Santo Domingo, 87-1-3, Doc. No. 113, Güemez y Horcasitas to Torrenueva, Havana, 18 April, 1738; S. P. F., Spain, Spanish Consuls, 222, Cayley to Newcastle, Cádiz, 21 January, 1738; *ibid.*, Cayley to Newcastle, Cádiz, 23 January, 4 February, 11 February, 25 February, 1738.

of the counter orders which Keene did not know had been sent in the preceding November. The bad state of Spanish finances and the resolution of the government at Madrid to send a flota to America would not, Keene thought, allow a prudent administration to think of bringing any potent enemies upon its back, yet he was not sure that the tranquillity of the American possessions and the security of navigation would depend upon the forces which the Spaniards knew the English had in the new world.[61]

Thus the attempt of Spain to secure by violent means what she held justly belonged to her was gradually abandoned. But Georgia remained a source of contention. However the right might have been, the English could not give up Georgia. Only the weak condition of Spain, according to the admission of the English themselves, kept the Spanish from fighting for it. These two facts were tacitly recognized by both parties. On this basis alone could the extraordinary behavior of Don Miguel Wall, international adventurer, be overlooked. A thorough search of the military records of Great Britain for the proper years fails to reveal any trace of a court martial. It is obvious that Savy designed to betray the interests of England and that the bad condition of his own affairs led him to betray those of Spain. His reports about the Spaniards were verified subsequently—indeed, nothing but blindness could have prevented their disclosure without his mediation—and he himself evidently pardoned. In 1740 he was made a captain-lieutenant of one of the regiments of foot raised in America to coöperate with Wentworth and Vernon against the Spaniards in the inglorious campaigns against Cartagena and Havana.[62] There he again stored his goods on the vessel *Martha* and made an attempt to desert, doubtlessly to give information to the Spanish as he was under sentence of death in South Carolina, whence it was claimed he was now bound, and could not be expected to return there for that reward. He brazenly boasted, however, that he had already cost the English a million pounds and hoped to cost them that much more. Savy was arrested by Admiral Vernon and

---

[61] S. P. F., Spain, General Correspondence, 130; Add. MSS, 32797, Keene to Newcastle, Madrid, 23 February, 1738.
[62] *Gentleman's Magazine*, 1740, p. 204.

thereupon disappeared from the story of American affairs.[63]

As soon as the excitement from Wall's and Patiño's attempt against the existence of Georgia had died down the problems arising from navigation in American waters claimed increasing attention. In 1737 Ambassador Keene was literally presenting bundles of claims for ships which had succumbed before the *guarda costas*. Two years later when the world was hopeful that the Convention of Pardo would at last solve these vexing problems, Spain insisted that the Georgia boundary question, in which the Spanish considered themselves the grieved party, should take precedence over the problems of navigation, where the English looked upon themselves as the victims. The English insisted upon the precedence of the latter for the same reasons. Hence the diplomatic higgling which John Savy accentuated served to foment the agitation which resulted in the desultory War of Jenkins' Ear. The incidents which Savy sponsored had far more immediate bearing upon the international situation than the more or less uncertain removal of an ear eight years prior to the outbreak of war. It was merely a capricious circumstance of history which gave to the war that followed the name, "The War of Jenkins' Ear" instead of "The War of Savy's Treachery."

---

[63] John Tate Lanning, "Don Miguel Wall and the Spanish Attempt against the Existence of Carolina and Georgia," *The North Carolina Historical Review*, X (July, 1933), 186-213.

CHAPTER V

SPANISH ALARUMS AND ENGLISH EXCURSIONS
IN EUROPEAN DIPLOMACY

THE TENSE negotiations which the southward thrust of the English frontier occasioned in America were only those of Europe in miniature. Exasperated to the breaking point by the reports from Florida, in the fall of 1736 the Spanish ambassador in England, Geraldino, according to instructions, made bold to lay before the court in London the complaints of his government—in memorials so strong that the pacifistic Walpole ministry was aroused from its lethargy and the war faction thrown into frenzies of delight. Profoundly as the establishment of a buffer colony in 1732-1733 had affected Spain, her surprise was not so great as when she suddenly began receiving messages from Governor Sánchez that an English fort was built only twenty-five leagues north of St. Augustine in Spanish territory, and another among the "Uchees and Talapoosees,"[1] and that Indians were constantly falling upon both the Spaniards and their allies at the instigation of the new neighbors. No less were her surprise and chagrin at the appointment and support of James Oglethorpe, who promised to take St. Augustine or "leave his bones before its walls." The Spanish policy was designed to remove imminent danger, if not the whole colony of Georgia, by an unequivocal statement of Spain's long uncontested right to, and occupation of, the Atlantic coast. English opinion on Georgia between 1734 and 1736 may tend to throw some light upon the utter shock of the Spaniards at the militant and surprised attitude assumed by the English upon the presentation of a memorial claiming Georgia as a part of Florida.

In 1734 the erection of forts inside of the Altamaha was urged upon the Board of Trustees in order to prevent the Spaniards erecting one there, but, said one of their number, "that being without our limits (for that river is our southern boundary) it

---
[1] Yuchis and Alabamas, members of the Creek Confederacy.

cannot be done."[2] The same board was unanimous in its opposition to the erection of Frederica beyond the Altamaha and finally approved that site because it was the southern boundary and would be auspiciously located to watch the galleons in case of a rupture with Spain. Besides such a weighty concrete argument might induce Parliament to raise its stipend, "but none of us had thoughts of settling more southward, knowing nothing then of the St. John River."[3] Sir Robert Walpole evidently did not believe that the colony of Georgia was of any advantage to England. Consequently he thought that the Georgia charter gave the Trustees too much power and made them independent of the crown, and surprisingly "that there was a spirit in all the Colonies to throw off their dependency on the Crown of England." The Georgia Trustees were ready to disavow the acts of Oglethorpe, and refused to accept a bill for five hundred pounds because it had been spent in building forts across the Spanish limits.[4] At the same time they complained against the "manifest neglect of the Duke of Newcastle in not attending the papers dispatched to him" concerning Georgia.[5] Obviously, official England could not sanction a move which the Trustees themselves did not approve. Soon, however, they were asserting that the two forts were "indeed in Carolina," although they could hardly justify Oglethorpe in spending their money for national defense.[6]

With the English themselves in such a state of general doubt, the territory that the Spaniards called Florida was the occasion of numerous letters from Governor Francisco Moral y Sánchez, emphasizing the attempts of the English to debauch the Indians of the Apalache region, and recurring with ever-increasing

---

[2] Egmont, *Diary*, II, 141, January 6, 1734/5.

[3] *Colonial Records of the State of Georgia*, XXI, 115, Eveleigh to Verelst, South Carolina, 24 March, 1735. "I understand Mr. Oglethorpe designs Strenuously to insist wth person's that Shall be appointed by Augustine to settle the Boundary's between the two Governm[ts], That the River S[t] Juan shall be the place, I have wrote him Several Letter's (in One of which) I offer'd some Reasons to incline the Spaniard's to consent thereto." Also Egmont, *op. cit.*, II, 282-83, "Oglethorpe's letter of 10 April instructs Dempsey what to say to the governor; . . . that our territory extends southward to the river St. John, the northern side thereof belonging to us, and the southern, where Fort St. Augustine is, to Spain." 16 June, 1736. See chap. 3.

[4] Egmont, *op. cit.*, II, 289-90.

[5] *Ibid.*, p. 288.

[6] *Ibid.*, p. 293.

uneasiness to the defenseless condition of St. Augustine.[7] Fort Picolata he constructed at his own expense. For such service he wished reward either in rank or money. In the following year Cristóbal Gregorio Portocarrero Count of Montijo, ambassador at London before Geraldino, dispatched to Patiño a statement that Oglethorpe had been voted twenty-six thousand pounds with the view of conducting families to Georgia, building forts, and maintaining a strong garrison "on the sole pretext of defense against the savage Indians."[8] Soon Governor Moral y Sánchez renewed his reports—this time with actual news. The English were committing every excess, even murdering Spanish soldiers, and had just consummated an agreement with the Yuchis and Talapoosees. So pressing did he consider the matter that similar letters and a plea for improvement in the defenses were sent also to the viceroy of Mexico and to the governor of Havana.[9] The worst of the governor's news was the erection of forts, especially at St. Simons—all a guarantee of English sovereignty and a constant menace to Florida.[10] The king and his government replied with alacrity to the governor of Florida, and simultaneously dispatched a letter to the governor of Havana in order to strengthen St. Augustine and to place the Spanish colonies in a general posture of defense. The movement of the English presaged a struggle. Notwithstanding this response the king and council were constantly plied with letters of news, supplication, and advice from the governors of St. Augustine and Havana, and even from the minister plenipotentiary in London.[11]

The Spanish Secretary of State, Don Joseph Patiño, was a man essentially militant, and the extravagance of any visionary scheme did not act as a deterrent upon him.[12] His decision was to strike suddenly and with force in America and to lose none of the advantages of diplomacy in Europe. For the latter purpose he had a capable but questionable agent. Don Tomás

---

[7] A. G. I., Audiencia de Santo Domingo, 86-6-5, Indice de las representaciones que el Governador de la Florida remite a S. M. en la presente coyuntura.

[8] *Ibid.*, 87-1-1, Montijo to Patiño, London, 15 April, 1735.

[9] *Ibid.*, 87-1-1, Docs. 18 and 19, Sánchez to Patiño, St. Augustine, 23 May, 8 July, 1735.

[10] *Ibid.*, 87-1-1, Doc. 15, Sánchez to Patiño, St. Augustine, 5 March, 19 October, 1735; 86-5-21, the same to same.

[11] A. G. I., Audiencia de Santo Domingo, 87-1-1, 86-6-5, *passim.*

[12] See chap. III.

Geraldino, who succeeded Montijo as minister plenipotentiary in London, was readily accepted by the English court. He was personally amiable with the Duke of Newcastle and with Sir Robert Walpole. Yet the very pro-British leanings of Geraldino made him a burden. Being conversant with the supine disposition of the Walpole government, he knew to what extent threats could be employed without risk and therefore fell readily into Patiño's embryonic but dangerous scheme.

Matters were rapidly approaching a crisis. By the Countess of Montijo, Geraldino sent two letters from Governor Sánchez of Florida to Patiño.[13] Since these letters included a minute account of the excesses committed by the English, especially by Indians of their allegiance, and the progress of the colony of Georgia, Patiño issued instructions to his ambassador to present the most efficacious and vigorous offices to the English court on both the depredations and the limits of the colony.[14] Copies of letters for his guidance were likewise sent. These representations Geraldino promised to make with all promptitude and to give an account of their issue.[15]

Some days after giving this notice, the ambassador's first famous memorial was presented. The memorial evinced great disappointment in the result of the promise of his Britannic Majesty's ministers given in September, 1735, that Oglethorpe's departure for Carolina would be conducive to the establishment of the most perfect understanding between Carolina and Florida. Quite contrary to these hopes, however, the governor of St. Augustine, who had been instructed by letters sent with Oglethorpe to contribute to so salutary a design, had the mortification to see a fortress situated within eight leagues of St. Augustine attacked by the Georgians on March 3, 1736, who, after killing a soldier of the garrison, cut off his head and carried it away in triumph! As if to confirm the step, the inhabitants of Georgia immediately thereafter built and garrisoned a fort within Florida, twenty-five leagues from St. Augustine "at

---

[13] A. G. I., Audiencia de Santo Domingo, 87-1-1, Doc. No. 34, Geraldino to Patiño, London, 28 June, 1736. All possible information about the English population and fortifications was likewise transmitted to the government. *Ibid.*, Docs. No. 36-38.

[14] A. G. I., Audiencia de Santo Domingo, 87-1-1, Doc. No. 44, Patiño to Geraldino, San Ildefonso, 28 August, 1736.

[15] *Ibid.*, 87-1-2, Geraldino to Patiño, London, 13 September, 1736.

the mouth of the River of St. Simon." The inhabitants of Carolina, the memorial emphasized, who had built a fort on the same spot had caused it to be demolished by order of the court of England at the instance of Spain.[16]

At the same time that the governor of St. Augustine supplied his government with this information, he called attention to the report of the Spanish lieutenant at Fort San Marcos in the province of Apalache that the English were then employed in building a fort in Spanish territory among the Yuchi Indians, and that they brazenly announced their intention to construct another among the Talapoosees, northwest of St. Augustine. This move the memorial in question set forth unequivocally, but it appeared diminutive in comparison to the news that a party of three hundred English had appeared on the frontiers of the province, displayed their standards at Coweta, the principal settlement, and called upon the natives to join them in making war on the Spaniards. According to the report, the governor of St. Augustine, because of the continual incursions from Georgia, did not hesitate to believe the report which the English gave out that they intended to raze Fort San Marcos and to besiege St. Augustine itself.

The King has ordered me to represent to His Britannic Majesty, that such a Behavior in the Inhabitants of Georgia, seems designed rather to interrupt the Peace and good Understanding which subsist so happily between the two Crowns than to establish the Continuance of it; and as the Facts are of themselves notorious and can't fail of making an Impression on His Britannic Majesty's just and equitable Mind, I thought I could not acquit myself of His Majesty's Orders better than by submitting them to the Royal Consideration of His Britannick Majesty, according to the Account given by the Governor of St. Augustine; to which I am to add, that the Colony of Carolina being situated in 32 Degrees of Latitude, and 294-½ of Longitude, and the Colony of Georgia being to the Southward of the other, it is indisputable that the latter is within the Territory of the King my Master, and even the former according to the Treaty of Peace of the Year 1670, and by the 7th Article of which the Demarcation for the said Province and that of Florida was fixt exactly at 33 Degrees and 50 Minutes of Latitude, and 339 Degrees and 20 Minutes of Longitude; altho' the Town

---

[16] The English uniformly held that this fort was accidentally destroyed by fire and was not therefore vacated at the suggestion of Spain. See chap. II.

called Carolina was tolerated, because it was built before the aforesaid Treaty; and as by the 8th Article of the Treaty of Peace concluded at Utrecht in 1713, it is agreed, That the Limits and Demarcations of the West Indies should remain on the foot they were in the Reign of King Charles the Second, of Glorious Memory; the King my Master hopes, and does not doubt but His Britannic Majesty, from an Effect of His Justice and Equity, upon his being informed of what I have the honour to communicate to your Excellency, will be pleased to give His Orders Immediately for causing the Inhabitants of Georgia to be punished, who shall be found guilty of having interrupted the Peace between the two Nations, and for causing the Limites to be observed, which have been adjusted by the aforesaid Treaties, which subsist between the two Crowns and that the Forts which have been built on the Territories of the Demarcation of Florida may be forthwith demolished; This is what I am to beg your Excellency to represent to His Britannic Majesty, and to let me know His Royal Resolution thereupon.[17]

With dispatch Geraldino sent his report to Patiño. He also gave notice of his conference with the Duke of Newcastle in which he again insisted upon a response for his king. Taking advantage of a casual interview with Sir Robert Walpole, Geraldino succeeded in widening the scope of his office by eliciting a promise of an early reply from Walpole and by attempting orally to undermine Oglethorpe, who, the ministry had promised Geraldino a year earlier, would not be allowed to execute hostile plans in Georgia.

This almost vehement memorial came as a shock to the Duke of Newcastle, who was thoroughly conversant with Geraldino's complaisant disposition. Although little impressed by the English right to the country in dispute, Newcastle turned to that group of men which, although best acquainted with the facts, was most likely to render a partial verdict—the Trustees of Georgia.[18] He simply transmitted a copy of the memorial to that group and called for an investigation and statement of the case to be laid before the queen for consideration.

In about two weeks the Trustees took the matter into con-

---

[17] S. P. F., Spain, Entry Books, 141; S. P. F., Spain, Foreign Ministers, 58; C. O. 5/656; C. O. 5/668; A. G. I., Audiencia de Santo Domingo, 87-1-1, Doc. No. 53, Geraldino's memorial to the Duke of Newcastle, London, 21 September/2 October, 1736.

[18] C. O. 5/656, Newcastle to the Trustees of Georgia, Whitehall, 27 September 1736.

sideration and solved every point at issue in accordance with their own predilections.[19] Although by October 6, they had agreed on the points in consideration, a letter was not submitted to the queen until October 20,[20] and the real answer to the Duke of Newcastle was not supplied until much later.[21]

Meanwhile, no answer was forthcoming and Geraldino was becoming exceedingly anxious. In his anxiety he went to Newcastle and displayed his inquietude over the tepidity and delay of the ministry in furnishing some answer for his court. Proceeding to Robert Walpole, he received the same reception as well as the same securities—that the government did not intend to permit settlements without the limits prescribed in the American treaties; that letters had been received from Georgia written by the governor of St. Augustine showing that although there have been some discord between the two peoples, good correspondence was now reëstablished. Being supplied with the dates of these letters, the Spaniard confessed himself in great doubt. In the same letter he poured out his invective against a dilatory procedure which depended upon the selfish whims of the Georgia Trustees for the fate of a Spanish province as important as Florida.[22]

Long before any answer was made, the Trustees had solved this problem of the memorial to their satisfaction after this fashion:

And as to the first Matter of Complaint, the Trustees have received full Evidence that none of the New Colony of Georgia were concerned in attacking any Fortress in the Territories of the King of Spain on the 3d of March last, or at any time. But the same was done by the Indians in Revenge of Injuries and Hostilities offered to them by the Spaniards, as specified in the Trustees said Representation.

As to the Complaint received by the Governor of St. Augustine from the Lieutenant of the Fort of St. Mark. The Trustees have received Evidence, That the Forts which they have built are all within the Territories of the King of Great Britain, and erected at the Desire of the Indians, being necessary for the Defence and

---

[19] Egmont, *op. cit.*, II, 300-304.

[20] C. O. 5/670, Trustees to the Queen, 20 October, 1736.

[21] Add. MSS, 32794, N. P., CIX, Martyn to Newcastle, London, 9 February, 1736/7.

[22] A. G. I., Audiencia de Santo Domingo, 87-1-1, Doc. No. 2, Geraldino to Patiño, London, 18 October, 1737.

Peace of the Country and no Forts have been built by the Trustees within the Territories of the King of Spain; nor in any of the Indian Nations belonging to them.

As to the further Complaint that a Party of three hundred English had appeared on the Frontiers of the Province of Apalache, and that having set up a Standard of War in a Town of Indians called Apalachicola, they had summoned the chief Town of the above said province, called Caveta, to join them in order to make War against the Spaniards; acquainting them at the same Time that they were resolved to demolish the Fort of St. Mark, and afterwards to beseige St. Augustine.[23]

The answer to this assertion was a flat denial: "We are building no forts on any land belonging to Spain, nor are we tempting the Indians to quit the amity of the Spaniards."[24] Whatever ground there might be for the assertion was, they held, the work of a lawless trader of Charles Town.

The rather clumsy efforts of the Trustees to make good their title to all of Georgia and the region as far south as Fort King George at least display more reason. The following summary from the *Diary* of the Earl of Egmont, one of the Trustees, is a clear statement of their position on such extension:

Assertion 2.—That the new settlers in Georgia have built a Fort upon his master's territories in Florida, 25 leagues from St. Augustine.

Answer.—This we say that, admitting the fort to be built, it is land belonging to King George.

Assertion 3.—That in proof the land on which this fort is built belongs to the king his master, a fort that has been built there by the order of the late King George in 1724, is demolished and the garrison recalled.

Answer.—Our answer will be that there was a fort from which the Government of Carolina recalled the garrison because it was at a great distance, and hard to supply with provisions, but the late King George was so far from approving the recall of that garrison that in his 108th instruction to Governor Johnson he ordered the fort should be restored, and if demolished new built, and was much pleased at what had been done. That the reason mentioned by his Majesty for restoring the fort is that the entrance of the Allatahma river be preserved.[25]

Assertion 5.—The memorial asserts that all the Province of Geor-

---

[23] Add. MSS, 32794, N. P., CIX, 252.
[24] Egmont, *op. cit.*, II, 300.   [25] *Idem.*

gia belongs entirely to the King of Spain, his territory extending to 33 degrees north latitude, but by toleration the English were suffered to enjoy Charlestown. That in 1670 a treaty made between Spain and England (Article 7) settled each Prince's possessions to be enjoyed without molestation, and that by the 8th Article of the Treaty of Utrecht that treaty in 1670 was confirmed, and each Prince to remain in possession of what had then been settled.

Answer.—We shall show that the King of England was in possession of Carolina and Georgia (then part of Carolina) before the Treaty of 1670. That in 1666 King Charles II made a grant of all the land lying 36 degrees north latitude to 29, so that the river of Allatahma, at least, if not lands beyond it, belongs to England, the mouth of that river being exactly in thirty degrees. That Sir Francis Drake took Fort Augustin, and afterwards the Indians of Georgia beseiged it and took the town, but not able to take the fort for want of cannon, retired over the Allatahma, and ever since kept possession of that country. Now the Treaty of Utrecht confirming the treaty of 1670 leaving both kings in possession of what they then enjoyed, and the King of England enjoying all the lands from 36 degrees to 29, the claim which the memorial makes to Georgia as belonging to the King of Spain is groundless.[26]

The report of the Trustees was promptly sent to Andrew Stone, secretary to the Duke of Newcastle.[27] The answer finally sent by Newcastle to Geraldino was short and non-committal, and to the effect that the Trustees had given no order for forts without the English limits; that having endeavored to preserve peace with the neighboring nations, they could not believe any person in their service would have acted in the manner described—and this, they believed, a more thorough examination of the facts would reveal.[28] "This, sir," wrote the Secretary of State, "is all the answer I can at present give to your letter, and until we receive a more particular answer from the Indies to the inquiries which his Majesty has ordered to be made there touching the several points contained in your letter."[29] A copy of this letter was placed in the hands of Benja-

---

[26] *Ibid.*, p. 301.

[27] *Ibid.*, p. 304.

[28] Add. MSS, 32793, N. P., CVIII, Newcastle to Keene, Whitehall, 26 November, 1736, ". . . et elle est persuadée qu'après qu'on aura plus exactement examineé l'affaire il paroitra clairement que ces Raports on ete repandus sans fondement. . . ."

[29] S. P. F., Spain, Entry Books, 141; S. P. F., Spain, Foreign Ministers, 58, 113.

min Keene, ambassador at Madrid.³⁰ The English had nothing to lose by dilatoriness. They were vaguely anticipating an attack in force in Georgia, and Oglethorpe was consummating a successful treaty with the governor of St. Augustine.

Anxious inquiries had not yet reversed their order and had not begun to flow in the other direction, for Geraldino upon receiving Newcastle's preliminary answer sought and obtained an interview with Sir Robert Walpole, who assured him that Georgia was a Parliamentary project and that the government could not give an extended answer to his memorial until the excesses reputed to Oglethorpe—who was now expected in England—had been verified. It was not the intention of the crown, Walpole continued, that English subjects should injure neighboring provinces, and proper orders against such an occurrence would be sent to America. So emphatic was the prime minister's tone that his interviewer was led to believe that such orders would be carried out. Even this assurance, however, did not prevent a little judicious advice to the effect that the governor of St. Augustine ought to be given arms and men enough to make himself respected. Such a step would give the English ministry a motive through which to disapprove the peopling of Georgia and might lead to measures looking towards the abandonment of that already occupied.³¹

The return of Oglethorpe did not expedite the negotiation. Great was the chagrin and perplexity of the Spanish embassy to learn that Oglethorpe had appeared before the Trustees and announced that perfect harmony and good correspondence was established with the governor of St. Augustine. This was news to the Spaniards. To Geraldino, who now sought him eagerly, Oglethorpe insinuated the same tidings. Returning to Newcastle with all haste in expectation of a more categorical answer to his office, Geraldino found the secretary cautious, promising to inform him of everything and declaring that his Majesty's intention was not to permit excesses by the inhabitants of Georgia.³²

---

³⁰ Add. MSS, 32793, N. P., CVIII, Newcastle to Keene, Whitehall, 26 November, 1736.

³¹ A. G. I., Audiencia de Santo Domingo, 87-1-1, Doc. No. 62, Geraldino to La Quadra, London, 6 December, 1736.

³² A. G. I., Audiencia de Santo Domingo, 87-1-2, Doc. No. 5, Geraldino to Torrenueva, London, 31 January, 1737.

The project of Patiño opportunely came into the hands of the English government,[33] and during the period in which memorials contesting the right to Georgia and complaining of the depredations of its inhabitants were being passed in London, the court of Madrid was kept busy avoiding embarrassing questions. Keene was called upon (in cipher) to investigate the report that a "considerable body of troops and train of artillery" were ready to march, and to exert himself to prevent the fruition of so important a design.[34] That ambassador and official of the South Sea Company replied:

I had attention to the vulgar reports of an approaching war with England and of some intentions of sending troops to the Florida; but upon the strictest examination I do not perceive they have any thoughts here, or indeed much power in their present circumstances, to attempt to give us uneasiness without provocation, and I think I have taken such care to be informed of affairs of this nature by different checks and canals, that it will be very unlucky if they escape my observations and knowledge.[35]

Although inclined to treat the reports of the minister with confidence, the English government hurried to get and to transmit the best information concerning the views of the Spanish court and the possible reasons for suspecting that there was brewing any scheme for molesting either the possessions, trade, or navigation of the West Indies. It is little wonder that these extra precautions were urged in the light of the reports from Commodore Dent about Patiño's attempt to extirpate the Georgians. Keene was to insinuate his knowledge without seeming to lend credence to the reports and to follow up the advantage thus gained by reference and force (and the colonial agreement), thus securing a countermand for the orders sent to the West Indies.

---

[33] See chap. IV. C. O. 5/388, pp. 72, 73, 79, 80; S. P. F., Spain, General Correpondence, 126, 127, *passim; ibid.*, 246, pp. 2-6, 9, 19, 20, 29, 47, 55, 169, 175; C. O. 5/638, p. 14; *ibid.*, 639, pp. 57, 58, 77; *ibid.*, 654, *passim;* Add. MSS, 32794, N. P., CIX, 337-41; *ibid.*, 32795, N. P., CX, 22-24, 90, 131-33, 303-9; *ibid.*, N. P., CXI, 36-37, 46-48; S. P. F., Spain, Foreign Ministers, 59 pp, 58-65. There is a very misleading account, the only authority in existence, in W. B. Stevens, *A History of Georgia*, I, 151.

[34] S. P. F., Spain, General Correspondence, 129, Newcastle to Keene, London, 3 February, 1736/7.

[35] Add. MSS, 32794, N. P., CIX, 163, Keene to Newcastle, 11 March, 1737.

No doubt the information supplied by the Trustees of Georgia that all disputes with the governor of St. Augustine had been adjusted considerably lessened the apprehensions of the English. Oglethorpe and his obliging friend, the governor of St. Augustine, settled, to the satisfaction of the English at least, most of the points which might have caused war. But the great question, the delineation of limits, was referred to Europe. In a confidential dispatch to Keene, Newcastle recalled that these questions, by an article of the Treaty of Seville, had been referred to commissaries whose work the Spanish court had impeded. Obviously the Spaniards could hardly proceed justly to war over the heads of plenipotentiaries they had helped to create and to thwart. Recognizing the possible gravity of the matter, the secretary called upon Keene to use his utmost endeavors to secure counter orders to report to the English governors and ship commanders in the threatened regions.[36]

Even when supplied with information from Consul Cayley of Cádiz that the Spaniards had sent out a man-of-war and a store-ship loaded with four hundred soldiers designed for St. Augustine, Keene had too much confidence in the explications of La Quadra[37] to apprehend anything contrary to the tenor of a "so ready and positive declaration from His Catholick Majesty."[38]

The death of Count Montijo left Spain without an ambassador in London. The work of the office had fallen into the hands of the Spanish commercial agent, Don Tomás Geraldino. Although embarrassed at the offices of this agent, the English ministry knew that he was much preferable to the appointment of an unknown candidate. Accordingly every pressure was brought to bear in Madrid to secure his appointment as minister.[39] Subtle insinuations finally produced the desired effect with La Quadra. Keene then recorded his success jubilantly in a letter to Newcastle,[40] who replied:

[36] S. P. F., Spain, General Correspondence, 129; Add. MSS, 32794, N. P., CIX, Newcastle to Keene, London, 24 March, 1736/7.

[37] Don Joseph Patiño, who had died, was replaced by Don Sebastián de la Quadra, later Marqués de Villarias.

[38] Add. MSS, 32795, N. P., CX, Keene to Newcastle, Madrid, 17 June, 1737.

[39] Add, MSS, 32795, N. P., CX, Keene to Newcastle, Madrid, 17 June, 1737.

[40] *Ibid.*, Keene to Newcastle, Madrid, 1 July, 1737.

His Majesty was extremely well pleased at M. Geraldino's being appointed Minister here; For I may inform you, that he appears upon all occasions to be in the best Disposition imaginable; tho notwithstanding what he pretends, he certainly wrote to his Court for Orders to make a strong Declaration upon the Affair of Georgia, and the Design of sending Mr. Oglethorpe to South Carolina, hoping, I believe, by that means, to prevent Mr. Oglethorpe's going.[41]

The appointment of Tyry in the place of Geraldino as agent for the affairs of the South Sea Company, however, did not appeal to the secretary. The candidate's parents were Irish, and he was reported to have gathered information for the Spanish concerning the English fleet while it lay at Portsmouth. If he were not born in the United Kingdom, no just objection could be offered; moreover, Geraldino undertook to answer for him, and his appointment was secured.

In Madrid, Keene sought in vain to find out the real design of the soldiers embarking from Cádiz. "A person well informed of matters of that nature," probably Keene's leading spy, his "purple friend," assured him that the troops were merely intended to strengthen a weak garrison at Havana. In spite of the reports of the newspapers[42] that some independent companies were being sent to Georgia to seize and garrison the two forts built against the will of Spain, La Quadra declared that there need be no apprehension of a Spanish attack on any of his Britannic Majesty's possessions, and this declaration the ambassador at Madrid ventured to trust. This view was soon more officially answered by Torrenueva, "a weak . . . man without any good or bad intentions towards us," on whom La Quadra had placed the unpleasant work of dealing with Georgia.[43] Newcastle rejoiced at this news.[44]

The arrival of Oglethorpe occasioned the representatives of Spain no little embarrassment. The ambassador early in the spring wrote the Marqués de Torrenueva that in a conference with Newcastle he learned of the treaty between Oglethorpe

---

[41] S. P. F., Spain, General Correspondence, 129, Newcastle to Keene, London, 12 September, 1737.

[42] *Gaceta de Madrid*, 8 January, 1737; A. G. I., Audiencia de Santo Domingo, 87-1-3, Doc. No. 4.

[43] Add. MSS, 32795, N. P., CX, 324.

[44] *Ibid.*, pp. 164, 324.

and the governor of St. Augustine. The founder of Georgia, the minister continued, was causing a great deal of anxiety to the ministry (which fain would let the matter drop) by his adventure in Parliament; however, he managed to see the treaty whereby the English agreed to vacate the fort on the St. Johns. A neutral ground was thereby established, and the question of limits was referred to the two courts for a determination of their respective rights. Taking advantage of this opening and the threatened Spanish invasion, the general ingratiated himself with Parliament and secured an appropriation of ten thousand pounds to perfect his settlement. Believing in menaces (so deep-seated was his certainty of Walpole's pacificism), Geraldino was convinced that if the garrison at St. Augustine were made formidable while the English were uneasy and corresponding measures taken elsewhere, there could be no more opportune time for forcing upon the English ministry that which it was willing to give if able—a crisis and break with the Georgia Trustees and complete abandonment of the newly occupied colony. This was indeed novel advice for a minister whose selection was so heartily approved by England.[45] In Spain the Royal Council had met in solemn conclave as a result of Oglethorpe's arrival at the St. Johns. The king, consequently, instructed Geraldino to resort to the cunning methods of the spy to learn of any projects before the governments of South Carolina and Georgia or any men or munitions dispatched to "Nueva Georgia."

The militant activity of the Trustees and their most conspicuous member forced the Spaniards to take advantage of every circumstance which they could possibly turn to their account to thwart the success of their opponents. Just when the ambassador was writing to Madrid for instructions to pass a strong memorial, circumstances which had their inception in the machinating brain of the deceased Patiño began to play into the hands of the Georgians. In an interview with Newcastle on April 26 the astonished diplomat learned that news had arrived from Jamaica, Carolina (with a request for aid), and other quarters that a design was brewing at Havana, where troops were embarking for St. Augustine, to dislodge the Georgians from their settlements; that instructions had

[45] A. G. I., Audiencia de Santo Domingo, 87-1-2, Doc. No. 14; 87-1-3, Doc. No. 6, Geraldino to Torrenueva, London, 28 March, 1737.

been sent without his knowledge to Benjamin Keene to pass offices to the Spanish government setting forth the ill consequences which would follow such a course and demanding their countermand in conformity with the existing good correspondence. Geraldino was not called upon to make the same overtures, Newcastle distinctly repeating then, as on former occasions, that the orders which might be given Oglethorpe would be such as to protect and not to prejudice the interests and limits of Spain. This profession of sincerity he promised to transmit to Spain. Returning the next day, the Duke asked him if he had written, and further informed him that news of the same import had just been received by Keene from Havana. The armistice which was drawn up previously, in October of the preceding year, between the governor of St. Augustine and Oglethorpe and upon which the English now relied was promptly disavowed—neither one having the power to make it. A copy of this treaty was included in the report to Madrid for the complete information of the government. By private means Geraldino learned and reported that a meeting of the Privy Council was held on April 24 to consider the proposition of the Trustees of Georgia that a regiment of infantry be formed immediately for the defense of Georgia.[46] Yet his Catholic Majesty's representative could but admire the consummate craftiness with which Oglethorpe turned these circumstances to his advantage.

In the first instance, Geraldino was informed that his office was superfluous in the light of the amity established by Oglethorpe with the governor of St. Augustine, news of which arrived in letters from Oglethorpe. Questioned by the Spaniard, Newcastle could not name the dates of those letters and was annoyed the next day when Geraldino appeared for an answer. This was a question of fact and not an affair of two days, he said. Reërecting a fort on Spanish territory, where in deference to Spanish wishes one had already been destroyed, was fact sufficient to establish his point, retorted the astute Geraldino. The dispatch which carried this information to Madrid likewise depicted graphically the fate of Jamaica, Bermuda,

---

[46] A. G. I., Audiencia de Santo Domingo, 87-1-2, Doc. No. 28; 87-1-3, Doc. No. 14, Geraldino to Torrenueva ("con copia del Tratado de Armisticio concluydo entre Dn. Diego Oglethorpe y el Govern^{or}. de San Augustine en 8 de Octubre de Año passado"), London, 2 May, 1737.

Española, and the probable disposition of the indispensible colony of Florida.[47]

Meanwhile the Trustees were petitioning Walpole. Beautiful harbors, the key to North America, the shield of Virginia and Carolina, the hope of strategy against Spanish men-of-war which must ply the Bahama Channel, surrounded by 2,500 French regulars and an ever increasing garrison at St. Augustine—these were some of the artifices to which they resorted in attempting to secure a regiment of seven hundred men for Georgia.[48] It was noised abroad that in London Oglethorpe was devoting himself with much zeal and solicitude to this same object. The news of the Savy-Patiño menace played propitiously into his hands. The desperate Spanish minister turned to Horace Walpole and implored him to intercede with his brother, Sir Robert, to stay the efforts of Oglethorpe and the Trustees. Horace promised to see his brother and report to Geraldino anything which might be decided upon before putting it into execution. To the Duke of Newcastle he renewed his solicitations of the previous week for an answer to his memorial. It was promised with all possible dispatch.[49] On the fourth of the following month, busy Señor Geraldino renewed his efforts to find the disposition of the government on Oglethorpe's "pretensions." After two interviews he decided that the ministry, by the exigencies of Parliamentary politics, had succumbed to the Georgia faction. It appeared to him as if Parliament had taken a resolution to make James Oglethorpe commander-in-chief of the troops of Carolina and Georgia. Although assured by Walpole that the general's conduct would be altogether in the interest of peace, he gathered that the dread project was likely to succeed; moreover, an affair handled with such secrecy was difficult to comprehend.[50] Definite news of the appointment of Oglethorpe, along with a view of the forces of Great Britain in America, followed two weeks later.[51]

---

[47] A. G. I., Audiencia de Santo Domingo, 87-1-1, Doc. No. 55, Geraldino to Patiño, London, 29 May, 1737. *Ibid.*, 58-1-25, Consejo Real, 4 March, 1737; *ibid.*, 87-1-2, Doc. No. 9, Torrenueva to Geraldino, Madrid, 8 March, 1737.

[48] Add. MSS, 35909, Hardwicke Papers, DLXI, 74, Georgia Trustees to Walpole, London, 22 June, 1737.

[49] A. G. I., Audiencia de Santo Domingo, 87-1-2, Doc. No. 65, Geraldino to Torrenueva, London, 27 June, 1737.

[50] *Ibid.*, 87-1-2, Doc. No. 69, Geraldino to Torrenueva, London, 4 July, 1737.

[51] *Ibid.*, Doc. No. 71, Geraldino to Torrenueva, London, 18 July, 1737.

The English misunderstood the anxiety and injured feelings of the Spanish. "I doubt not," Keene buoyantly wrote,

that the answer Your Grace has given to Mr. Geraldino, with regard to his apprehensions upon the nomination of Mr. Oglethorp to be commander-in-chief in Carolina, has perfectly effaced him, and engaged him to represent that matter to his court in a proper manner. . . .

The demand for smoothing the feathers of Geraldino the right way was urgent, for the Spanish administration shifted its attitude with the whims of its foreign employees. If La Quadra pressed, however, Keene proposed to satisfy him with the "solid reasons" of "Your Grace."[52]

One week before this letter was penned, instructions for a second memorial, which had been requested by the ambassador at the court of London, were completed in Madrid.[53] The Spanish court was not satisfied with the assurance that the returning commander-in-chief would be given authority for defense only. The government could not look with indifference upon the return of one who in his former sojourn had caused so much trouble and offense, especially with his present instructions. On August 1, Geraldino replied that he would forthwith pass offices in accordance with the royal order concerning Oglethorpe, the settlement, and the expected evacuation of Georgia.[54]

To determine the firmness of the English government in the support of the Trustees—which the Spaniards thought altogether contingent upon party politics—seems to have been the object of what the English called "blustering memorials."[55] At a dinner at Cider House, the restless Oglethorpe informed Vernon, Dr. Stephen Hales and Sir William Heathcote that in a conference with Sir Robert Walpole, Geraldino had "insolently renewed" his complaints against Georgia. Those complaints bristled with talk of war.

---

[52] Add. MSS, 32795, N. P., CX, 164, Keene to Newcastle, 22 July, 1737.

[53] A. G. I., Audiencia de Santo Domingo, 87-1-2, Doc. No. 70, the king to Geraldino, Madrid, 15 July, 1737.

[54] *Ibid.*, 87-1-2, Doc. No. 72, Geraldino to Torrenueva, London, 1 August, 1737.

[55] A. G. I., Audiencia de Santo Domingo, 87-1-2, Doc. No. 72, Geraldino to Torrenueva, London, 1 August, 1737, ". . . a descubrir el animo de este Govierno en la pretención de Dn. Diego Oglethorpe apoyado de los Directores de la nueva colonia nom^{da}. Georgia. . . ."

He told him [Walpole] he had a second memorial to deliver him, by order of his master, the purport of which was to complain of no answer being returned to the first memorial given last year on the subject of the settlement of Georgia by English subjects, which country belonged to Spain from the southward up northward as far as 33 degrees and 50 minutes north latitude; that England has been encroaching on the Spanish dominions ever since the revolution, but his Majesty of Spain finding himself in good condition is resolved to re-annex all that formerly belonged to the Spanish Monarchy; that he hoped there had been time enough given since the presenting of the last memorial for the English settled in Georgia to remove; that as he had given himself up to God's service, he was desirous to see his own dominions restored to him without Christian bloodshed, but if otherwise it would not lie at his door; that unless the English remove by fair means, his Governors knew how to oblige them thereto by force, and if His Majesty of Great Britain should send over troops, and particularly Mr. Oglethorpe to command them, he should take it for a declaration of war.

Fitzgerald [Geraldino] then offered to present Sir Robert the memorial, which he declined to take, telling the other the proper person to receive it was the Secretary of State, to which Fitzgerald said the Duke of Newcastle was out of town, and he looked on this refusal as a put-off. Sir Robert then bid him present it to the King himself, which Fitzgerald expressed himself averse to for reasons which, said Mr. Oglethorp, it is not allowable to me to tell, though Sir Robert informed me of them, who added he had never met with such treatment from a foreign Minister in his life, and knew not how to behave under it.[56]

Sir Robert Walpole having refused to receive Geraldino's memorial, that minister delivered it to Lord Harrington, Secretary of War. Meanwhile, however, he had dropped the pretensions to Carolina, claimed only Georgia, and generally softened the document down to smoother terms.[57]

The new memorial began with a reference to the provisional answer of the Duke to the memorial of the previous year. Then Geraldino displayed in no uncertain terms the confidence of his Catholic Majesty in English promises, despite the diligence with which the establishment of Georgia was carried on contrary to them. The Spanish government expected a limitation of the arbitrary views of the directors of Georgia. An explicit

---

[56] Egmont, *op. cit.*, II, 426. The entry is for 3 August, 1737.
[57] *Ibid.*, p. 428.

answer having been deferred, all offices on the matter, all orders to the governors of South Carolina and Florida for regulating limits and the demolition of English forts on Spanish territory, and the answers given by the English to various overtures having been examined, the proceedings of the Georgians, and particularly of Oglethorpe were found highly disagreeable. The Catholic King was no less surprised at the violation of the seventh article of the Treaty of Utrecht than at the infraction of the American Treaty. Immediate issuance of orders suspending the establishment of Georgia and asking for the demolition of the forts complained of were unequivocally solicited, inasmuch as the least delay in an affair of such importance as the return of Oglethorpe with increased authority could but produce bad consequences. Since numerous inquiries were reaching Madrid concerning preparations at Havana, Geraldino protested that in consequence of the fundamental laws of the Indies, and the general instructions of the commander of the Spanish forces and the governor of St. Augustine for the preservation of the king's possessions, his Catholic Majesty's government could not disavow any steps which they might take to recover territories seized contrary to existing treaties.[58]

Every faction was now thoroughly stirred up; to the ministry this bellicose attitude brought consternation; to the Prince of Wales and the war faction, no little delight. On August 3 it was certain that the Privy Council "would not give way to the menaces of Spain." On August 7 Oglethorpe came to sharp and warm words with Walpole concerning the memorial,

... which had so terrified Sir Robert, by apprehensions of the Spaniards falling out with England, in case any forces should be sent under Mr. Oglethorp to Georgia (for the memorial threatened nothing less), that Sir Robert proposed to Mr. Oglethorp the dropping the design of sending him over with a regiment and his accepting a regiment in England in lieu thereof, at which Mr. Oglethorp fired and asked him what man he took him to be, and whether he thought he had no conscience, to be the instrument of carrying over 3,000 souls to Georgia, and then abandoning them to be destroyed by the Spaniards, for the consideration of a regiment. He also desired to know whether Georgia was to be given up, yea or

---

[58] S. P. F., Spain, Foreign Ministers, 58, 59 and Entry Books, 141; Add. MSS, 32795, N. P., CX, 311; A. G. I., Audiencia de Santo Domingo, 87-1-2, Doc. No. 73, Geraldino to Harrington, London, 28 July/8 August, 1737.

nay? If so, it would be kind and just to let the Trustees know at once, that we might write immediately over to the inhabitants to retire and save themselves in time. Sir Robert replied he did not see the necessity of that.[59]

Oglethorpe forced a crisis by demanding £30,000 when he only hoped to get twenty. Thus placed under duress, Walpole sought out the great imperial troublemaker who "spoke with great freedom to Sir Robert, who told him he was not used to have such things said to him. Mr. Oglethorpe replied, Yes, he was when he was plain Mr. Walpole; but now he was Sir Robert, and Chief Minister, he was surrounded by sycophants and flatterers who would not tell him the truth."

Having thus got off to a good start, Oglethorpe proceeded to observe that he was done with being Don Quixote for Georgia on behalf of which he had spent £3,000 of his own money. He thereupon proposed a general colonial militia, only to have himself named General of the Forces of South Carolina and Georgia after a plot to embalm him in Parliament and another to make him governor of South Carolina (where he had long been unpopular) had been frustrated.

While everybody was thoroughly wrought up over the memorial, Oglethorpe kept a vigil over the Cabinet Council in order to turn every fortune or seeming misfortune to his advantage. The council decided not to give way to "the menaces of Spain." The Trustees were fairly secure in moments of intense feeling. The Prince of Wales could be counted upon as an opponent of the government.[60] Sir Robert Walpole was usually backward in the affairs of Georgia, but others were very forward: all the Scots lords, Henry Pelham, Earl of Pembroke, and Sir Joseph Jekyl.[61] The Trustees and the worsted merchants in London made common cause in heaping ridicule upon the government.

We all of us think it a melancholy thing to find the low credit the nation is in with foreign princes on account of our facility in bearing insults, which proceeds from Sir Robert Walpole's natural ti-

---

[59] Egmont, *op. cit.*, II, 429.

[60] The Prince of Wales had been banished from the court by the king because aside from his political conduct, vexatious to ministry and sovereign alike, he had taken the princess away from Hampton Court for travail. *Ibid.*, pp. 339-41.

[61] Egmont, *op. cit.*, II, 434.

midity, and his apprehension of not sitting so firmly in the seat of Chief Minister in case of a war, which he colours with the inability of the nation to enter into war.[62]

Since the founder of Georgia served as a connecting link between government and Trustees, it was upon the receipt of information from him concerning the king's meeting in council that the Trustees decided to present a memorial (with seal affixed) to the king setting forth the fact that in view of the Spaniards' increasing envy of the Georgia ports commanding the homeward passage from the West Indies, and the recent augmentation of armaments and men in the Spanish colonies, the Trustees found it necessary to supplicate the king for the forces necessary to protect the settlers whom the Board could not protect.[63]

Cognizant of the English ministry's docility and the unlikelihood of its calling his bluff, and convinced of the justice of the Spanish cause in Georgia, Geraldino almost succeeded in scaring Walpole into submission. Newcastle, on the other hand, although showing very little sympathy, realized the ministry could not back down on Georgia. And, paradoxical as it may seem, Newcastle was at times the prime minister during the Walpole era. Fain would Walpole have dropped him from his ministers, but he could not—Newcastle's influence carried fourteen extreme royalist members of Parliament.[64] Walpole, indeed, was not entrenched beyond the possibility of dislodgment. The letter from the Trustees, Oglethorpe discerned, made a good impression at the council meeting, and the Lords were warm in their praise of it.

At last, on September 2 the English ministry responded in a long letter written in French—the accepted medium of diplomatic intercourse—Newcastle showed more firmness and more unequivocal assurance than had been the wont of his fainthearted colleagues. Geraldino had at least advanced one step in his program! The delayed response which was so constantly bewailed was attributed to the amicable settlement between Oglethorpe and the governor of St. Augustine as well as to La Quadra's declaration to Keene that no person whatever had

---

[62] *Ibid.*, p. 429.
[63] *Ibid.*, p. 428; *Colonial Records of the State of Georgia*, I, 296.
[64] Egmont, *op. cit.*, II, 486.

been authorized to make preparations against Georgia, but that, on the contrary, Spain wished all disputes settled amicably. Admittedly the tenor of the last memorial was a little surprising. The Georgians, ran the reply, upon the strictest inquiries would be found not to have violated the treaties according to the allegations. The attack upon the Spanish fort originally complained of was a mere retaliation for the burning of an Indian woman and other outrages—none of the attackers were of the English allegiance. The fort deprecated in the memorial was abandoned solely because of unwholesome conditions and not because of any orders from the English court, for that ground "then and now belongs to England."[65] Moreover, the forts reported by the governor of St. Augustine among the Yuchis and Alabamas were built upon English territory by orders of His Majesty. The standard so obnoxiously displayed at Apalachicola and the summons to the Indians at Coweta to join in an expedition for the demolition of Fort San Marcos were due to an irresponsible South Carolina trader. Regulations were immediately forthcoming for the prevention of such disorder and vagabondage. The governor of St. Augustine, it was alleged, had not instituted sufficient investigations for his complaints. Thus the response summarily dismissed the preliminary points of the memorials and answered at length the more sweeping claim—the right of Spain to all Georgia.[66]

To the king of Spain's claim to Georgia and South Carolina, excepting Charles Town because it was built before the Treaty of 1670, Newcastle replied that in neither the Treaty of 1670 nor in that of Utrecht did there appear mention of any limits or demarcations. In fact the seventh article, upon which Spain rested her case, contained no specification or rule beyond possessions then held.[67] Deeming it a notorious fact that England was in possession not only of South Carolina (which he pointed

---

[65] S. P. F., Spain, Foreign Ministers, 59, pp. 59-60.

[66] *Ibid.*, p. 61.

[67] Conventum praterea est, quod serenissimus Magna Britannia Rex, Hevedes et Successores Ejus cum plenario Jure summi Imperii, Proprietatis et Possessiones Terras, omnes et Regiones, Insulas Colonias, ac Dominia in Occidentali India aut quaves parte America sita, habebunt, tenebunt et possidebunt in perpetuum; quacunque dictus Magna Britannia et Subditi Ejus, improsentiarum tenent ac possident, ita ut, eo nomine, aut quacunque sun Pratensione, nihil unquam amplius urgeri, nihilque controversiarum in posterum moveri possit aut debeat.

out the Spaniards themselves admitted) but also of Georgia, it was only necessary to prove them so when the treaty was framed. The kings of England had issued charters granting the country between 36° 30' and 29° inclusive. These grants, in which the government took every care to include Georgia in 1732, he said, had long been publicly known and acquiesced in. He feigned great surprise at Geraldino's declaration[68]

that in consequence of the fundamental laws of the Indies, and the general instructions which the commanders of his troops and the governor of Florida have, for preserving entire the possession thereof even by force, his Catholic Majesty cannot disavow the measures they may take for recovering all the territories that may be seized contrary to the tenor of the treaties and to the demarcations and possessions of his Catholic Majesty.

Especially was this overt threat a shock, he said, when he recalled the express denial of military preparations made by La Quadra on the first of June when Keene sounded him concerning an American expedition. As a last proof of amity, he agreed to the appointment of commissaries to settle the limits dispute in a manner acceptable to the two courts. Assuming, therefore, that the Spaniards did not intend to attack in America, he promised that no American officers, governors, or any persons would encroach upon Spain and that explicit instructions to that effect were being sent, but "his Majesty, at the same time, cannot but declare his resolution to defend and support his just rights, and those of his subjects established by his authority within the limits of his dominions, that shall be attacked."

Soothing ruffled feelings and uprooting the umbrage taken at Oglethorpe's voyage to South Carolina was more delicate. Assuming a tone of righteousness for Oglethorpe, the crown insisted on sending out whatever governor it chose so long as he remained within the confines of propriety and no proofs of misbehavior were adduced. For full measure, however, the government related that Oglethorpe was being subjected to the peace stipulations in America like all governors there, and anyone acting contrary to them "would not fail to receive marks of his displeasure." So frequent and strong were the pro-

---

[68] 28 July/8 August, 1737. S. P. F., Spain, Foreign Ministers, 59.

testations of peace in this document that they sound almost weak.[69]

In Spain, Keene was oblivious of these diplomatic transactions, merely writing "in the Gazets I find there is a notion that a blustering Memorial has been presented by M. Geraldino upon the colony of Georgia, but as I have heard nothing of it from the office, I suppose it is without foundation."[70] His placidity was, however, to be of short duration. The London government redispatched Keene's servant to him in all haste with Geraldino's "very extra-ordinary memorial" and the answer made to it.

The inability of the English ministry to understand the foreign and American policy of the Spanish government was most natural and inevitable. Indeed, that wriggling government faced the task of reconciling three distinct policies. Patiño's bequest was a plan to proceed *a des voyes de fait* without an attempt at an amicable adjustment. Now his successor, Sebastián de la Quadra, upon solicitations from the English ambassador concerning Spanish preparations and designs in America, replied,

> That His Catholick Majesty had not authorized any person whatsoever, or the Governor of Havana, to make any military Preparations and that it was not His Catholick Majesty's Intentions to disturb his Neighbors; But on the contrary, if any Dispatches should arise between the Governors of the respective Countries, about the Limits of their respective Jurisdictions, His Catholick Majesty's Mind was, that instead of proceeding *a des voyes de fait*, such Disputes should be amicably adjusted, and settled, between the two courts.[71]

A full answer had been prepared to Geraldino's first memorial when La Quadra made this declaration. It was therefore withheld in the light of this suggestion of an "easy and unexceptionable" manner of adjusting disputes. The English ministry thought to avoid the pains of a discussion in particulars,

---

[69] Add. MSS, 32795, N. P., CX, 215-322; S. P. F., Spain, Entry Books, 141, Foreign Ministers, 59, Newcastle to Geraldino, Hampton Court, 2 September 1737.

[70] S. P. F., Spain, General Correspondence, 128, Keene to Newcastle, Segovia, 16 September, 1737.

[71] S. P. F., Spain, General Correspondence, 128, Keene to Newcastle, Segovia, 16 September, 1737.

but it was disappointed in its hopes when the second office declared that the king of Spain could not disavow the acts of any of his duly constituted officers in America in recovering territory seized contrary to the treaties. Newcastle's answer was now absolutely necessary. The ambassador at Madrid was supplied with a copy and urged to use it both as a basis for his discussions of the English forts near St. Augustine and of the Spanish claim to all Georgia.

The ambassador was further required to interview La Quadra and to express in no uncertain terms the surprise which, after the declaration made by the Spanish secretary himself, Geraldino's letter occasioned. Keene was likewise instructed to say that the Spanish claims were without foundation, even from the treaties, which the Spaniards cited with so much precision in support of this contention,

. . . and indeed it can hardly be imagined, if the Court of Spain had the Right, which is now pretended, to that Country, or had ever thought of laying claim to it, that such an active minister as Mon. Patiño would have taken no notice of it, when the colony of Georgia was established, which is now several Years ago; Or that he would not have made some remonstrances, or offer'd some Reasons against that Establishment.

In the instructions to Keene there appeared a note of mildness. In spite of the peremptory nature of the Spanish memorial, the English saw fit to conceive their answer in as moderate terms as were consistent with the support of the British title to Georgia and the resolution to defend and maintain British rights and properties. The cause of this moderation under duress is discernible in the instructions to the representative at Madrid to offer to settle differences by reference to commissaries, or in any amicable manner agreed upon by the two courts as La Quadra suggested. Newcastle could not but add to this overture his fond hopes that nothing hostile, as threatened, would engage the attention of the Spanish governors in America, and that any uneasiness at Madrid about Oglethorpe's voyage ought to be allayed by the answers already given on that point.

Although the idea of a vigorous memorial originated with Geraldino, he began insinuating after the delivery of his memorials that he was powerless to soften the expressions therein, but that notwithstanding them, he was persuaded that the Spanish governors in America would not proceed to hostilities and that the affair there would be amicably accommodated. It was necessary, however, to pay some heed to what had been presented in writing in so solemn a manner. The king of England accordingly ordered that a battalion be sent from Gibraltar and some ships for the defense of Georgia be dispatched at once. In response to any questions which might arise as a result of this step, Keene was ordered to say that, although unaware of any destination he had instructions to give the strongest assurance that no just cause of jealousy nor any attempts against the Spanish possessions were intended, and to add, as if from himself, that in the light of the memorial the Spaniards could not be surprised that sufficient troops for the prevention of invasion were sent. The example of the king of Spain in reinforcing the garrison at Havana with four hundred men lent cogency to this argument.

An account of all offices contingent upon these instructions was demanded. The confidence of the government in La Quadra, and his statement that no hostilities were on foot, led the English government to suspect Torrenueva or some other minister. In such an event Keene was to make every effort to increase the already growing prestige of La Quadra with the Catholic King. Keene's manifold task likewise included gleaning intelligence of any hostile movements in America from those people who had made disclosures to him concerning Miguel Wall, whom the English government still rightly believed to have been sent to Havana with directions from Patiño to put his designs into execution.

Geraldino, however, appeared reasonably satisfied with the reply to his memorial and endeavored to excuse a technical error concerning the demarcation between Georgia and Florida on the grounds that the stipulation asserted to be in the seventh article of the Treaty of 1670 was in reality in a convention, unknown to the English government, between the two crowns shortly before that time.[72] Although satisfied with the answer

---

[72] Geraldino wrote to his court to enquire whether there were any such treaties, saying that he understood the ministry in England needed something to justify its resolution against Georgia before the next session of Parliament in order to avoid disputes with the opposition and the Trustees. S. P. F., Spain, Supplementary, 246, Torrenueva to Geraldino, Madrid, 28 November, 1737.

given concerning Oglethorpe's voyage, the Spanish minister hoped that the government would of its own accord lay aside the design of sending him to South Carolina. In reply to this it was only possible to reassert the reply to the memorial—that an officer or an official could not be impeded or degraded without committing an offense.[73]

Meanwhile the Spanish ministry underwent a similar flurry. Consternation at first sight was the result of the memorial of August 8. Although admittedly the document looked like pure threats, the Spaniards learned that the English ministers appeared satisfied with Geraldino's explanatory answer. Geraldino, however, feared that this complaisance was a mere ruse in order to gain time to place Georgia in a state of vigorous defense in case it were attacked, or to begin negotiations in order to retain all or part of that colony. The Spanish diplomat now became convinced that the ministry, although naturally inclined to delays, would continue its temporising and subserviency to the Trustees of Georgia, which he in turn sought to encourage by pointing out that the negotiation was not only an affair of menaces but one of grave potentialities. Of comforting news for Madrid there was very little. The English intention of sending six hundred men from Jamaica to join Oglethorpe's command was a portent of evil omen for Florida, but it would leave Jamaica subject to Negro insurrections. More ominous still for the Spaniards was the rumor that the government at London was considering the nomination of a military captain-general with jurisdiction over the Carolinas, Pennsylvania, Virginia, and New England, both for mutual defense and expansion.[74] The latter the Spaniards dreaded.[75] In conference with the Duke of Newcastle and Sir Robert Walpole, Geraldino found his office had created amazed uncertainty—that a meeting of the council was to be held on it and that the

---

[73] S. P. F., Spain, General Correspondence, 129; Add. MSS, 32795, N. P., CX, 303-9, Newcastle to Keene, Hampton Court, 12 September, 1737.

[74] Lanning, "The American Colonies in the Preliminaries of the War of Jenkins' Ear," *Georgia Historical Quarterly*, XI (June, 1927), pp. 144-52; Add. MSS, 32694, N. P., IX, 3-4; C. O. 318/3, 170-76, 185,319; *Journals of the House of Burgesses of Virginia, 1727-1740* (edited by H. R. McIlwaine), p. xiii; *Journals of the Council of Colonial Virginia* (edited by H. R. McIlwaine), II, 904.

[75] A. G. I., Audiencia de Santo Domingo, 87-1-2, Doc. No. 74, Geraldino to Torrenueva, London, 15 August, 1737. An accompanying folder contains La Quadra's reply and the king's reasons for opposing the establishment of Georgia.

appointment of Oglethorpe should not be taken as a cause for the alarm which had been taken. This Geraldino did not believe. Responding that the appropriation of twenty thousand pounds sterling indicated an object of great moment, he compelled the pacific ministry to deny ever having admitted that Georgia was in Spanish territory, and to promise to take no steps without informing the Spanish government.[76] Meanwhile the Spanish diplomat anxiously awaited the answer which the Trustees were virtually framing. Response, he was assured, would be forthcoming with all solicitude and punctuality.[77]

On September 23 Geraldino supplied his superior with the reply—a document already in the hands of Keene at Madrid. Having declared that the treaty between Oglethorpe and the governor of Florida was null and void, Geraldino at Hampton Court heard from Newcastle doubts as to whether or not the limits of America had ever been determined; that although the ministry favored an amicable arrangement through commissaries, it would be necessary to finish the matter before the next sessions of Parliament in order to avoid unusual discord and hostility with the opposition. To Sir Robert Walpole he attributed the same sentiments.[78]

La Quadra, informed of the full contents of this communication from London, replied to the official making the report that he had remitted the matter to Count Montijo, president of the Council of the Indies, and at the same time required the assistance of several members of that council to examine the affair secretly in order to expose Newcastle's suggestions with more profundity and to determine whether the Catholic King ought to prosecute or abandon his obligation.[79] At last, thoroughly acquainted with the misunderstanding over the Georgia boundary, and professing to preserve good correspondence

---

[76] A. G. I., Audiencia de Santo Domingo, 87-1-2, Nos. 76-76, Geraldino to Torrenueva, London, 22 August, 1737; La Quadra to Torrenueva, San Ildefonso, 17 September, 1737.

[77] *Ibid.*, Docs. Nos. 79, 80, 81, 82, Geraldino to Torrenueva, London, 29 August, 5 September, 9 September, 1737.

[78] *Ibid.*, 87-1-2, Doc. No. 82, Geraldino to Torrenueva, London, 28 September, 1737.

[79] A. G. I., Audiencia de Santo Domingo, 87-1-2, Doc. No. 82-2, La Quadra to the Marquis Virrens, 14 October, 1737; A. G. S., legajo 7633 (enumeración antigua). In this legajo at Simancas are the lengthy reports made by some ten different men, which were requested by La Quadra.

between the two crowns, La Quadra decided that it was first incumbent upon the Spaniards to suspend the expedition preparing under the governor at Havana and to give every facility to the Council of the Indies in its examination of the demarcations and possessions in Florida.[80] The expedition was thereupon suspended.[81] The Spanish minister in London was at the same time plying his government with missives concerning a conference, and reporting the progress of English troops in the colonies.[82]

The pacific disposition of the La Quadra ministry was not disclosed as a comfort to England's ambassador, Benjamin Keene. Appealing to La Quadra, Keene was sent to Torrenueva, onto whom responsibility for American affairs seems to have been shifted in the crisis. Torrenueva gladly agreed with Keene. Montijo seemed well pleased with the suggestion for a peaceable settlement. In Madrid Torrenueva became reticent, and Keene explained that he had probably been reprimanded by La Quadra for his over-exuberance in the matter, but he let it be known that he stood for the cultivation of friendship between the two crowns and that the Georgia dispute ought to be settled through negotiation.[83]

Immediately the English grew surer and bolder. The Dutch were seeking English coöperation in their protests against Spanish depredations.[84] Horace Walpole, probably encouraged by this situation, wrote to Keene from the Hague professing not to understand what was meant by settling the affair of Georgia in an amicable manner. To him that matter was already determined. Refutation of a point-blank demand for the surrender of the colony, couched in such unequivocal language, needed only time for Spain to acquiesce in the justice of English pretensions.[85] Both La Quadra and Montijo admitted receipt of the papers on Georgia, but since, as they said, getting at the bottom of the affair required time and diligence, Keene decided not to press the matter, as the Spaniards might suspect

[80] A. G. I., Audiencia, de Santo Domingo, 87-1-2, Docs. Nos. 82, 83. The document dated Buen Retiro, 11 October, 1737, is signed by La Quadra.

[81] *Ibid.*, Docs. Nos. 82-83.

[82] *Ibid.*, Doc. No. 83, Geraldino to Torrenueva, London, 10 October, 1737.

[83] S. P. F., Spain, General Correspondence, 128; Add. MSS, 32796, N. P., CXI, Keene to Newcastle, 14, 21 October, 1737.

[84] Add. MSS, 32796, N. P., CXI, 34.

[85] *Ibid.*, Horace Walpole to Keene, the Hague, 7 November, 1737.

a good cause. Perhaps they were awaiting news of English armaments, since they were getting ready four ships of force which, Keene averred, might be as likely designed against the Dutch as the English. To this urbane minister it made little difference whether Spain intended to make an impartial examination or whether she intended to resort to force; he reported, comfortingly, that Spain was never in a worse condition for attacking the English.[86]

Instead of a rapprochement, the chasm broadened.[87] Newcastle joined Horace Walpole, who was probably emboldened by the Dutch. He professed not to understand what the ambassador meant by speaking of an amicable settlement by negotiation; the mere statement of the fact was sufficient demonstration of the English right to Georgia.[88]

The depredations of the *guarda costas* at this juncture began to weigh exceedingly heavy in negotiations.[89] There was no certainty about La Quadra now. He promised one time after another to submit an answer to the papers relating to Geraldino's memorial, but he was apparently driven to consult Montijo, who was "a double in cases that embarrassed him."[90] Yet Montijo distinguished himself by his keen discernment of the ludicrousness in the whole situation. He professed much knowledge of American affairs and was apparently consulted upon every step taken, but he informed Keene that neither La Quadra, Torrenueva, nor he "had given orders to Geraldino to present his second bullying memorial." There remained, then, only the king and queen who could possibly have interfered, and this they might have done upon reading Geraldino's dispatches and receiving no answer to the first memorial, or this may have been a trick of the ministry to shift the responsibility.[91]

---

[86] S. P. F., Spain, General Correspondence, 128; Add. MSS, 32796, N. P., CXI, Escorial, 28 October, 1737.

[87] Add. MSS, 32796, N. P., CXI, 114-16, Newcastle to Keene, Whitehall, 4 November, 1737.

[88] *Ibid.*, p. 120. The Spanish peace move was founded upon these words in Newcastle's answer to Geraldino's memorials: "Et pour donner a Sa Majeste Catholique . . . un poura entre les deux Cours." *Ibid.*, p. 243, Keene to Newcastle, Madrid, 13 December, 1737.

[89] Add. MSS, 33007, Diplomatic Papers, III, 122.

[90] Add. MSS, 32796, N. P., CXI, 130-34, Keene to Newcastle, Madrid, 18 November, 1737.

[91] *Idem.*

Keene's conjectures were not without foundation. Torrenueva informed the ambassador in London that his Catholic Majesty immediately agreed to settle the limits of Florida by commissaries according to the treaties. He further suggested that the English representatives in Madrid, or any persons selected as proper to be sent to the court, be authorized to examine the much-mooted points in Madrid, since it was there that the treaties of 1670 and 1729, the bases of the settlement of the limits, were negotiated. The plan had some rough places from the English point of view. The conferences for the determination of the differences were to last only six months,[92] during which time neither of the parties was to occupy or to people the territory of the new forts erected in the eighteenth century and particularly during the late voyages of Oglethorpe. Holding that the region was peopled and fortified in manifest contradiction of the treaties and just limits, the Spaniards requested its evacuation and the demolition of the forts prior to the conferences to be held for the regulation of limits. Such steps alone could serve as proof of a desire for the establishment of good correspondence. To these measures England had pledged herself by the eighth article of the Treaty of Utrecht, a solemn pledge of all the European nations, whose guarantees still subsisted. Written instances were to be enforced by those of mouth until Geraldino obtained a speedy and precise answer.[93]

So ardently did Spain now desire to secure this amicable settlement that Keene was given "all the assurances imaginable" that Newcastle's response to Geraldino's two memorials would be entirely satisfactory. Torrenueva was even more effusive in his professions that it was the king's intention to avoid any coolness or interruption in the friendship either through the Georgia affair or the depredations dispute.[94] Rather be-

---

[92] S. P. F., Spain, Supplementary, 246, Torrenueva to Geraldino, Madrid, 28 November, 1737.

[93] S. P. F., Spain, General Correspondence, 130, Torrenueva to Geraldino, 23 December, 1738. This letter is also included in La Quadra's letter to Keene, El Pardo, 15 March, 1738, and Keene to Newcastle, Madrid, 17 March, 1738.

[94] Add. MSS, 32796, N. P., CXI, 191; S. P. F., Spain, General Correspondence, 128, Keene to Newcastle, Madrid, 2 December, 1737. The depredations question was becoming decidedly acute. "Upon the whole, my Lord, the State of our Dispute seems to be that the Commanders of our Vessels do always think they are unjustly taken, when they are not taken in actual illicit Commerce; even though

latedly, however, it was discovered that the American Treaty of 1670 formed no concrete basis for adjustment. At that date the accommodation of European affairs was of primary importance, and America is alluded to in the treaty only in a cursory, general, and complicated manner.[95] Only a revalidation of the rights of possession and prohibition of all commercial intercourse were specified. Continued intelligences were conveyed to the English minister that the *consultas* of the Council of the Indies which La Quadra had commanded would be satisfactory.[96] As if to remove all room for apprehension, the dispatch, which was received in London with joy,[97] continued:

> To conclude, My Lord, it is hardly to be conceived that a country destitute as this is at present of foreign Friends and Allyances, deranged in its Finances, whose Army is in a bad Condition, its Navy in a worse if possible, without any Ministers at heat (unless Montijo should get the Reins into his hands) to push Their Catholick Majesties on to any extravagant Enterprises, or of Capacity enough to re-establish their Affairs, I say it is hardly to be conceived, that a Country in their Circumstances can have any premeditated design to fall out with us at present, notwithstanding the blustering steps they have taken about our Colony of Georgia.[98]

Yet there was no certainty about the diplomacy of this period. While these professions of good faith were en route to Keene, the Georgians were gaining fresh ground below the Altamaha. The Spanish ministers simultaneously were sending anew polemic instructions to their ambassador in London. On December 23 Keene learned by accident that Torrenueva had "some time since" sent an instruction to Geraldino demanding the evacuation and demolition of the forts built by Oglethorpe before the opening of the negotiations. Keene thought this step was taken without La Quadra's knowledge, and excused his

---

Proofs of their having traded in that Manner be found on board them: and the right of seizing, not only the Ships that are trading to their Parts, but likewise of examining and visiting them on the High Seas in order to look for Proofs of Frauds they may have committed. And till a Medium be found out between these two Notions, the Government will always be embarrassed with Complaints." Add. MSS, 32796, N. P., CXI, 221, Keene to Newcastle, Madrid, 13 December, 1737.

[95] "Quod autem ad utrasque Indias. . . ." Add. MSS, 32796, N. P., CXI, 213.
[96] *Ibid.*, CXI, 227.
[97] *Ibid.*, CXI, 286, Keene to Newcastle, Madrid, 11 and 19 December, 1737.
[98] *Ibid.*, CXI, 443.

failure to anticipate it in his correspondence on this ground, for about December 20 La Quadra declared himself unable to report his Catholic Majesty's sentiments on Georgia.[99]

Caught in the pacifism of the Walpole ministry, Geraldino hesitated to carry out Torrenueva's orders. That ambassador reported that in his extra-judicial conversations with the English ministers he had found them in a disposition to name a commissary to act jointly with Keene, but was unable to obtain any more positive answer.[100] Later he reported that Newcastle had acquainted him of the English government's intention to name such commissaries. Against this transpiration Geraldino thought it proper to withhold his office, being persuaded that the affair would be more expeditiously dispatched at Madrid,[101] and that the commission would soon be sent to Keene.[102] Thereupon he ceased to refer to Georgia.

An investigation of this disobedience now took place. The decision was very formally to transmit to Keene in Madrid the office which Geraldino was to have presented in London in reply to Newcastle's answer to the Spanish memorials. The English ambassador was bluntly informed that the Madrid government was highly displeased at Geraldino's failure to carry out the royal orders, and that he would be forthwith censured for his conduct and ordered to comply with his original instructions immediately.[103] The task of examining Geraldino's conduct and correspondence fell to the Conde de Montijo. In a long document[104] he recommended the instance which was made to Keene. At his suggestion Geraldino was ordered not to confer extra-judicially or confidentially with the English ministers upon a closed order; that absolute compliance with the treaties was the only acceptable basis of negotiations; that

---

[99] Add. MSS, 32796, N. P., CXI; S. P. F., Spain, General Correspondence, 130, Keene to Newcastle, Madrid, 23 December, 1737.

[100] A. G. I., Audiencia de Santo Domingo, 87-1-2, Doc. No. 107; 87-1-3, Doc. No. 22, Geraldino to Torrenueva, 23 January, 1738.

[101] Ibid., 87-1-2, Doc. No. 108; 87-1-3, Doc. No. 21, Geraldino to Torrenueva, London, 30 January, 1738.

[102] A. G. I., Audiencia de Santo Domingo, 87-1-2, Geraldino to Torrenueva, London, 6 February, 1738. The same information is in the *consulta* of Montijo, Doc. No. 109, in the same legajo.

[103] S. P. F., Spain, General Correspondence, 130, La Quadra to Keene, El Pardo, 15 March, 1738.

[104] A. G. I., Audiencia de Santo Domingo, 87-1-2, Doc. No. 109, 3 March, 1738.

the demolition of the forts was the essential and fundamental prerequisite of the same; and that the political exigencies of the English ministry and parliament ought not to be the concern of the officers of Spain.[105]

Keene was incredulous. Arriving at El Pardo too late to interview La Quadra, he desired to know from Torrenueva whether the king had insisted that orders be sent, prior to the opening of the commission, for the evacuation and demolition of the forts said to have been built by Oglethorpe. The answer was that there was enough to treat aside from these last intrusions into Spanish territory. This the Englishman could not concede unless informed that the English had admitted that the claim to the whole province of Georgia had some sort of foundation. Geraldino could not prove such to be the case, for had he not desired to be instructed as to treaties in which the demarcations might be found without having his curiosity satisfied? If the transplantation of all Georgia and the demolition of the forts were made prerequisite conditions, what, Keene inquired, could be the business of the hourly approaching commission? Baffled, Torrenueva asked what orders he had from London to put this question to him. The response was that it was the duty of every minister of common sense to send what information he could to his court, especially any pieces of extraordinary importance. It was thereupon admitted that the instructions sent to Geraldino consisted of two points: the naming of commissaries, and the demand that orders be sent for the demolition of what the Spanish called the new encroachments. With the first instruction Geraldino complied, but with the second he did not, much to the chagrin of the Spanish ministers.

Apparently the Spanish government at this juncture softened its attitude on Georgia, dividing the country into three classes: (1) that to which England had a clear title, (2) the disputed area which was to be the subject of the commission, and (3) lastly the region occupied by Oglethorpe or his followers since the end of the conferences at Seville—the region which Spain wished to see evacuated antecedently to the new commission.[106]

---

[105] A. G. I., Audiencia de Santo Domingo, 87-1-2, Doc. No. 110.

[106] La Quadra referred to "Georgia en los territorios de la Florida." A. G. S., 396: 7.634; 397: 7.635; 398: 7.636; tres tomos, "de las memorias manuscritas

With La Quadra Keene held practically the same discourse. This official very strongly insisted, however, that it was agreeable to reason and equity that Oglethorpe's recent advances should be abandoned by the English prior to the commission and matters left as they were before his momentous voyages. To him what that gentleman had done was a novelty in contravention of the treaties. The improvement of an estate, ran the retort, was in a sense a novelty, but such a one that the neighbors had nothing to say so long as one kept within one's own bounds. Had not England a right to that territory in King Charles II's time, and was not the delay in erecting forts solely an English concern? But to Keene's opponent such a right might be forfeited after a considerable number of years without such occupation, an argument which Keene did not fail to remind him would fall hard upon many leagues of Spanish-American land without either forts or subjects. Keene added that both British and Spanish tenure was previously as well as then determined by the Treaty of 1670, which rendered useless all investigations of first discoveries prior to that date. In spite of the conciliatory position taken by the ministers of the Catholic King, Keene lamented the lack of results and reverted dolefully to the days of Patiño, when business was expeditiously conducted. But he forgot to what purpose some of Patiño's work was designed.[107]

Here Oglethorpe, who had admitted his intentions of making the St. Johns River the southern boundary of his march colony, now had an opportunity to make his voice heard. He was called upon by the Duke of Newcastle to state what forts there were in Georgia and which ones had been demolished. The crux of the Spanish grievance was Oglethorpe's Fort St. George. Oglethorpe's counter policy was one of cunning, subterfuge, and falsification. After the repeated remonstrances of the Spaniards that this fort stood athwart the navigation of the St. Johns River, and upon assurances that this step would guarantee the continuance of friendship, and that the surrounding country would not be occupied by the Spanish, Oglethorpe agreed in the Treaty of 1736 to abandon the disputed fortifi-

de D. Joseph de la Quintana, sobre la Junta de comissarios Españoles é Yngleses en Sevilla enquadernada en porta."

[107] S. P. F., Spain, General Correspondence, 130, Keene to Newcastle, Madrid, 17 March, 1738.

cation. The garrison was then apparently withdrawn and the palisades taken away. That the post had been abandoned both Governor Moral Sánchez and the Marqués de Torrenueva admitted. But suddenly in 1738 they began making demands for its evacuation which belied their previous admission.

Oglethorpe, who had undertaken without success to convince the Spaniards that Fort St. George was on the Altamaha by confusing it with Fort King George (generally conceded as English territory), was not above victimizing English ministers in England where the Spaniards in Florida had been too sharp for him. For the sake of legality it was suddenly important to convince Newcastle and Walpole that Fort St. George had never been given up, for they were in a mind to relinquish to the persistent Spaniards all of Georgia that they could. The soldiers were too illiterate and too distant to contradict Oglethorpe. Besides the Trustees, who knew no better, would have supported the Machiavellian ruse in which the general was about to indulge. After naming a few forts which had been demolished, the great frontiersman, after deliberately speaking of "Fort King George or Fort St. George," continued subtly to draw the veil of haziness over the entire question by holding that the dismantled fortress stood upon "that Part of the Altamaha nearest to the river which the Spaniards call St. Johns." Thus was the legality of the English title to the St. Johns established. It was at the price of duping the Prime Minister. Having thus disposed of his dilemma, the general turned his attention to the Spanish right.[108]

Although the Spaniards claimed all Carolina as far as thirty-three degrees and thirty minutes north latitude, to Georgia's founder they had no color of a right to anything beyond the St. Johns with the possible exception of the Spanish fort St.

---

[108] Forts mentioned were Fort Moor, Fort St. George, Johnson's Fort, Fort Argyle, and several others. Add. MSS, 32795, N. P., CX, 250-51, Horace Walpole to Keene, The Hague, 3 September, 1737; 303-10, Newcastle to Keene, Hampton Court, 12 September, 1737; 32794, N. P., CIX, 255-60 (Oglethorpe-Moral Sánchez Treaty of 1736); A. G. I., Audiencia de Santo Domingo, 87-1-2, Doc. No. 19, Geraldino to Torrenueva, London, 11 April, 1737 (enclosure No. 1); Moral Sánchez to Montijo, St. Augustine, 14 October, 1736; Doc. No. 99, dated Madrid, 28 November, 1737; Doc. No. 100, Torrenueva to Güemez y Horcasitas, Madrid, 28 November, 1737; ibid., 87-1-3, Doc. No. 8, dated Madrid, 10 April, 1737; C. O. 5/654, fols. 131-32; Add. MSS, 32797, N. P., CXII, 292-94, Oglethorpe to Newcastle, 2 April, 1738.

Francis de Popa.[109] Relying on the *status quo* established in the Treaty of 1670, and reverting to the fuliginous title of the charter of King Charles II to the lords proprietors of 1668, he found England possessed of the region included in that charter. Neither did the independent company withdraw from Fort King George until 1727, and then on account of provisions. And by royal order the post was reoccupied in 1734-35, having been occupied in the interim by Indians of the English allegiance.[110]

By the spring of 1738 the various circumstances were coming into a vortex which bespoke danger to Anglo-Spanish relations. Geraldino's conciliatory and suave policy was rudely jarred by the orders extraordinary from Madrid and the polemic instructions demanding evacuation of the disputed territory and the fortresses in Georgia prior to the meeting of the commissioners.[111] Good wishes for amity between the two crowns could hardly erase the impression created by this procedure. Newcastle was demanding to know what passed between Keene and the Spanish ministers, and desiring that they be informed unequivocally that the dissatisfaction with Spain was universal and national, and not mere malice of the Parliamentary opposition, as the Spaniards probably thought.[112] Keene spared no efforts to show that resentment in England did not proceed from party intrigues, but from the "just resentment of the whole nation."[113] Yet it was held "pretty plain they would not fall out with us notwithstanding their late blusterings about Georgia."[114] England was, nevertheless, whether for party reasons or for reasons of need and danger, anticipating armed conflict and preparing for any eventuality. That the Dutch would then abandon the English for their own private advantage was early recognized.[115] Yet His Majesty's government inquired in cipher

---

[109] Oglethorpe contended that even this fort was west and not north of the river.

[110] C. O. 5/635, Oglethorpe to Newcastle, Frederica, 2 April, 1738.

[111] S. P. F., Spain, Supplementary, 247; S. P. F., Spain, Foreign Ministers, 59, Geraldino to Newcastle, London, 7 April, 1738 (in French).

[112] S. P. F., Spain, Supplementary, 247, Newcastle to Keene, Whitehall, 13 April, 1738.

[113] Add. MSS, 32797, Keene to Newcastle, Madrid, 7 May, 1738.

[114] S. P. F., Spain, General Correspondence, 130, Keene to Stone, Madrid, 15 April, 1738.

[115] Add. MSS, 32797; S. P. F., Spain, General Correspondence, 130, Keene to Stone, Madrid, 15 April, 1738.

as to the number and condition of the garrisons in Spanish ports, their stores, ammunition, naval strength, and the condition of the Spanish settlements in America.[116] The English also hastened to issue letters of marque and reprisal to both the English and the colonials. From Spain came representations like a medley in chagrin and consternation.[117]

The rumor of war turned all eyes to France and the prospect of the immediate operation of the *pacte de famille*. Waldegrave, British ambassador at Paris, reported that no warlike anticipatory steps had been taken and that the French court was ill-disposed towards Spain. La Mina, Spanish ambassador in France, in broaching the subject had been answered coldly, and informed that France had no treaty with Spain. The rumor, therefore, was La Quadra's strategic move to keep the Dutch from making common cause with England. Yet England could not expect redress. Spain would attempt to offset her demands by counter-claims. An economic boycott and unrestricted privateering, too, presaged an advantage to Spain.[118] La Quadra soon set the English ambassador at rest by informing his friend that France had not "interposed herself in the Disputes betwixt us and Spain." Similar assurances came from M. Champeaux, French ambassador in Madrid,[119] yet it appeared that France had held out hopes to Spain while Champeaux was kept in the dark by his own court.[120]

Wild rumors soon began to fly in London. Newcastle dispatched information to Spain requiring all British merchants forthwith to withdraw ships and effects from the ports of Spain.[121] The Spaniards were apprised of the steps of Waldegrave in Paris, but it was the opinion of even the Spanish moderates that in the affair of Georgia Spain could not bring herself to any compliance without prejudice to herself—a point well known to the English government.[122] Then came news

---

[116] Add. MSS, 32797, Newcastle to Keene, Whitehall, 28 April, 1738.

[117] S. P. F., Spain, General Correspondence, 130, Geraldino's memorial, 28 April, 1738.

[118] Add. MSS, 32797, Waldegrave to Newcastle, Paris, 10 May, 1738.

[119] Add. MSS, 32798, N. P., CXIII, Keene to Newcastle, Casa del Monte, 19 May, 1738.

[120] *Ibid.*, 29 May, 1738.

[121] *Ibid.*, Newcastle to Keene, Whitehall, 1 June, 1738.

[122] S. P. F., Spain, Supplementary, 246, Geraldino to St. Gil, London, 3 June, 1738.

that warlike preparations were under way in the land of the Catholic Kings; ships began to move from Cádiz to the West Indies under the utmost secrecy, whereas Great Britain had "given itself continually the utmost pains to advise them of their danger" which would serve to put the damper on the use of threats.[123] The departure of Oglethorpe was a similarly dark prospect for the opposition. While the English fleet was equipping, it was published in London that the Spanish troops transported from Havana had seized Georgia, a false rumor which both amused and perplexed the Spaniards who knew better.[124]

As midsummer approached, Spain still frantically tried to enlist the support of France and to frighten England with the shadow of the *pacte de famille*,[125] while England went deliberately about granting letters of marque and reprisal and ordering attacks on Spanish ships without the incidental declaration of war.[126] This situation was to obtain until the outbreak of the desultory War of Jenkins' Ear, which gradually merged into European politics in the War of Austrian Succession. Meanwhile the diplomatic stage was cut across by a sincere effort of the friends of peace to effect a reconciliation in the Convention of Pardo—an attempt which revealed the real nature of his Majesty's opposition as well as that of the "Oglethorpians" among the Trustees.

---

[123] Add. MSS, 32798, N. P., CXIII, Keene to Newcastle, Madrid, 9 June, 1738. See also Add. MSS, 32797, Keene to Newcastle, Madrid, 27 January, 1738.

[124] S. P. F., Spain, Supplementary, 246, Geraldino to la Mina, London, 16 June, 1738. A complete list of letters to and from Thomas Geraldino on the affair of Georgia for the period of this chapter is in S. P. F., Spain, Foreign Ministers, 59.

[125] A. Baudrillart, *Phillippe V et la Cour de France*, IV, 159.

[126] See J. F. Jameson, *Privateering and Piracy in the Colonial Period*, p. 356.

CHAPTER VI

GEORGIA IN THE CONVENTION OF PARDO: THE FIRST PHASE

ENGLAND AND SPAIN approached the diplomatic crisis of 1739 with statesmanship as docile as their problems were perplexing. In diplomacy the personal factor is always important, yet Spain was ruled by "three or four mean, stubborn people with little minds and limited understandings."[1] That pungent, uncomplimentary appraisal embraced Sebastián de la Quadra, Foreign Minister, Joseph de la Quintana, Secretary of Marine and Indies, and Casimiro Uztáriz, economist and First Commissioner of the War Office.[2] Queen Elizabeth Farnese manipulated the court with an assertive hand. Count Montijo, president of the Council of the Indies, who felt, as Ambassador Keene put it, that "if Spain would accumulate all her grievances against us [the English], she might make as much to do as we did; that there are faults on both sides; our contrabandists ought to be punished, and some of their governors hanged," was the most reasonable.[3] Rather late in the tension of 1736-1739 La Quadra shifted the onus of responsibility onto the Marqués de Torrenueva to whom the officious Keene likewise paid his respects.

From this gentleman I shall proceed to Torrenueva, a weak, embarrassed, timid man, without any bad or good intentions towards us, but who not having much practice in the affairs of the Indies, is led away by those he consults with. M^r. Geraldino's correspondence with him or his office is not according to former custom, and is according to M^r. de la Quadra's throwing off from his shoulders all that he can possibly get rid of.[4]

English officialdom is likewise unique. The minister, Sir Robert Walpole, was easy, good-natured, and desirous of peace al-

---
[1] Add. MSS, 32796, N. P., CXI, 241.   [2] *Idem.*
[3] Temperley, "Causes of the War of Jenkins' Ear," *Royal Historical Society Transactions*, 3rd ser., III, 204.
[4] Add. MSS, 32796, N. P., CXI, 241.

most to a fault; moreover, his was an age in which the standards of political corruption were different from if not worse than those of today. Walpole was at the head of a relentless political machine about which there hinged a great deal of vituperative, if ineffective, criticism. The Duke of Newcastle, an efficient and well-balanced official, was the principal secretary of state.[5] To the student who probes beneath the surface of English affairs during the reign of Walpole, Newcastle's influence and preponderance must appear more and more conspicuous. Walpole was a master of the groups. For that reason Newcastle's control of the extreme royalists made him a factor to be reckoned with. Keene, the ambassador at Madrid,[6] was fat, good-natured and agreeable, yet resolute and adroit enough when occasion required. The Spaniards and others whom he bribed and garnered into the English service in Madrid and contacted through "channels" (referred to unemotionally as just another fact in the day's work) were dubbed his "Purple Friends" or his "Friend No. 101." Keene, however, was an

[5] For the formative years of his life see S. H. Nulle, *Thomas Pelham-Holles, Duke of Newcastle, passim*.

[6] Although Keene is herein loosely referred to as minister or ambassador, he was given that title only late in his career. Coming first into prominence under the patronage of Sir Robert Walpole, he was sent to Spain as agent of the South Sea Company in 1723 and served that post until the War of Jenkins' Ear. His business connection did not deter him from holding, nor his patrons from extending to him, governmental posts. Made Consul-General at Madrid in 1724, three years later he was raised to the rank of Minister Plenipotentiary. In that rôle he signed, in conjunction with his collaborator sent to Spain for that purpose, the Treaty of Seville in 1729. With Stanhope's return Keene was left the exclusive minister for ten years. At that time his most important diplomatic undertaking, the Convention of Pardo, was signed. Disappointed at the ingratitude for his work in 1729, the later tardiness of the government in giving him the Order of the Bath, and the storm of popular condemnation that roared about his ears at the time of the Convention made his native land distasteful to him. He served in Parliament for Maldon in Essex and Looe in Cornwall from 1740 to 1746, but he eagerly seized the occasion to go off to Portugal. After serving and enjoying life there for two years, he was again deposited on Spanish soil with a large and important diplomatic docket. After the treaty of 1748 he was exalted to the rank of ambassador. He died in Madrid, as he himself would have thought proper, on December 15, 1757. Although his power was such as to contribute substantially to the overthrow of a Spanish government during these last ten years, he had already reached the peak of his career when diplomatic methods held out some promise in Spain. The most important English ambassador in Spain during the eighteenth century, he was one of Walpole's and Newcastle's most able servants. Sir Richard Lodge (ed.), *Private Correspondence of Benjamin Keene*, i-xxxvii.

agent of the South Sea Company and at the same time a representative of the English crown. Although such a position was aboveboard and not then considered incompatible with the performance of his duties, serving two public masters and one private one augmented Keene's difficulties.

The channels of profitable commerce are devious and the English merchants found one method or another around the highly monopolistic Spanish colonial system. Since European merchants outside of Spain could not send goods to the Spanish West Indies on their own account, their goods were sometimes carried over under the reputed ownership of Spaniards.[7] Precarious was a trade so dependent on individual honesty and so withdrawn from the sanctions of government. English merchants occasionally found themselves divested of their goods without explanation or money, particularly wheat and barley of which the fleets were frequently in dire need. Seizure was the penalty upon proof of undeclared or illegally declared goods. Such business was discreditable, costly, and vexatious, and nothing short of one hundred per cent profit made it worth while.

It devolved upon England to infringe on the Spanish trade and to tap the stream of precious metals that flowed from the perennial and inexhaustible mines of America. In such a design what device could have more charms than trade, for the English were left free to engage in illicit, and sometimes compulsory commerce with the Spanish coasts without interference from England. Defense was one of those many burdens of proof and action the English were quite content to let rest on Spanish shoulders. Long before, William Paterson, the adventurous speculator, had bethought himself of the occasion of the will of Charles II to propose the seizure of the strategic ports of Hispanic America in order to rid the world of Spanish prohibitions and exclusions which the English only regretted they were unable to make. Throwing open the ports to all nations, England could collect moderate duties and become the "emporium of Europe."[8] Although the suggestion was as hairbrained as

---

[7] *Memorials Presented by the Deputies of the Council of Trade in France*, p. 26.

[8] William Paterson, *A Proposal to Plant a British Colony in Darien; to Protect the Indians against Spain; and to Open the Trade of South America to all Nations* (edited by Saxe Bannister), pp. 155-60.

Paterson's inexplicable Darién experiment, it had a substantial basis. In 1701 a proposal to the same effect was made to King William. Repetitions occurred at least in 1702 and 1709.

Opportunely located and ever active, the Jamaicans led the fleets of elusive sloops that darted in and out of the Caribbean coasts, plying highly remunerative trade. Of the same nature were the merchants of Barbados, Bermudas, and Bahamas. The Jamaican sloops, slipping out of Kingston or Port Royal, dropped suddenly into the mouths of streams between the Río de la Cacha and the Chagres. The Spanish fleet system had made of Cartagena and Porto Bello distributing centers, but runs between New Spain, Porto Rico, Hispaniola, and Cuba widened the range of these enterprising merchants. Avoiding the numerous taxes imposed by the Spanish government upon legitimate trade, these men could naturally undersell competitors, and effect a quicker turnover in flour, manufactured articles, and woolens. Not only in "shoes, and ships, and sealing wax," but in Negroes they could undersell the market. DeFoe's sentiment that a war with Spain must pay was enthusiastically sanctioned by a pamphleteer who exclaimed that the privateers had had such success that, favored by war, "Jamaica will be the richest spot in the universe."[9] The *British Merchant*, inclined to moderation rather than exaggeration, estimated the Jamaica sloop trade at £200,000 to £300,000 per annum.[10]

In logwood cutting along the bays of Campeachy and Honduras, where a party of Spanish soldiers might swoop down any day and blot them out or put them in chains, these resolute men from England, New England, and Jamaica cut blithely away, their arms close by, prepared for any eventuality. Is the profit not great and the advantage to the mother country

---
[9] Charles Leslie, *A New and Exact Account of Jamaica* (3rd ed., Edinburgh, 1740), p. 376.

[10] An official source fixed the sums sold as follows: "August, 1706-August, 1707, of which the modest computation is 1,400 negroes at £56,000. 4,000 bayes at £48,000. 10,000 perpitts at £45,000. 8,000 sayes at £36,000. 4,000 scarletts at £20,000. 1,000 mixt serges at £3,500. In sundry goods as laces, worsted stockins, wax, hatts, lynnens of all sorts, by the lowest computation can't have been sold for lesse then £66,500. Total £275,000. Besides ye above goods we supply ye Spaniards with great quantitys of flower which brings in return only silver." *Calendar of State Papers* (hereafter cited as *C. S. P.*), Colonial, XXV, 111.

formidable?[11] The Board of Trade was early petitioned to appoint a governor for the Bay of Campeachy and to list it among the British colonies.[12]

For nine years before 1706 the galleons had not arrived. Intervals of this kind made illicit commerce inevitable. Down by the gulf stream from the north there came a steady flow from Maryland, New York, Pennsylvania, and New England. These merchants sold their flour and other provisions to logwood cutters, at Curaçao and St. Thomas, to the French, and to the very Spaniards themselves. Such men the Jamaicans loved as little as they loved honest Spanish officials—both were their enemies. But the Jamaicans themselves, in cutting through the ever-dear Spanish monopoly, were flying in the face of the Treaty of 1670 which was revived in the Treaty of Utrecht. When the crisis came, it was found impossible to curb these American traders. The spirit and vigilance of the colonies were such that "neither the Laws of their Islands, nor the Laws of England, nor the Laws of other Nations, can restrain them from trading wherever they foresee Advantage."[13] Another imperialist put it that "Colonies and Plantations are both Strength and Riches to their Mother Country, while they are strictly made to Observe the Laws of it."

The accumulated grievances other than the Georgian projects which led to the Convention of Pardo can be traced indirectly to the beginnings of the Spanish colonial system and directly to the Peace of Utrecht. Taking advantage of the general negotiations of 1713, the Spanish ministers, at the behest of vast, chafing and improperly supplied colonies, signed the *asiento*[14] compact with the eager Robert Harley, Earl of Oxford, who was impelled by the clamor of the South Sea Company

---

[11] The story of the incessant disputes about logwood can be traced more fully in the volume edited by Sir John Alder Burdon, *Archives of British Honduras*, passim.

[12] C. S. P., Colonial, fourteenth series, XX, 439-40.

[13] *Popular Prejudices against the Convention and Treaty with Spain, Examin'd and Answer'd*, p. 23.

[14] *Asiento* merely signifies a contract, but the *asiento de negros* was not a new proposition, having been held at one time by the Genoese, at another by the Portuguese, and by the French Guinea Company during the War of Spanish Succession. M. Postlehwayt, *The National and Private Advantages of the African Trade Considered*, p. 111.

for Spanish colonial trade. By this arrangement, the South Sea Company agreed to send forty-eight hundred slaves annually for thirty-eight years to designated ports in Spanish America. For this privilege the Company was to pay thirty-three and one-half pieces of eight a head on that number whether imported or not. Few interested parties approved of the treaty. The British merchants opposed it, the Spanish merchants were outspoken, and even the British Board of Trade seems to have sympathized with all. Like the English politicians of the early eighteenth century, they impotently drifted on with the agreement, laying the foundation for a diplomatic entailment from which it was impossible to get free.[15]

The *asiento* contract afforded the coveted privilege of breaking into the Spanish trade monopoly through one vessel of five hundred tons which quite sufficed to dazzle the English imagination. The South Sea Company was allowed two vessels as tenders, yet returns, as other companies had learned, were disproportionate to capital or expectation. The companies holding the *asiento* before had uniformly sustained losses, but despite the lesson the legend of the riches of the Indies in trade persisted. Instead of a source of boundless wealth, the contract had proved such a burden that the French company would not labor under it.[16] The profits were whittled to one-half by turning over the required twenty-three eightieths to the Spanish crown, and by the British and American interlopers.

The Jamaicans continued naturally and stubbornly to sell on the Spanish Main. Undaunted by the Spanish authorities, why should they quail before the bureaucratic South Sea Company? In the ensuing feud between the Jamaicans and the company, the private trade, reduced to peril by the company's identification with the government, continued to whittle down the *asiento* profits. Soon open charges that South Sea Company factors supplied the Spaniards with information were being hurled about. The company itself, however, was hostile to Spain and kept up a running dispute with Madrid over its dues, and the South Sea ship *Prince Frederick* was seized and confiscated by Spain, as was later the *Wool Ball*. Total company claims ranged upward of £250,000. Though the company paid

---

[15] *Report of the Commissioners for Trade and Plantations*, II, 578-80.
[16] *British Merchant*, III, 209, 254-66.

full duties for the specified number of slaves, the actual shipment seldom reached half that number.[17]

Many officials of England, including Keene at the court of Spain, were at one time or another connected with the South Sea Company or concerned with the affairs of Georgia. The Spanish governors frequently connived with schemers in order to supply the wants of the colonies. Soon, instead of the two tenders allowed the *asiento* vessel, whole flotillas replenished the lawful cargo as fast as it was sold. Without a more direct communication with Madrid it was hard to control the Spanish privateers (from which the governors sometimes made profits) which swarmed the Spanish Main. The realization of high prices generally for contraband traffic made it difficult for Spain to control her governors and *guarda costas* and England her merchant privateers. Spain could not acquiesce long in the abuse of concessions she had made. Unlimited foreign competition and the practical impossibility of retaining the American trade for her own galleons explain the eager adoption of monopolist ideals by the rising political schools of Uztáriz and La Quadra. Although perhaps bearing no relation to that sovereign, during the reign of Philip V, Spain, taken with a new sense of her national dignity, after the Peace of Utrecht so tightened her efforts at policing the American waters that only a national catastrophe, with which the English imperialists were becoming more and more willing to accommodate her, would suffice to conform her ideas to her size. The peace of 1721, ending one of the frequent, meaningless wars resulted in mutual restorations, the king of England holding onto the *asiento* contract and the Spaniards gaining their codfishing rights around Newfoundland.[18] Besides, Uztáriz, whose first literary attempt at the rejuvenation of a nationalistic commercial policy appeared in 1724,[19] now stood high in Spanish councils—perhaps higher than his merits warranted. His work, far from being a detached scholarly tome, passed beyond the

---

[17] G. B. Hertz, *British Imperialism in the Eighteenth Century*, pp. 9-13; *Present State of the Revenues and Forces by Sea and Land of Spain and France Compared to those of Great Britain*, p. 26. A prolonged dispute between the King of Spain and the company reached a crisis in 1733. The company had refused to honor pieces of eight except at the current rate of exchange while the King had insisted on 4/6.

[18] Board of Trade Papers, Plantations General, X, L 40.

[19] *Theórica y práctica de commercio y de marina* (Madrid, 1724).

range of a disquisition and became an exhortation to Spain to invigorate her navy, encourage manufactures, reform customs and promote trade. In perfecting his case, he made brilliant use of the mercantilism of Louis XIV and Colbert, analyzed what a group of Spanish thinkers superior to himself had done, and showed familiarity with the English navigation and trade acts. Although mild and ineffective wherever engaging any powerful institution, he pressed the case against England (in denying fishing rights to the Guipuscoans and Biscayans in Newfoundland) far enough to advise asking the Pope for a dispensation permitting another form of abstinence on fast-days.[20]

Of first significance was the fact that the Spanish governors issued instructions to the *guarda costas* to guard the coasts against illicit commerce. By dickering with the smugglers, the Spaniards found a method of inveigling them. Sometimes these ships acted as pirates towards Englishmen while holding the credentials of the Spanish government. They often became careless in discriminating between smugglers and vessels plying in good faith between England and the English West Indies. Spanish courts confirmed the captures by condemning ships and cargoes and impressing English seamen.

As the crisis of 1718 raised the head of the volcanic eruption of the Anglo-Spanish mixture in the Caribbean, Colonel James Stanhope, member for Derby who had served as envoy to Spain, began to speak in bulk of English claims, relating that he had presented more than twenty-five memorials to the Spanish court without the slightest redress.[21] Looking upon so many documents as formidable, Stanhope began to present his protests in bundles. That was a distinction that fell to the lot of Keene. Depredations began to figure seriously in Anglo-Spanish affairs around 1726. Merchants inundated the House of Commons with petitions against Spanish maritime onslaughts. The House itself echoed with the stirring resolutions of indignant members.[22] The policy of the British government, already inert in the hands of the master, Walpole, who desired

---

[20] For a revised opinion of the influence of Uztáriz see E. J. Hamilton, "The Mercantilism of Gerónimo de Uztáriz," *Essays in Honor of T. N. Carver*.

[21] *Cobbett's Parliamentary History of England* (hereafter cited as *Parliamentary History*), VII, 582.

[22] Journals of the House of Commons, XXI, *passim*.

the fruits but not the costs of war, found expression in the memorable expedition of Vice-Admiral Francis Hosier to the perimeter of the Caribbean and the border of Spain's empire. He had instructions[23] to surprise and capture both fleets—the galleons and the flota—and any isolated ships, and to inform the Spanish governors that he intended committing no hostilities unless it should be necessary in order to protect British property. His orders carried the peculiar provision that he was to use "his best Endeavours by Persuasion, or even by force to get them and their Cargo into his Possession; declaring in the strongest manner to the Commander-in-Chief, that his orders were to carry them to a Port of Safety, and that his Majesty's Design was to restore to everybody what belonged to them. . . ." That, to the ribald Englishman of the eighteenth century, was the height of effeminacy, and he inquired with supreme irony to know whether "a *British Squadron* was ever fitted out before, at a vast Expence, for a long and hazardous Voyage, to play the *Pedants*, and *endeavour to* persuade."[24] Stanhope was next called upon to "endeavour to persuade," and accordingly went directly to Madrid where he required the service of Keene. The Treaty of Seville[25] was the result of the negotiations, but the Parliamentarians were unsatisfied, and it only augmented English vexations. Their harangues continued and, with regard to Carolina, one document merely replaced another as a basis for argument.

But there was a possibility that the sore spot of navigation and depredations would at last be healed. The king on April 2, 1730, commissioned John Goddard, Benjamin Keene, and Arthur Stert as commissaries to adjudicate differences. By the eighth of the same month Newcastle had designated the Board of Trade to receive claims of the British subjects. During April and May numerous advertisements of the Board appeared in the *London Gazette*, one informing the public that the claims, accompanied by Spanish translations, were to be authenticated in the Court of Admiralty at the expense of the king. When Goddard and Stert departed to join Keene in Spain, they left behind their secretary, John Crookshanks, to press matters.

---

[23] Dated March 28, 1726.

[24] *Some Farther Remarks on a late Pamphlet, entitled Observations on the Conduct of Great Britain by Caleb D'Anvers*, p. 19.

[25] 9 November, 1729.

Soon they received from that worthy 102 claims, and seventy-two cases of lost ships. All this he did before the voluminous papers of the South Sea Company were ready. On December 21 the Spanish government had not yet appointed commissaries to review the English documents. When they were appointed, they frequently acted without conferring with the English. In the next year the old irritation still chafed. Newcastle droned out to Keene that far from the disorders ceasing,

> the number of *Spanish* Privateers, or rather Pirates, under the Denomination of *Guardia costas*, increases daily; and that the gain which the *Spanish* Governors in *America* make by countenancing these unlawful Practices, and sometimes being ourselves Sharers in the fitting out of those Privateers is such a Temptation, that unless the Court of *Spain* takes some more effectual Method, as by punishing those who have most notoriously offended that way, and making them answerable for the *Disorders* and *Irregularities* committed by ships to which they grant Commissions, or which are harboured in their Ports with Impunity, there will never be an end of the unjustifiable, and, as it too frequently happens, barbarous Practices.[26]

A cedula of the king of Spain early in the next year commanding the governors not to permit any abuse to Englishmen or their ships sailing in the American seas was nullified by the proviso "as long as they keep their proper distances and are not concerned in any illicit trade. . . ."[27]

No satisfaction or reparation could be obtained. "Spanish insults and depredations" was the refrain of countless protests through the ensuing years while Walpole, "that indefatigable Minister who, for many years hath rock'd the publick cradle, and endeavored to lull that forward Babe, the Nation, to rest," allowed them (according to the opposition) to be submitted to a supine government. The difficulty, of course, was summed up by Montijo. There were abuses on both sides. Some abuses the officials could not end and others they preferred to wink at. These burdensome depredations seemed in some measure to have discontinued in the year 1736, but in the following year they were renewed with greater violence than ever, while every

---

[26] Newcastle to Keene, 18 November, 1731. Marchmont, *A State of the Rise and Progress of our Disputes with Spain*, p. 11.

[27] Journals of the House of Commons, XXII, 86.

report smacked of the preparations that were making at Havana by the order of the court of Spain for the destruction of Georgia.[28]

> Oh, England! At what a State of Contempt and Cowardice are you arrived? England that destroyed the *Spanish* Armada in 1588, and . . . is now in danger of being destroyed by *Spanish* Pyrates,

came the Jeremiad from the wailing pen of "L.D."[29]

In 1737, after five years of relative quiet, the diplomatic pot suddenly began to boil again. Why? The conniving Elizabeth Farnese, in trying to get English assistance in the seizure of the Duchy of Tuscany was refused, and there was a noticeably increasing vigilance on the part of the *guarda costas*. Walpole's biographer lays the new depredations at the feet of the queen, who issued the vindictive instructions for America.[30] At any rate scores of merchants trusted their perplexing claims against Spain to His Majesty's justice. They naturally resented the disastrous implication that the discovery of logwood, cocoanuts, and pieces of eight (all of which could be found in the British possessions) meant illicit commerce, especially when the search was made in a way proscribed by the Treaty of 1667 which, although they so believed, did not pertain to America. That such goods were not proof of illicit trade the Ministry had been endeavoring to establish—and with indifferent success—for many years.[31] On this issue La Quadra did not equivocate. Citing Article VIII of the Treaty of 1670, which precluded mutual trading in America, he protested loudly enough

> That these words plainly shew the little grounds of the proposition you have advanced, that his Britannic Majesty's subjects have a right to a free commerce and navigation in the West-Indies, the only navigation that can be claimed by them being that to their islands and plantations, whilst they steer a due course and their ships are liable to seizure and confiscation, if it be proved that they have altered their route, without necessity in order to draw near to the Spanish coasts.[32]

---

[28] *Parliamentary History*, X, 486; *Gentleman's Magazine*, X, 639.

[29] *Reasons for a War Against Spain*, p. 37.

[30] Statement of Horatio Walpole in Coxe, *Memoirs of the Life and Administration of Sir Robert Walpole*, I, 561.

[31] George Lyttleton, *Considerations Upon the present State of our Affairs, at Home and Abroad*, p. 5.

[32] La Quadra to Keene, 10/21 February, 1737. *Parliamentary History*, X, 1181-82.

Newcastle virtually admitted the situation was coming to a head when he observed that the trouble lay in the assumption of English merchants that unless they were actually taken in illicit commerce, despite proof of their having engaged in it and having been found aboard, they were unjustly taken; and in the assumption of the Spaniards on the other hand that they have a right not only to seize ships continually trading in their ports, but to search them on the high seas for proof of fraud. Between these two opposing theses both governments were continually embarrassed.

Newcastle abandoned remonstrances, therefore, and issued peremptory demands for the first time in 1737.[33] He called upon Keene early in November to insist on the immediate punishment of the officials responsible for eluding and rendering of no effect the orders and cedulas sent to America to stop the "violences, depredations, and cruelties" and to obtain reparations for them. Without this response the only solution could be satisfaction for English subjects according to the treaties and the law of nations.

Ambassador Keene continued to press for an answer to this memorial. Meanwhile the English evinced great dissatisfaction with the rejection by the Spanish officials of the very favorable Oglethorpe Treaty.[34] In spite of Spanish hostility to the colonization of the Georgia country, the ministry under the guidance of Montijo expressed its willingness to submit the question to commissaries on the basis of the treaties of 1670 and 1729, with the proviso that no new forts or posts would be established and that the outposts would be abandoned as a preliminary step to the negotiation. Thus the idea of a convention of boundary commissioners, which remained an all-important topic from November, 1737, to June, 1738, replaced the stillborn Georgia treaty of 1736.[35] There appeared to be

---

[33] Temperley, "Causes of the War of Jenkins' Ear," *Royal Historical Society Transactions*, 3rd ser., III, 204.

[34] A. G. I., Audiencia de Santo Domingo, 87-1-2, Doc. No. 96, Crown to Geraldino, Madrid, 28 November, 1737.

[35] *Ibid.*, Doc. No. 96; S. P. F., Spain, Supplementary, 247, Geraldino to Newcastle, London, 27 March/7 April, 1738; A. G. I., Audiencia de Santo Domingo, 87-1-2, Doc. No. 92, Memorandum of the Conde de Montijo, San Lorenzo, 9 November, 1737; Doc. No. 104½, Torrenueva to Geraldino, Madrid, 28 November, 1737; Doc. No. 106, Geraldino to Torrenueva, London, 23 January, 1738; Doc. No. 107, Geraldino to Torrenueva, London, 30 January, 1738; *ibid.*, 87-1-3,

a great eagerness in Madrid to promote the negotiations over "New Georgia and the territories usurped by the English nation ever since the beginning of the century," yet Geraldino's instructions were arbitrarily written, dated, filed, and finally dispatched.[36] On the other hand, the English ambassador clamored for the satisfactory responses to his overtures which he never received.

Keene was especially disgruntled when La Quadra overlooked him completely in giving his reaction to Newcastle's response to the Spanish memorials. After a suave explanation to the English minister La Quadra expressed the readiness of his government, as Geraldino was already instructed to do in London, to agree to settle the American disputes through commissaries and to approve the appointment of Keene or any person the English government thought fit to be charged with that mission. Keene's complaints were answered with an embarrassed look. "It is not at all surprising," he wrote to Newcastle, "that your grace cannot well conceive the present form of this administration when we who are here can hardly comprehend it."[37] He was baffled that La Quadra relinquished some authority by shifting the responsibility onto Torrenueva for whom he had not the least esteem.

Upon request, General Oglethorpe furnished information which he thought would be most useful to the commissaries appointed to settle the differences concerning the Spanish claim to Georgia and Carolina. He reverted to the old pretensions, but his cardinal point was a staggering one from the Spanish point of view. Since the English were in actual and quiet possession of Georgia, it was incumbent upon the Spanish to make out and prove their rights. Could they be so audacious as to

---

Doc. No. 23, Geraldino to Torrenueva, London, 6 February, 1738; enclosure, Torrenueva to Geraldino, Madrid, 24 February, 1738; Doc. No. 24, Torrenueva to La Quadra, Buen Retiro, 8 February, 1738; Doc. No. 25, Torrenueva to La Quadra, 16 February, 1738; *ibid.*, 87-1-2, Doc. No. 109, Montijo to the king, Madrid, 3 March, 1738; Doc. No. 110, Royal order to La Quadra, Buen Retiro, 13 March, 1738; Add. MSS, 32797, N. P., CXII, 166-71, Keene to Newcastle, Madrid, 17 March, 1738.

[36] S. P. F., Spain, Supplementary, 246, Torrenueva to Geraldino, Madrid, 27 December, 1737.

[37] S. P. F., Spain, General Correspondence, 128; Add. MSS, 32796, N. P., CXI, Keene to Newcastle, 30 December, 1737.

General James Edward Oglethorpe

desire his Majesty to relinquish what he stood possessed of unless the Spaniards could show a better right than that under which he was possessed? The implication was that the Spaniards would have to show superior force. The onus of proof was the lot of the plaintiff.[38]

The English secretary firmly refused to abandon the forts in question for the stipulated period of six months, as the Spaniards requested, since that identical procedure was all that Spain could expect in case the commissaries rendered a decision favorable to her. The Spanish conditions were inadmissible. They would render unnecessary the treaties of 1667 and 1670. Could any encroachments by either side be discovered through an impartial examination of the facts by commissaries named by both sides? That was as far as Newcastle would go,[39] but he professed himself prepared to accept the six months probationary period, and was desirous of securing peace.[40] Nothing more could be said.

To Torrenueva's charge that the "Ministers in England would have been glad of some instrument that might justify the determination to be taken on the affair of Georgia, and that it might be done before the meeting of Parliament, in order to prevent the disputes that might be raised by the contrary party on this affair," Newcastle, who claimed to have insisted on England's "undoubted right to Georgia,"[41] retorted: "Absolutely without foundation." When approached on this subject Geraldino dissembled, but Keene was ordered "to contradict in the strongest manner the . . . false and groundless assertion in Mon. Torrenueva's Letter" if any credit was given to it.[42] Again the Spaniards had bungled in their efforts to exploit English partisan intrigue.

The twin problems of Georgia, navigation and depredations

---

[38] Add. MSS, 32797, N. P., CXII, 51-52.

[39] Add. MSS, 32797, N. P., CXII; S. P. F., Spain, Supplementary, 247, and Foreign Ministers, 59, Newcastle to Geraldino, Whitehall, 11 April, 1738; S. P. F., Spain, General Correspondence, 132, Newcastle to Keene, Whitehall, 12 April, 1738.

[40] *Idem.*

[41] Add. MSS, 32796, N. P., CXI, Newcastle to Geraldino, 1 September, 1737.

[42] Add. MSS, 32797, N. P., CXII; S. P. F., Spain, General Correspondence, 132; S. P. F., Spain, Supplementary, 247, Newcastle to Keene, Whitehall, 12 April, 1738.

in American waters, the merchants by numerous petitions did not permit the king's government to forget. In Parliament an outspoken and vehement resolution was offered against the Spanish maritime procedure, demanding a cessation of depredations, satisfaction for losses already suffered, security for the free navigation of British subjects in the future, and beseeching the king to use his utmost endeavors to that end. The ministers, logically not sympathetic, escaped merely by sanctioning the strong language of the resolution, defeating by 163 to 224[43] a motion from the polemic faction to recommit. In the exciting debate there appeared the screeching anti-Spanish motto of the opposition: "No search." In a feverish speech on February 10/21, 1738/9, Carteret had reached his peroration in these electrifying words:

> There is one point in dispute, my Lords, betwixt us and the Spaniards, which, if adjusted, must either leave us in the quiet and uninterrupted exercise of navigation and commerce, or must leave to Spain an absolute and uncontroulable sovereignty of these American seas. The Spanish court says, "We have a right to search your ships"; but "No search" are the words that echo from shore to shore of this island. This, my lords, is what we ought to insist upon; for without this concession, all other concessions from the Spanish court are to no purpose. . . .
> "No search," my Lords, is a cry that runs from the sailor to the merchant, and from the merchant to Parliament, my Lords, it ought to reach the throne.[44]

Meanwhile the signs of conflict grew more ominous. Bellicose resolutions of the House of Commons were dispatched to the English minister, with orders to write a letter thereupon to La Quadra. The government immediately issued letters of marque and reprisal to merchants.[45] A fleet under Admiral Sir Nicholas Haddock was made ready and sailed for the Mediterranean, May 28, 1738.[46] Already, however, Keene had found a note of mildness in some conferences with the Spanish secretary and was led to hope that the Spaniards would drop the insuperable conditions they would have annexed to the opening of the com-

---

[43] *Parliamentary History*, X, 729-1322.
[44] *Ibid.*, X, 754.
[45] *Acts of the Privy Council of England*, Colonial Series, III, 636.
[46] S. P. F., Spain, Supplementary, 248, fol. 68.

mission, but he held that the Spanish court was thoroughly apprised of Great Britain's firm resolution to "Maintain every inch of Ground that belonged to us by Treaty."[47]

Although La Quadra had emphasized the pacific intentions of his government by stating that "His Catholic Majesty would readily agree with the King in following any amicable means that may be thought of for finishing all the Disputes in general between the two Crowns, in such a manner that all past motives of complaint may be adjusted and buried in oblivion,"[48] Geraldino in London had no instructions for effecting a settlement. Lord Harrington, Sir Robert Walpole, Sir Charles Wager, and the Duke of Newcastle, whose agent, one Stert, was negotiating with Geraldino, however, were impatiently awaiting them.[49]

[47] Add. MSS, 32797, N. P., CXII; S. P. F., Spain, General Correspondence, 130, Keene to Newcastle, Casa del Monte, 7 May, 1738.

[48] S. P. F., Spain, General Correspondence, 130, Keene to Newcastle, Casa del Monte, 29 May, 1738.

[49] S. P. F., Spain, Foreign Ministers, 59, 132, Geraldino to Newcastle, London, 1 June, 1738; S. P. F., Spain, Supplementary, 247, fol. 218; Add. MSS, 32798, N. P., CXIII, fols. 165-81. Arthur Stert, who felt that he would be appointed plenipotentiary because he was one of the commissioners of 1730-1733, began unofficial conversations with Geraldino and managed to draw up the tentative results in April 1738. After the Spanish claims of £180,000 had been deducted from the British claims of £343,277 Spain still owed more than £140,000. Geraldino was permitted to confirm such an agreement with Stert's committee of Lord Harrington, the Duke of Newcastle, Sir Charles Wager, and Sir Robert Walpole. Later ship claims were deducted from the English claims on Spain. The Spanish, demanding the same proportional reduction, found they still owed £95,000 (third article of the convention) which they expected the South Sea Company to pay directly from what (£68,000) it owed Spain. Bristowe and Burrell, agents for the Company, would acknowledge the debt only when the king of Spain made known his policy in the matter of *represalia*. The English regarded the failure of the Company to pay insufficient cause for the suspension of the *asiento* (which La Quadra threatened); moreover, the Spanish soon seized upon the presence of Haddock's squadron as an excuse for not paying the £95,000. The fourth article of the convention provided that if any restorations were made on separately mentioned ships, these sums were to be deducted from that due England. The cases of the *Success* and the *Santa Teresa* (seized in Dublin) were referred to the commissioners and no vessels seized after December 10, 1737, were included. S. P. F., Spain, 94/131, Stert's plan; *ibid.*, Doc. of 16/27 June, 1738; *ibid.*, Keene to Newcastle, Madrid, 22 July/2 August, 1738; *ibid.*, Geraldino to Newcastle, London, 17/28 August, 1738; *ibid.*, 94/133, Villarias to Keene, Madrid, 17 May, 1739; A. G. S., leg. 2335/6904, *passim;* leg. 2335/6906, Newcastle to Geraldino, London, 16/27 August, 1738; *ibid.*, Bristowe and Burrell to Geraldino, London, 25 January/5 February, 1739.

Upon request they at last agreed to wait on Geraldino.

Finally Geraldino received orders

> . . . to represent to your majesty, that though it is indisputable that the new forts erected since the beginning of the present century, on his majesty's territories and more particularly by Mr. Oglethorpe under the more specious title by which he calls them Georgia, ought to be demolished previous to the conferences, the king, being willing to give the greatest proof of his desire to contribute to the union and good correspondence between the two crowns, agrees that your majesty may send to Madrid two commissaries at least with authority to settle all the limits between the provinces of Florida and Carolina according to the tenor of the Treaties.[50]

The response of Sir Robert Walpole was that in case the Spanish court signified its acceptance of the plans evolved, he would be willing to appoint the commissaries.[51] The rumors which were afloat in London concerning a Spanish attack on Georgia did much to fan the flame. St. Gil at the Hague anxiously inquired of his colleague in London concerning the report, which he utterly discredited, that four thousand Spaniards had landed in Carolina and had taken both Carolina and Georgia. While awaiting reports from Spain, St. Gil assured the ministers of the justice of the Spanish proceeding against the coming of the expected answers from the British court "where the literal sense of the Spanish tongue is used to be either adulterated or misunderstood."[52]

Geraldino responded punctually that it was reported in London that five thousand Spaniards had landed in Georgia and that the news had been quickly contradicted. Then rumor added, the ambassador pointed out, that two Spanish men-of-war had taken one English ship transporting three hundred men from Gibraltar to Carolina, "but this too is a lie, and fomented by Mr. Oglethorpe, who being still at Portsmouth, has written it hither with the same sinister intention as he has invented many other things which have all proved false."[53] La

---

[50] S. P. F., Spain, Foreign Ministers, 59, 132; S. P. F., Spain, Treaty Papers, 67; Add. MSS, 32798, CXIII, Geraldino to Newcastle, London, 29 May, 9 June, 1738.

[51] Add. MSS, 32798, N. P., CXIII, fol. 186.

[52] S. P. F., Spain, Supplementary, 246, St. Gil to Geraldino, The Hague, 17 June, 1738.

[53] *Ibid.*, Geraldino to St. Gil, London, 24 June, 1738.

The Convention of Pardo

Quadra, however, probably did not understand the agitation in London, and he never opened his mouth in the first instance concerning Admiral Haddock's appearance with a fleet at Spain's back door,[54] but he soon received the information that Oglethorpe had instructions to do "nothing contrary to the treaties"[55]— an elusive and useful phrase.

Both parties had now expressed an earnest desire to preserve good correspondence, and to appoint commissaries,[56] but suddenly La Quadra seemed to awake from a lethargy.[57] Messengers were exchanged, but, instead of the satisfactory answer which Geraldino expected, it was found that La Quadra had acquainted Keene that "there were such great incongruities in the account sent him by M^{on}. Geraldino, and so much to the king his master's prejudice, that he did not know how to lay it before him."[58] He was sure that the king would not like having certain projects chalked out, from which there could be no deviation. The acceptance of the plan proposed by Stert and later authorized by the British government was now to be accompanied with four conditions: that the agreeing to the plan and the nomination of the plenipotentiaries be one and the same act; that the Carolina-Florida dispute be linked with other matters for discussion and remitted at once to the consideration of commissaries; that the plenipotentiaries were to set out from London a month after their appointment and begin the conferences in Madrid within two months and bring the affair to a close in eight months; that during the conference in lieu of a fixed rule matters were to "go on in the same manner they are in at present, without any innovation or alteration."[59]

For a time it appeared that the negotiations would break

---

[54] Add. MSS, 32798, N. P., CXIII, Keene to Newcastle, Madrid, 23 June 1738.

[55] S. P. F., Spain, Supplementary, 247, Newcastle to Keene, London, 23 June, 1738.

[56] S. P. F., Spain, General Correspondence, 132, Newcastle to Keene, London, 14 and 21 June, 1738.

[57] S. P. F., Spain, Supplementary, 248, fol. 69. Geraldino was able to promote the negotiations without interruption because of La Quadra's new appointment as Councillor of State, the most honorable post in the Spanish government. Add. MSS, 32798, N. P., CXI, fol. 205.

[58] S. P. F., Spain, Supplementary, 248, fol. 69.

[59] S. P. F., Spain, Doc. dated 22 July/2 August, 1738.

down. Keene was ordered to hand in a memorial demanding a categorical answer to the project submitted by London. If no answer were forthcoming, he was ordered to leave Madrid immediately.[60] As the storm approached, however, the British consuls in Spanish ports took precautions, for which rather insincere conduct Keene was reproached by the Spanish government. With ships unable to enter the ports, commerce was at a standstill; yet it was thought that Spain would not make war on England on account of the Spanish king's "chimerical projects against Corsica and Tuscany."[61]

After numerous delays and objections by the officials at Madrid, the Spanish conditions, made agreeable to Newcastle's answer, were delivered by Geraldino. Matters in Georgia were to remain *in statu quo* "without increasing the fortifications, or taking any new posts, agreeable to the offer made by his Britannic Majesty in the Duke of Newcastle's letter upon this subject of April 11 of this year." Plenary powers were already in Geraldino's hands.[62] Having got in touch with the British ministry, he appeared too ready to conciliate the English and hastened the convention through, signed the document early in September, 1738,[63] with the Lord Chancellor, Lord Harrington, Sir Robert Walpole, and the Duke of Newcastle,[64] who dispatched a copy to Madrid. Secretary La Quadra soon let Keene know, though not by the king's order, that "Don Tomás Geraldino" had exceeded his "instructions and powers in pretending to conclude and sign the convention of the twenty-ninth past."[65]

The Spanish attempted to regain some of the diplomatic advantage which Geraldino had relinquished by insisting that the ratification of the second article[66] and the powers to be

---

[60] Add. MSS, 32798, N. P., CXIII, 21 July/1 August, 1738.

[61] *Ibid.*, fol. 244.

[62] S. P. F., Spain, General Correspondence, 132, "Plainpouvoir de sa Majesté Catholique a Geraldino," 1 August, 1738.

[63] S. P. F., Spain, Treaty Papers, copy of convention signed 29 August (old system), fols. 246-53.

[64] Add. MSS, 32799, N. P., CXIV, fol. 85.

[65] S. P. F., Spain, General Correspondence, 132, Keene to Newcastle, Segovia, 29 September, 1738.

[66] "Le Reglement des Limites de la Floride et de la Caroline lequel, suivant ce que a été convenu derenièrement, devoit être decidé par des commissaires de part et d'autre sera parcillement commis aux dits Plenipotentiares pour obtenir un

granted in consequence of it were to import that the plenipotentiaries were to treat in general upon all the pretensions which each crown had upon the other. To limit Spain's counter power was Keene's task, and, learning that the Spaniards were forewarned of his advantage, he lost his patience. Although pretending to know of no well-founded pretensions the Catholic King could have on England, he insisted that to admit such general treatment would "open a door to all the fanatical and capricious Disputes that could possibly be invented, and entirely frustrate the ends proposed by the future conferences; that if the two Nations had been ten Years in War against each other, he could not have made another sort of Proposition."[67] Keene, however, treated the matter with such warmth that La Quadra desisted, but he made it clear that the negotiations were to be confined to limits, commerce, and navigation, as specified in various treaties.[68]

The Spanish secretary was upset over the expression, "South Carolina (which is supposed to comprise the colony of Georgia)." He insinuated that Geraldino had been over-reached and that by the parentheses the English hoped to include Georgia within South Carolina with a design to support their title to all the disputed territory under the general denomination of South Carolina. No such *supercheries*, he was assured, were intended. The name of the disputed territory could not alter the facts, yet the king would not agree to the ratification of this article "which Mʳ. Geraldino had signed without authority, and much to his master's Prejudice,"[69] until the English could prove their intention to treat fairly with him.

Accord plus solide et effectif; et pendant les temps que durera la Discussion de cette affaire, les choses restoront aux sus dits Territoires de la Floride et de la Caroline dans la Situation ou elles sont à present; et on ne commencera point d'Ouvrages nouveaux et il ne sera faite aucune Innovation de parte ou d'autre respectivement sur les Frontiers de la Caroline Meridionale (dans laquelle on entend etre comprise la colonie de la Georgie) ou sur les Frontiers de la Province de la Floride appartenante au Roy d'Espagne; et pour cet effet Sa Majesté Britannique, et Sa Majesté Catholique feront expedier les Ordres necessaires immediatement aprés la Signature de cette Convention." S. P. F., Spain, Treaty Papers fol. 190.

[67] Add. MSS, 32799, N. P., CXIV, fol. 147; S. P. F., Spain, General Correspondence, 131, Keene to Newcastle, Segovia, 13 October, 1738.
[68] *Ibid.*, fol. 148.
[69] *Ibid.*, fol. 149.

One fact which cast a gloomy shadow over the Anglo-Spanish diplomacy of the period was the *pacte de famille*.[70] The concord of the Escorial, the first of the agreements, was not very effective, but its substance was known to Newcastle in February, 1734, and this knowledge exercised an ominous effect upon the negotiations of 1737-1739. The Marqués de la Mina, Spanish ambassador at Paris, in the early summer of 1738 found the Cardinal in a good disposition for a rupture between Spain and England.[71] Portentous messages passed between Geraldino and La Mina. The uncertainty of Anglo-Spanish affairs alone probably kept the Spanish from attacking Curaçao,[72] the Dutch depot of the Caribbean. The relative certainty of French succor served as a barrier to a reconciliation, for La Quadra learned from Paris that before admitting the conditions the English might propose, the aid of France should be counted upon. The King of Spain, therefore, would be doing himself an injustice to humor English pride if they pretended to anything beyond the dictates of reason and the limits of the treaties.[73]

Meanwhile the depredations issue was pressing. The rather faint efforts of the Spanish officials to obtain compensation for English merchants were fruitless. Many Spanish governors did not so much as acknowledge the letters and orders sent them. Keene presented twenty-eight bundles of claims to the Spanish government in less than a year! The growing popular agitation was becoming more and more articulate and every situation was shot through with dire forebodings. England increased her seamen from ten to twenty thousand and issued letters of marque and reprisal for which her disgruntled merchants were clamoring. Military and naval orders smacked of war. Orders for impressment on a large scale, the sure sign of immediate action, were sent out. Parliament was prorogued and voted £3,750,000 for combating injuries. Walpole was still noncommittal. But the time was ripe for the appearance of one Robert Jenkins of the *Rebecca* in Parliament. There under the auspices of the war faction he exhibited his detached and pickled ear,

---

[70] Baudrillart, *Philippe V et la Cour de France*, IV, 155 *et seq*.
[71] Add. MSS, 32798, N. P., CXIII, fol. 263.
[72] *Ibid.*, 32799, N. P., CXIV, fol. 102, *passim*.
[73] *Ibid.*, La Mina to La Quadra, Paris, 8 September, 1738.

credit for its removal eight years before going without a challenge to the Spanish captain, Juan de León Fandino. In the strangely apt speech that he made he recalled how, after being mangled, he expected the threatened death and recommended his soul to God and the revenge of his cause to his country. Whether this speech was prearranged or not, it was a happy one for the polemic faction. Excitement ran high. One Parliamentarian exclaimed: "Our countrymen in chains! and slaves to the Spaniards! is not this enough, Sir, to rouse all the vengeance of a national resentment?"[74] Countered a ministerial pamphleteer: "Many tuns of Logwood, even Ears, or even the life of a Man (whatever compassion he deserves) are not worth a general war. . . ."[75]

To Keene the situation was hopeless. "I am persuaded they have gone all the lengths they will go towards avoiding a war, and bringing on a reconciliation between the two crowns."[76] Had not La Mina on September 8 indicated the certainty of French aid? The tendency was confirmed by the information secured through Keene's bribes and through the statements of the ministers themselves. The method used to procure information throws some light upon eighteenth-century diplomacy.

Your Grace would have had some other circumstances of the Transaction between this Court and France were it not that La Quadra has carry'd on the correspondence with La Mina in his own hand. But my friend is as alert as possible, and as the term of my last Draught for his gratification is expired, I have sent M. Wall a Bill on you for 540 Pounds, the odd fifty having been disbursed in procuring Intelligences I sent your Grace from Aranjuez of

---

[74] *Parliamentary History*, X, 572, 786. See p. 270 for the case of Robert Jenkins, its authenticity, and psychological influence. For protests against imprisoning English sailors in Spanish dungeons, particularly those of Cádiz, see S. P. F., Spain, 94/133, Keene to Newcastle, Madrid, 26 January, 1739; *ibid.*, 94/134, Keene to Newcastle, 20/31 March, 1739.

[75] *An Appeal to the Unprejudiced, Concerning the Present Discontents Occasioned by the late Convention with Spain*, pp. 29-30.

[76] *The Merchants Complaint against Spain: Containing. . . . III. A Dialogue between Henry VIII, Edward VI, Prince Henry, Queen Mary, Queen Elizabeth, and Queen Anne; wherein the inbred Hatred of Spain to England is plainly proved to be Hereditary and that the only method to treat with Spain, is by point of sword (being the advice of Lord Chancellor Bacon on his Death-bed to Queen Elizabeth)* . . . (London, 1738), pp. 22, 23, 40; *An Impartial Account of Many Barbarous Cruelties Exercised in the Inquisition in Spain, Portugal and Italy* (London, 1738).

what was doing in the Council of the Indies, and other small Gratifications.[77]

Yet the day before this letter was written, the Convention, as it was agreed upon in London, was ratified, but with certain conditions. A proviso for clarification was added to the second article which dealt with Georgia, stipulating that during the time the adjustment of the limits of Florida was being conducted by the plenipotentiaries, matters in the Carolina-Florida region were to come to a halt, precluding all augmentation of forts or establishment of new posts. Necessary orders to that end were to be dispatched immediately after the signing of the Convention.[78]

Ambassador Keene and his successor as Consul-General in Spain, Abraham Castres, were appointed by the British government as plenipotentiaries. They appealed jointly to the British government.

We beg leave to observe [they wrote] that the two principal and most important Points to be examined and finally adjusted in our future Conferences will be the Limits of Georgia, and the Freedom and Security of the Navigation of His Majesty's Subjects in America. . . . As to the first Point which regards the Limits of Georgia, we humbly hope we shall receive full Instructions from your Grace upon it and beg leave to represent that we have nothing to offer upon this matter, having had little or no Information hitherto of the real state of our Disputes with this Court upon this important Subject.[79]

Uncertainty still filled the air. The king of Spain refused to announce his plenipotentiaries, already nominated, because he was not sure that England would accept the conditions imposed in Spain to the agreement arranged in London. The English, too, were becoming less frightened at the *pacte de famille*. As they grew more incorrigible, the significance of La Mina's letter[80] waned. The illness of the Cardinal and the con-

---

[77] Add. MSS, 32799, N. P., CXIV, Keene to Newcastle, 13 October, 1738.

[78] S. P. F., Spain, General Correspondence, 132; S. P. F., Spain, Treaty Papers, 67; Add. MSS, 32799, N. P., CXIV, "Copia de Ratificazion de la Convencion. Que para no equivocar el principal fin de este Articulo. . . ." fols. 246-47.

[79] S. P. F., Spain, General Correspondence, 131, Keene and Castres to Newcastle, Segovia, 13 October, 1738.

[80] La Mina's letter of 8 September, 1738, gave the assurance that in case of war Spain could expect the succors of France.

THE CONVENTION OF PARDO 147

sequent uncertainty of affairs had an influence upon European councils which was not expected to make England more conciliatory, and Spain was no longer in a mind to humor her.[81]

The conditions proposed in the Spanish ratifications were at first held inadmissible by the English government.[82] Newcastle hastened to send a revised draught of the Convention to Keene at Madrid.[83] The alteration in the second article, however, referring to Georgia, was held to be of little consequence. Since the limits of South Carolina and Florida were referred to plenipotentiaries, it was never intended, as the Spanish feared, to determine by the Convention that Georgia was a part of South Carolina. Although agreeing to a fresh draught the cabinet would not consent to the exchange of ratifications.[84]

The French, who were interested in the commercial possibilities of the Spanish possessions, were wily enough to take advantage of the new situation. Since Madrid expected French aid, the French ambassador, La Marck, continued to press the Catholic kings to accede to the New Treaty of Vienna, which would have repaid France amply for her aid. La Marck was tactfully told that since the Austrian emperor did not have a minister in Madrid, it would be better to treat the matter at Paris—a step which was regarded as an *honnête excuse*.[85]

When informed that the English court objected to the Spanish conditional ratifications transmitted to Geraldino, La Quadra was surprised, holding that that court must be sensible that Geraldino had exceeded his instructions.[86] His decision to insist on the Spanish right to suspend the *asiento* contract, announced four days before the signing of the Convention, however, almost broke down negotiations.[87] He was eager

---

[81] Add. MSS, 32799, N. P., CXIV, Keene to Newcastle, San Ildefonso, 15 October, 1738; *ibid.*, Walpole to Keene, Fontainbleau, 27 October, 1738.

[82] S. P. F., Spain, General Correspondence, 132, Newcastle to Keene, Whitehall, 13 November, 1738.

[83] Add. MSS, 32799, N. P., CXIV, fol. 249.

[84] *Ibid.*, fol. 236; second article of Newcastle's; S. P. F., Spain, Supplementary, 248, fols. 72-73.

[85] Add. MSS, 32799, N. P., CXIV, Keene to Newcastle, Madrid, 22 December, 1738.

[86] S. P. F., Spain, General Correspondence, 133, La Quadra to Keene, Madrid, 22 December, 1738.

[87] "His Catholic majesty reserves to himself, in its full force, the right of being able to suspend the Assiento of Negroes, and for dispatching the necessary orders

to secure the £68,000 obligation of the South Sea Company whose affairs had been excluded from the Convention.[88] In the same letter he gave notice of the appointment of Don Joseph de la Quintana and Don Estéban Joseph de Habaria as the Spanish plenipotentiaries.[89]

Momentarily war was averted, but much to the regret of the English, La Quadra apparently had fallen under the influence of Don Casimiro Uztáriz, first commissioner of the War Office, and son of the distinguished mercantilist, and neglected the sane counsels of Montijo.[90] Both countries had primary interest in the settlement, Spain to stop the English advance in Georgia, and England to stop the depredations in the Caribbean, and the negotiations went on apace. The English plenipotentiaries hoped to settle the Caribbean problem and to sign the treaty before the affair of Georgia, in which Spain could demand concessions, could be broached, and thereby deprive Spain of a great diplomatic advantage. Fearing that the Spaniards would make some difficulty in agreeing to this, Keene and Castres appealed to Newcastle for all the reports and papers relating to the English right to Georgia.[91]

One alteration was made in the second article of the Convention in order to remove the apprehensions of the Spaniards. In place of "And no new works shall be begun; and no Inovation made on either Side, respectively, upon the Frontiers of South Carolina (in which the Colony of Georgia is understood to be comprehended)[92] or upon the Frontiers of the Province of Florida belonging to the King of Spain"[93] was written the

---

for the execution thereof, in case the [South Sea] company does not subject herself to pay within a short term the 68,000£ sterling, which she has confessed is owing on the duty of Negroes, according to the regulation of 52d. per dollar, or on the profits of the ship Caroline; and likewise declare [s] that under the validity and force of this protest, the signing of the said Convention may be proceeded on, and in no other manner." *Parliamentary History*, X, 1028.

[88] S. P. F., Spain, Treaty Papers, 68, La Quadra to Keene, Madrid, 10 January, 1739; Add. MSS, 32800, N. P., CXV, Keene to Newcastle, 13 January, 1739.

[89] S. P. F., Spain, General Correspondence, 133, La Quadra to Keene, Madrid, 10 January, 1739.

[90] Add. MSS, 32800, N. P., CXV, Keene to Newcastle, Madrid, 13 January, 1739.

[91] *Ibid.*, Keene and Castres to Newcastle, Madrid, 13 January, 1739.

[92] The Spaniards thought the English might use this parenthetical phrase as a blanket title to Georgia.

[93] S. P. F., Spain, Treaty Papers, 67, fol. 213.

following: "And during the Time that the Discussion of that Affair shall last, Things shall remain in the aforesaid Territorys of Florida & of Carolina in the Situation they are in at present, without increasing the Fortifications there or taking any new Posts."[94] Proper orders to this effect were sent to the governor of Florida and the viceroy of New Spain.

The famous Convention was, then, signed on January 14, 1739, by La Quadra and Keene and the ratifications immediately exchanged.[95] Two commissaries of each country were to meet in Madrid to arrange the issue of depredations and to settle the boundaries of Georgia. Thereupon began an English attempt to put an immediate stop to the activities of the *guarda costas*.[96] Whole bundles of claims were submitted to the commissaries.[97]

La Quadra instructed the Spanish commissaries, Don Joseph de la Quintana and Don Estéban Joseph de la Habaria, to negotiate on the basis of the American Treaty of 1670 by which he hoped to confine the English to the territory they then held.[98] They were to convince the English that they did not, in 1670, hold possession of such parts of the territory as were in dispute. Proofs of English possession in 1670 by means of legitimate documents were to be produced before any recognition of such

---

[94] *Ibid.*, 68, fols. 226, 333, 380; A. G. I., Audiencia de Santo Domingo, 86-6-5, 25 February, 1739.

[95] A. G. I., legajo, 2262, Doc. 183; Add. MSS, 32800, N. P., CXV, fols. 68-70; S. P. F., Spain, Foreign Ministers, 59, *passim*; S. P. F., Spain, General Correspondence, 133, Keene to La Quadra, Madrid, 19 February, 1739. Keene expected compliance with the Georgia article and agreed to proceed "a l'Execution de cet Article avec la même exactitude. . . ." S. P. F., Spain, Treaties, 503, Ratifications, 14 January, 1739.

[96] Add. MSS, 32800, N. P., CXV, fol. 72.

[97] S. P. F., Spain, General Correspondence, 133, Stert to Keene, London, 15/26 January, 1738/9.

[98] A. G. S., Sec. de Estado, 2731, 7.632, instructions for the Spanish commissaries, signed, 5 December, 1738. Also 2529, 7.627 "de fechas de nombramientos de comisarios para dha. Junta, 7 Papeles instructivos sobre el mismo [Georgia], Asiento año 1739." La Quadra had secret papers on which to base the claim that all English forts built since 1720 should be demolished and the following places restored to Spain: "Lugar de Talaje, Bahía de Santa Helena, Santa Catalina, Zápala, Asao, Guadalquina, Assabow, San Felipe, Santa María, San Juan, Isla de Providencia," and the provinces of Guale and "Camacu," embracing South Carolina and Georgia; A. G. S., Sec. de Estado, leg. 7633, Memoria de Montijo, punto 11; Memoria de Barcía, punto 6.

possession, and by no means were the commissioners to recognize the English usurpations of territory contrary to the Treaty of 1670.[99] Having exceeded their bounds of that year, "the pretensions of the English were pulled up by the roots." The constant incursions and excesses of the English were also in contradiction to the treaties.

The debate in the English Parliament which followed the Convention was the high peak of the pre-war diplomacy in England. The patriots and imperialists, including the Trustees of Georgia, were resolved to ruin the effects of the Convention before they knew a word of its provisions, in which, according to a contemporary, "England was never more misled and unreasonable."[100]

The negotiations were complicated by domestic politics and by the interjection of the South Sea Company's affairs. Although it was common gossip among men of affairs that Georgia might be used merely as a pawn in obtaining the Convention of Pardo, Trustees Alderman George Heathcote, Robert Hucks, Robert Moore, and John White subscribed to Walpole's casual attitude and increased Oglethorpe's difficulties when they observed that "if we may have peace with Spain by giving up Georgia, it were a good thing." But such timidity was more than counterbalanced by the ardent labors of Henry Archer, Martin Bladen, the Earl of Egmont, and Henry Towers. Walpole began by an appeal to the Parliamentarians to do nothing rash to embarrass and confound the pending negotiations with Spain. Secretly he broached Henry Archer, Georgia trustee, and pressed him to second the motion of thanks, to be made the following day, to his Majesty for the speech from the throne. Archer declined under the apprehension that this procedure might in some way tie his hands and prevent him from supporting Georgia in case of an attempt to give it up to the Spaniards in the Convention. Walpole replied that he was amazed that so incredible a rumor should have been given such general

---

[99] *Ibid.* On the contrary, "atendidos en justicia y razon les privan aun de lo que por el expresado tratado se les cedió y concedió por esta corona. Pues no debe, no puede segun dro. mutual y el de gentes abrigarse; aun defenderse nadie con lo que le concede un contrato recíprico, sin que haga primero ver haberle por su parte punctualmente observado. . . ."

[100] *Appeal to the Unprejudiced Concerning the Present Discontents Occasioned by the late Convention with Spain*, p. 6.

credence; that in spite of the fact that there was no such design, "the Gentlemen of Georgia were his Enemies." This Archer countered by saying they looked upon him as their patron and support.

I told M^r. Archer [wrote the Earl of Egmont in his *Journal*] that I thought he had acted a wise part; that our Situation was very difficult, The Minority menacing to refuse us support unless we joyn'd them *tête baissé* against the Ministry; And on the other hand, no money to be expected if we disobliged S^r. Robert: But since we found ourselves threaten'd or courted by both sides, it would become us to stand on our leggs, & make no strong professions to either. He said he thought so too, & added that he found S^r. Robert was very serious, & under consternation what would be the issue of the Convention when laid before the house. I told him S^r. Robert had some reason, if L^d. Carteret's prophecy be true, who told me yesterday, that this affair of the Convention & the giving Georgia up would hang him.[101]

The Georgia faction was skillful enough to sell its support of the Convention to Walpole for a large subsidy to Georgia. The first petition for eight thousand pounds was granted, but it was necessary to go through Parliament and not to subvert the work of the commissioners too early. In this manner Walpole stalled the Trustees. Probably the hostility of the Carolinians against Georgia engendered a spirit of opposition in England that made the money grant difficult to procure. Egmont thereupon hastened to prepare a paper on the reason for preserving and supporting the colony. In spite of the fact that by the second article of the Convention the limits of Florida and Carolina were to be determined at Madrid, there were apprehensions that by a secret article the commissioners in the Spanish capital were to receive orders to deliver up Georgia.

That was very consistent with S^r. Robert Walpole's saying the Trustees should have no money this session, and his declaration thereof to Girildini ye Spanish Minister; but very contradictory to his promise that we should have money which he desired Mr. Henry Archer to assure the Trustees, and to his message to us by the same

---

[101] *Colonial Records of the State of Georgia*, V, 112-13. Add. MSS, 9131, fols. 199-273; N. A. Brisco, *The Economic Policy of Robert Walpole*, p. 25; P. Vaucher, *Robert Walpole et la Politique de Fleury, 1731-1742*, pp. 228-302; Egmont, *Diary*, pp. 10-45.

Gentlemen, that he should take it as a favour if we would make out his Majesties right to Georgia.[102]

Instead of becoming timorous the Trustees raised their petition from eight to twenty thousand pounds.[103] Some favored drawing up the defense, but others demurred, fearing to lay open the weakness of the claim to the government, and apprehending that secret orders had already been issued for surrendering Georgia. Sir William Heathcote accordingly moved to ask what the Spanish demands were, but this embarrassing move was not seconded.[104]

The Trustees' decision not to take upon themselves the defense of Georgia was privately imparted to Walpole by Towers and Archer, who agreed to serve as private persons if given access to the documents. Walpole said he knew nothing of the Spanish claims beyond that in Geraldino's memorial. Although not as well qualified as the king's advocate, the attorney general, and other crown officers, Walpole had a reason for this procedure. The Earl of Egmont believed

> . . . that S^r. Robert having advanc'd too far in subjecting his Majesties Title to Georgia to be litigated by the Spaniards, and yielding the same to be treated on by Commissioners, and being sensible of this mistake, he was now willing to get off, by taking the Sense of Parliament thereon, which should it be known that he employ'd the Chief Officers of the Crown in the defence of the Kings Title, might appear to Monsieur Giraldini a treacherous proceeding; whereas by employing the Trustees of Georgia in that work, the Opposition that might be made in Parliament to the giving up, or even suffering the kings Title thereto to be question'd would appear to proceed from others, & not from himself, and so make him stand in a fairer light to the Court of Spain, which he was very unwilling to displease, and who think the Parliament does nothing but by his direction.[105]

The Trustees were not indolent in pressing their petition for twenty thousand pounds. Oglethorpe's letter disclosing the want of troops and the debts of the colony were passed about among the members of Parliament. Walpole finally agreed to sanction the appropriation, and, upon urgent solicitation, promised that

---
[102] *Ibid.*, p. 98.
[103] *Ibid.*, p. 107.
[104] *Ibid.*, pp. 108-9.
[105] *Ibid.*, p. 113.

the plenipotentiaries were to be given directions from London and that Georgia was not to be given up.[106] The minister, however, was feeling about. He disclosed to certain Trustees that the Spaniards would give up everything, even searching English ships at all, to have Georgia surrendered to them, and added that he could see no reason why an inconsiderable part might not be conceded to them without injury to Georgia or England.

This shews how ignorant he was of the situation of the Colony and importance of it; for if any part of it were to be given up, it must be what ly's next to the Spaniards, and that includes the harbour of Jekyls Sound, which is the best on all the continent; And so M^r. Tracy reply'd, adding that when that was gone the rest would not be worth keeping, and observing he could not give a better reason why we should preserve the Colony in our hands, than the Spaniards eagerness to have it from us.[107]

The Trustees on February 14 decided on a list of papers relating to Georgia which they intended to lay before Parliament[108] in order to prevent the possible surrender of any part of Georgia. Walpole, taking alarm, would not allow the Trustees to make the motion for laying the paper before that body until the Convention had been accepted. Whereupon one of their number, Henry Archer, informed Walpole unequivocally that the Gentlemen in the Georgia trust were unanimous for keeping the colony out of Spanish hands, and that without satisfaction on that point, they were resolved to oppose the Convention.

S^r. Robert hearing this, call'd to Col. Bladen, and ask'd him whether England had a right to Georgia? yes, reply'd the Col^o. Can you prove it, said S^r. Robert, and will you undertake it? the Col^o answer'd he would. Then, said S^r. Robert, By G—d the Spaniards shall not have it.[109]

---

[106] *Ibid.*, pp. 117-19.
[107] *Ibid.*, p. 118; Egmont, *Diary*, III, 22.
[108] *Colonial Records of the State of Georgia*, V, 119.
[109] *Ibid.*, p. 121.

CHAPTER VII

GEORGIA AND THE FAILURE OF THE CONVENTION OF PARDO: THE DIPLOMATIC COLLAPSE OF 1739

WALPOLE's loud oath that the Spaniards should not have Georgia in 1739 might have been a species of political subterfuge. Was he not, indeed, beset by domestic foes who sought any means to embarrass him? And many were the jingoes to be placated; moreover, no such brilliant diplomatic opportunity as the now jeopardized Convention of Pardo had presented itself within the century. Duplicity, too, was not beyond the great Sir Robert. As evidence that the public regarded him with suspicion, the clamor against his foreign policy went merrily on. Great pressure was brought to bear on the Trustees by the opponents of the Convention as the debate in Parliament approached. The city of London, the merchants, the trading towns were petitioning against the agreement and asking: What are the Trustees doing? Could they actually be duped by Walpole? Could they expect support when they did not support themselves? Feeling their honor impugned, Egmont urged at the board meeting that the question of Georgia be detached from all other matters so that no one might be in doubt about how to vote. He then moved, "That a petition be presented to Parliament that they will be pleased to interpose, that the Colony of Georgia may not be affected by the 2nd Article in the Convention, which refer'd the settling of the Limits of Carolina & Florida to Plenipotentiaries."[1] The motion was spiritedly seconded by Lord Limerick. The friends of Walpole among the Trustees did not oppose, but merely deferred. Not content with this agreement, after some debate they arranged for the Earl of Shaftesbury to move the house to call for the papers on Georgia. By the interposition of Parliament they hoped to bind up Walpole in case he had made any in-

---
[1] *Colonial Records of the State of Georgia*, V, 123.

discreet promises to the Court of Spain about Georgia.

On February 24 certain Trustees endeavored to filibuster in board meeting until after the House of Lords had debated on the Convention. This move, which Horace Walpole openly favored, was finally thwarted.[2] The Trustees met to defeat any objection to their petition, but none arose. Once more the claims to Georgia were braced up by "Some Observations relative to the Boundaries of Florida and Carolina, to be discuss'd by the Plenipotentiarys, in Consequence of the late Convention with Spain."[3] Reviewing the history of the dispute the "Observations" showed that the Trustees felt it incumbent upon them to procure some vote in Parliament for the greater security of their possession "whereby their Property may be exempted from any examination by the Plenipotentiarys appointed for the future Treaty." Such procedure would absolutely render ineffective the second article of the Convention.

It is not to be doubted that either House of Parliament may, if they please, come to some Resolution that the Crown of Great Britain has an undoubted Right to all the Lands comprehended within the charters of Carolina and thereupon address the King not to enter into any treaty that may call the same into question, but such a Resolution would not give us a Title if we had not one already; and it is very Natural to Imagine upon Notice of such a Measure taken here by the Parliament, the Spaniards, who are much stronger in that Neighborhood than we, would immediately endeavor to Obtain a Possession by Force of Arms, to which they have no Title, and of which they might probably be convinced by an Amicable Conference.[4]

At last on March 6 the House of Commons met for the purpose of taking the foredoomed Convention into consideration. The interest taken in the subject was so intense and political feeling so highly strung that more than four hundred members were in their places at eight o'clock in the morning. After resolving itself into a committee of the whole, the House spent the whole day in hearing merchants[5] and witnesses against the

---

[2] *Ibid.*, pp. 127-29.

[3] Add. MSS, 35907, Hardwicke Papers, DLIX, fols. 70-74; *ibid.*, 33009, N. P.; S. P. F., Spain, General Correspondence, 134.

[4] Add. MSS, 35907, Hardwicke Papers, DLIX, fols. 70-74; *ibid.*, 33009, N. P.; S. P. F., Spain, General Correspondence, 134.

[5] Merchants' petitions against the Convention came from London, Bristol (the

Convention of Pardo. Documents were read the following day. Consideration of the king's speech from the throne came on March 8, with a House fuller than had been known for many years. Horace Walpole, diplomat and brother of Sir Robert, moved for the address of thanks for the king's "careful and prudent negotiation with Spain to preserve the trade & possessions of his subjects." He added that the outbreak of war between England and any great continental state would occasion a new blow from the Pretender and his followers. That prediction of Horace Walpole came true. So intense was the opposition of the minority that the debate lasted from half past eleven until ten o'clock at night. They spoke with immense scorn of the possibility of the recurrence of a Jacobite movement in England. Then the court carried the address by the narrow margin of 260-232. Before giving their votes, the Trustees insisted that the word *possessions* replace *rights belonging to Great Britain in the West Indies.*[6] Walpole yielded to humor them and secured their votes, but from that day the minority was enraged, considering the Trustees the mere tools of the ministry.[7]

Unscrupulous and vehement were the attacks on both the peace and the Convention. William Pitt deemed the Convention

A stipulation for national ignominy; an illusory expedient to baffle the resentment of the nation; a truce without a suspension of hostilities on the part of Spain; on the part of England a suspension as to Georgia of the first law of nature, self-preservation and self-defence; a surrender of the rights and the trade of England to the mercy of plenipotentiaries. . . .[8]

Henry St. John Viscount Bolingbroke and William Pulteney Earl of Bath, by a *coup de théâtre* attempted to withdraw the opposition from the House of Commons and to create such a

---

Merchant Adventurers), Edinburgh, "Dumfermline," Dundee, Montrose, Stirling, Lauder, Cupar, Kinghorn, Glasgow, Lancaster, and Aberdeen. Journals of the House of Commons, XXIII, *passim.*

[6] *Colonial Records of the State of Georgia*, V, 131; Egmont, *Diary*, III, 32.

[7] Newcastle to Keene and Castres, Whitehall, 20 March, 1738/9. Newcastle forwarded the addresses of Parliament to the plenipotentiaries to the effect that the "utmost regard will be had to the Rights, belonging to His Majesty's Crown and Subjects in adjusting and settling the Limits of His Majesty's Dominions in America."

[8] *Parliamentary History*, X, 962-1325.

sensation all over England that Walpole would be scared into refusing the passage of the Convention, something their presence could not have prevented. Sir William Wyndham, the opposition leader, was probably not a party to Bolingbroke's and Pulteney's scheme, but he insisted that the majority was determined by "arguments we have not heard" and appealed to a future Parliament to judge the conduct of himself and friends, while the "insolence of enemies without and the influence of corruption within threaten the ruin of the constitution." It was Walpole himself who squelched the attempted motion that Wyndham be committed to the Tower, but he delivered a stern speech, flinging into Wyndham's teeth his old devotion to the Stuart cause.

> For I remember [he said] that in the case of their favorite prelate the same gentleman and his faction made the same resolution. They went off like traitors as they were; but their retreat had not the detestable effects they expected and wished, and therefore they returned. Ever since they have persevered in the same treasonable intention of serving that interest by distressing the government.[9]

The House broke up in the greatest excitement since the Excise Bill or the South Sea Bubble. About sixty members, however, had temporarily seceded, although Sir John Barnard and others stood at their posts.

Many were the objections invoked against the negotiation in a veritable maze of pamphleteering, speaking, and letter writing. Keene was ridiculed for accepting the Spanish reservations. He was obligated, they pointed out, to the King of Spain for being styled "Don Benjamin, by which I conceive he hath made him a Gentleman; for which we are much obliged to him."[10] Those who felt that King Charles owned the western hemisphere could prove a better right to St. Augustine than the Spanish to Georgia,[11] which had been for a hundred years England's unquestioned property.[12] What good were a thousand treaties compared to ownership?[13]

To have formed an Agreement with them signed on both sides,

---

[9] J. McCarthy, *A History of the Four Georges and of William IV*, II, 225-27.
[10] *National Disputes, Extracts from the Craftsman*, p. 229.
[11] *Ibid.*, p. 247.
[12] *Observations on the Present Convention with Spain*, p. 28.
[13] *Ibid.*, p. 29.

while it appears that they insist that Georgia be left defenceless, and at the same time refuse to disown this illegal practice of searching, is a Piece of Conduct of so extraordinary a Kind that my Reader must furnish me with words to characterize it.[14]

Every pamphlet called out another. Would you go to war, asked the ministerial supporters, for reparation when you can have it without hostilities by acquiescing in the peaceful solution of the Ministry.[15] "Is it possible that we can have any amongst us who would disguise their Pursuits by a false cry, and only seek to wound the Ministry through the Sides of the Spaniards?"[16] Tipping the balances in favor of the Convention was the pertinent idea that England could not begin a war also with France and that she ought therefore to conciliate Spain.[17] The opposition was mortified and the ministry surprised, consequently, when Spain came to acceptable terms.[18]

Would they [inquired an Englishman in the guise of a Spaniard writing a friend in Madrid] if their circumstances would have suffer'd them to have used stronger Arguments, pusillanimously have resorted to a Convention? . . . *Jack English* truly makes a fine figure, and is of great Weight in the Balance of Power, when he is forced to come cringing to a Convention; and to treat about points that never would have come upon the Tapis but for their own Supineness and Ignorance in Policy. . . .[19]

A pamphlet dedicated to a devastating arraignment of every part of the Convention, irrespective of its merits, insisted that the second article contained an "extraordinary concession" in that a large tract of land in "South Carolina" had been purchased by His Majesty's government only when the ministry declared it to be a frontier, where a new colony would protect the others from the insults and depredations of the Spaniards, give an advantage in war, and shadow the treasure fleets passing back to Spain within sight of the coast. Georgia had been planted at great expense, and subsidized each year by Parlia-

---

[14] *Idem.*

[15] *The Grand Question Whether War, or No War, with Spain, Impartially consider'd,* pp. 31-32.

[16] *Popular Prejudices against the Convention and Treaty with Spain,* pp. 162, 174.

[17] *A Series of Wisdom and Policy Manifested in a Review of our Foreign Negotiations and Transactions for several Years past* (London, 1735), No. 8, p. 62.

[18] H. Walpole, *The Convention Vindicated,* pp. 5-6.

[19] *A Letter from a Spaniard in London to his Friend at Madrid,* pp. 12-13.

ment. Many Salzburgers and other persecuted inhabitants of the Catholic provinces of Germany had taken to the woods to enjoy the protection of the English in their civil and religious liberty. Now, when the region had been bought and improved by the public, the Spaniards having acquiesced for many years in the English title, the "Spanish neighbours of Florida" began to long for the morsel, and a memorial was delivered demanding its surrender. Although the Spaniard's "right to this country is no better grounded than their visiting our ships, yet as either from their natural Haughtiness, or their opinion of our Supineness" they pushed their exorbitant claims so far that the ministry condescended to stop the improvements in the province, to expose its inhabitants (who had been transported out under stout promises of protection) to the mercy of relentless enemies!

Since England did not demand Floridá of the Spaniards, the attack continued, the cessation of all activity could affect only the English adversely. Since England had no intention of invading Florida, what difference did it make whether the Spaniards increased their fortifications or not, asked the bitter pamphleteer. Moreover, the Spaniards having already fortified themselves adequately, only the newly arrived English, who needed to take all possible measures for their safety, found themselves defenseless just when the king of Spain demanded the delivery of the colony and an attack like that planned by Patiño and Savy was imminent. Could anyone expect such desertion of a people, so placidly inserted in the second article of the Convention, even at the end of ten years unsuccessful war? The "modest neighbours" who had only demanded Georgia in this same article had even prevented fortification at Charles Town, the capital, where the insufficient forts were in ruins and the government on the verge of increasing and repairing them. Quantities of munitions and stores shipped to St. Augustine just before the Convention made it "no extravagant surmise" to predict an attack on Charles Town.[20]

During the struggle Walpole's difficulties were increased by the conduct of Geraldino. On terms of confidence with the patriots, he went about declaring that Walpole was trying to deceive the English people as well as the Spanish government.[21]

---
[20] *Observations on the Present Convention with Spain*, pp. 32-35.
[21] McCarthy, *op. cit.*, II, 211.

Reports circulated that the Spanish minister gave out everywhere that his court would on no account whatever acquiesce in the English possession of Georgia.[22] One of these rumors was to the effect that Geraldino had told Lord Lovel that the king of Spain would sooner part with Madrid than Georgia. On the day for foreign ministers at court, March 15, General Wade went to inquire into it. Geraldino, being taken aside, protested against what he deemed a great injustice. All the foundation he could presume for the report was a conversation at Mr. Nungent's where Lord Lovel was present. After a great deal of talk on the Convention, they at last came to Georgia. Geraldino kept silent until solicited to talk. Then he expressed apprehension that the king of Spain, by the treaties of 1667 and 1670, had a right to a great part of Georgia. Notwithstanding, the Spanish minister held that he had stated several times, particularly to Sir Robert Walpole, that the King of Spain would be contented with the southern side of the river Altamaha if the English kept to the northern side.[23]

A trustee, Robert Tracy, having made this report in writing to the Earl of Egmont, was informed that Spanish occupation of the southern bank might mean sufficient Spanish fortifications to control the navigation of the stream. That the lands to the south should be left uninhabited by either Spanish or English was the utmost in the possible concessions. Egmont felt that the petition of the Trustees to Parliament, their declaration to the ministry, and the stand of the minority had produced this declaration from Geraldino, for he lent credence to Lord Bathurst and Tracy.

By inserting the word *possession* in the Commons address the Georgia Trustees bound England not to give up an inch of territory and defeated the ensuing treaty,[24] but unanimity among the Trustees was lost. Heathcote, White, Moore, and Hucks absented themselves from the meetings. Hucks at one time asserted that in case of a debate to give up Georgia he would divide the House against it even if there were but three members to join him, yet he was now asserting that peace with Spain at the price of Georgia would be a good thing.[25] It

---

[22] *Colonial Records of the State of Georgia*, V, 136.
[23] Egmont, *op. cit.*, III, 35 ; *Colonial Records of the State of Georgia*, V, 135-36.
[24] *Colonial Records of the State of Georgia*, V, 131 ; Egmont, *op. cit.*, III, 32-33.
[25] *Colonial Records of the State of Georgia*, V, 135.

FAILURE OF THE CONVENTION OF PARDO 161

soon appeared that Walpole did not intend to preserve the word *possession* in place of *just rights*. He had suffered it to pass so far only to ensnare the Trustees into voting for the Convention. This compromise the minority unsparingly flung into their faces.[26] The ministry carried the Convention in the House with the precarious vote of 244 to 214.[27] In the House of Lords Carteret repeated his "no-search" doctrine, attacked the Convention article by article, and contended with great plausibility that trade winds and the proximity of the islands of the West Indies compelled English craft to pass within sight of Spanish territory. Although on March 1 the Lords passed an address of thanks for the Convention by a vote of ninety-five to seventy-four, thirty-nine of these peers signed a resolute condemnation of it.[28]

One Spanish plenipotentiary, Joseph Quintana, succeeded Torrenueva as Secretary of State for the Indies and Marine, and this temporarily halted negotiations.[29] Geraldino finally demanded, however, that the Duke of Newcastle dispatch the proper orders to the governor of Carolina and the commander of the king's troops in Georgia according to the second article of the Convention.[30] This Newcastle did, sending at the same time a copy of his response to Geraldino and full powers for the English plenipotentiaries.[31] They were acknowledged on April 23. Nothing then stood in the way of opening the conferences on the following Saturday.[32]

The conferences in Madrid did not open auspiciously. James Lord Waldegrave, the English ambassador in Paris, began to make ominous reports. His "Friend 101" had begun to discover

---

[26] *Idem.*

[27] Journals of the House of Commons, XXIII, 277.

[28] *Parliamentary History*, X, 1241-43.

[29] S. P. F., Spain, General Correspondence, 133, Keene to Newcastle, Madrid, 9 March, 1739; Add. MSS, 32800, N. P., CXV, fol. 174.

[30] S. P. F., Spain, Treaty Papers, 68, fol. 384; S. P. F., Spain, Foreign Ministers, 59, Geraldino to Newcastle, 13/24 March, 1738/9. "Je prie votre Excelence de me faire savoir si Sa Majeste Britan, que a fait expedier les siens au Governeur de la Carolina et au commandant de ses troupes dans ce Payz. . . ."

[31] S. P. F., Spain, General Correspondence, 134, Newcastle to Keene and Castres, Whitehall, 20 March, 1738/9.

[32] S. P. F., Spain, General Correspondence, 133, Keene and Castres to Newcastle, Madrid, 23 April, 1739; Add. MSS, 32800, N. P., CXV, Keene to Newcastle, Madrid, 16 March, 1739.

things. The French ambassador had advised the Spanish government "no longer to have patience" with the English—an easy task in the light of the fact that the queen had abandoned herself to France.[33]

The efforts of the English plenipotentiaries to thwart the Spanish claim to Georgia by giving precedence to depredations and illicit commerce were hardly designed to placate the Spanish. Keene perceived the sore spot and recommended a remedy.

What would it avail, says Montijo, if we should hang up half a dozen of our governors in America to please you, or because they deserve it, if you [the English] do not treat your contrabandists with equal rigour? You only hear of your ships being taken, but give no attention to the damage we suffer essentially by your interlopers.[34]

With this sentiment La Quadra and even the Dutch minister were in accord. Naturally Keene was not enthusiastic about the successful termination of the impending negotiations since the country was run, he averred, "by three or four mean, stubborn people of little minds and limited understandings, full of Romantick Ideas they have found in old memorials and speculative Authors who have treated of the immense grandeur of the Spanish Monarchy."[35]

Admiral Haddock, according to the understanding between England and Spain, was to have withdrawn from the Mediterranean. The Spanish accordingly unarmed the greater part of their ships, gave liberty to their officers to leave their regiments and, remarked the English plenipotentiary, "will be ashamed either to trust our word, or to discover their lightness in having altered their military Measures before the Departure of Admiral Haddock."[36] In the mobbish clamor against the Convention, Newcastle, it seems, succumbed to pressure and ordered Haddock back to the Mediterranean, from which, a few days after the signing of the Convention (in which his presence was a great argument), he had been instructed to depart. This was

---

[33] Add. MSS, 32800, N. P., CXV, fol. 338; S. P. F., Spain, General Correspondence, 133, Keene to Newcastle, 4 May, 1739.

[34] Add. MSS, 32800, N. P., CXV, Keene to Newcastle, Madrid, 16 March, 1739.

[35] S. P. F., Spain, General Correspondence, 133; Add. MSS, 32800, N. P., CXV, fols. 288-94.

[36] Add. MSS, 32800, N. P., CXV, fol. 299.

a step to reassure British public opinion that the King of Spain would do as he had promised as well as a vulgar surrender to the opposition. The King of Spain was offended, and confidence in the British ministers to control the public in England was undermined.[37] Moreover, complaints against the countermanded orders and presence of the fleet continued to roll in. La Quadra, now Marqués de Villarias, and Montijo resented the presumption.[38] The commissioners, however, were allowed to pay their visit of ceremony preliminary to opening the conferences.[39] In spite of this warning, however, the Spaniards, according to the consul in Cádiz, continued to disarm their men-of-war.[40]

Both commissions came to Madrid abundantly supplied with well developed arguments.[41] The English Secretary of State appealed to all the logical sources for information to brace up the English claims. These papers the English commissioners received with exultation.[42] Walpole was not willing to concede that the English position was perfect. On March 21 Egmont recorded:

After this we joyn'd the other Gentlemen at diner where M^r. Sloper & S^r. Hen. Gough also came. After dinner I met Capt. Dempsy, and told him S^r. Robt. Walpole said publicly in the house of Commons, that there had not yet been a shovel of Earth dug towards building Forts in Georgia. The Capt. swore G— d— him what did he mean to say so? That Fort Frederica is so strong it cant be taken without Canon, having bastions, covert way, Palisadoes & ditch, and when he was there, 20 cannon mounted. That he also assisted in building Fort S^t. Andrews, a strong place, but left it before he had seen it finish'd.[43]

---

[37] *Raisons Justifications* . . . , p. 80.
[38] *Ibid.*, pp. 300-37.
[39] A. G. S., legajo 6733 antiguo, "Lo que S. M. manda expressar en la primera conferencia a los ministros plenipotenciarios."
[40] S. P. F., Spain, General Correspondence, 133, Cayley to Castres, Cádiz, 10 May, 1739.
[41] A. G. S., "legajo 7633 antiguo, papeles de Junta de Georgia—[Manijo, Barcía, Layssequilla, Quintana, Montijo], relazion de los papeles que comprenden quatro legajos . . . Indices de los Papeles tocantes a las conferencias entre plens. de S. M. y los del Rey B. G. refleciones." Secretaría de Estado 396.7.634, 635, 636, "que son tres tomos de las memorias manuscritas de D. Joseph de la Quintana sobre la Junta de comisarios Españoles e Yngleses en Sevilla. . . ."
[42] S. P. F., Spain, General Correspondence, 133, Keene and Castres to Newcastle, 23 April, 1739.
[43] *Colonial Records of the State of Georgia*, V, 144.

From Colonel Martin Bladen of the Board of Trade came the only defensible thesis. Even he was shocked that by the first charter the English had arrogated unto themselves regions the title of which they could not defend in the second one. He advised against claiming all the country north of the thirtieth degree, since Popple's map, regarded as the most exact then extant, placed St. Augustine ten minutes and the St. Johns forty north of that degree. Bladen doubted the latitude, but lamented the specific detail of the map as a source of disputes and delays. Under the circumstances he considered couching the second article in the terms of one of the charters to the Lords Proprietors by Charles II as the most effectual and capable of support at home and abroad. The grant to Edward Earl of Clarendon, with other Lords and Gentlemen "who had sought the King's leave *'to transport and make an ample Colony of his Subjects in the Parts of America not yet cultivated or Planted, and, only inhabited by some barbarous People, who have no knowledge of Almighty God*' " included the area from "Luske Island in the thirty-sixth degree of northern latitude to the River St. Mathias [St. Johns] within one and thirty degrees" and so "west in a Direct line, as far as the South Seas aforesaid." In the second charter, two years later, the "Bounds of Carolina are extended *South and Westward as far as the Degree of Twenty-nine, inclusive, Northern Latitude.*" Quite naturally Bladen could not understand why, after saying they intended to take territory "only inhabited by some barbarous people," the Proprietors weakened their claim by taking in the whole twenty-ninth degree of northern latitude. One glance at the map, he emphatically pointed out, showed that the grant not only included St. Augustine, but the Gulf of Mexico, where the Mississippi and other rivers discharge themselves into that gulf, and where both the Spaniards and French had made settlements. The second boundary being indefensible, he proposed to support the claim from the first charter. Since some maps showed the "St. Mathias" flowing northwest and others southwest, to avoid ambiguity he hit upon the idea of designating the point where it empties into the sea. Another support lay in the fact that this was the boundary of King Charles I's grant to Sir Robert Heath.[44] "Here, therefore," he cautioned the Duke of

---

[44] Both charters said "within thirty-one degrees."

Newcastle, "I would stop for how desirous soever Your Grace, or I may be to extend the British Dominions in America, yet I apprehend the best way of asserting our Right is to carry it no farther, than our vouchers will support us." The alert Bladen left it to the Duke to decide whether or not to include words "which bordereth upon the coast of Florida," but "I confess upon reading the Charter, they struck me, as if they had been prophetically inserted so many years ago, to decide the present dispute at home (tho perhaps not abroad) and let us know, by authority of the Great Seal, where the Frontiers of Florida begin."[45]

This was one method of approaching an historically difficult situation. The second charter was to be overlooked because it took in St. Augustine and the top of the Spanish empire, yet new laws and new charters in the ordinary course of events supersede old ones. If validity could not be claimed for the first charter because it was inexpedient, how could it be claimed for the second?

The English government then proceeded to draw up a project treaty, the ninth article of which described the English possessions according to the royal charter of 1662, which corresponded with the charter of April 25, 1732, to the Trustees of the colony of Georgia. To meet the situation in case Spain proposed anything radically different from the suggestions, four counter projects were devised in advance.[46] The Treaty of 1670, which confirmed the possessions held in that year in America, was accepted by both parties as the basis of the negotiations.[47] The English faced a difficult problem in proving that Spain had not occupied territory to Santa Elena and another one to prove English possession below Charles Town. What right did the English have to make the grant of 1662 to Clarendon and others? The instructions of Newcastle to Keene and Castres answer the question.

---

[45] C. O., 5/654, fols. 205-7, Bladen to Newcastle, Albrohatch, 25 April, 1739.

[46] S. P. F., Spain, General Correspondence, 134; Add. MSS, 33009, Diplomatic Papers of the Duke of Newcastle, V, Newcastle to Keene and Castres, Whitehall, 7 May, 1739.

[47] At Madrid, in May, 1670, Godolphin signed a treaty in which Spain confirmed the possessions then held respectively in America. He probably signed this before he had news of the South Carolina settlement. See J. Dumont (ed.), *Corps Universal Diplomatique*, VII, 138.

That the Crown of Great Britain had a right to make the Grant cannot be controverted; Since tho' It may perhaps be difficult to prove that the British Subjects at that Time actually occupied Lands to the utmost Extent of that Grant, yet as the Crown of Great Britain was in possession of South Carolina at that Time, and that the Lands were not possessed or occupied by the Subjects of any other Power,[48] and were never till lately, claimed by any other Power, the Crown of Great Britain as first Discoverer and Possessor, had a Right to dispose of them. And the grant having been accepted by the Proprietors, and the Lands in the greatest Part, possessed and occupied by virtue of that Grant, It cannot be imagined, that the Subjects of Great Britain, properly authorized for that Purpose by His Majesty, or any of His Predecessors, were not at Liberty to occupy and possess the remaining Part of those Lands, as well as to hold, and enjoy the other Part of them, by virtue of that Grant.[49]

After the formal reading of full powers on May 5, the plenipotentiaries adjourned to meet May 26. Meanwhile the presence of Haddock's squadron, Spain's refusal to pay the £95,000 and her threat to suspend the *asiento* pact, brought the negotiations to a most delicate point. The French fleet under d'Antin was called to protect the flota from Cádiz to America.[50] The English ambassador was instructed to cause all English merchants to withdraw from Spanish ports.[51] The Spanish inquired if the English ambassador were responsible for the precautions taken in these ports, and the Spanish king ordered his plenipotentiaries to call attention to the revoking of orders for Haddock's return after the Convention was signed.[52] Keene wrote that nothing less than flattery and cajolery could make the Spanish queen so blind to the interest of her own nation. Rumor seeped through to Consul Cayley at Cádiz that the conferences had broken up.

Spain wished to have the Georgia question settled first; England, that of depredations. Each wished to negotiate where

---

[48] An error in fact.
[49] S. P. F., Spain, General Correspondence, 134, Newcastle to Keene and Castres, Whitehall, 8 May, 1739.
[50] Add. MSS, 32801, N. P., CXVI, fol. 23.
[51] *Ibid.*, p. 38.
[52] S. P. F., Spain, General Correspondence, 133, Keene and Castres to Newcastle, Madrid, 18 May, 1739; Keene to Newcastle, Madrid, 9 June, 1739.

injured, but never where it was the aggressor. In the conference held in Madrid on June 3, 1739, the British plenipotentiaries asserted that the point relating to navigation as laid down in the Convention[53] ought to be examined and decided before any other. They asserted that in the Convention of Pardo, visiting, searching, taking ships, and seizure of effects were the first points enumerated in the full powers of the ministers on each side who signed the Convention. In the second place they held that grievances of each side in this respect were by nature, as well as in the bad consequences they might draw after them, such as deserved the first attention of commissioners whose principal view should be to prevent for the future all occasion for misunderstanding. No mention was made, they added, in the whole Convention of any other limits than these of Florida and Carolina.[54]

On the same day Quintana and Habaria responded in elaborate argument.[55] The first step recommended by the Spanish was an exchange of memorials containing the pretensions on both sides, because a reciprocal statement of pretensions was held to be preliminary to a decision as to which grievances required a preference in the debates. Here the British insisted on the point of navigation and the Spanish strongly defended the prior and exclusive point relating "to the limits and territories seized and possessed by the British nation contrary to the express tenor of the treaties." In confirmation of the preliminary exchange of memorials they cited a similar frictionless exchange of grievances by the commissaries at Seville, April 24, 1732. By this precedent, the spirit of the treaties, and the necessity of finding out which the English ports and colonies were before attempting to regulate the navigation there, they supported the priority of limits over navigation in the debates. England herself had, moreover, in 1670 taken great "care to assist her right to the ports and colonies which her subjects were at that time possessed of in America before any mention was made of the point of navigation, which latter would have been

---

[53] Journals of the House of Commons, XXI, 393-94, articles vi and viii.

[54] S. P. F., Spain, General Correspondence, 133, Keene and Castres to Newcastle, Madrid, 9 June, 1739.

[55] A. G. S., legajo 7633 antiguo, "Copia a la letra del papel entregado por los plenip^{os}. de S. M. en junta de 3 de Junio de 1739. . . ."

entirely needless without some previous regulation of the bounds to which it might extend."[56]

Among the particular reasons adduced for the priority of limits was the fact that English enroachments were complained of antecedently to all other grievances, Spanish representations for a settlement having been constant since 1722. The Spanish government had even insisted that it be settled preliminary to the Convention. Like the English, they concluded by hoping that the strength of such arguments would convince the English of the justness of the Spanish proposal; that the exchange might no longer be retarded, and the days for conferences fixed for settling the boundaries and then for adjusting other grave concerns.[57]

The English representatives wrote in all haste to London that they apprehended that the Spanish plenipotentiaries intended to divert the English from consideration of navigation, which they knew to be the English objective, or to secure a diplomatic advantage by advancing a plausible pretense for introducing the Georgia question. It was only when the two positions were found to be identical and apparently irreconcilable that the differences were submitted in writing. There the Spanish allegations and arguments for the priority of the Georgia question were as strong as ever. Keene and Castres made every effort to overcome the obstacle, but they were not prepared to compromise. In fact they would have consented to suspend the conference "rather than to wear the reproach of having made our appearance there for no other purpose than to give the Spaniards an opportunity of trying whether Georgia is to be theirs or ours."[58] According to the agreement reached in the Conference, June 17, it was decided that each of the contesting powers should present a memorial on those headings which they considered most important, but this decision was not reached until after a warm debate.[59] The next meeting was

---

[56] A. G. S., legajo 7633 antiguo, "Copia a la letra del papel entregado por los plenip^{os}. de S. M. en junta de 3 de Junio de 1739."

[57] A. G. S., legajo 7633 antiguo; S. P. F., Spain, General Correspondence, 133, paper presented by the Spanish plenipotentiaries, 3 June, 1739.

[58] Add. MSS, 32801, N. P., CXVI, Keene and Castres to Newcastle, Madrid, 9 June, 1739.

[59] Add. MSS, 32801, N. P., CXVI, Keene and Castres to Newcastle, Madrid, 22 June, 1739.

Failure of the Convention of Pardo

deferred by the Feast of St. John the Baptist, according to the Spanish custom of *fiesta religiosa*.

On June 25 the Spaniards presented "their pretension upon the point of limits and territories entered and seized by the English nation in America contrary to the tenor of the treaties."[60] Reverting to the American Treaty of 1670, they agreed

That the most serene King of Great Britain, his heirs and successors, shall have, hold, and keep, and always possess in full right of sovereignty, seignory, possession, and propriety, all the lands, countries, islands, colonies, and dominions, lying and situate in the West Indies or any part of America which the King of Great Britain and his subjects now hold and possess, insomuch that neither can nor ought hereafter to be contested or called into question for them upon any account or under any pretence whatever.[61]

Beyond the provisions of the treaty they could not go. The English held, therefore, only what they could prove they possessed, either by the king or his subjects in that year. In consequence the Spanish plenipotentiaries insisted that England should

. . . evacuate all the settlements that she has lately made in Florida, and the islands of Providence, St. Catherine, Port Royal, St. Andrews, and the Fat Virgins, alias Paristron, as well as Turtle Island, which have all been seized by his Britannic Majesty's subjects since the signing and against the express tenor of the said Treaty of 1670.[62]

Not content with a mere enumeration they held that "all other islands or territories whatsoever," not held in 1670 should be evacuated.

The Spanish representatives knew full well that these strong demands would lessen British diplomatic assets when the depredations issue was approached.

His Majesty's ministers plenipotentiary protest that these pretensions shall not be meant to prejudice any others that may offer

---

[60] A. G. S., legajo 7633 antiguo, "Copia a la letra del papel de reflexiones sobre el plan de pretensiones en punto de limites, presentado por los Plenip⁰ˢ. de S. M. en Junta de 25 de Junio de 1739."

[61] S. P. F., Spain, General Correspondence, 133, memorial of the Spanish plenipotentiaries presented 25 June. Hertslet, *A Complete Collection of Treaties and Conventions*, II, 196-97, Art. VII.

[62] S. P. F., Spain, General Correspondence, 133, Spanish memorial of 25 June.

hereafter with regard to the present or any other points whatever founded either on treaties, conventions, or offers; all of which the said plenipotentiaries reserve to themselves the right of alleging and extending in virtue of the present protest.[63]

Keene and Castres at the same time supplied the Spanish with a paper containing their pretensions upon the point of navigation. The Spanish demands for the surrender of several English colonies appeared something of a perversion of the Convention. Since the Spaniards saw fit to tack the dispute about the Carolina-Florida limits onto that about depredations, and to demand territory the British considered theirs, the English plenipotentiaries endeavored to convince them that they had trespassed the bounds prescribed by the Convention. And in the case of Providence, the Bahama Islands, and Florida the Englishmen rested, holding it the business of the Spaniards to prove that they had encroached upon the Spanish dominions since 1670.[64]

In response to the Spanish memorial the English supported their case by the seventh article of the American Treaty of 1670 which guaranteed to them in perpetuity what they then held in America. They still further embarrassed their antagonists by blandly holding that there was nothing in the treaty to oblige the king of England to prove that his subjects had certain possessions at that time. Nor was there any foundation in the article for the other Spanish assumption that all the territory the English had acquired since that time constituted a manifest contravention of the treaty.

Although the two principal points of navigation and the Florida limits were emphasized by the English, they agreed, upon the insistence of the Spanish, to take up the additional case of the Island of Providence—not as a matter of obligation, but of magnanimity in order to keep bound the ties of friendship. Since, however, they thought they had just grounds "for asserting that Great Britain does not actually enjoy any Possessions in America which can be lawfully disputed; it is incumbent upon the Spanish Plenipotentiaries to produce proofs to the contrary supported by Treaties; & not the business of

---

[63] *Idem.*

[64] Add. MSS, 32801, N. P., CXVI, fol. 90; A. G. S., legajo 7633 antiguo, "Respuesta al papel presentado por los Yngleses en 25 de Junio de 1739."

those of His Majesty to produce the Titles, which they may have in their hands, to justify their Possessions; still less to abandon Places where the King's subjects have made Settlements, as the Spanish Plenipotentiarys pretend. . . ."

The Spaniards replied with insurmountable conditions.[65] Payment of the £68,000 claimed from the South Sea Company, the recall of Haddock and the fleet from the Mediterranean, the Spanish reply made absolute prerequisites of further negotiations. The plenipotentiaries also stiffened the requirements on the subject of search, informing the agents of England on July 1 that "Spain is obliged to insist on the Stopping, Visiting, and Searching of all Vessels which Navigate in the *American Seas*, as a right depending on, and inseparable from their Preeminences and Dominions in those Seas."[66] This demand, which elicited a thunderous negative declaration in reply, doomed and practically ended the conferences.[67]

Never were circumstances on both sides so inopportune for negotiations. Spain had not yet paid the £95,000 stipulated in the Convention. La Quadra was demanding the cessation of naval preparation in British ports. Newcastle was asking his ambassador to determine the number and whereabouts of the Spanish troops and ships, and whether in event of war more damage could be done to Spain in Europe or in the West Indies. Between England and France there loomed the *pacte de famille* and a probable commercial treaty between France and Spain.[68] La Quadra, now Marqués de Villarias, expressed his willingness to pay the sum stipulated, but held that proper orders for the Carolinians and Georgians, according to the agreement of the Convention, had not been dispatched.[69] In her obstinacy Spain was encouraged by France. To Van der Meer's office of conciliation in Madrid, France gave a friendly backing obviously to keep the Dutch from joining the English.[70]

---

[65] A. G. S., legajo 7633 antiguo, "Respuesta al Papel dado por los Yngleses en 1º de Julio de 1739."

[66] A. G., leg. 7633, "Respuesta al Papel dado por Ingleses en 1º de Julio de 1739." *Address to the Electors*, p. 61.

[67] *King of Spain's Reasons for not paying the £95,000 stipulated in the Convention signed at Pardo, 14 Jan., 1739, Examined* (London, 1739), p. 30.

[68] S. P. F., Spain, General Correspondence, 134, Newcastle to Keene, Whitehall, 14 June, 1739.

[69] Add. MSS, 32801, N. P., CXVI, fols. 60-66.

[70] *Ibid.*, fol. 65.

As they seem to be as indifferent upon the Consequences of a rupture with us [lamented Keene] as they are ignorant of those which must flow from their depending so much upon the House of Bourbon, there is but too much reason to fear, that all the Pains that have been taken to preserve the tranquility between the two Crowns will have been in vain.[71]

At last Louis Pierre Engilbert Comte de la Marck, the French ambassador, called upon Keene and emphasized the extreme heat of the Spaniards. To this suggestion Keene responded by pointing to the decrepit finances of Spain. La Marck ended by suggesting an amicable settlement of the point of navigation—a thing Keene already knew was impossible.[72] Apprised of the drift of affairs, Newcastle informed his plenipotentiaries that he had no further instructions except that after July 14 no more conferences were to be held with the Spanish plenipotentiaries. The Convention was doomed.[73]

The Spanish reply to the English point of navigation was a lengthy reiteration of the Spanish position, adding only that the English contention was inconsistent with the fifteenth article of the Treaty of 1670 which made it appear that the English were trying to defeat the basic American Treaty.[74] Newcastle's instructions to desist from the conferences arrived in Madrid July 5. This information was first transmitted to Villarias.[75] From the documents they submitted after the final conference on July 1, they declared

. . . Your Grace will perceive that far from closing with our just and reasonable Demands upon that head, the Spanish Ministers were endeavouring to perplex the main question, by raising doubts and difficulties with regard to Rights and pre-eminencies in the American Seas which would have thrown us into a Labyrinth of useless Disputes, had not Your Grace signified to us His Majesty's pleasure, to decline holding any further conferences with the Spanish Plenipotentiaries in the present circumstances.

In order to excuse these His Majesty's commands without giving the Spanish Plenipotentiaries a formal notice of what was intended,

---

[71] S. P. F., Spain, General Correspondence, 133, Keene to Newcastle, Madrid, 22 June, 1739.

[72] Add. MSS, 32801, N. P., CXVI, fols. 92, 93.

[73] S. P. F., Spain, General Correspondence, 134, Newcastle to Keene, Whitehall, 28 June, 1739.

[74] S. P. F., Spain, Keene and Castres to Newcastle, Madrid, 1 July, 1739.

[75] *Ibid.*, 9 July, 1739.

before I & Keene were able to speak to the Marquis de Villarias in the Manner Your Grace will see in my Dispatch of the 9th instant, we sent our Secretary on the 7th to the Spanish Ministers to acquaint them, that I, Keene having been indisposed for several days, it would be impossible for us to meet them at the Conference which according to agreement was to have been held the 8th instant, but that we should wait upon them ourselves in a day or two to make our further excuses for our non appearance upon that occasion. Accordingly on the 9th instant we went to pay each of them a visit at their own houses, in which after a suitable compliment, we declared to them that His Majesty had been pleased to command us to excuse ourselves from assisting at the Conferences in the present situation of affairs, adding that out of attention to their own persons (of whom we have indeed received very great civilities during the course of the negotiations) we had chosen this method of making this formal Declaration to them, not to put them to the trouble of going in vain to the Place appointed for holding the Conferences. They both expressed and particularly Don Estevan de Abaria a good deal of concern at the turn matters seemed to be taking, but they would not appear by their answers, to have been prepared for any such notification.[76]

With the breaking off of negotiations it became apparent that war was the only alternative. All diplomacy having been rendered futile, the Georgia agitation merged with the veritable bedlam of 1739 in England. The English ministry had recourse to backhanded methods while it was supinely swept into war by the combined fever of Georgians, merchants, imperialists, and jingoes. At this juncture, the beginning of the War of Jenkins' Ear, the diplomatic story of Georgia becomes no longer traceable. The threads can only be picked up and distinguished at the conclusion of the War of Austrian Succession and the signing of the Treaty of Aix-la-Chapelle, 1748.

Oglethorpe's dictum to dissemble and to hold (by force if necessary) now became the exclusive title whereby Georgia was retained in the English Empire. That title had at least the virtue of accommodating itself to the inexorable facts of the occupation of America by all the powers.

---

[76] S. P. F., Spain, General Correspondence, 133; Add. MSS, 32801, N. P., CXVI, fols. 104-6; Keene and Castres to Newcastle, 1 July, 1739.

CHAPTER VIII

FORCING THE HAND OF WALPOLE: THE DRAMA OF 1739 IN AMERICA[1]

THE HISTORY of the first half of the eighteenth century has been overlooked or at least obscured by the more glamorous events of the subsequent half century—so much so that the mention of the War of Jenkins' Ear evokes from the average individual either frank laughter or courteous blankness. Its place as the nucleus of colonial wars, as an experiment in Britannic imperial affairs, and as the zenith of the Anglo-Spanish struggle for control of that unremittingly important economic center, the Caribbean Sea, is not yet generally recognized. American participation, moreover, in the casual references thereto, has been treated more as the activity of the Lafayette Escadrille in the Riffian War than as a movement in which the North Americans created a universal resentment and a general fear, and placed wholeheartedly their ships and their men at the disposal of the empire. The disputed story of Jenkins' Ear to informed expansionists has always been a pathetic episode; to orthodox Whigs, a fabulous claptrap. This appendage and appellation was but one weapon in a large armory, but great movements as well as great men often carry forever what the merest trifle, through some strange but not infrequent prank of history, attaches to them. Let us now take a panoramic glance, from the perspective of our detailed information, at the tempestuous stage of Anglo-Spanish affairs on the eve of the War of Jenkins' Ear.

The South Sea Company was raising its discontent in ever louder strains, and this was a strain in close harmony with the polemic song of the Georgia Trustees. The Spanish commission and the American interlopers for years kept the company's

---

[1] The two subsequent chapters are of a general nature, designed to correlate the threads of the contest whether military or diplomatic and to embrace the maritime controversy.

returns disproportionate to the investment. The desperate company, instead of the two tenders allowed, blithely continued to dispatch whole flotillas loaded with goods to smuggle into New Granada. It had succumbed to the nebulous methods of its competitors. The *guarda costas*, sensing an opportunity in the growing and well nigh universal smuggling, sometimes acted as pirates towards Englishmen while holding the credentials of the Spanish government; moreover, they often became careless in discriminating between smugglers and vessels plying in good faith between England and the English West Indies. Parliament was inundated with petitions relating to barbarities committed on the persons of English sailors in Spanish prisons. "Spanish insults and depredations" formed the refrain of countless protests presented in bundles[2] by Keene at the Spanish court, while Walpole, "that indefatigable Minister who, for many years, hath rock'd the public cradle, and endeavored to lull that forward Babe, the Nation, to rest," allowed them to be submitted to a supine government.[3] Some abuses on either side officials winked at; others they were powerless to quell. In 1737, upon the presentation of the famous merchants' petition, Newcastle had abandoned remonstrances for peremptory demands.

To this perplexing problem Jamaican claims to cut logwood on the Central American coast and to gather salt on the coast of Tortuga added embarrassment and rent in twain the price of these commodities.[4] Over this strained Anglo-Spanish diplomacy the *pacte de famille* cast sinister shadows.[5] Popular agitation was becoming more and more articulate, and every situation was shot through with gloomy forebodings. An increased naval force, issuance of letters of marque and reprisal,[6] impress-

[2] Add. MSS, 32796, N. P., CXI, 65.
[3] *Parliamentary History*, X, 586; *Gentlemen's Magazine*, X, 639.
[4] Add. MSS, 32800, N. P., CXV, 1-2.
[5] Baudrillart, *Phillippe V et la Cour de France*, IV, 155; Add. MSS, 32801, N. P., CXVI, 291; *ibid.*, 32692, VII, 538. In 1743, in accordance with this arrangement they agreed on: "Art. 10. La Securete de la Florida ne pouvant etre entiere tandesque l'Angleterre aura l'Establissement et la Possession de la nouvelle Georgie: S. M. T. C. si oblige a procurer la Destruction des Forts de Georgie." S. P. F., Spain, Treaty Papers, 68, fol. 36.
[6] C. O., 5/318, III, 156-58; S. P. F., Spain, Foreign Ministers, 59, *passim*; Add. MSS, 3280, N. P., CXVI, 227. Newcastle dispatched letters of marque and reprisal to the colonial governors and ordered them to go to the aid of Georgia if

ment on a large scale, a £3,750,000 parliamentary appropriation, and general polemic instructions smacked unmistakably of war. In the meantime Walpole's enemies produced in Parliament one Robert Jenkins of the *Rebecca*, who displayed his detached and pickled ear, the forgotten removal of which, nine years previously, was attributed to the Spanish captain, Juan de León Fandino. After the Spaniard had torn his ear off, Jenkins related, he handed it back with this well-phrased insult: "Carry it to your king and tell his majesty that if he were present I would serve him in the same manner." Asked what he expected from his enemies Jenkins replied in seemingly well-coached language:

Gentlemen, after mangling me in this manner, they threatened to put me to death. I expected it, and recommended my soul to God, but the revenge of my cause to my country.[7]

necessary before he ordered Keene and Castres to abandon the Convention of Pardo. S. P. F., Spain, 94/134, Newcastle to the American governors, 15/26 June, 1739.

[7] That this episode was a figure of partisan imagination is no longer tenable. It is only the Parliamentary episode which remains obscure. For example, on March 16, 1731/2, Newcastle wrote Keene: "The King approved your repeated Instances for bringing the Pyrate Fandino to Justice, who has had so great a share in these depredations in the West Indies ———. He was not openly received and protected at Havana, but he constantly resorted to Baraccao, a Port in the Island of Cuba, and if the Governor there will not take care to have him seized and brought to Justice, the Court of Spain must not be surprised if some of His Majesty's Ships should pursue him; and endeavor to clear those Seas of so notorious a Pyrate, who does not even spare ships of their own nation." Add. MSS, 32776, N. P., CXV, London, 16 March, 1731/2. A somewhat critical and almost contemporaneous account of the Jenkins' incident is *The Danverian History of the Affairs of Europe, For the Memorable Year 1731*, pp. 40-42. Newcastle to Keene, 10 January, 1731/2, Add. MSS, 32776, N. P., XCI, 47; S. P. F., Spain, Treaty Papers, 67, *passim*; J. K. Laughton, "Jenkins' Ear," *English Historical Review*, IV (October, 1889), 741-749. The celebrated story of Jenkins' brilliant speeches in Parliament —models of "noble simplicity—" has come to us through William Coxe, Sir Robert Walpole's biographer, who claims to have relied on contemporary publications. He admits, however, that in the *Journals* only these two entries, both of them before the fact, can be found:

"March 16: Ordered, That Captain Robert Jenkins do attend this house immediately.

"March 17: Ordered, That Captain Robert Jenkins do attend, on Tuesday morning next the Committee of the whole house, to whom the petition of divers merchants, planters, and others, trading to, and interested in, the British plantations in America, in behalf of themselves, and many others is referred." *Memoirs*

The result as anticipated was a happy one for the opposition. The unbounded excitement boded no good for the pacifistic Sir Robert. Parliamentarians harangued about chains and slavery, rousing the vengeance of a national resentment. But concession was in the Spanish air. Count Montijo, now president of the Council of the Indies, informed Ambassador Keene that the intentions and dispositions of the Spaniards were never more opportune for either peace or war. Peace pleased Keene, and with La Quadra, January 14, 1739, he concluded the famous Convention of Pardo[8] wherein "the King of Spain agreed that we might send commissaries to his Sublime Porte, with power to determine within six months."[9] Six months! The imperialists could hardly endure six days. The Georgia-Carolina boundary, logwood cutting in Campeachy Bay, and the British right to free navigation were the issues. Excluding the affairs of the South Sea Company, the English preserved its interests by crucifying the American interlopers and were forced to reduce their damage claims from £340,000 to £95,000 to be paid in four months. Spain admitted the injustice of certain seizures which the English interpreted as a precursor of diplomatic victory. Georgia and Florida were to remain *in statu quo*.[10] This Pitt deemed an illusory expedient to baffle the nation.

In the outstanding debate which followed in Parliament, patriots and imperialists were resolved to ruin the effects of the convention before they knew a word of its provisions, in which, according to a contemporary, "England was never more misled and unreasonable."[11] The enthusiasm and petitions of merchants for war, eyes cast longingly in the direction of Zacatecas and Potosí, Newcastle's promise of a share in all booty to American colonists who enlisted—all lend especial credence to the story of exploitative designs of certain English

---

of the Life and Administration of Sir Robert Walpole, I, 579, 573-87. This is the extent of official documentation. The story, doubtless, has been carried along because it is intrinsically a good one.

[8] S. P. F., Spain, Treaties, 502, *passim*. See chap. V, VI, VII.

[9] *State of the Rise and Progress of Our Disputes with Spain*, p. 45. A. G. I., Audiencia de Santo Domingo, 76-6-24, Güemez y Horcasitas to Quintana, Havana, 20 June, 1739.

[10] S. P. F., Spain, Treaties, 67, fol. 213; *ibid.*, 68, fol. 384.

[11] *An Appeal to the Unprejudiced Concerning the Present Discontents*, p. 6.

merchants[12] and soldiers of fortune on Spanish America. Into caricature and song the sentiment found its way. The sentiment of the merchant, the self-constituted political liberator, the soldier of fortune, and the humiliated nationalist, is crowded into these lines:

> Our merchants and ears a strange pother have made
> With losses sustained in their ships and their trade;
> But now they may laugh and quite banish their fears,
> Nor mourn for lost liberty, riches and ears.[13]

To which Pope mechanically added:

> And own the Spaniards did a waggish thing
> Who cropped our ears and sent them to the king.[14]

But while the English mob was howling, the merchants petitioning, and the Georgia Trustees agitating, there was a more serious and sober group which saw the fallacy of conquered riches. It was not overwhelmed by the dazzling éclat and glory of military operations. Injuries and violences were crimes of private persons—piracies, not hostilities. Only the refusal of Spain to do England justice would make them the acts of the state.

Walpole was engulfed when Spain withheld payment of the £95,000 until the counter claim of £68,000 against the South Sea Company was adjusted, and on May 17, 1739, the *asiento* was suspended.[15] The Admiralty Out-Letters authorized all sorts of "Hostilities against the Spaniards."[16] Admiral Haddock was ordered to Spain's back door and Captain Sir Yelverton Peyton to convoy Oglethorpe's regiment to Georgia. On June 14, the privateering was authorized. The king, swept into the vortex of excitement, demanded war. Newcastle, who had

---

[12] See *A Proposition for Opening Spanish American Ports to All Nations: A Dissertation on the Present Conjuncture, Particularly with Regard to Trade*, pp. 22-26.

[13] R. Wright, *Caricature History of the Georges*, p, 116.

[14] Alexander Pope, *Poetical Works*, I, 300.

[15] Add. MSS, 32799, N. P., CXIV, 320-21; S. P. F., Spain, Foreign Ministers, 59.

[16] Admiralty Out-Letters, 55, fol. 445.

been uncompromising for two years, went into the war faction with the king who disliked the slow methods of diplomacy. Walpole then helplessly gave Vernon instructions to sail against Spanish America. Keene and Geraldino, personally ingratiated with Newcastle, were peremptorily ordered to return home. The English consuls were left to shift for themselves.[17] Egmont recorded that Geraldino was "in disgrace at his court for engaging her in a war, by giving false information that England would continue to bear with her usage of us; that he desired leave to come and dwell in England as a private person but had been refused."[18] Depredations, the fear of a Bourbon alliance, and dazzling ideas of conquest, then produced this situation. The comedians revived *Sir Walter Raleigh*, comparing Gundemar and Geraldino, and whenever any severe things were said about the ministry's transactions "or our backwardness to resent the insults of Spain, the audience clapped all over the house, to show they took the hint, and their aversion to the measures taken."[19] The formal declaration of war, October 23, 1739, was celebrated by the Prince of Wales in an ordinary tavern, and by the multitude in frenzies of acclamation at St. James's, Charing Cross, Chancery Lane, Wood Street, and the Royal Exchange.[20] And thus the might of the British public rang up the first curtain of an eight years' drama, and out of this war has issued in a clear and unmistakable stream the series of wars which were waged between England and France in the eighteenth century.[21]

The King of England in his speech from the throne on November 15, 1739, responding to the pressure of the opposition, called for "ready and vigorous support, which the repeated Injuries and Violences committed by that Nation upon the Navigation and Commerce of these Kingdoms, and their Obstinacy, and notorious Violation of the most solemn Engagements, have rendered unavoidable." Near the end of the speech, however, in the form of a mild and melancholic accusation from

---

[17] Add. MSS, 32801, N. P., CXVI, 185; S. P. F., Spain, Treaty Papers, 68, fol. 390.
[18] *Op. cit.*, III, 86, 91.
[19] *Ibid.*, p. 83.
[20] *Parliamentary History*, XI, 2-6.
[21] Temperley, "Causes of the War of Jenkins' Ear," *Transactions of the Royal Historical Society*, 3rd ser., III (1909), 197-98.

an unwarlike ministry, appeared the real sentiment of the government: "The Heats and Animosities, which, with the greatest Industry, have been fomented throughout the Kingdom, have, I am afraid, been One of the chief Encouragements to the Court of Spain to hold such a Conduct toward us, as to make it necessary to have Recourse to Arms."[22]

The more reasonable among the Spanish advocated sitting quiet, since their ports were well-fortified, and thus preventing extraordinary strain on an exhausted treasury while the English expended their energy and resources on an expensive and unsuccessful war.[23] In the light of this knowledge it was uniformly urged in England that most damage could be done in America. Spain, it was noticed, had winced most at the threat to arm privateers and grant letters of marque and reprisal. "Creating and perpetuating a race of pirates would sting Spain to the heart."[24] To the King of Spain in 1739 as to Phillip II, the Indies were still the "apple of his eye." At the time, "the very name of an attempt upon the Spaniards settlements in America will carry the face of a Golden Adventure, which will undoubtedly allure a multitude of brisk men."[25] But the King of Spain, too, after appealing to the outside world to judge the justice of his cause, ordered reprisals. An ironical Englishman phrased his intent:

> On ev'ry Thing *English* We order Reprisal,
> Ships, Chattels, Effects, wheresoever it lies all:
> Restraining our Subjects, for fear of Disaster
> From taking one Vessel but what they can master.[26]

Walpole, now displaying as great an inaptitude for the prosecution as for the declaration of war, delayed activities until the press informed the enemy of military and naval details, while according to a contemporary versifier

> In silent moan the honest farmer grieves
> To think his country no redress receives;

---

[22] Journals of the House of Commons, XXIII, 382-83; *The False Accusers Accused*, pp. 28, 41.

[23] Add. MSS, 32801, N. P., CXVI, 119.

[24] *Idem.*

[25] Add. MSS, 32894, N. P., IX, 3-4.

[26] *His Catholic Majesty's Manifesto justifying his Conduct in relation to the late Convention* (London, 1739), 4.

FORCING THE HAND OF WALPOLE

> Better these troops on the Spanish main were shown
> Than kept for fools to gaze at on their own.[27]

The pacific minister was flayed for suspected monopolization, organized corruption, and the application of secret service money to party purposes. The celebration of either Admiral Vernon's birthday or his victory at Porto Bello, he thought, would fill the streets with disagreeable cheering bands, and the night with mobbing. As early as 1740 pamphlets were asking to exchange him for one who would

> Speak what he thinks and freely plead the cause
> Of Britain's commerce, liberty, and laws;
> Exert his power to check corruption's swing,
> And serve at once his country and his king.[28]

An attack on the ministry in Parliament led by Pulteney and Pitt resulted in Walpole's resignation, February 2, 1742, but soon after his passing, the War of Austrian Succession eclipsed in national glamour the Caribbean War.

Since this was a purely American war, and as significant as any in the eighteenth century, it can readily be discerned that the importance of North American participation does not depend altogether upon the mere contingent of Americans in the fiasco at fever-ridden Cartagena. In its preliminaries and in its execution the continentals played an important rôle. In April, the month which marked the beginning of mobilization on the mainland, Robert Dinwiddie reported to the Lords Commissioners for Trade and Plantations that the mainland colonists owned and navigated 1,855 vessels. The annual value of their produce was £2,190,000; their fighting strength 135,000.[29] These facts the English war faction saw with genuine foresight as media through which England could usurp Spanish commercial interests in the American seas. The proximity of the Northern Colonies to the coveted Spanish West Indies made them a great nautical, commercial, and even greater psychological advantage.

---

[27] *The Mock Campaign*, p. 18.
[28] See Hertz, *British Imperialism in the Eighteenth Century*, p. 36.
[29] *Archives of the State of New Jersey* (edited by F. W. Ricard and W. Nelson), VI, 84-90.

Forty or fifty large and readily available American ships, one pamphleteer confidently asserted, would, without English aid, easily master St. Augustine, Cuba, Hispaniola, Porto Rico, and the whole trade of the discontented Spanish Americans. The vast American trade and shipbuilding industry, New England alone employing fifteen thousand sailors and supplying the French with three-fourths of their merchant ships, offered the British the ascendency and the Americans an advantage in case of a formidable Caribbean struggle.[30]

Robbed of the ammunition and stores from the English colonies, without ship-building materials, and unable to send succor to their friends, the Spanish and French squadrons would be starved out, and the Caribbean would be an easy but momentous prize for American energy and ingenuity.[31] Neither Spain nor England anticipated the British fleet and army later sent. No English colonial governor was reluctant to take proper precautions to stifle such pernicious trade between the British and Spanish colonies. The acts of specially-called legislative sessions, requiring that no vessel laden with provisions without its master giving bond could land in a port subject to a foreign prince, later became general in an embargo act of Parliament.

Stopping, retaining, and searching ships navigating the seas of America, said one Parliamentarian, was not only destructive to the *lawful* commerce of British subjects, but obstructed the free intercourse and correspondence between the plantations, a consideration of the highest importance, which "enormitys could not fail of bringing on war between the two nations." England felt touched in two very tender points, her pride and her pocketbook. The trade of the West Indies, then, in 1739 was largely in the hands of Yankee skippers and interlopers who characteristically did not worry over much about the legal aspect of getting their cargoes safely into West Indian ports, and this embittered the Spanish.

The colonies beheld with fear and trembling the interference

---

[30] *Present State of Revenues and Forces by Sea and Land of Spain and France compared to those of Great Britain*, pp. vii, 31-34, 40; *Archives of the State of New Jersey*, VI, 83-91; *An Account Showing the Progress of the Colony of Georgia*, p. 49.

[31] *Original Papers of the Expedition to Carthagena*, p. 13; *Pennsylvania Colonial Records* (edited by Samuel Hazard), 2nd ser., IV, 491; *Acts of the Privy Council*, colonial series, III, 160-70, 182-90, 730-36, 746.

with intercolonial trade, and an ever-increasingly dreadful Franco-Spanish alliance; moreover, the French subjection of the Southern continental colonies to establish easier navigation and freer communication between the French colonies, by uniting the Canadees, Choctaws, and others, would break the wedge formed by the mainland group.[32] Certain Southern ports were urged as strategic points from which to protect Carolina and Georgia, to control the Bahama Channel, to impede the transportation of the Spanish treasure; for if they were not used for this purpose they would become Spanish privateering centers.

History has unjustly overlooked the defense of Georgia by the war party.[33] Georgia could serve not only as a buffer to appease the anxiety and shield the sides of the Carolinas, but also as a commercial substitute for European rivals:

> Now bid they Merchants bring thy Wine no more
> Or from the Iberian or the Tuscan shore;
> No more they need the Hungarian Vineyards drain
> And France herself may drink her best Champaign.[34]

The Trustees of Georgia as well as the war faction (in whose interests they were ever vigilant) took every occasion to paint Georgia in glowing colors.[35] Not only was Georgia a veritable wonder garden of silk and wine, but of cattle, poultry, oak, hickory, and vegetables. This flourishing state found its expression in the envy of the Englishman in these words:

> The Spring which but salutes us here
> Inhabits there and courts them all the Year:

---

[32] C. O. 5/639, No. 38; C. O. 5/654, pp. 42, 45.

[33] The final rupture turned on this point. Add. MSS, 32081, N. P., CXVI, 17-18, 104-6; C. O. 5/654, pp. 32, 267, *ibid.*, vol. 639, *passim*; Add. MSS, 32794, N. P., CIX, fols. 250, 252, 255-59; S. P. F., Spain, Supplementary, 246, fols. 3-9, 169, 175; S. P. F., Spain, Foreign Ministers, 58, fols. 84-86; Add. MSS, 33009, N. P., CCCXXIV, 81 *et seq.*; *Observations on the Present Convention with Spain*, pp. 32-35.

[34] *True and Historical Narrative of the Colony of Georgia in America*, p. xii; see also *The Advantages and Disadvantages which will attend the Prohibition of the Merchandises of Spain* (London, 1739).

[35] *An Impartial Inquiry into the State and Utility of Georgia*, p. 20; *A State of the Province of Georgia*, p. 13.

Ripe Fruits and Blossoms on the same Tree live;
At once they promise what at once they give.[36]

These misrepresentations brought much to Georgia which might not have come her way—an orphan house, appropriations, increased garrisons, the extension of the boundary to Fort St. George on the St. Johns. Thus a false conception of Georgia, rather than the actuality, was the basis upon which they acted, for they felt it would be wrong to allow a ministry to sacrifice the hopes of thousands of industrious colonists, and the welfare of generations to come, for the sake of a dishonorable peace.

The English were not dogmatic about Georgia. Newcastle himself had his doubts. Winham urged in the House of Commons that some of Georgia must be ceded, else it would be ridiculous to refer the question to the plenipotentiaries before the Convention of Pardo. But there was never a doubt as to the course ultimately to be pursued. Newcastle remarked simply: "I fancy however the right may be, it will now be pretty difficult to give up Georgia."[37] Pitt, in March, 1739, attacked the results of the Convention as "an illusory expedient to baffle the nation . . . on the part of England, a suspension as to Georgia, of the first law of nature, self-preservation, and self defense."[38] Imperialism was closely followed by philanthropy and religion, as evinced in the aid secured by Whitefield from the most humble classes in England which was, perhaps, the purest motive that actuated the hatred felt for Spain. Although the aspirations of the English war faction were vicious and their contentions doubtful in law, they championed a demoralized army and navy, and from the English point of view, saved two provinces, strategic bases of great value, both against the Spaniards and against the French on the Mississippi. The English mind from the common laborer to the nobleman was affected by the imperialistic concept. It is significant that without the possibility of troops and naval assets from the Northern Colonies and without the fear of losing Georgia, there would probably

---

[36] J. E. Oglethorpe, *A New and Accurate Account of the Provinces of South-Carolina and Georgia* (London, 1733), p. 21.

[37] Temperley, "Causes of the War of Jenkins' Ear," *Transactions of the Royal Historical Society*, 3rd ser., III, 200.

[38] *Parliamentary History*, IX, 1113-14, 1272, 1283.

never have been a war with the familiar appendage, Jenkins' Ear.

In June, 1739, as the inevitability of war became clearer, the Atlantic seacoast, menaced by sea and land, was seized by a panic. It was widely rumored that the Governor of St. Augustine had issued a proclamation of freedom and sanctuary to all runaway slaves from the English plantations. Attempting to extirpate the Chickasaws, a body of three hundred Frenchmen and seven hundred Indians from Canada passed behind the Northern Colonies, but as usual were repelled. This threatening move was considered indicative of what was to be expected from the French and was communicated in all seriousness from one governor to another. The entrance of France becoming imminent, a general war threatening in Europe, and the French straining every nerve to prepare the Indians against that event, the colonial governors called upon the assemblies to reform the militia laws and put the coast in a posture of defense, Governor Gabriel Johnston of North Carolina adding:

I must not omit to inform you Gentlemen that the French and Spaniards have taken of late uncommon pains to debauch all the friendly Indians who live in the neighborhood of his majesty's Dominions. . . .[39]

Pursuant to royal instructions the Northern Colonies attempted to maintain good relations with the Indians by gifts and laws regulating Indian trade. The growing menace of the Six Nations afforded such baffling problems that in the fall of 1742 it was necessary for the colonies from North Carolina to Massachusetts to meet them in a conference where differences were adjusted and apparently amicable relations restored, although the exposed colonies continued to offer gifts.

Governor George Thomas of Pennsylvania, urging defensive measures, and confronted by a hostile Quaker assembly, pictured graphically the state of the province, and hoped to find the assembly "vigorously pursuing these laudable ends," but that body characteristically deferred action.[40] The assembly of Maryland, where the problem of defense was acute, although

---
[39] *Colonial Records of North Carolina*, IV, 471-72. See also A. G. S., 2336/6909, Marqués de Villarias to Geraldino, Buen Retiro, 22 June, 1739; *ibid.*, 2335/6907, Quintana to Villarias, Buen Retiro, 12 June, 1739.
[40] *Pennsylvania Colonial Records*, IV, 354-56.

often right in principle, showed a higgling and petty spirit in complying with the governor's urgent and conciliatory suggestions for defense. In the session held from May 26 to June 22 1741, Governor Samuel Ogle recommended the continuation of the fund for the purchase of arms and ammunition. An animated contest followed a lengthy committee report, but on June 15, by the votes of thirty-one to eight and thirty-two to seven the assembly refused to put the question of laying an export tax of three pence a hogshead on tobacco. Ogle's successor, Thomas Bladen, continued to press the measure, but the disagreement between the two houses made impossible its passage.[41] Frequent orders were, nevertheless, issued to the treasurers of the Western and Eastern Shores for the purchase of military equipment from London merchants at the expense of the province.

A general attempt to reorganize the militia was made, and in this, as over the enlistment of servants for the expedition to the West Indies, the Quakers in Pennsylvania became a bulwark. To the governor natural advantages, strategic position, extensive trade, population, and a French danger, enhanced the importance of the erection of posts and the rejuvenation of the militia. To the assembly, safely deposited behind New York, New England, and the Carolinas, these items were evocative of exactly the opposite reaction. The assembly questioned the ambition reputed to the French, disparaged the population of Canada, and did not agree with the governor that the example of New York and Boston in preparing for defense was worthy of emulation. Both factions exhausted every conceivable argument.[42] The assemblymen finally pointed out that it would be needless to press them further.

Elsewhere the response was instantaneous, either by legislation, as in North Carolina, or by proclamation as in Maryland, where all officers in the province were required frequently to muster and to discipline their men for an emergency and to have all persons not exempt by law enlisted. To secure unity in case of an insurrection, military activity was increased. Virginia appropriated money, required frequent small and semi-

---

[41] *Archives of Maryland* (edited by W. H. Browne and B. C. Steiner), XXVIII, 228-53, 312-13; XL, 424, 426; XLII, 16, 34-77, 88, 152.

[42] *Pennsylvania Colonial Records*, IV, 369-75, 380-84, 387-88, 401-2, 404-5, 407.

annual general reviews, and imposed heavy penalties for disobedience in any emergency. Rhode Island, New York, and Massachusetts did likewise. Connecticut now found impetus for a long delayed enactment, requiring the enlistment and presence at musters of all able-bodied men between sixteen and fifty and dividing the militia into thirteen regiments.

Naval preparation was even more imperative. Rumours of mysterious Spanish craft spread with incredible rapidity. From Georgia to New England Spanish vessels found their way, raiding plantations, stealing Negroes and shooting women, so that every accessible point on the coast was aware of its jeopardy.[43] Individuals were called in to testify on news of the designs of Spanish privateers, which according to the *Journal of the Sloop Revenge* took at least five ships along the northern coast. Another took so many ships that it landed its prisoners at Sandy Hook to return to Havana. The *Boston Weekly News-Letter* reported that the mysterious black sloop continued to menace the coast of New York and New England. The Council at Boston, quaking with fear, hailed an officer and his Spanish guest before it, fearing that he was sent to discover and give intelligence of the country. Such opportunities to impress upon the assemblies the need of defense the governors did not overlook, because many thought, "our seafaring brethren and business are exposed and discouraged and the people on the sea coasts in fears of suffering loss of their estates, if not their lives, every hour."[44] New York and Boston responded with appropriations for fitting out vessels, offering fifty pounds to each injured sailor.[45] New Jersey requested of the admiralty a ship for protection. North Carolina also humbly sought one to be stationed at the Cape Fear where it was the governor's plan to station the militia and embark them for Jamaica.[46] Rhode Island equipped old Fort George, impressed men for service

---

[43] Jameson, *Privateering and Piracy in the Colonial Period*, p. 484; B. Norton, "Journal of a Privateersman," *Atlantic Monthly*, VIII (1861), 353-59, 417-24; *Colonial Records of the State of Georgia*, supplement to vol. IV, 225-28; *The Public Records of the Colony of Connecticut* (edited by J. H. Trumbull and C. J. Hoadly), VIII, 379, 381, 438.

[44] *Ibid.*, p. 275.

[45] *Archives of the State of New Jersey*, XII, 93-94.

[46] *Colonial Records of North Carolina*, IV, 421, 477-79; *Acts of the Privy Council*, colonial series, III, 421.

there, built watch houses at Castle Hill, Breton's Point, Sachmast Point, Point Judith, Watch Hill and Portsmouth, and required individual towns to erect beacons. She likewise ordered the sloop *Tartar* built.[47] Connecticut renovated the fort at New London and built a substantial sloop, the *Defense*. Vernon dispatched ships from the Caribbean.

Equally panic-stricken were the Spanish. Any moment the English ships in Jamaica might sally forth and repeat the exploits of Drake or Morgan.[48] As early as 1738 Governor Manuel de Montiano reported to his government that the English, preliminary to attacking, had given orders to the Indians to kill all the Spaniards they could, recited the English strength with a feverish hand, and anxiously prayed for forces to show his grave resentment.[49] Oglethorpe did certainly order a thousand Indians to annoy the Spanish. A troop of horsemen was sent out to prevent surprises and to secure intelligences. At this aggression St. Augustine shrank from a city to a mere fortified castle.[50] The projected trip of Oglethorpe to Coweta to draw, as the Spanish thought, some of the nations of Indians away from their dependence on Spain brought the Spanish under still greater apprehension.[51] Always Cuba was in jeopardy.[52]

Between 1739 and 1741, while Spain had about a half hundred privateers afloat, 316 vessels, each valued at £3,500, en route to or from the ports of the Northern Colonies were seized by the Spanish.[53] The exploits of the Spanish privateers are obscured in the English sources, but from the results neither their bravery nor their activity can be reproached.

On June 15, 1739, three months before war was declared, Newcastle directed the colonial governors to grant commissions of marque and reprisal to those applicants fitly qualified for arming and fitting out ships of war, a virtual recognition that

---

[47] *Colonial Records of Rhode Island*, IV, 566-68, 575.

[48] A hundred or more pertinent documents in A. G. I., 76-6-17, *passim*.

[49] A. G. I., Audiencia de Santo Domingo, 86-6-5. Montiano to King, St. Augustine, 31 August, 1738; King to Montiano, Madrid, 30 June, 1739.

[50] C. O. 5/654, 223.

[51] *Ibid.*, p. 225.

[52] *Archivo Histórico Nacional de Madrid*, legajo 2263, Doc. No. 187.

[53] For a list of ships taken in the War of Jenkins' Ear see *Gentlemen's Magazine*, IX, 495; X, 95; XI, 689; XIII, 23, 419, 699; XIV, 260, 311, 366, 367, 424, 533-36, 592, 647.

war was inevitable.[54] Massachusetts alone commissioned thirty-two; Oglethorpe, several which gave good accounts of themselves. Governor Morris of New Jersey wrote Sir Charles Wager, first Lord of the Admiralty:

> The people of New York, Rhode Island, etc., are very fond of having leave to make reprisals on the Spaniard. . . . I wish the success may answer the expectation; if it does not I'm afraid they'l turn thieves and Pyrates.[55]

Seamen, Negroes and sailmakers were supplied the king's ships from the colonies.[56] The sloop *Revenge* of Rhode Island, and the *Squirrel*, were outstanding offensive agents—to the latter being attributed, before 1742, two Spanish privateers valued at one thousand pounds, a ship with stores, ammunition, and twenty thousand dollars, valued at eight thousand pounds, "a French ship, 1387 Pistoles, 2091 in Silver, 200 Ounces Plate, 700 Barrels of Flower, Cocoa, Gold and Silver Lace for Carthagena . . ." valued at four thousand pounds.[57] The *Revenge*, commissioned June 2, 1740, sailed south, recaptured a vessel off the coast of North Carolina, at Obricock, a Spanish vessel and its prize, and the *Sarah*, off the coast of Cuba. These steps were taken largely to legalize armed protection, and not to carry on systematized warfare, and for the most part at the urgent insistence, or direct expense, of the prominent merchants, which accounts for the fact that by 1743 only 392 Spanish ships valued at £1,749,600 were taken. By this same date prizes taken by American privateers alone, aside from those which escaped unnoticed, were valued at £1,335,100. The British did not seek to discredit the importance of these merchant warriors of America. For example on July 2, 1740, an English magazine reported:

> Every ship from the West Indies brings that the privateers belonging to our Colonies continue taking Prizes of Great Value. It is something strange that the *British* Men do not as usual come in for a share.

---

[54] C. O. 318/3, fols. 157-58.
[55] William A. Whitehead, ed., *The Papers of Lewis Morris*, IV, 66.
[56] E. Ames (ed.), "Participation of Massachusetts in the Expedition Against Carthagena," *Massachusetts Historical Society Proceedings*, XVIII, 370-73.
[57] *Gentlemen's Magazine*, XI, 497, 696.

Again on November 30, 1742: "Advice is come since our last of his Majesty's Ships having taken four Prizes, and our *American Privateers* Ten."

For striking episodes of bravery and cunning not even the burning of the *Philadelphia* or the deeds of the dashing privateers of the American Revolution and the War of 1812 excel those of the Americans in the War of Jenkins' Ear. In 1739 a Rhode Island privateer took a port and plundered a town on the northern side of Cuba. In 1740 Captain Massward, commanding the disabled *John* of New York, was chased by a Spanish privateer until it was dark, at which time he set fire to a tar barrel, and putting it into a tub, sent it adrift, leaving the Spanish privateer to follow it. Captain Bayard with a New York sloop came into port near Santiago, Cape Verde Islands, but a French man-of-war followed him, took the Spanish treasures aboard, and notified the American that the Spaniards were under his protection. During the night Captain Bayard sent a small boat alongside the French vessel. The occupants, feigning to be natives, informed the French that a formidable English vessel of war had been observed just outside the harbor. Realizing that his conduct would be hard to justify, the French captain quietly stole away and left the field clear for Captain Bayard.

Losing their nautical ethics, these privateers indiscriminately made prizes of Dutch ships in both European and American waters, whereupon Newcastle strictly enjoined the executives to secure close observance of instructions from those having letters of marque and reprisal. Colors of American privateers were made uniform with those issued in Great Britain. Prizes were awarded either by commissioners upon the receipt of authentic accounts of transactions or by admiralty courts. Imprisoned Spanish officers in New England were cared for by private individuals and reimbursed by the government. Some escaped and became a menace to the coast. They were suspected of aiding clandestine importation of Spanish goods, but the colonial governors made every effort to prevent smuggling.

In every part of the world frequented by Europeans, Americans, no less than Englishmen, between 1739 and 1744 fell with telling effect upon Spanish commerce, privateers, and men-of-war. The historians of American privateering would do well to pause briefly and place them in their proper perspective. Few Americans know that the Northern Colonies played a vital part in the War of Jenkins' Ear; still fewer know that the first great surge of American privateering, which added the last crushing blow to mercantilism and contributed to the abolition of the Spanish fleet system in 1748, occurred before the American Revolution.[58]

The outburst of enthusiasm which greeted the declaration of war in England had its counterpart in the American colonies. With news of war, riders were authorized to "arrest horses" and by relays to get "His Majesty's express . . . with utmost dispatch" to the various provinces where they were pompously read before the populace, garrisons, and lines of militia, assembled in the "handsomest manner." This ceremony was followed by regal marches to the town houses. Joy was expressed by repeated acclamations of "God save the King!" to the discharge of cannon and volleys from the troops along with the consumption of some barrels of beer in drinking to his royal health.[59]

The response to the natural and just call to furnish troops was extraordinarily quick and cheerful, not altogether because of war fever, but primarily for a chance to share in the prospective booty, the trade of Spain, the mines of Mexico and Peru, and to defend the commerce of New England.[60] The final plan was a conjunct military and naval expedition under Charles Lord Cathcart and Admiral Vernon.[61] Both officers were adjured to coöperate to the limit of their ability and to preserve the best correspondence (a lesson perhaps learned for

[58] References to the exploits of these privateers in both the *Colonial Records* and in the *Gentlemen's Magazine* are numerous.

[59] *Archives of Maryland*, XXIII, 194-99; *Public Records of the Colony of Connecticut*, VIII, 296; *Massachusetts Historical Society Proceedings*, XVIII, 199, 374-75; *Colonial Records of Rhode Island*, IV, 581.

[60] The first elaborate plan for American participation was submitted by Governor Spotswood of Virginia to Lord Townsend. It became the weapon of the war faction and was adopted almost *in toto* by the ministry and its advisers at Hanover Square. Add. MSS, 32694, N. P., IX, 3-4; C. O. 318/3, 170-76, 185-319; *Journals of the House of Burgesses of Virginia*, 1727-1740, p. xiii; *Journals of the Council of Colonial Virginia*, II, 904.

[61] C. O. 5/41, fols. 9-164, includes many official records of the American troops, letters relating to American field officers, method of handling American levies, papers of Cathcart, Blakeney, Gooch, and journals of Captain Knowles and Lord Elibank. C. O. 5/42, fols. 42-184, embraces the returns of Colonel Gooch's regiment.

naught from Penn and Venables) in the expedition that had Havana, if practicable (and, thereafter Vera Cruz, Cartagena, and Panama), as its prime object.[62] A Council of War to be consulted in crises, composed of Cathcart (Wentworth), three officers next in rank, Vernon, three sea officers next in rank, and Governor Edward Trelawney of Jamaica, was created to introduce sanity and experience into these tropical councils albeit they only introduced insane confusion. Proclamations of freedom to the Spanish Americans, too, were grandiloquently authorized.[63] It was to be the most formidable fleet and army ever assembled in America.[64]

It was opportunely recalled that the British colonies on the continent of America had participated in an expedition against the French in King William's time, and again in the expeditions against Nova Scotia and Canada during Queen Anne's War, and, somewhat reluctantly admitted that they had "most heartily concurred."[65] Queen Anne's instructions to Lord Peterborow, Lord Shannon, and those of Cromwell to Penn and Venables for their West Indian campaigns were dusted off and given a respectful perusal by a somewhat bewildered officialdom.[66] The mainland colonials were to join the expedition at the general rendezvous at Port Royal in Jamaica, and together they were to attack the heart of Spanish America, the West Indies. Even the governors of the Leeward (200 men) and Virgin Islands were directed to call for volunteers to accompany Vernon and Cathcart.[67] The governors of Jamaica were charged with raising and provisioning by martial law if necessary[68] 500 Negro workers (with a right to share in all booty), and required to hold an independent company ready for serv-

---

[62] Instructions to Our Trusty and Well-beloved Charles Lord Cathcart. 27 May, 1740. C. O. 318/3, fols. 260-69.

[63] Instructions to Cathcart, 1 July, O. S., 1740. C. O., 318/3, fols. 281-89. Staff for the Expedition to the West Indies, C. O. 318/3, fols. 301-2.

[64] Cathcart considered the Americans the primary advantage in the struggle. Add. MSS, 32692, N. P., VII, 544.

[65] C. O. 318/3, M. Bladen to Lord Harrington, 14 December, 1739.

[66] C. O. 318/3, fols. 259, 270-72, M. Bladen to Andrew Stone, Hanover Square, 16 May, 27 May, 1740. Bladen to Newcastle, 27 May, 1740.

[67] C. O. 318/3. Minutes of the Meeting at Hanover Square, 3 March, 7 March, 1739/40. Governor John Hart to Lord Cathcart, Bath, 28 February, 1739/40.

[68] C. O. 318/3, fols. 275-76, M. Bladen to the Duke of Newcastle, 23 June, 1740.

ice with Cathcart.[69] Newcastle, secretary of the Southern Department, in a letter of January 5, 1740, informed their excellencies, the governors of the Northern Colonies, to be prepared for inviting his "Majesty's subjects . . . to enlist in the glorious Expedition on foot for attacking the most considerable settlements in the West Indies. . . ."[70] All governors in their general instructions were invited to seek advice from Governor Spotswood of Virginia, named Quartermaster-General.[71] Newcastle likewise forwarded a list of twelve instructions to be supplemented upon the arrival in America of Colonel William Blakeney, named Adjutant General of all the forces employed, urging the subjects of each province "cheerfully to enlist," and giving them every assurance of protection, respect, and lucre, on a parity with British soldiers. No especial quota or detailed instructions were sent, the recruits being left to the zeal of the governors. However, general orders were issued to the effect that the colonies were to provision and transport the troops to the common rendezvous. The expense of the return trip, upon termination of the campaign, was assumed by the government in London. Clothing, blankets, arms, commissions, and £7,437 8s. 6d. in specie, for thirty companies were supplied through Colonel Blakeney.[72] Irish Catholics were to be rejected as Papists unfit to fight. The Americans were to be constantly suspected for this reason. The proclamations calling for volunteers, to be organized into companies of one hundred men each, were prepared in advance and almost uniformly accompanied the publication of the declaration of war, the acme of excitement.[73] The Duke of Newcastle was advised to order Ogle-

---

[69] C. O. 318/3, fols. 279-86, Letter to Governor Trelawney of Jamaica, June, 1740.

[70] Add. MSS, 32693, N. P., VIII, 21, 25, 132, C. O. 5/5, 157.

[71] C. O. 318/3, fols. 252-58, Instructions to our Trusty and Welbeloved Alexander Spotswood Esqr. Major General of our Forces. 2 April, 1740. King's instructions to the governors or lieutenant-governors of New Jersey, Massachusetts Bay, New Hampshire, Rhode Island, New York, Virginia, Pennsylvania, North Carolina, Maryland, Connecticut.

[72] C. O. 318/3, fols. 201-8, 245-57, 281-90.

[73] Draught of Instructions for the Governors on the Continent of North America to levy troops for His Majesty's Service. 19 January, 1739/40. Minutes of the Meeting at Hanover Square, 21 January, 1739/40. C. O. 318/3. Blakeney brought to New York for the American troops £8,000, clothes for twenty-five sergeants,

thorpe, as soon as he had obeyed his original instructions, to hold himself in readiness to join Lord Cathcart with the artillery and stores sent him, and with as many men from his regiment as could be spared.[74] Spotswood was not permitted, however, to make levies on South Carolina, Georgia, and Nova Scotia.[75]

The provincial executives had the explict orders of the British government to call and impart their instructions to the council of the province, and to appoint to military stations "only men of interest in their locality and well disposed toward the service."[76] The nomination of officers rested upon the governor and his council except in Virginia where in addition, Major General Spotswood was consulted.[77] The colonies reciprocated by the appointment of their best military possibilities of higher rank to share disaster beneath the sun-baked walls of Cartagena. The appointment of Governor Spotswood, an officer "long settled in North America and engaged in Affection to protect their Persons and secure their interests," was auspicious.[78] Massachusetts and Connecticut appointed committees for his and Colonel Blakeney's entertainment. The other officers recommended by the governors had commands in the militia, or were young doctors, lawyers, merchants, and naval commanders. All were gentlemen of the first rank in the provinces where the companies were raised. Their names were, and

---

ten drummers, and five hundred enlisted men, thirty blank commissions for captains (signed by the king), twenty-eight blank commissions for lieutenants (signed by the king), thirty blank commissions for ensigns (signed by the king), 3,000 muskets and appurtenances, 3,000 bayonets, 3,000 cartouch boxes, 45 barrels of fine powder, 46 wt. of musket shot, 9,000 musket flints, 120 halberds, 20 reams of cartridge paper, 120 partisans, 60 drums, 100 tents with furniture, 11 camp colors, 11 sets of staves for the same, 11 bell tents, C. O. 318/3, fol. 251. *Documents relative to the Colonial History of the State of New York* (edited by E. B. O'Callahan), VI, 162; Ames (ed.), "Participation of Massachusetts in the Expedition against Carthagena," *Massachusetts Historical Society Proceedings*, XVIII, 368, 369; *Pennsylvania Colonial Records*, IV, 395.

[74] C. O. 318/3, M. Bladen to the Duke of Newcastle, 19 January, 1739/40.

[75] C. O. 318/3. Draught of Instructions to Colonel Spotswood. 19 January, 1739/40.

[76] *Archives of Maryland*, XXVIII, 214.

[77] C. O. 318/3. Minutes of the Meeting at Hanover Square, 15 March, 1739/40.

[78] He had offered his services eleven years before. Add. MSS, 32694, N. P., IX, 3-4; *Pennsylvania Colonial Records*, IV, 396; *Archives of Maryland*, XXVIII, 216, 219; *Journals of the House of Burgesses of Virginia, 1727-1740*, p. xiii.

still are, those of the best families, the Washingtons of Virginia; the Duxburgs, Spragues and Thomases, one of whom, Benjamin F. Thomas, in 1881 was a judge in the supreme court of his state of Massachusetts; the Holtons, one a member of the governor's council, the Coltrains and the Innes of North Carolina. Captain Thomas Laurie of Pennsylvania was secretary to the governor.

In April, 1740, the fife and drum of the recruiting sergeant were heard from Massachusetts to the Carolinas. Its music was well understood from the placards placed by sheriffs on doors of churches and town houses, and from newspapers and other advertisements. Legislative action, aside from Pennsylvania and Maryland, was exemplified in the words of Governor Johnston of North Carolina to the Duke of Newcastle, November 5, 1740: "I must in justice to the Assembly of the Province inform your grace that they were very zealous and unanimous in promoting this service." Massachusetts offered a bounty of seventy pounds to captains who enlisted. To enlisted men Maryland, Connecticut, New Hampshire, and Massachusetts offered five pounds; Rhode Island, three. The total number of pounds was not to exceed five hundred in Maryland nor fifteen hundred in Connecticut. New York and Maryland each appropriated £2,500 to encourage volunteers. This meager incentive was braced up by something more enticing. Maryland offered her soldiers exemption from military duty for a period after their return, freedom from arrest for debt, taxes, and ferriage fees.[79] For example, Thomas Walker of Ann Arundel County, rebuffed in arresting an indebted soldier "did in a very arrogant Manner curse his Majesty, King George, in these Words, viz. God Damn King George and all Souldiers." Acts laying duties on slaves were general. Legislative encouragement reached its climax when the Rhode Island assembly invited commissioned officers to dine with the court, and other officers and soldiers

---

[79] *Pennsylvania Colonial Records*, IV, 424; Ames (ed.), "Participation of Massachusetts in the Expedition against Carthagena," *Massachusetts Historical Society Proceedings*, XVIII, 376; Massachusetts, General Court, *Provincial Statutes*, II, 1061, section II; *Archives of Maryland*, VI, 580, 582-84, XLII, 124, 125, 127, 128; *Colonial Records of Rhode Island*, IV, 573; *The Public Records of the Colony of Connecticut*, VIII, 296; *Documents relative to the Colonial History of the State of New York*, VI, 154, 168, 171.

to be "treated by the sheriff with liquor, to the value of £15, both at the charge of the colony.

"God save the King."[80]

The provincial troops, according to instructions, were to consist of four battalions up to 3,000 men, formed in companies of a hundred men each, four sergeants, four corporals, two drummers, besides commissioned officers, one captain, two lieutenants and an ensign; the Maryland, New Jersey, and Rhode Island field officers, men of experience from England, and one sergeant for each company from the four independent companies at New York.[81] The eight English field officers, three of whom were personally selected by Cathcart, received ten shillings a day less than officers of their rank in the British regiments, but not without protest. The British themselves furnished thirty lieutenants (officers of from three to thirteen years service in the army)—half the number necessary for the American regiment,[82] as well as the five adjutants required. Disgruntled from the outset by the condescending treatment accorded them, nevertheless, the American troops immediately began to desert in New York, and, because the officers went both uncommissioned and unpaid, four companies were disbanded.[83] So anxious were the young Americans to receive commissions, the reward for the first completion of a company, that recruiting took on the nature of competition and some extra-legal procedure. When only one commission remained in New Jersey, two officers completed their companies on the same day. Private offers of money to raise troops were refused in Boston. In other colonies committees to "beat for volunteers" and to "take names" were appointed. The captains of such companies were elected by the men. In Virginia the magistrates of the various counties were to impress the "able-bodied persons, fit to serve his Majesty who follow no other lawful calling or employment." The Rhode Island assembly required the officers to assemble the volunteers for service in the expedition against the Spaniards, to collect two companies, and to discharge the rest.

---

[80] *Colonial Records of Rhode Island*, IV, 579.

[81] C. O. 318/3, fols. 326, 246. Minutes of the Meeting of Admiralty, 27 February, 1739/40.

[82] C. O. 5/41, fols. 7-13.

[83] C. O. 5/41, fols. 97, 99, 100.

Pennsylvania, dominated by the Quakers, was precipitated into a crisis when Governor Thomas sanctioned the Duke of Newcastle's instructions, April 5, 1740, urging enlistments, provisions and transportation to the Capes of Virginia by the end of August. The regular session of the assembly had adjourned without considering appropriations for the expedition, but all the governors were prepared for such an eventuality in a set of secret instructions empowering them to provide victuals and transports in case the assemblies refused to make provision.[84] The governor of Pennsylvania retaliated by issuing a writ for a special session, July 28, by giving encouragement to the enlistment of indentured servants, even deigning to shake hands and to converse with them. To the protests of the assembly he retorted that he considered such condescension magnanimous. Considerable money in the treasury, jeopardized private property, and a ripe and unreaped harvest, were excuses offered by the assemblymen. On the other hand the activity of the assembly, the wealth and population of the province and ready enlistments substantiated the executive. Their original position was that war was diametrically opposed to their principles, but they demonstrated the sensitive spot to be economic and parsimonious rather than religious when on August 22, 1740, they actually issued a warrant to the Treasurer for the appropriation of three thousand pounds with the stipulation that their servants be released, which inconsistency the governor did not fail to note. Every conceivable argument was advanced. If the governor was determined and opinionated, he was sincere and politic, and he authorized the officers to release such servants recruited en route to other provinces as could be persuaded to return to their masters. The council, answering the officers' petition, advised them according to the king's instructions to retain the security and trade of the provinces by refusing to discharge the indentured servants. The climax of the struggle came in a point blank challenge of the governor's veracity.[85] Thus we find a striking parallel of colonial opposition to imperial control in subsequent crises.

In some provinces servants had been retained and were not

---

[84] C. O. 318/3, M. Bladen to Newcastle, 24 January, 1739/40.

[85] *Pennsylvania Colonial Records*, IV, 435, 437, 440, 441, 448, 452, 454, 455, 456, 459-61, 466, 467, 591, 593, 598.

returned until encouragement had been given freemen to enlist, but Virginia prohibited the enlistment of either indentured or bought servants.[86] Governor Clark of New York suggested enlistment as a method of removing obligations, and Governor Morris of New Jersey was thoroughly in accord with its legality.[87] From petitions of widows and descriptions of deserters, one can see that practically every kind of able-bodied man, from Negro to aristocrat, was accepted.

Writing to the Duke of Newcastle, Colonel Blakeney voiced the surprise of all the colonial governors at finding themselves restricted to a specific number of companies.[88] A dispute over a commission in New Jersey was settled by mustering the American companies before a British lieutenant and two justices of the peace. Withholding commissions, wrote the governor, with genuine prescience, "has put a great damp upon the thing, and will render the raising of future levyes very difficult to be done if his Majesty should have any occasion for them." Some provinces, however, raised and dispatched more companies than they had commissions.[89]

Aside from an insufficient number of commissions, there were practical and concrete obstacles to enlistment. Ancient means of communication, inadequate transportation, and the lack of credit and confidence rendered financial flexibility impossible. The impossibility of negotiating bills of exchange limited North Carolina to four hundred men and New Jersey to three hundred, and was the subject of governmental investigation in Massachusetts.

In the meantime training went on. In the latter part of August there was a general muster and review of the troops. Pressure upon the king's subjects in the Northern Colonies, encouragement of volunteering by servants, as well as the animosity and rancor called forth in Pennsylvania and Mary-

---

[86] W. W. Hening (ed.), *Statutes at Large of Virginia*, V, 94-95.

[87] *Documents relative to the Colonial History of the State of New York*, VI, 165; Whitehead, *op. cit.*, IV, 97.

[88] C. O. 5/41, fol. 95.

[89] Add. MSS, 32695, N. P., X, 210; *State Records of North Carolina*, XI, 42, 43; *Colonial Records of Rhode Island*, IV, 576, 578; Whitehead, *op. cit.*, IV, 103-4; Henry Stevens, *Analytical Index to the Colonial Documents of New Jersey*, VI, 117, 166-67; Ames (ed.), "Participation of Massachusetts in the Expedition against Carthagena," *Massachusetts Historical Society Proceedings*, XVIII, 375.

land, made the problem of desertion acute, especially as certain demagogues in Maryland asserted that the soldiers might with impunity desert. Governor Ogle called attention to his resolution to apply with the utmost vigor the act of Parliament for punishing mutiny and desertion. Most of the colonies relied on existing laws. Virginia and Connecticut passed separate laws. Others took extreme measures, Rhode Island offering ten pounds and Pennsylvania three for the arrest of a deserter.

In spite of the handicap of insufficient commissions and uncertain exchange, the colonies exceeded expectations. In the meantime, the death of Governor Spotswood of Virginia resulted, by virtue of Newcastle's foresight, in Lieutenant Governor Gooch's elevation to his place in the West Indian expedition.[90] Upon issuing the thirty commissions, Colonel Gooch requested the Southern group to be "off the Capes of Virginia," from which they sailed in October with the northern companies. The Maryland troops assembled at Annapolis. From the several certificates, discharges, charter parties, and other vouchers it appears that three companies of three hundred men, including three British lieutenants and three corporals from New York, constituted the Maryland quota. Virginia furnished four companies of four hundred men, which assembled at Hampton. Pennsylvania furnished eight companies of eight hundred men which the governor reported completed early in the summer. They were assembled at Philadelphia. The North Carolina contingent of four hundred men, three hundred of whom were from the counties adjoining Virginia, was supposed to sail with this group, but was delayed by Governor Johnston at Cape Fear the day after Colonel Gooch had left the province. Gooch announced, however, that they would proceed immediately to Jamaica. On October 23, 1740, Colonel Blakeney wrote the Duke of Newcastle: "4 companies from Virginia, 8 from Pennsylvania, 3 from Maryland, all gone with Col. Gooch [except those of Maryland who followed him]." Spotswood and Blakeney, empowered to raise as many as sixty horses on the mainland[91] for the train, obviously had no difficulty. To Newcastle, Blakeney bared his chagrin and disap-

---

[90] C. O. 5/41, fol. 90, Blakeney to Newcastle, New York, 25 June, 1740.
[91] Minutes of the Meeting at Hanover Square, 23 January, 1739/40. C. O, 318/3, fol. 314.

pointment upon his discovery at the Capes that Gooch, without even leaving a message, had proceeded to Jamaica a fortnight ahead of him.[92] With the arrival of the North Carolinians, the Americans mustered thirty companies, six without arms; but the soldiers on the seventeen vessels that brought them when divorced from "rum and fruit, began to be sickly."[93] By the time all the colonials reached the rendezvous two hundred were already in the hospital.

The Massachusetts troops, five companies, were collected at Boston; those from New Jersey at Perth Amboy and New Brunswick; those from Connecticut, two companies, probably at New Haven; those from New York, four companies, at New York City, one being sent on English ships; those from Rhode Island at Providence. After proceeding from New York to the first rendezvous off the Capes of Virginia, troops from these places sailed with Blakeney. On December 12, he reported the arrival of the contingent in Jamaica, thus completing the roster of troops raised in North America except those from North Carolina, who sailed independently by Florida and the Bahamas, and were daily expected until they joined the fleet.[94]

The attitude of the British government, exemplified in the dispatch of only thirty commissions, and in the review of American captains and their companies by British lieutenants,[95] was responsible for keeping the Americans as low as thirty-six heterogeneous companies. The American officers had labored honestly but vainly to command the respect of British military circles. That reward they deserved, Admiral Knowles to the contrary notwithstanding.[96] Only the personal leadership of such

---

[92] C. O. 5/41, fol. 106, Blakeney to Newcastle, Hampton, 22 October, 1740.

[93] C. O. 5/41, fols. 107, 110.

[94] C. O. 318/3, fols. 185-319; *Archives of the State of New Jersey*, XII, 136; *Colonial Records of North Carolina*, IV, 421, XI, 43, 44, XV, 752; *Archives of Maryland*, XLII, 162-163; *Pennsylvania Colonial Records*, IV, 460; *Documents relative to the Colonial History of the State of New York*, VI, 171; Stevens, *op. cit.*, V, 179; *Public Records of the Colony of Connecticut*, VIII, 295, 324, 354, 420; *Colonial Records of Rhode Island*, IV, 576. Virginia and Massachusetts did not send the preponderance of troops as intimated by Ames(ed.), "Participation of Massachusetts in the Expedition against Carthagena," *Massachusetts Historical Society Proceedings*, XVIII, 365, 374.

[95] C. O. 318/3, 248.

[96] Add. MSS, 32695, N. P., X, 473-74; H. W. V. Temperley, "The Relations of England with Spanish America," *Annual Report of the American Historical Association, 1911*, I, 237; *Original Papers of the Expedition to Panama*, pp. 10-11; *Original Papers of the Expedition to the Island of Cuba*, p. 44.

men animated many to enlist and to share disease and defeat under the dilatory Wentworth beneath the tropical skies over Cartagena. The loyal response of governors, councils in particular, and assemblies as a rule, shows how a policy of confidence instead of one of suspicion would have forced rebellion into the remote future and perhaps averted it.

It is the occasion of some bewilderment to find a general lack of knowledge of the loyal and truly affecting legislation of the English colonies in the War of Jenkins' Ear. Yet this event entailed many new laws, recommended by the governors to the assemblies with uniform insistence and fervor, becoming the subject of at least two acts in every mainland province with the single exception of Pennsylvania, whose discrepancy was atoned for by dispatching to Cartagena almost twice as many men as any other province. The raising of men and the general order for provisions and transports to the main rendezvous in the West Indies were the primary tasks before the assemblies throughout the summer of 1740. Discordant notes in Maryland and Pennsylvania were directly attributive to religious disharmony.[97] In the former the Protestant-Catholic elements counteracted each other; in the latter a Quaker experiment in government was in full sway. Some of the colonies, especially North Carolina, too poor to appropriate money, made sacrifices, from which we would have winced in the World War, to supply their troops.

Various were the expedients to which the colonies had recourse when pressed by Colonel William Gooch, successor to Governor Spotswood, to provide transports and supplies for the voyage to Jamaica. The Boston assembly voted sixty pounds to each captain. Governor Thomas of Pennsylvania upon the advice of Colonel Gooch prematurely prorogued the assembly, which reluctantly consented to his previously arranged writs of council. The mortified assemblymen fixed time limits, however, which rendered impossible the negotiation of a bill of exchange between London and Philadelphia. Foiled by the sale of the bills to willing citizens who feared a retardation of the expedition and trusted to His Majesty's justice to be repaid, the Quakers attacked the method as repugnant to their religious principles, vicious, low, and dishonest. Exorbitant inn

---

[97] See I. Sharpless, *A Quaker Experiment in Government, passim.*

keepers, "Drunkenness and Disorders," however, forced the billeting of the recruits in villages adjacent to Philadelphia.

A new emission of bills being frustrated by the imperial government in North Carolina, a bill was soon forthcoming, August 22, 1740, for commissioners to arrange transportation and a levy in proclamation money and payments in kind, ranging from pork to beeswax, to be paid at quit rent stations or specially erected warehouses, and inspected and acknowledged by a county commissioner. The assembly commended Governor Johnston for his "mild and prudent administration," and lamented its inability to promote the service more extensively. The governor in turn praised their liberality in view of the circumstances, sanctioned their petition for a man-of-war on the Cape Fear, and promised frugal management of levies.

The supply asked for from Virginia, five thousand pounds, was willingly and promptly granted. The special session lasted only eight days and the bill granting the supply, borrowed on the security of revenues arising from liquor and slaves, was the only one offered. Through the able management of Governor Lewis Morris, New Jersey appropriated, July 1, two thousand pounds, and New York banished all scruples of financial stringency when Governor Clarke generously offered two years of his overdue salary on a loan. Connecticut and Rhode Island stipulated that committees be appointed to draw upon the treasuries and to contract with private individuals to transport and victual the troops.

The Maryland assembly was the most obstinate. Considerable acrimony arose over the appointment of agents to hire vessels and the exemption of masters of vessels from suit for transporting soldiers who might be in debt, but they ultimately appropriated five hundred pounds secured by duties on fermented beverages, Irish servants, and Negroes. Details of total expenditures, £1,483 12s. 10d. were presented by Chairman Benjamin Tasker. The French menace forced the province to buy more and more arms in London, and increased between 1740 and 1745 the futile but vociferous debate on a three pence tax a hogshead of tobacco for that purpose.

The most important direct contribution of the mainland colonies to the expedition, however, was the constant line of ships loaded with provisions, especially wheat and meat, which New England, Pennsylvania, and other colonies kept plying between the provinces and the scene of operations.[98] Upon these supplies the expedition depended, and this very factor allowed the commanders to draw out the campaign and extend its horrors. Tobias Smollett, versatile physician and author of *Roderick Random*, gave the source of Vernon's and Wentworth's supplies, but the gift is to the disparagement of their quality. "Especially," he says, conditions were unhealthful,

. . . as our provision consisted of putrid salt beef, to which the sailors gave the name of Irish horse; salt pork of New England which though neither fish nor flesh savoured of both; bread from the same country, every biscuit of which like a piece of clockwork moved by its own internal impulse, occasioned by the myriads of insects that dwelt within it, and butter served out by the gill, that tasted like train oil thickened with salt.[99]

Vernon and Wentworth engaged in acrimonious debate over the importation of fresh provisions from North America. The latter charged that the naval officers impressed so many colonial sailors engaged in the northern trade that no merchant dared undertake to bring supplies. Vernon denied the insinuation, but Wentworth reiterated it. At last on July 14, 1742, Vernon was compelled to proclaim the freedom of men to engage in bringing supplies from New England.[100]

---

[98] Vernon depended upon the colonies for flour, biscuit, rice, butter, cheese, beer, cider, peas, potatoes, corn, pork, beef, poultry, and turtle. C. O. 5/41, fol. 109. *Calendar of Treasury Books and Papers*, IV, 106, 107, 175, 183, 225, 257, 268; *Colonial Records of North Carolina*, IV, 536, 537, 539, 541, 548, 549, 569, 573, 574, XXIII, 151-57; Ames (ed.), "Participation of Massachusetts in the Expedition against Carthagena," *Massachusetts Historical Society Proceedings*, XVIII, 373-74; *Pennsylvania Colonial Records*, IV, 431, 596; *Journals of the House of Burgesses of Virginia, 1727-1740*, pp. xxxiii, 437-38, 441, 442; *Journals of the Council of Colonial Virginia*, II, 905-6; Hening, *op. cit.*, V, 121-123; *Archives of Maryland*, XL, xvi, 458-60, XLII, 4, 10-14, 16-17, 94, 96, 97, 99, 100, 117, 127-239, 155-62, 177-79, 197-98, 238; *Documents relative to the Colonial History of the State of New York*, VI, 166, 215; *Public Records of the Colony of Connecticut*, VIII, 324, 325, 420; *Colonial Records of Rhode Island*, IV, 573-74, 578, 582, 585.

[99] M. Stover, "Vernon Medals," *Massachusetts Historical Society Proceedings*, LII, 201.

[100] C. O. 5/42, fols. 145-47.

CHAPTER IX

AMERICA AND JENKINS' EAR

AT THE discharge of cannon, in public drinkings to health, the colonies, engaged in recruiting men and awaiting developments, celebrated the capture of Porto Bello, November 22, 1739, and English imperialism vented itself in these words:

> There while Vernon sate all glorious
> From the Spaniards late defeat
> And his crews with shouts victorious
> Drank success to England's fleet.[1]

The *Boston Post Boy* characterized it as a glorious event which "inflamed every loyal and honest Heart here with a warmpth unfelt before in this infant country."

Upon his arrival at Port Royal, Jamaica, Thomas Wentworth, commander after the death of Lord Cathcart at St. Rupert's Bay,[2] found Vernon's fleet and 3,600 Americans (whose orders to rendezvous at Port Antonio had been changed to Port Royal) regimented under Colonel Gooch and encamped on the island where they had been since the middle of December, while English coffee houses and newspapers published every detail of the expedition. Although most of the Americans sailed from the Capes of Virginia, their movements on the mainland coast were entirely at the discretion of Gooch and Blakeney. While the troops awaited provisions, recourse was had to such meager things as Jamaica could supply. The rank and file, indentured servants, Negroes, and tramps, guiltless of drill or discipline, became disorderly and mutinous. The plunder, for the distribution of which the commander of the expe-

---

[1] Pedro J. Guiteras, *Historia de la Isla de Cuba*, I, 412; Hertz, *British Imperialism in the Eighteenth Century*, pp. 57-58.

[2] The melancholy task of reporting the tragic news to the Duke of Newcastle fell to Cathcart's nephew. C. O. 5/42, fol. 88, Hugh Whiteford to Newcastle, Dominica, 24 December, 1740.

dition had such minute instructions,³ was not so rapidly forthcoming. By meting out a more diluted drink for the sake of health and temperance, Admiral Vernon added the words "old grog" to the sea service.

Tropical conditions had already begun to take an even greater toll from the Americans than from the Englishmen. Wentworth's returns of January 11, 1741, indicated the death of eleven commissioned officers and men, with a sick list of 351.⁴ Havana, the original object of the invading expedition, slowly but inexorably glided from the horizon. Reports came in like a crescendo, one warning that the fortifications of the city had been augmented, with a battery of twenty-four guns newly posted on the hill behind the city supporting the garrison of five hundred.⁵ A Spaniard, taken prisoner to New York, reported a new boom-chain thrown across the mouth of the harbor at Havana, and raised the figure for the garrison from five hundred to 3,335;⁶ moreover, inclement weather and increasing sickness forced the French to return to Brest, made slow measures certain ruin for the British, and forced the decision to attack Cartagena without delay both by sea and land. Coming to anchor first in Iras, Tiberon, and Doña María bays, the squadron finally anchored at Playa Grande, two leagues to windward of Cartagena, in what is now Colombia, then the best fortified town in South America. A number of men-of-war, 150 guns, eight hundred regulars, an additional garrison of four thousand men besides a number of Indians and Negroes, and the very surf itself which washed the walls of the city, constituted a strong defense. Furthermore, Don Blas de Leso, taking advantage of ample warning, prepared the forts, covered the streets with sand, and placed a boom across the narrow channel, a league to the west of the city and the only practical approach. Situated on one side was the Castle of San Luis containing four strong bastions, eighty-two guns, three motors, and flanked by redoubts with twenty-six additional guns. On the other side was the Baradera fascine battery of fifteen guns, while facing the entrance of the harbor on a low lying

---

³ Instruction to Lord Cathcart, 7 July, 1740. C. O. 318/3, fols. 291-94.
⁴ *State Records of North Carolina*, XV, 754.
⁵ C. O. 5/41, fol. 38.
⁶ C. O. 5/41, fols. 91, 93.

island stood Fort St. Joseph, with twenty-one guns.[7]

Of the formidable English command[8] approximately 3,600 were Americans from the Northern Colonies,[9] used for the first seven days along with detachments of Negroes to cut fascines and pickets. In an attempt to take the first strategic point, Boca Chica Castle, a detachment of the fleet rendered untenable Battery de Chamba, as well as forts Santiago and San Felipe. For several days the landing of materials and the setting up of a camp at an ill-chosen spot before Fort San Luis were greatly retarded by the disposition of the Negroes to scamper off every time a shot from the harrassing fascine battery on the Baradera side came near them. Here American troops were first brought into action. To erase this Negro impediment three hundred sailors and two hundred Americans, under the command of Captains Lawrence Washington and James Murray, were landed about a mile to leeward of the Baradera under the very muzzles of a masked battery of five guns. After the first wave of consternation when the battery poured a hot fire upon them, they promptly rushed it and then actually seized the Baradera battery itself, spiked the guns, and set everything

---

[7] See *Journal of the Expedition to Carthagena*, pp. 5, 37; Stover, "Vernon Medals," *Massachusetts Historical Society Proceedings*, LII, 197; J. W. Fortescue, *History of the British Army*, II, 61-62; Jacobo de la Pezvela y Lobo, *Historia de la Isla de Cuba*, II, 380; F. R. Hart, "Attacks on the Spanish Main by Admiral Vernon," *Journal of American History*, II, 326.

[8] Eight regiments of eight hundred each and some scattered detachments amounted to 7,000, while the force was augmented by 3,600 Americans, 500 Jamaicans, and sailors and marines enough to bring the total to 12,000. C. O. 5/41, fols. 32-33.

[9] List of forces raised in North America for the expedition, officers included:

	Companies	Men
Pennsylvania	8	800
New England	5	500
New York	5	500
Virginia	4	400
North Carolina	4	400
New Jersey	3	300
Maryland	3	300
Rhode Island	2	200
Connecticut	2	200
		3,600

C. O. 318/3, fol. 303.

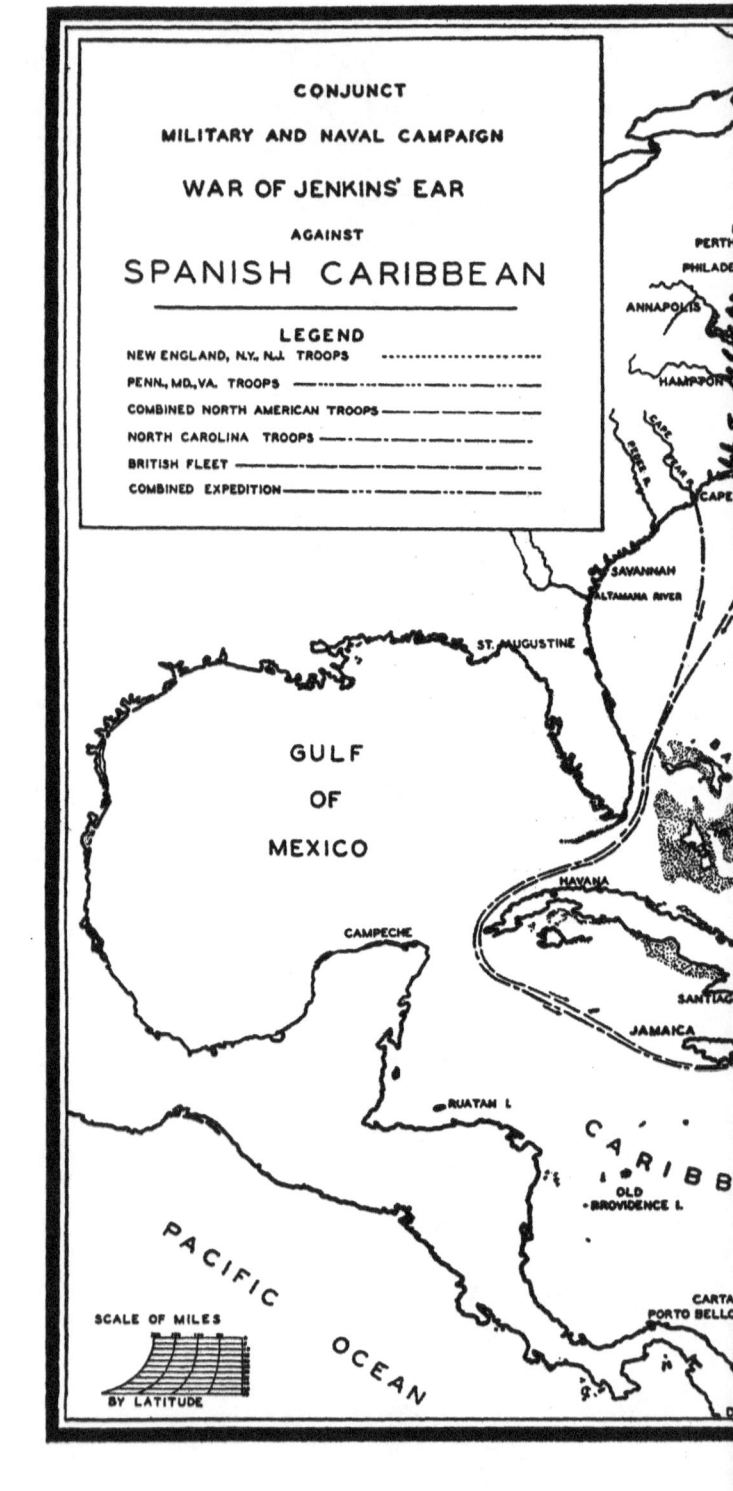

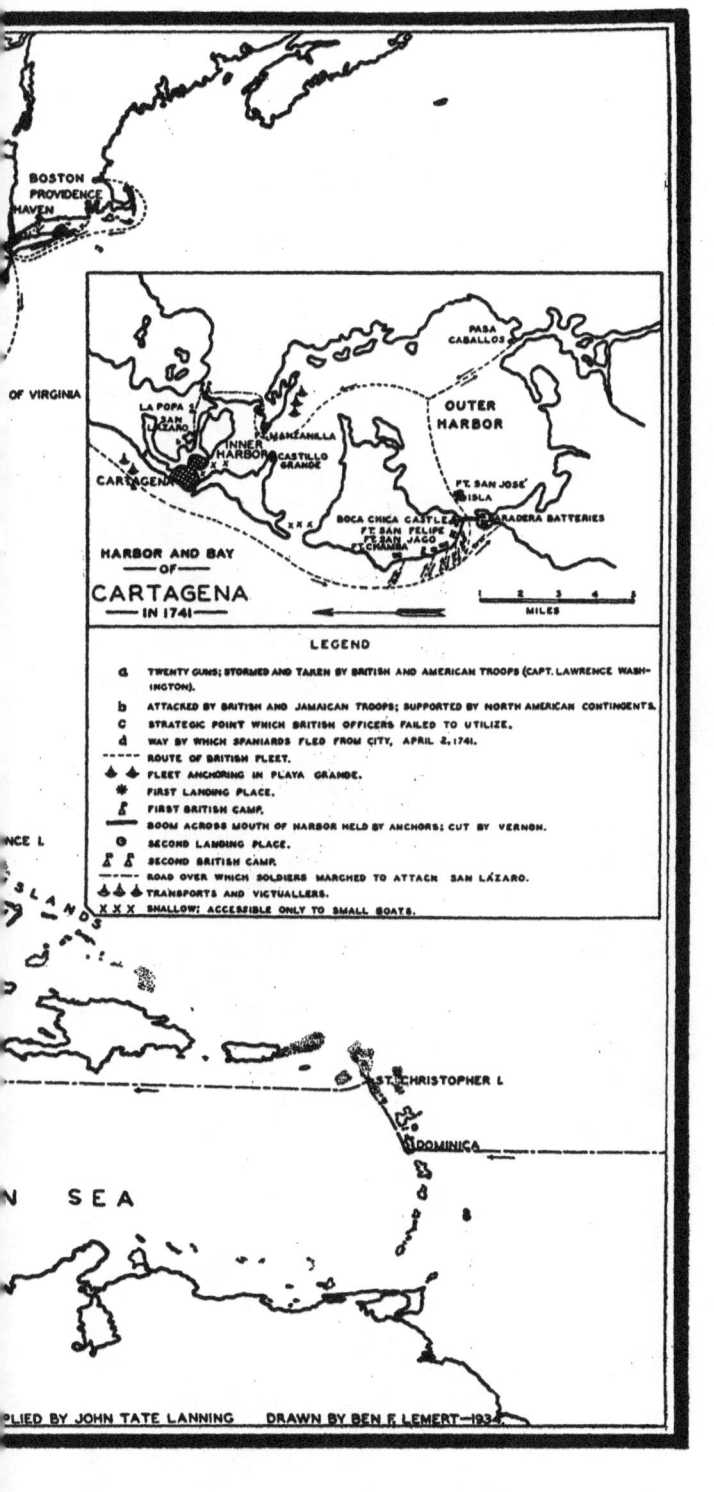

else on fire. For their gallant behavior the American officers were heartily commended.

Immediately after this action two hundred Americans joined an equal number of Jamaicans and parts of Cavendish's and Bland's regiments to clear the ground for a camp just east of the main camp.[10] Irascible then as well as now, a few marauding colonials climbed up to the top of the Convent Madre la Popa and, taking care not to disclose their presence to the Spaniards, sent word to the English that they were in possession of it.[11]

Between March 23 and April 2 forts and batteries were sufficiently cleared away for Wentworth to open fire on Boca Chica, but the camp was directly in line with the shots from the guns at the fort, bringing havoc, killing and wounding one hundred on the first day. The guns were silenced only by the help of a furious cannonade from the fleet. The general then stormed the castle and evicted the Spaniards who scarcely fired a shot. While the Spaniards on the other side were partaking of the panic, Vernon cut the chain boom, effecting an entrance to the harbor, and dispatched the *Spence* with the Spanish Admiral's flag and news of another glorious victory.[12]

All the men were now reëmbarked to be carried to the head of the harbor for the major assault on Fort San Lázaro, a small square fort of six guns to a side and the last great bulwark before the city. Those Americans serving on shore were taken back on the transports. On April 5, boats for landing being inadequate, a short pause followed the slightly resisted landing of about fourteen hundred English soldiers and Colonel Grant's grenadiers just above Fort Manzanilla where the Americans were ordered to join them with tools. Advancing without tools to throw up works or "negroes to reconnoitre the woods" on the flanks, and forced by a lagoon on the left and a thick copse on the right to march only one platoon in front, the English found the road barred by seven hundred men. A party of Americans coming up during the attack was ordered to flank the troops on the march and to fall upon the rear of any small

---

[10] *Original Papers of the Expedition to Carthagena*, p. 37; *An Account of the Expedition to Carthagena*, pp. 38, 49, 55; *Journal of the Expedition to Carthagena*, pp. 12, 14; *Gentlemen's Magazine*, XIV, 40; W. L. Clowes, *The Royal Navy, A History*, III, 67, 71, 72, 73.

[11] "A Journal of the Expedition that sailed from Spithead," C. O. 5/41.

[12] Stover, "Vernon Medals," *Massachusetts Historical Society Proceedings*, LII, 198.

parties lodged in the coppice at the right. Of the 1,140 Americans landed six hundred were employed upon no other service than the less dignified working parties.[13] Moving forward with great alacrity, pouring in a volley, then wheeling to the right and left to make room for the next platoon, the troops readily drove back the Spaniards, and Fort San Lázaro alone awaited their onslaught.

Wentworth now paused to bring ashore stores, arms, ammunition, and men, including a detachment of Americans and Negroes to clear the ground for the encampment about a mile from Cartagena. As the Americans were suspected of being Irish Papists, both chiefs thought it best to employ these "cutters of wood and drawers of water," as Lord Elibank deemed the colonials, strictly on board the fleet and not in an assault on San Lázaro. Wentworth's demand for reinforcements, confirmed in a council of war and made absolutely necessary by the increasing deaths among the regulars, induced Vernon to give orders that all the Americans "that can be trusted" be placed in Wentworth's corps, a plan designed to make the attempt, but the naval officer, who had quarreled with Wentworth, thought it only another of "many pretenses of fruitless delays."[14]

Several urgent and curt notes from Vernon and Ogle persuaded Wentworth to advance on the enemy's lines before San Lázaro from the North and South simultaneously, with five hundred grenadiers, five hundred of Wolfe's marines, and one thousand European and Jamaican soldiers, guided by Spanish deserters. They were followed at a considerable distance by a large number of distrusted Americans, loaded with woolpacks, scaling ladders, and hand grenades which could only be used after the troops were in possession of the breastworks.[15] At four o'clock in the morning the air, speaking tragedy, was close and still as the red columns disappeared silently into the darkness, leaving behind scores of men with yellow fever, some tossing and raving, others waiting helpless and ghastly for the final hour.

---

[13] *Journal of the Expedition to Carthagena*, pp. 26-28.

[14] *Journal of the Expedition to Carthagena*, pp. 4, 30, 33, 37, 38, 43; *An Account of the Expedition to Carthagena*, p. 39, Stover, "Vernon Medals," *Massachusetts Historical Society Proceedings*, LII, 196, 197.

[15] *Gentlemen's Magazine*, VI, 385.

On the southern hill Wynward's men, very improperly supported and guided by a renegade Genoese who admitted he had never been to San Lázaro, scrambled with dogged persistence up an ascent so steep that they were forced to crawl on their hands and knees until they suddenly found themselves facing a Spanish volley at the nerve-trying range of thirty yards. This was the time for a rush, which had it been made by a few trained or enthusiastic troops, must have resulted in victory; but as if in a parade, the officers wheeled their platoons, advancing in perfect order, to the right and left, and they fired dutifully on although they were consistently mowed down.

Overlooking the advantage of La Popa Hill for bombarding the fort was the tragedy of Grant, who was shot early in the action, no less than that of Wynward. The English faced the fire of the Spaniards who had retreated over the drawbridge, and returned it in vain, but with perfect order and steadiness. They called for scaling ladders on the right, the death of Grant impeding the progress on the left. The American soldiers who had charge of the ladders, which were too short by ten feet to be of any use, found themselves knocked down from above and without any arms to defend themselves. Notwithstanding the utmost endeavors of their officers to prevent it, they cast the ladders down, and with characteristic pioneer individualism, either took up firelocks or put themselves under cover from the shot of the enemy. The American soldiers who were commanded with arms were in no wise wanting in their duty.

With no artillery to silence the guns at Cartagena, which at dawn opened fire on Grant's columns, Wentworth at eight o'clock ordered Wolfe's marines to cover the retreat. His decision was augmented by the unerring aim with which the Spaniards picked off the officers, and by the precision with which a column of Spanish infantry issued from the fort and cut off the English. Unfaltering courage did not allay the hopeless disheartenment of the men nor diminish the significance of Grant's philippic: "The general ought to hang the guides, and the king ought to hang the general." Both American officers and men were listed among the appalling casualties, six hundred and fifty-four in number. As coöperation was absolutely essential to the continuance of the enterprise, it was unanimously decided, after several heated exchanges of messages in a stormy council of war, to reëmbark.[16]

The failure of the dead men to bring off their firelocks, and the Americans their worthless scaling ladders, elicited from one partisan pamphleteer the remark "That Numbers of Drums and Colours were left behind in the Retreat." Only the death of the lieutenant colonel of the American battalion which left five tents and some tools and arms prevented his being censured. The twelve hundred North American troops, conscious of the stigma attached to them since the British first laid eyes on them, and later characterized by the British as many degrees worse than "raw, new raised, undisciplined men," and their officers as "Blacksmiths, Taylors, Shoemakers, and all the Banditti the Country affords," bore heroically this "Heap of Billingsgate . . . to villify the American regiment."[17]

To the American soldier his treatment seemed more than mere defamation. Officers were frequently separated from their men, companies divided between the land encampments and the ships where they were sometimes ill-used, beaten, and kicked about at the whim of the sailors. In response to the demands of the men for relief from their sufferings the officers of the American regiment presented a memorial to Vernon and Wentworth, including among their enclosures evidence of the death of an American soldier, occasioned by brutal assault of an English sailor.[18] It is little wonder that the rank and file, hastily raised and without inquiry into their respective circumstances, inadequately trained and poorly cared for, should not give a dashing account of themselves, especially when they

> Heard nightly plunged amid the sullen waves
> The frequent corpse, while on each other fixed
> In sad presage, the black assistants seem'd,
> Silent, to ask whom fate would next demand.[19]

The officers were either "cadets of good families in North Britain" and men of long service, or American assemblymen,

---

[16] Clowes, *op. cit.*, III, 67-75; Fortescue, *op. cit.*, vol. II, chap. III; *Journal of the Expedition to Carthagena*, pp. 38, 39, 45-46; *Gentlemen's Magazine*, XI, 331-32; *State Records of North Carolina*, XV, 752-60; *Archives of the State of New Jersey*, XII, 96.

[17] *Journal of the Expedition to Carthagena*, pp. 39, 45-46, 55-56.

[18] C. O. 5/42, fol. 116, Memorial of Gooch's officers, 3 February, 1741/2.

[19] From James Thomson's *The Seasons*.

planters, commanders of militia, or younger sons of the principal families of professional men, such as lawyers and physicians —all outstanding figures in their respective provinces. Competitive recruiting, while all strained to command military recognition, eliminated all but the best.[20]

The eight hundred thousand pound Spanish loss in ships, guns, and fortifications was only exceeded by the English. For ten days they remained quartered in filth, without cooks, doctors, or provisions. Thousands died with fever, while the fierce tropical sun burnt overhead, or the dense tropical rain poured down in gray streams and the air was filled with a thick, close heat capable of sapping the energy of the most healthy. As discipline vanished, the soldiers, with the abandoned listlessness or finality of marooned sailors, simply dragged their comrades on deck and dropped them overboard to make within a few hours a charnel house, the revel of scrambling sharks and of croaking and flapping birds. The slightly better disciplined sailors daily made their way silently in little boats to the shore and planted their human cargoes beneath the heated sands. Not more than a thousand men remained fit for duty. The *Boston Weekly News Letter*, July 2, 1741, noted the death of eight thousand men and remarked with simple dejection: "The officers and Soldiers from North America behaved themselves with much Bravery but many of them are dead."[21] It was finally

---

[20] *Journal of the Expedition to Carthagena*, pp. 54, 55; C. O. 318/3, fols. 252-57.

[21] The returns of Gooch's regiment are stark with tragedy. At Cartagena the four American Battalions numbered 2,203. Between April 25 and May 30, 1741, enlisted men and non-commissioned officers amounted to 2,568, while in that short time 400 died of sickness and wounds. By 19 June, 138 others had succumbed, Gooch, apparently in despair, had returned to America, and the officers had reported 1,194 wanting to complete their commands. From January to 30 May, 3 lieutenant colonels, 1 major, 12 captains, 29 lieutenants, 7 ensigns, and 2 staff officers had died. Returns for the period from July 29 to August 26 disclosed that sixty additional men were dead, 2,220 privates (centinals) and non-commissioned officers still enlisted, and 1,322, lacking. Other returns on October 3 revealed 1,442 wanting to complete the regiment. Soon thereafter 272 private men were recorded as sick, while at the end of the time between November 1 and December 5, only 119 (of the 1,455 centinals) were fit for duty, 405 were sick, 214 dead, and 1,785 wanting for the command. The inexorable figures marched steadily on until it was discovered that of 1,316 effective enlisted men 456 were ill. The privates and enlisted men by August 31, 1742, had dropped to 1,141 as 229 were recorded sick with so many others debilitated that only 319 could report for duty. Among the casualties since 3 August, 44 had died, 19 had deserted, and 72 had been discharged. Now 2,380 men were lacking! By October 17, 1742, the total of non-

resolved on May 5 to return to Jamaica, and the fleet sailed away from the scene of horror two days later. Thus began the end of the designs on Spanish America.

Neither an expedition against Havana, the nucleus of Cuban commercial and military strength, where the squadron of Don Rodrigo de Torres lay in port, nor one against Panama, urged by the British government and Governor Edward Trelawney of Jamaica, held out such prospects for a successful attack as Santiago de Cuba. Vernon, Wentworth, Ogle, and (Brigadier) John Guise, therefore, agreed to attack it, and dispatched a squadron on June 25, 1741, manned partly by Americans, to reconnoitre. The death of one hundred men weekly and muffled wrangling among army and navy officers rendered increasingly doleful English prospects of success. Vernon upbraided Captain Trevor for receiving the sick soldiers of the American regiment into the hospital for seamen at Port Royal, threatened to charge the liabilities upon that officer's wages, and called attention to the army hospital at Kingston and the strict orders for the American regiment to be regarded in every respect as a component part of the British army. These reasons were also supplied the attorney-general at Jamaica, who directly intimated that the colonial troops had not received equal attention. Vernon pressed the removal of these men, lent to man his ships, until Wentworth promised to repay the naval contractor the expenses accrued from the care of the American soldiers "inadvertently sent" to the navy hospital. The hero of Porto Bello himself graphically depicted the need of the scorbutic colonials for speedy relief from this overwhelming suffering. Lack of fresh provisions, and the very smell of the earth in quarters ashore, created a list of Americans who required being sent to army hospitals. Vernon criticised Wentworth for not establishing such infirmaries.[22]

Meanwhile occasional reconnoitring vessels, manned by

---

commissioned officers and men amounted to only 768, fifty-nine others were dead, and 314 had been discharged. It would be difficult to imagine a more tragic undertaking. C. O. 5/42, fols. 16, 24, 25, 29, 32, 42, 45, 51, 62, 68, 69, 99, 116, 143, 144, 170, 180, 182.

[22] *State Records of North Carolina*, XV, 557; *Original Papers of the Expedition to Panama*, pp. 2-6; *Original Papers of the Expedition to the Island of Cuba*, pp. 189-90.

Americans, were designed to procure intelligence of the movements of the Spaniards and to prevent surprises. Vernon requested Governor Trelawney to order a detachment of four score soldiers of the American regiment, officers included, speedily to supply the outguard of the expedition, the *Strafford* and the *Tilbury*, which were short of their complement. He surmised that Torres' fleet was already superior to anything the English could muster for the preservation of the trade of Jamaica and the mastery of the sea, and apprehended through intercepted dispatches the daily approach of Spanish and French reinforcements. The more imminent that danger, the more inclement the British officers reported the climate. Vernon was therefore reluctant to lessen his man power by disembarking the Americans and receiving them back at the discretion of the general.

Supposing Santiago to be impregnable by sea, Vernon, in order to attack overland, dropped anchor, July 18, 1741, sixty-five miles from Santiago in Walthenam Bay, renamed by him Cumberland Harbor, across the narrow entrance of which was extended a substantial boom along with six large vessels to guard the transports. On July 25 a scouting party of a hundred Americans, a hundred Negroes, ten seamen and a guide, fell in with a Spanish advance guard, hastily drove them off and secured eleven horses and a seasonable supply for the officers, some ammunition, a lot of jerked beef,[23] and three letters from the governor of Santiago. "Old Grog" now urged Wentworth to make a forced march with a thousand men and a thousand bearers, and to administer a quick, bold, decisive blow to capture Santiago by surprise, the fleet meanwhile coöperating by blockading the harbor. He thought it necessary, in order to facilitate the design on Santiago, to retain the Americans to make up his complement and to dispatch some cruisers to watch the "potential fleet of decidedly dangerous strength" which lay at Havana. George Lowther, the ex-buccaneer, drafted and commissioned by the English, presented an elaborate plan for taking the city by a running naval attack through the mouth of the harbor, the ships passing in such sequence as to catch

---

[23] *Original Papers of the Expedition to the Island of Cuba*, p. 41.

the Spanish unloaded. His idea was not radically different from that which proved successful many years later when other Americans called on Santiago with hostile intent.[24] Not even the *sang-froid* of a pirate could make a more resolute fighting man of Wentworth.

On the morning of August 7, a few seamen, armed with swords and pistols, and some Negroes and Americans, serving as musketeers, were ordered to open a communication between Wentworth's camp on the Augusta River and the fleet; to march in three open files, with muskets rested on their arms to avoid ambuscades and surprises. Serious charges against the continentals were voiced credulously by Wentworth to Vernon, who did not consider their merely being Irishmen sufficient inducement for lending credence to charges of designs to desert. Captain Lawrence Washington was able to report that these Irishmen and servants, anticipating a chance for more activity, went on the service in a manner both orderly and cheerful.[25]

In the march on Santiago the calculating, meager-spirited, and woefully inactive General Wentworth, faced by a mere path in the jungle capable of being quickly rendered impassable by swollen streams either for advance or retreat, and by the prospect of dragging guns, wasted more men than would have been required to take the contemptible land defenses of Santiago. Thus he abandoned the chance which would have sent delight through the hearts of Drake, Hawkins, or Morgan. After Vernon, by personal inspection, assured himself that there was no way to take it by sea, a council of war came to a decision November 20, and the fleet quit Cumberland Harbor for Jamaica, November 28.[26] Sane strategy would have dictated a telling blow at Don Rodrigo de Torres at Havana, at the center rather than the extremities of the island. Torres, by electing to do so, could have come out and destroyed Vernon's scattered fleet, encumbered by the transports; but the "enterprise was as ill-conceived as it was pusillanimously attempted."

The diminished man power of the English dictated replenishment or abandonment of the expedition. Accordingly, both

---

[24] "Lt. George Lother's plan for taking St. Iago de Cuba," C. O. 5/42, fol. 170.
[25] *Original Papers of the Expedition to the Island of Cuba*, pp. 59, 71, 72, 101, 128, 142.
[26] *Ibid.*, p. 85.

General Wentworth and the Duke of Newcastle prepared circular letters and, after ordering no impressments of Americans on supply ships, Vernon ordered the *Ludlow Castle* and the *Seashore* to convoy ships with recruiting officers "to the governors of the Northern Colonies" who issued proclamations. Captains Winslow and Hopkins carried to the mainland Wentworth's instructions to raise as many men as possible with all dispatch and send them to Cuba in batches of not less than fifty.[27] A share of lands taken, free leave to return, transportation, and the retention of arms and clothing were some inducements offered for enlistment. The attitude toward the Americans and the treatment accorded them, rumors of which leaked through to the colonies, were damaging to the empire and certainly not conducive to frequent volunteering, wrote Governor Morris of New Jersey. Connecticut, Massachusetts, Pennsylvania, and other states responded in various ways.[28] Probably five hundred recruits were dispatched to the scene of operations.

Even after the collapse of the undertaking in Cuba, the curtain was not yet to fall on this awful drama. Leaving the sick men in the hospital, in which two hundred and fifty died in a single night, the fleet arrived in Jamaica and immediately, February, 1742, cruised off Hispaniola to meet the convoy of three thousand men from England. Even in British Jamaica the sick increased so rapidly before the inexorable march of tropical disease that hospitals, hospital ships, and all normal facilities overflowed as Vernon resorted to building huts for the suffering. Even so he could not keep pace with the parade.[29] The plan of action presented by Lowther, the ex-buccaneer, and finally resolved upon after lengthy debates, was to land at Porto Bello, and to march across the isthmus to Panama with three thousand soldiers, five hundred Negroes, and four hundred friendly Mosquito Indians. Hearing that the Spanish

---

[27] Wentworth's Instructions to Winslow and Hopkins, Camp in the Sole of Cuba, 12 August, 1741. C. O. 318/3, fol. 317.

[28] C. O. 318/3, fol. 317; *Original Papers of the Expedition to the Island of Cuba*, 44; *Original Papers of the Expedition to Panama*, p. 7; *Documents relative to the Colonial History of the State of New York*, VI, 197, 212, 215; Ames (ed.), "Participation of Massachusetts in the Expedition against Carthagena," *Massachusetts Historical Society Proceedings*, XVIII, 378; *Pennsylvania Colonial Records*, IV, 499; *Public Records of the Colony of Connecticut*, VIII, 439.

[29] C. O. 5/42, fol. 122.

reinforcements were en route to Cartagena, Vernon cruised off that coast to decoy the enemy, and finally arrived at Porto Bello with a thousand of his men sick or dead. Wentworth impoliticly conveyed his decision of impracticability, deduced from Lowther's report of the Mosquito coast, to Governor Trelawney, whose private request for passage back to Jamaica was Vernon's first knowledge of the doomed nature of the expedition.[30]

Inadequately supplied by Newcastle, unable to convince the general that swifter and more adventurous tactics with a formidable force should at least repeat the exploit of Morgan, and embroiled in a controversy in which Governor Trelawney and Sir Chaloner Ogle were prevented from slashing each other only by the timely intervention of Wentworth, both Vernon and Wentworth were, on September 23, ordered to return to England; and the strife was terminated. Sailing on the *Boyne*, October 18, Vernon was soon followed by Wentworth and the remnants of the army. In the meantime the five hundred men left at Jamaica had died and were replaced by eight hundred more. Of the regiments which sailed from St. Helen's under Cathcart in all the pride and confidence of strength, only one man in ten remained to return; of the Americans only three in forty—a truly appalling figure.[31]

Military and naval chiefs intended to settle the Americans in Cuba, hoodwinking themselves that such was the American desire. They actually renamed many places as a prelude to annexation, but finally, in view of the Cuban fiasco, annexed the island of Ruatan in the Bay of Honduras. Trelawney effected the sending of Captain Hodgson and thirty-four Americans, along with the Caledonia Indians, to aid the one hundred British already there, and to incite the Mosquito Indians to a general uprising. Settlement would prevent the island's becoming a "Receptacle for Pirates," open branches of trade with Mexico, protect the logwood trade, and stifle the increasing Dutch and general foreign trade—matters of national moment. Wentworth himself on July 22, read plans for the settlement

---

[30] "Reasons for laying aside the attack on Panama," C. O. 5/42, fols. 133, 136.

[31] *Original Papers of the Expedition to Panama*, 119, 121. For a few examples of the appeals of widows see *Journals of the House of Burgesses of Virginia, 1747-1749*, pp. 20, 21, 57, 87, 163, 174, 157, 255.

of the island in case the council of war continued the project.[32] A second council of war, after hearing European complaints of preparing an American settlement, and consulting the inclinations of some of the Americans concerning it, decided to send transports convoyed by the *Litchfield* and *Bonitta*, with the four companies of Americans under Major Caufield, with a chief engineer, ordinance stores, and utensils, to settle and defend the island. The expedition sailed August 13, 1742, and arrived August 23. Organization of distinct civil and military branches of government had been entrusted to Governor Trelawney and General Wentworth. The returns of Colonel Gooch's American regiment indicated that 221 American officers and men were on the island.[33] These men, however, became so discontented that their plight was conveyed to Wentworth and the Duke of Newcastle.[34] As for the commanding officer himself, Major Caufield, he desired to have the disgruntled Americans sent away. Not even mixing them with the other soldiers allayed their resentment at the service to which they were put. So effective were they in voicing their sentiments that their English commander loudly cried they were absolutely unfit further to serve his Majesty.[35]

The significance of this settlement, the attempts to arouse the Indians, and the stationing of war vessels at Ruatan had not been appreciated. The measures had not only the effect of securing the alliance of the Mosquito Indians, but proved both the British government's desire to annex the area and its approbation of the officers' conduct in sending forces. The knowledge thus acquired caused the British government to take clear and decisive steps to determine her sovereignty in 1749. The expedition thus became the basis of British Honduras.

War in the eighteenth century was indeed strange. The English Admiral in the Caribbean, with instructions to destroy and sink all enemy ships encountered in the Caribbean, attempted to encourage trade between the British colonies and

---

[32] C. O. 5/42, fol. 156.
[33] C. O. 5/242, fol. 182.
[34] C. O. 5/242, fol. 184, Wentworth to Newcastle, London, 23 November, 1743.
[35] C. O. 5/42, fols. 141, 185, Caufield to Trelawney, Ruatan, 19 March, 1742/3, 3 May, 1743.

the Spanish West Indies. Vernon on December 1, 1741, reported with gusto that he had seized the remaining two of the original Spanish quicksilver ships with 3,900 quintals, and next we find him without any apparent sense of contradiction, observing: "I have now had the Pleasure to lay a solid Foundation for restoring the lost *Spanish* Trade to this Island, by reestablishing a good Correspondence both at Porto Bello and the *South Keys*," the back entrance to Havana and Santiago. A. Manning & Company agreed to supply the Viceroyalty of New Granada with slaves during the war, and Vernon conducted negotiation with Vera Cruz looking to the opening of a traffic with that important port. Some years before an Englishman, while en route to Cartagena as an agent of the South Sea Company in charge of the *asiento*, was caught and delayed in Jamaica for eight years by the declaration of war. As he waited for instructions he deliberately decided to make use of his intimate knowledge of the Caribbean coasts through the channel of "private trade." The paradox of his success did not altogether escape him:

Whilst we were trading upon the Coast, Admiral Vernon was knocking down their Castles at *Porto-bello* and Chagre, which at first seemed to me very preposterous. However, I found trade answer as well if not better, at that Time than any other during the War; for the Spaniards are in some measure to be compared to our *Spaniel Dogs*, the more you beat them the more they fawn upon you; for there is no Nation in the World so proud and haughty in Prosperity, nor so mean and dejected in Adversity.[36]

Believing the Americans went upon the expedition principally to seek a new habitation,[37] and that the return of any but unserviceable Colonials would be detrimental to the crown and kingdom, Vernon kept the news of the movement of the British troops from them but finally appointed, October 12, 1742,

---

[36] *Original Papers of the Expedition to the Island of Cuba*, 6-8, 182-83; *Original Papers of the Expedition to Carthagena*, 44, 125-26, 139; *Original Papers of the Expedition to Panama*, 23, 41-43, 118, 142, 153, 177-78, 186-87, 190-91, 192, 218.

[37] H. H. Bancroft, *History of Central America*, II (vol. VII of his *Works*), 601; *Original Papers of the Expedition to the Island of Cuba*, 44, 95, 96, 97, 110; *Calendar of Treasury Books and Papers*, IV, 296, 302, 402, 441, 443, 449, 472, 474, 502, 508, 663, 678, 711, 737, 804, V, 479; R. White, *The Case of the Agent to the Settlers on the Coast of Yucatan; and the late Settlers on the Mosquito Shore*, p. 3, sec. 1, p. 10.

Captain Lawrence Washington

the *Gibraltar* and *Shoreham* to convoy the languid and infirm[38] soldiers northward.[39] Among them was Lawrence Washington. Sincere, able, and loyal, he won the admiral's friendship, a Vernon Porto Bello medal, and was inclined upon regaining his health to go to England and seek preferment in the British army. His marriage with Anne Fairfax in July, 1743, however, banished all thoughts of a military profession. He, therefore, erected a plain, substantial mansion upon the most prominent eminence along the Potomac front of his Hunting Creek estate, and named it Mount Vernon in honor of the unsuccessful hero of the Caribbean.

[38] For example, *The Boston Evening Post*, December 17, 1750.
[39] Returns of the colonial troops in the Expedition to Cartagena, *State Records of North Carolina*, XV, 752-60.

CHAPTER X

THE SEAL OF OGLETHORPE'S DIPLOMACY

WHILE ENGLAND contemplated and executed a distinct Caribbean expedition, the little colony of Georgia baffled and stalled the Spanish for four years. Georgia, the debatable land in dangerous proximity to St. Augustine and Havana, met with some defeats and won no offensive campaigns; but a mere handful of men under the leadership of the indomitable, but domineering and opinionated Oglethorpe, achieved more than all England's mighty fleet in the West Indies. Only the troops of South Carolina and Georgia had been required by the exigencies of home defense to be exempted from that campaign.

Rightly suspecting even before the war that the French and Spaniards were trying to debauch the friendly Indians most capable of ranging the woods for intelligence of the movements of the Spanish, the Georgia Trustees sought by candor, gentleness, and presents "to engage them firmer in the British interest," and as a final measure enacted legislation prohibiting unlicensed and fraudulent trade. While the Creeks were fairly well under the sway of Georgia, the Choctaws, a warlike race of five thousand fighting men, were in amity, secured by intermarriage and trade, with the French. French efforts to seduce the friendly Indians, and the improvement and enlargement of their settlements and defense, elicited from the South Carolina assembly a memorial deploring beseechingly the defenseless condition of the province, the seething disposition of the slaves, and the probability of French absorption of the Carolina and the Bahama Channel trade.

The arrival of news in March, 1735, that the Spaniards intended to attack Savannah—which was destitute of fort, battery or shelter—created great consternation. The Spanish squadron, delayed for eight days in Havana, was caught by orders from Spain to forbear hostilities since negotiations with prospects of amicable adjustment were pending. Although the campaign came to naught, its results were far-reaching.[1] The King of England, on August 19, 1737, ordered a regiment to Georgia, a force which was negligible in comparison to the Spanish strength at Havana or St. Augustine. By 1739 the Cherokees, tampered with by the French, were very insolent. Intelligences of the French and Indian expedition from Canada against the Indians in amity with Georgia and Carolina were received by Governor William Bull of South Carolina from Governor George Clarke of New York, and communicated, August 26, 1739, to Stephens in Georgia, General Oglethorpe having gone to Coweta. South Carolina immediately implored his "Majesty's Gracious and timely Succour." Oglethorpe bombarded the governors of the mainland colonies with news of war and perfervid petitions for aid. They were too frightened to ignore the challenge.

Frequent intelligences of Spanish bribes to create a rupture between the Creeks and English impelled a personal visit from Oglethorpe to the Indian conference, including Chickasaws and Choctaws, at Coweta, five hundred miles from Frederica, to prevent such seditions and designs. With seven thousand red warriors and the destiny of Georgia hanging in the balance, he, with Lieutenant Dunbar, Ensign Leman, and Cadet Eyre, proceeded up the Savannah to Ochee Town, met the friendly Indians with saddle and sumpter horses, and overcame the almost insurmountable difficulties of a trackless wilderness. They slept on the bare ground and under an open sky, or in a case of a beating rain, under a rude shelter of poles and leaves, crossed rivers by fording, by rafts, or by swimming, until they were met forty miles out by an Indian deputation and escorted to Coweta.

On August 11 a council opened with pomp and prescribed rites. After agreement on stipulations for trade, Oglethorpe drank the hilarious Faskey and smoked the reassuring Calumet. Due deliberations among the Indians resulted in a unanimous declaration to adhere to their ancient love for the King of

---

[1] This affair was due to an English traitor, John Savy, and the Spanish Minister, Patiño. C. O. 5/388, fols. 72, 73, 79, 80; S. P. F., Spain, General Correspondence, 126, 127, *passim; ibid.*, 246, fols. 2-6, 9, 19, 20, 29, 47, 55, 169, 175; C. O. 5/638, fol. 14; *ibid.*, 639, fols. 57, 58, 77, *ibid.*, 654, *passim*; Add. MSS, 32794, N. P., CIX, 337-41; *ibid.*, 32795, N. P., CX, 22-24, 90, 131-33, 303-9; *ibid.*, N. P., CXI, 36-37, 46-48; S. P. F., Spain, Foreign Ministers, 59, pp. 58-65. See chap. IV.

Great Britain. In conference they repeated their territorial agreement with the Trustees, disparaged the claims of Spain and declared what territories did by ancient right belong to the Creek nation—stipulations of mutual interest and respect.[2] Such diplomacy was more important than that of European monarchs.

Following this invaluable service, executed with such vigor, Oglethorpe lay sick with a fever at Augusta, where Cherokees and Chickasaws complained threateningly of an epidemic of smallpox, thinking it merely the effects of English rum. Information received here of remote Rhode Island's privateering commissions both astonished and perplexed Oglethorpe. It strained his nerves to observe periled and defenseless Georgia, ignorant of actual or meditated war, and yet to be unable to fortify until receipt of news from the Convention of Pardo. It was known in Georgia, however, by September 8 that war would come and officially heralded by Oglethorpe on October 3. Dispatching a troop of rangers in pursuit of the rebellious South Carolina Negroes, Oglethorpe at a general meeting before the courthouse issued a proclamation for granting letters exmarque and reprisal, and spoke vehemently of the designed of pedition against Florida. Failure at St. Augustine would find his bones before the walls thereof! This declaration was accompanied by the discharge of cannon, and three defiant and "handsome volleys" from the arms of the free holders. As volunteers clamoured for the privilege of marching against the Spanish, four hundred Cherokees and six hundred Creeks were called to the southern frontier to coöperate. The militiamen were reviewed, arms and ammunition issued, fortifications repaired and strengthened, especially those of Amelia Island, and vessels detailed to guard the coast.

Gun reports, denoting the murder of two unarmed highlanders, October 17, on Amelia Island, by a group of skulking

---

[2] Oglethorpe's reason for the trip was to keep the Indians from attacking the French. See *An Account showing the Progress of the Colony of Georgia*, pp. 13, 18, 35, 45, 47, 48; *Gentlemen's Magazine*, X, 151; *Colonial Records of the State of Georgia*, IV, 398-99; C. O. 5/640, W. Stephens to Verelst, Savannah, 10 September, 1739; C. O. 5/1059-1060; C. O. 5/641, Doc. No. 59; C. O. 5/323, 344, 346; C. O. 5/1324-1325, 1337, 1423, 1426; G. A. Wood, *William Shirley, Governor of Massachusetts, 1741-1756*, p. 126; *Documents relative to the Colonial History of the State of New York*, VI, 70-71, 147-48, 198-99, 211-12, 214, 219, 243, 245; *Colonial Records of North Carolina*, IV, 271-72; *Colonial Records of the State of Georgia*, IV, 619.

Spaniards, drew out a detachment of Oglethorpe's regiment.[3] Foiled in the pursuit of the perpetrators, the general swept down the St. Johns, drove in the outguards, burnt three outposts, and marched toward St. Augustine, ravaging and precipitating groups of Indians and Spaniards into flight, and even ordered Dunbar to attack forts St. Francis and Picolata, the reduction of which would have required artillery.

A detachment of the regiment and a contingent of Creeks and Chickasaws on New Year's Day, 1740, surprised and burnt Fort Picolata, invested Fort St. Francis de Popa (Pupo), and silenced its brisk fire with the second discharge of four pieces of artillery. Being twenty miles from St. Augustine, in the midst of territory well stocked with cattle and horses, and commanding the ferry across the St. Johns to Picolata, Oglethorpe strengthened the fort and occupied it with a garrison.

Realizing the precarious situation of Georgia and South Carolina, and the comparatively secure one of the Spaniards, Oglethorpe appealed to the home government entreatingly, but in vain, for men and equipment. He even fortified Frederica at his own expense. But only the materializing of the designs on St. Augustine held forth security. Now was the opportune time to strike, while Vernon delayed the Spaniards in the West Indies, and the galleys guarding the St. Johns were at Havana for supplies, leaving a needy garrison. Urgent invocations and the personal visit of Oglethorpe to Charles Town finally induced the reluctant South Carolina legislature to contribute a regiment of four hundred men under Alexander Vanderdussen.[4] He made inducements to his allies, and stipulated what generous considerations they might expect in any emergency, sent runners to the Indian allies who responded with three hundred warriors, and then returned to St. Simons Island industriously equipping troops and collecting the requisite munitions of war.[5]

While awaiting general mobilization, Oglethorpe, with four hundred men of the regiment and a band of Creek and Cherokee Indians, hastily invaded Florida, repossessed himself of Fort St. Francis de Popa, reduced Fort Diego and replaced

---

[3] C. O. 5/654, fols. 326, 249, 251 ; *Gentlemen's Magazine*, X, 129 ; *Colonial Records of the State of Georgia*, IV, 406-7, 426-28.

[4] Carroll (ed.), *Historical Collections of South Carolina*, II, 359.

[5] W. Stephens, *A Journal of Proceedings in Georgia* (3 vols., London, 1742), II, 150.

its garrison—fifty regulars, Indians, and Negroes—by sixty men under Lieutenant Dunbar. Facing about, he returned May 9, to the general rendezvous, the mouth of the St. Johns, where he was joined by the expected forces, save horsemen, pioneers, and Negroes—in all about fifteen hundred effective men.

Exact information about the number of troops, the stone fort, Castle St. Augustine, its sixty-yard curtain, nine-foot parapet, twenty-foot rampart, and armament of fifty cannon was obtained from prisoners. St. Augustine itself was girdled by a line of entrenchments with ten salient angles, in each of which field pieces were mounted, with a garrison well exceeding a thousand men. The plan was to take the island before St. Augustine "sword in hand," fall upon the over-burdened castle, demand its surrender, and greet its refusal with a shower of "Grenado-Shells," or, alternatively to seige the city, the summer's blockade being highly conducive to its success. The arrival of six Spanish half-galleys, armed with long brass nine pounders, two hundred regular troops, and two sloops of provisions, cast gloomy shadows on English prospects, especially since the premature attacks on Fort St. Francis de Popa and Diego had driven in the detachments and cattle.[6]

Lack of defense on the sea side made it advisable to rendezvous off shore, to bar the North Channel, and to order Captain Warren to land two hundred sailors on Anastasia Island in order to erect batteries and to bombard the town. As the land forces advanced, Sir Yelverton Peyton with the navy was to close in, thus instituting an attack on all sides. Moving upon the city about the middle of May, 1740, the English drove in the garrison of Moosa, burned the gates of the city, and reconnoitred its defenses. In the main attack, June 5, to the great disgust and perplexity of the land officers, the signal to the navy evoked no response. The water had proved too shallow to dislodge the Spanish galleys which were arranged so effectually as to prevent the ascent of the English barges and to preclude the landing of troops on Anastasia Island. Upon a second

---

[6] Patrick Tailfer, Hugh Anderson and D. Douglas, *A True and Historical Narrative*, p. 65; G. Cadogan, *Spanish Hireling, Detected*, pp. 57, 58; *Collections of the Georgia Historical Society*, III, 108, 109; *An Account Shewing the Progress of the Colony of Georgia*, p. 44; G. R. Fairbanks, *History and Antiquities of the City of St. Augustine*, pp. 144, 145.

signal, the mystified general withdrew, and finally resorted to a siege. Rigid vigilance and incessant scouting were the order of the day. Colonel Vanderdussen took possession of Point Quartel, and Oglethorpe of Anastasia Island, and erected batteries. The haughty answer of the "Don" (to Oglethorpe's challenge to surrender) that he would fain kiss his lordship's hands drew forth a furious but futile cannonade. The half-galleys in the harbor prevented all ingress by the fleet. A naval attempt against them proving impracticable, the besiegers gradually became lax and uncertain.[7]

Now was the opportune moment, and the Spanish seized it. Don Antonio Salgrado with a superior force issued from the city, fell silently upon Moosa, and by a slaughterous hand-to-hand combat with Palmer's command temporarily took the fort and relieved the city from the prohibition which had hitherto stopped all intercourse with the surrounding country. The withdrawal of the ship guarding the Matanzas River permitted the entrance of seven hundred additional fighting men and a large supply of provisions to sustain the defenders. The last vestige of hope for starving the enemy now vanished, and the fatigued and dispirited army despaired of forcing a surrender. The Carolina troops marched away in large numbers.[8] Short provisions and the approach of the usual hurricanes forced the withdrawal of Sir Yelverton Peyton who was no longer willing to hazard his fleet. Reluctantly a depressed Oglethorpe arranged to call off his men, but through indomitable and pathetic pride marched away with colors flying and drums beating. Carrying away the bones which he had sworn to leave before the walls of St. Augustine if he did not capture it, Oglethorpe arrived in Frederica, July 10, 1740 [9] The men repaired to their respective homes, but the campaign immediately be-

---

[7] A. G. I., Audiencia de Santo Domingo, 87-3-12, Montiano to the Crown, St. Augustine, 9 August, 1740. This is a detailed account of the English siege and the enclosures are (1) folio, copia de un papel que el dia 14 de Junio se encontro en el fuerte de Mazo fijado en un palo y original de remitio al Rey; (2) 4 folios, copia de las cartas de los Generales Dn. Diego Oglethorpe y Dn. Vicente Pierse.

[8] For contrasting accounts see Jones, *History of Georgia*, I, 333, which work contains a lucid account of the expedition; D. Ramsay, *History of South Carolina*, I, 143; McCrady, *History of South Carolina*, 224-29.

[9] "My letters say the General charges it wholly upon the sea officers, they upon him, and Colonel Vanderdussen upon both of them." Add. MSS, 32695, N. P., X, 209.

came, and has to a certain extent remained to this day, the subject of caustic and Jacobinical, sympathetic and defensive literature.[10]

The problem of defense was now rendered increasingly acute, twenty-five prominent Georgians petitioning for ships, rangers, artillery, and fortifications, to equal the increased strength of the Spaniards. The ensuing two-year interval General Oglethorpe employed in strengthening his fortifications on St. Simons Island. This was a lucky move that was successfully to parry the Spanish counter blow. Besides, the General was frequently engaged in defending the southern borders, keeping faithful Indian allies harassing St. Augustine, and in working out an elaborate and ingenious system of defense, perfected by signals and canals. A lull in the storm was overcome by clamours for recruits, men-of-war, half-galleys, and boatmen, when eight hundred additional men arrived at St. Augustine, May 12, 1741.

A desperate invasion of Georgia and South Carolina, whose sovereignty and right the Spanish always contested, was the avowed intention of the Spanish authorities. Its beginning depended upon the outcome of the Vernon expedition. The letters of Governor Bull of South Carolina, who had ignored the bemoanings of Georgia to Vernon, Wentworth, and Trelawney depicting the dismal prospects of an impending Spanish invasion, elicited high sounding resolutions and preparations from a council of war.[11] A letter from a South Carolina merchant confirmed the opinion of the naval command at Kingston that the northern stationed ships would have dispersed that cloud already. The arrival of two letters from Governor Bull, however, and an affidavit from Stephen Budon, who left Oglethorpe in the very midst of the Spanish invasion on July 7, impelled Vernon, after a hastily summoned council of war, to issue instructions, September 8, 1742, to Captain Roderick of the *Shoreham*. He, with additional men-of-war, was instructed to convoy transports bearing five hundred soldiers to the succor of Georgia and South Carolina, imperiled at St. Simons

---

[10] A. G. I., Audiencia de Santo Domingo, 87-3-12, Montiano to the Crown, 30 March, 1741. Description of seige and damage. Maps are in letters of 9 August, 1740 (transferred to Depósito Hidrográfico at Madrid).

[11] C. O. 5/42, fol. 164; *Documents relative to the Colonial History of the State of New York*, VI, 222.

Island. By that time rare good fortune, strategy, and grim determination had sent the Spaniards, as the chronicler buoyantly avers, off "rowing and sailing to St. Augustine."[12]

General Güemez y Horcasitas, Governor of Havana, now free from Wentworth, dispatched artillery, a fleet of fifty-six sail, and eight thousand men, part of whom were dispersed and did not reach St. Augustine, to join the command of Don Manuel de Montiano. First intimations of this redoubtable and menacing invasion were suggested to Captain Dunbar at Fort William when a Spanish fleet of fourteen sail attempted an entrance. Rebuffed, they entered at Cumberland Sound. Oglethorpe with a small fleet followed Captain Horton with Indians and troops to Cumberland. Lieutenant Tolson, with the strongest boat, ran up a river for safety. The next day at St. Simons Island, he falsely reported the death of Oglethorpe to the Spaniards, upon whom in reality he had inflicted damages necessitating their return to St. Augustine.[13]

On July 5, with a leading gale and a spring tide, thirty-six Spanish vessels in battle formation ran into St. Simons harbor, and after an obstinate engagement of four hours passed all batteries and shipping, got out towards Frederica, and landed 4,500 men. The English commander got off to Charles Town only Thompson's ship, a guard schooner, and a prize sloop. The others he destroyed and recommended their owners' cause to his majesty, the king. On July 7, a party of Spaniards under Captain Antonio Barba marched toward the town. Some Indians, rangers, and a highland company advanced to attack them in the defiles of the woods. Three platoons and a company of the regiment were placed near a meadow through which the enemy had to pass. Upon receipt of news that the whole Spanish army was advancing, Captain Dunbar with a company of grenadiers was ordered to join the Indians and regulars and harass the approaching Spaniards.

The English took up a position forming an ambuscade. The Spaniards halted within a few hundred yards of this place, stacked their arms, and began preparations for cooking. Suddenly the snort of a horse, frightened by the gay uniforms of

---

[12] C. O. 5/42, fols. 165-66; *Original Papers of the Expedition to Panama*, pp. 179-82; *Gentlemen's Magazine*, XII, 601.

[13] A. G. I., Audiencia de Santo Domingo, 87-1-3, Doc. No. 80, Diario que sigue el yneriero en jefe Don Antonio de Arredondo en la presente expediczion.

the regulars, gave the alarm. The Spaniards ran to their arms and were shot down in great numbers by the still invisible detachments. In vain they tried to form. Soon they fled with the utmost precipitation, leaving accoutrements on the field. So excited were those who secured arms that while in rapid retreat they fired their arms over their shoulders at their pursuers, pruning the trees instead of hitting the enemy. From the blood spilled upon this lowland, where the Spaniards lost five hundred men, it is today known as Bloody Marsh.[14]

Marching in the direction of the firing, Oglethorpe met a cowardly retreating detachment from which he learned that the English were routed. Soon learning the truth, he marched with participating contingents down to a causeway, thus hindering the dispersed Spaniards from returning to camp. Deeming it imprudent to attack those who had retired into the fort, the general withdrew to Frederica, leaving only small parties of Indians and rangers to harass the enemy. General Montiano, lending credence to Oglethorpe's clever artifice, a decoy letter to a French deserter asking him to lure the Spaniards over where the hidden batteries were, immediately embarked all the troops, confined all the French on board, and left behind numbers of cannon and quantities of equipment. Those dead of their wounds still remained unburied. The Cuban squadron of twenty sail thereupon stood to sea. It was soon followed by the St. Augustine squadron which halted long enough to destroy the plantation at Jekyl. A ruse was usually sufficient to ward off the few nibbling attempts at outlying fortifications, especially Fort William. These efforts were the postlude.

The menace to English America was not confined to the debatable land. After the storm abated, shivers of dread were experienced all the way to Massachusetts. Mindful of their obligations to Oglethorpe, and appreciating the deliverance vouchsafed at his hands, the governors of New York, New Jersey, Pennsylvania, Maryland, Virginia, and North Carolina addressed messages mellifluously congratulating him upon his success and consequent great renown, and expressing their solemn gratitude to the "Supreme Creator of Nations" for placing the destiny of the Southern colonies under his able direction.

---

[14] *Collections of the Georgia Historical Society*, I, 281-84.

The reluctance of the strong Spanish to attack again increased the requests for reinforcements, enhanced work on fortifications, and instituted greater caution and discipline. Oglethorpe, energetic, active, and alert, reinforced by two hundred men from Virginia under Major Heron, anticipated Spanish reinforcements in the spring. With a portion of his regiment, detachments of Creek warriors, rangers, and highlanders, he landed in Florida by night, March, 1743, drove in the outguard and placed his command in ambush, thus attempting to rouse the wary Spanish, who "were so weak there was no provoking them" to fight.

This Anglo-Spanish war began, was conducted, and ended in indecision. Wentworth hesitated before San Lázaro and lost through yellow fever. Don Manuel de Montiano paused before Frederica and lost through bad fortune. The clarity of the issue of the war and its very indecision nevertheless constitute its importance. Hopelessly jumbled up with the *pacte de famille*, fought solely upon the supreme issue of modern times—commercial supremacy and imperial domination—it was the opening curtain of the polemic drama, ending only in 1782, acted by England and France in the eighteenth century. And as such should it not require a readjustment of opinions and a shift of perspective in the colonial history of America? American privateering, military activity, and the great surge of imperialism, indeed, were not limited to Massachusetts or to Virginia. The reaction of all these colonies during the war first clearly foreshadowed their attitude in, and afforded an excellent parallel to, subsequent colonial wars. The attitude of the colonials reflects to a hitherto unappreciated degree both eager response and strikingly typical opposition to imperial control, which, without sane and sincere attempts at amelioration, might disrupt the empire. That was an imperial lesson assigned in the French and Indian War and learned in the American Revolution.

CHAPTER XI

THE END OF A HALF-CENTURY OF NEGOTIATIONS

BUT FOR the brief periods of Geraldino's nervous activity in London during the year 1736 and the supreme agitation which forced Walpole's hand in 1739, Anglo-Spanish affairs were not spectacular in the first half of the eighteenth century. In the course of the war of 1739, which became the War of Austrian Succession, hostilities lapsed in America, but the same old fears continued to be urged. In 1744, Oglethorpe, now living in Westminster, appealed to the government for an augmentation of troops in Carolina and Georgia. Fearing a combined advance of French and Spanish from the Mississippi, he made special efforts to hold the Chickasaws to English allegiance.[1]

Two years before the peace of Aix-la-Chapelle, Newcastle took steps to restore the ancient amity between Spain and England through Portugal.[2] Keene, then ambassabor to Portugal, was given credentials to the king and queen of Spain as ambassador extraordinary.[3] Equipped with private instructions, he met with one disappointment after another.[4] The domestic situation in Spain prevented success. The War of Austrian Succession had recemented the old and disagreeable alliance between Spain and France, and in 1743 Elizabeth Farnese renewed the *pacte de famille*. The queen who succeeded Elizabeth Farnese on July 9, 1746, eclipsed her in power and wielded an influence over Ferdinand VI as Portuguese as Elizabeth's over Philip V had been Italian. Benjamin Keene, pulled

---

[1] Add. MSS, 32702, N. P., XVII, fol. 347.

[2] Add. MSS, 33009, Diplomatic Papers of the Duke of Newcastle, V, fol. 49. See chapter on the final struggle, in Bolton, *Arredondo's Historical Proof*. . . , pp. 85-110.

[3] Lodge, *Private Correspondence of Sir Benjamin Keene*, xii-xvi.

[4] Sir Richard Lodge, *Studies in Eighteenth Century Diplomacy, 1740-1748* (London, 1930), chap. 7; Sir Richard Lodge, "Sir Benjamin Keene, K. B.; A Study of Anglo Spanish Relations in the Earlier Part of the Eighteenth Century," *Transactions of the Royal Historical Society*, 4th ser., XV, 1-43.

bodily from British Parliamentary politics which he found distasteful, instead of entering upon the easy life of an ambassador rewarded for past services, under the direction of Newcastle, was thrown into a violent diplomatic contest looking to the defeat of the encroaching French influence and the establishment of the old anti-Bourbon alliance. With a commission to cross from Portugal (where he was happy) over into Spain at the first moment the Spanish authorities would permit him to do so, Keene was frustrated because the English could not give up Gibraltar without arousing that terrible English disapproval which he and his directors had felt so violently in 1739. It was equally difficult to grant an Italian principality to Ferdinand's brother because that step would alienate the allies, Austria and Sardinia. Yet one of the two was necessary.

There was, moreover, an upheaval in the English government. The Duke of Bedford took Newcastle's place in the Southern Department while Chesterfield and Newcastle took the Northern Department. Upon the appointment of plenipotentiaries, preliminary articles were prepared to serve "as a base in Treaty of Peace, Union, Amity, and mutual Defense."[5] Article III concerned the adjustment of boundaries in America, stipulating in a vague way the maintenance of the *status quo*.[6]

Always in the van of any movement in the interest of Georgia, the Trustees were on hand when it appeared that their title might again be called into question.[7] Fearing a revival of the Georgia limits in the Congress, they, as an indispensable duty, authorized their secretary to lay before the Duke of Bedford the agreements made with the Spanish before the beginning of the war, purporting to show title to the Altamaha, as well as sovereignty over the Creeks, Chickasaws, Cherokees, and Choctaws, who acted under British orders during the war.[8] It was pointed out that the first regular regiment was sent out

---

[5] Add. MSS, Diplomatic Papers, V, 78, 102-10, 114, 191, 223.

[6] S. P. F., Spain, Treaty Papers, 68, Preliminary Articles, Article III.

[7] The Spanish had no such private agency to keep alive interest in Georgia. This accounts for the paucity of material in Spain for these last years. A. H. N. Papeles de Estado, Legajo 4267.

[8] C. O. 5/656, fol. 60. Among the papers submitted was "Some Observations on the Right of the Crown of Great Britain to the North West Continent of America," *ibid.*, fols. 66-107. These papers were almost completely taken from the files of 1736-1739.

to Georgia in 1737 at the behest of the Trustees after Ambassador Geraldino had made an absolute claim to 33° 50', a claim which included all of Georgia and most of South Carolina. When it appeared that the troops might be withdrawn in 1748, the Trustees recalled the old threat (which they had never heard the Spaniards had retracted) and apprehended that removal would be regarded as a tacit acknowledgment of the Spanish claim. This would expose the Georgians, especially the foreign Protestants encouraged to go there, "to the Rage of their inveterate and irreconcilable Enemies."[9]

Unfortunately for the Georgia projectors, this candor found its way into the *Hague Gazette* and the *Utrecht Gazette*, and a paragraph on the same subject was printed in the *Whitehall Evening Post*. The Duke of Bedford directed the papers to be sent to the Trustees, who manifested the utmost concern that a document of such importance from their office should find its way into any foreign gazettes at such a highly critical juncture. The papers, taking no notice of a simultaneous resolve that soldiers from the independent companies in South Carolina were to be stationed in Georgia, made it appear to prospective colonists that the colony was defenseless. The Trustees now proclaimed loudly in answer to the "invidious remarks" of the *Whitehall Evening Post* that they had not one doubt as to the safety of the people or of the possession of the province being maintained, and that after the strictest investigation they were entirely ignorant of the means through which the journals secured the information.[10] They were especially afraid that this news might spread into Germany.[11]

In 1753 the twenty-one years of the royal charter granting "all the Lands, from the Northern Stream of the River Savanah to the most Southern Stream of the River Altamaha" to his "Majesty's indigent subjects and persecuted foreign protestants" would expire. The Trustees thereupon supplicated the king for a renewal of the charter, emphasizing the old claims, the defense of South Carolina, and the preservation of channel and gulf trade routes. What a boon to Spain its abandonment would be![12]

[9] C. O. 5/668, fol. 299.
[10] C. O. 5/668, fols. 120-21; *ibid.*, 688, fols. 85-91.
[11] *Ibid.*, fol. 330.
[12] Add. MSS, 33029, N. P., CCCXLIV, 72-75.

By 1747 not everyone was in accord with the Trustees. Governor James Glen of South Carolina in a letter to the Board of Trade wrote:

> Some time ago the People of this Province were annually alarmed with Accounts of intended Invasions, & ever in time of profound Peace they were made to believe that the Spaniards had prepared embarkations for that purpose at St. Augustine & Havana, or that the French were marching by land from Louisiana with more men than ever were in that country to drive us into the Sea.

To Governor Glen these were the devices of artful men.[13]

Little, therefore, stood in the way of peace in America, but for a while it seemed that the insistence of the English on a prolonged *asiento* contract might arouse the apprehensions of the Spanish and block the peace.[14] The secret Treaty of Aix-la-Chapelle provided for the restoration of all conquests, including the West Indies.[15] In order to compensate the South Sea Company for the interruption of its concessions during the war, the *asiento* contract, permitting the importation of slaves to the West Indies, and also the trade of the annual English merchant ship, was renewed in the treaty. The last day for hostilities was fixed on August 9, 1748.[16] Since this treaty, however, did not deal adequately with Anglo-Spanish affairs, Keene signed a separate treaty with Carvajal at Madrid, October 5, 1750. Reproducing almost verbatim the Treaty of 1715, it cancelled the four-year renewal of the *asiento* contract, and mutually dropped all claims between the two crowns. The South Sea Company was awarded £100,000 to be paid either at Madrid or London within three months. There appears to be no evidence to show the sum was ever paid. While Keene had been held up to opprobrium as "Don Benjamin" after the Convention of Pardo, he was now hailed as a national hero with the same words. The self-same Benjamin had the extreme pleasure of signing the ultimately disappointing Treaty of Aranjuez on June 14, 1752, which he thought meant a divorce

---

[13] C. O. 5/372, Glen to Board of Trade, Charles Town, 1 February, 1747.

[14] S. P. F., Spain, Treaty Papers, 103, *passim.*

[15] *Ibid.*, "On restituera de part d'autre toutes les Conquetes, qui ont été faites depuis de commencement de la presente Guerre, tant en Europe qu' aux Indes Orientales et Occidentales, en l'Etat qu' elles sont actuellement."

[16] S. P. F., Spain, Supplementary, 250, fol. 153. Later a neutral ground was suggested.

between France and Spain, an achievement of the utmost importance to England, for the boundary disputes in America which evaded adjustment at Aix-la-Chapelle threatened to involve England in a war not alone with Spain but with France. Priding himself on the treaty "which cost me more pains than all the business I ever did on my own account," Keene was openly annoyed when the Duke of Newcastle had the melancholy task of explaining to him that the king refused to grant him the Order of the Bath.[17]

The Treaty of 1748 suspended the marauding expeditions between Georgia and Florida which had broken up all English settlements south of the Altamaha before that year. These expeditions, however, were renewed in 1755. Oglethorpe, ever alert to any chance, appealed to the government to raise his regiment to full strength.[18] The English settlers meanwhile again pushed into territory which even their government recognized as Spanish, and the Spanish ambassador at the Court of St. James obtained an order commanding the English settlers to retire from the territory of Florida. The governor, Don Alonzo Fernández de Herreda, sent a company of dragoons to emphasize compliance. Upon a summons the English agreed to retire, but they never did so.

Another sign of quiet, however, was faintly appearing in the horizon—the end of the Seven Years' War. The Englishmen were not clamoring for annexation of St. Augustine and the peninsula, with the probable exception of those who wished to attach them in order to remove a menace and a receptacle for runaway slaves. They did wish to hold Mobile Bay and Pensacola Bay, which would connect the empire and prove of great advantage to the colonies on the Ohio and to the western parts of Carolina and Georgia; but to make them the most valuable of all the settlements, the French would have to be expelled.[19]

In 1763 the provinces of the Floridas were ceded to Great Britain in exchange for Havana and the western portion of Cuba, which had been captured from the Spanish. The treaty was concluded on November 3, 1762, and ratified on February 10, 1763. By the treaty, British subjects in Cuba were allowed

[17] Lodge, *Private Correspondence of Benjamin Keene*, p. 415.
[18] Add. MSS, 32797, N. P., CXII, 185-86.
[19] Add. MSS, 35910, fol. 29.

to settle their affairs, to recover their debts, and to bring away their persons and effects. In consequence, the treaty reads:

> ... his Catholic Majesty cedes and guarantees in full right, to his Britannic Majesty Florida, with Fort St. Augustine and the bay of Pensacola, as well as all that Spain possesses on the continent of North America to the east or to the southeast of the River Mississippi; and, in general, everything that depends on the said countries and lands, with sovereignty, property, possession, and all rights, acquired by treaties and otherwise. ... [20]

In the same year the boundary was officially extended from the Altamaha to Saint Marys River.[21] In 1770 De Brahm's *Survey of America* listed the boundaries of Georgia as 30° 26' 49" north and south and 35° 30' west and east.[22]

At the end of a half century, the only radical change that had been effected in Georgia through diplomacy was the cession of Florida. Apparently Georgia shared the usual fate of the American colonies in European diplomatic stakes—restoration of all conquests. But Georgia's position was different; merely to be left *in statu quo* was the crowning achievement of Oglethorpe's policy. Spanish diplomatic victory would have necessitated a great retrocession. While the imperialists and merchants steadily infringed on the Spanish domain, ever nearing the sweeping and majestic claims of the English royal charters, time was gained, and suspense not infrequently maintained by diplomacy. It is little wonder that Spain in 1763 abandoned La Florida with few qualms.

Oglethorpe spoke with uncanny prescience when he openly said in 1736 "that although he should receive orders from his King and court to fix the boundary limits ... of the Carolinas, he would delay the execution of it so that there should never be a sign of these limits."[23] Once, at least, the tortuous course of Hispanic diplomacy played directly into the hands of its greatest European antagonist.

---

[20] A. B. Hart and E. Channing (eds.), *American History Leaflets*, No. 5, "Extracts from the Treaty of Paris of 1763," p. 9.

[21] Add. MSS, 35910, fol. 134.

[22] King's MSS, 210, I, 73.

[23] Egmont, *Diary*, III, 91.

BIBLIOGRAPHY

As THE BULK of this study is based on manuscript materials, it has appeared too laborious to cite the thousands of separate items. Among the most important papers, however, are the Additional Manuscripts in the British Museum, including the Newcastle Papers, which frequently, but not always, are originals of many papers in the Public Record Office. In the latter archive there is a vast amount of pertinent material—foreign, domestic, and colonial. Whenever these have been published, due recognition has been made. Any work on eighteenth-century England also leads one into a veritable maze of pamphleteering and consequently to familiarity with various minor London libraries and archives.

In the *Archivo Histórico Nacional*, the *papeles de estado* include the Spanish foreign papers of the century to 1728. Thereafter these papers are to be found in the rich, unexploited, *Archivo General de Simancas, secretaría de estado*. Always challenging the investigator, the *Archivo General de Indias* offered up a treasure in the form of *expedientes*, all documents in an official file on a given case.

The greater number of references is the result of original investigation during a residence of twelve months in London, Paris, Madrid, Simancas, and Seville.

A. PRIMARY SOURCES

I. GUIDES TO MANUSCRIPTS

1. Printed

Andrews, C. McL., *Guide to Materials for American History to 1783 in the Public Record Office of Great Britain*, Washington, 1912.

Andrews, C. McL. and Davenport, F. G., *Guide to the Manuscript Materials for the History of the United States to 1783 in the British Museum, and in the libraries of Oxford and Cambridge*, Washington, 1908.

Ballister, Rafael, *Bibliografía de la Historia de España, Catálogo Metódico y cronológico de las fuentes y obras principales relativas a la historia de España desde los orígenes hasta nuestros días*, 8 vols., Gerona, 1921.

Calendar of State Papers, Americas and the West Indies, preserved in the Public Record Office, edited by C. Headlam, Commission for Printing State Papers, Colonial Series, Calendars, 27 vols., London, 1860-1927:

Ford, Worthington Chauncey, ed., *List of the Vernon-Wager Manuscripts in the Library of Congress*, Washington, 1904.
González, Joaquín, *Archivo Histórico Nacional, en Guía*, Madrid, 1898.
Hill, Roscoe R., *Descriptive Catalogue of the documents relating to the history of the United States in the Papeles procedentes de Cuba deposited in the Archivo General de Indias at Seville*, Washington, 1915.
List of Colonial Office Records, preserved in the Public Record Office [and at Cambridge], London, 1911.
List of Volumes of State Papers, Foreign, preserved in the Public Record Office, London, 1904.
Lanzas, Pedro Torres, *Archivo General de Indias, en Guía*, Seville, 1918.
Martínez, Mariano Alcocer, *Archivo General de Simancas*, Valladolid, 1923.
Molins, A. E. de, *Ensayo de una bibliografía de España y América*, 8 vols., Madrid, 1902.
Pascual de Gayangos, *Catalogue of Manuscripts in the Spanish Language in the British Museum*, 4 vols., London, 1875.
Pérez, L. M., *Guide to the Materials for American History in Cuban Archives*, Washington, 1907.
Robertson, J. A., *List of Documents in Spanish Archives relating to the History of the United States*, Washington, 1910.
Sabin, Joseph, *A Dictionary of Books Relating to America from its Discovery to the Present time*, 8 vols., New York, 1868-1876.
Shepherd, W. R., *Guide to the Materials for the History of the United States in Spanish Archives*, Washington, 1907.
Winsor, Justin, *Calendar of Sparks Manuscripts in Harvard College Library, with an Appendix showing other manuscripts*, Cambridge, 1889.

2. Manuscript

Additional MSS, Catalogue of British Museum, 1882-1887, London, 1889.
———, *1888-1893*, London, 1894.
Archivo histórico nacional Catálogo I, etc., Madrid, 1903.
Bibliothèque Nationale Catalogue de l'histoire de l'Amérique, Paris, 1903.
Catalogue of King's Pamphlets, 9 vols.
Catalogue of Manuscript Maps, Charts, and Plans, and the Topographical Drawings in the British Museum, 3 vols. (1844-1861).
Catalogue of Maps, Prints, Drawings, etc., in the King's Library, 2 vols. (1829).
Catalogue of Newspapers in the British Museum, 4 vols.
Catalogue of Printed Maps, Plans, and Charts in the British Museum, 2 vols. (1885).
Classified Catalogue of Manuscripts, British Museum, 108 vols.
Massie, J., *List of Commercial Books and Pamphlets*.

BIBLIOGRAPHY

II. UNPUBLISHED

Public Record Office.[1]
Admiralty In-Letters, 232, 233, 4108, 5273, 5275, 5276.
Admiralty, Marine Office, 512.
Admiralty Out-Letters, 55-59.
Colonial Office Papers, 5.
  America and the West Indies, 5, 12, 21, 41, 42, 195-200, 283, 362-372, 384-389.
  East Florida, 540.
  Georgia, 636-642, 654-657, 666-671, 681, 686-692.
Colonial Office Papers, 318-3.
  Plantations General, 3-10.
Colonial Office Papers, 524.
  Plantations General, 10, 40.
State Papers Domestic.
  Regencies, 321, 323.
State Papers Foreign.
  Spain, Foreign Entry Books, 140-143.
  Foreign Ministers, 58-59.
    General Correspondence, 125-136.
    News Letters, 92.
    Spanish Consuls, 217-227.
    Supplementary, 245-250.
    Treaties, 500-505.
    Treaty Papers, 67-68, 103.
British Museum.
Additional Manuscripts.
  Newcastle Papers, 32691-32695, 32702, 32714-32722, 32738-32802, 32806, 32817, 32819-32820, 32824, 32826-32832, 32834-32840, 32843, 32845, 32847-32854, 32857-32860, 32866, 32868-32869, 33028-33030, 33811-33812, 33983.
  Diplomatic Papers of the Duke of Newcastle, 33005-33025.
  Collection de differents Memoires apartenants a Guerre qui s'en dernièrement allumée en l'Année 1739, entre l'Angleterre et l'Espagne, 21438.
  Coxe Papers, 9131, 9145.
  Hardwicke Papers, 35406, 35884, 35907-35910.
  Miscellaneous, 11759, 14036, 15494, 15903, 16367, 17648A, 22680, 28456, 29973, 35406, 36807.
Egerton Manuscripts, 770, "Demostración del derecho que tiene el Rey Catholico al territorio de Nueva Georgia. . . . Por A. de Arredondo."

---

[1] The system of citations used is that employed by each archive and is not, therefore, uniform.

Harleian Manuscripts, 1589.
King's Manuscripts, 205, 210-211.
Lansdowne Manuscripts, 1049: 242, 324, 2954, 3271, 3376, 3394, 3397, 3476, 4059, 4065.
Sloane Manuscripts, 3861, 3986.
Stowe Manuscripts, 256, 792.
Bodleian Library.
Ashmolean Manuscripts, 48.
Rawlingson Manuscripts, A, 271.
Houses of Parliament.
Journals of the House of Commons XXI-XXIII, 1726-1739.
Journals of the House of Lords, XIX, XXIII, XXIV, XXV, XXVI, XXVII, XXVIII, 1739-1762.
Archivo General de Indias (enumeración antigua).
Audiencia de Santo Domingo; estante 58, cajón 1, legajo
 25, 58-1-31, 58-1-32, 58-1-33, 79-4-14 y 15, 79-5-3, 79-6-17, 79-6-18, 79-6-24, 79-6-25, 79-6-26, 79-6-27, 79-6-30, 80-3-16, 81-2-5, 81-4-9, 82-6-22, 84-3-19, 84-3-20, 84-3-21, 84-3-22, 86-5-21, 86-5-22, 86-6-5, 87-1-1, 87-1-2, 87-1-3, 87-3-12.
Capitanías Generales, legajos 1439, 2263.
Archivo General de Simancas.
 Secretaría de Estado, legajos 2335 (6904-6909), 2336, 2366, 2577: 7.617, 7.618; 2538: 7.619, 7.620, 7.621, 7.622, 7.623; 2529: 7.624, 7.625, 7.626; 2530: 7.627, 7.628, 7.629, 7.630; 2731: 7.631, 7.632; 2732: 7.633; 396: 7.634; 397: 7.635; 398: 7.636.
Archivo Histórico Nacional.
 Papeles de Estado, Sección IX, legajos, 1701-1730, 4265-4270.
Archives du Ministère des Affaires Etrangères.
 La Correspondance d' Angleterre, 1731-1741, 44 vols.

III. PUBLISHED
1. Pamphlets

Alvarez, Francisco, *Noticia del establecimiento y población de las colonias Ingleses en la América septentrional; sacada de varios autores*, Madrid, 1778; the date has been altered by pen to 1608.
An Account of the Expedition to Carthagena, with explanatory notes and observations, London, 1743.
An Account of the Late Application Made by the Merchants of London, London, 1742.
An Account Showing the Progress of the Colony of Georgia in America from its First Establishment, London, 1741.
Address to the Electors; Ten Years' Transactions with Spain, London, 1739.

Advantages and Disadvantages (The), which will Attend the Prohibition of the Merchandises of Spain, London, 1739.
Advantages to Great Britain and Allies from Approaching War, London, 1727.
An Appeal to the Unprejudiced, Concerning the Present Discontents Occasioned by the Late Convention with Spain, London, 1739.
Articles of Alliance between England and Spain, Signed June 10, 1680, and Article of Alliance between England and Holland, signed March 3, 1678, London, 1860.
A[she], T[homas], *Carolina, or a Description of that Country*, London, 1682.
Authentic Papers Relating to the Expedition against Carthagena, London, 1744.
Both Sides of the Question: An Inquiry into a Certain Doubtful Character [Oglethorpe] Lately Whitened by a C—l M—l, London, 1742.
Brief Account of the Establishment of the Colony of Georgia, under Gen. James Oglethorpe, February 1, 1733, London, 1733.
Brief Account of the Causes that Have Retarded the Progress of the Colony of Georgia in America, attested upon oath being a proper contrast to a state of the Province of Georgia attested upon oath and some other misrepresentations on the subject, London, 1743.
Brief Description of the Province of Carolina, on the Coast of Florida, and More Particularly of a New Plantation begun by the English at Cape Feare . . . 29 May 1664. . . . Together with a Most Accurate Map of the Whole Province, London, 1666.
British Merchant; or Commerce preserv'd, in answer to [DeFoe's] Mercator; or Commerce retriev'd, London, 1713.
British Sailor's Discovery; or, The Spanish Pretentions Confuted, Containing a Short History of the Discoveries and Conquests of Spain in America, London, 1739.
Cadogan, George, *Spanish Hireling Detected, being a Refutation of the Several Calumnies and Falsehoods in a Late Pamphlet Entitled, An Impartial Account of the Late Expedition against St. Augustine under General Oglethorpe*, London, 1743.
Campbell, John, *A concise history of Spanish America. . .* , London, 1741.
Casinas, El Marqués de, *Details of what Occured in the British Expedition, Entrusted to the Care of Brigadier Don Manuel de Montiano, from the 15th Day of June, on which the Convoy Arrived from Havana at St. Augustine, the Whole Being Contained in a Journal, Kept by the Marquess of Casinas, etc.*, Georgia Historical Society Collections, Savannah, 1913.
Catholic and British Majesties Conduct Compared, London, 1739.
Common Sense: Its Nature and Use, Applied to the Spanish Affair, London, 1738.

Conduct of Admiral Vernon Examined and Vindicated, London, 1744.
Conduct of the Late Administration with Regard to the Spanish Affair, London, 1742.
Considerations on the American Trade before and since the Establishment of the South Sea Company, London, 1739.
Cowley, J., *The Sailor's Companion*, London, 1740.
Coxe, Daniel, *A Collection of voyages and travels in three parts*, London, 1741.
———, *A description of the English Province of Carolana, by the Spaniards call'd Florida, and by the French la Luisiane, as also of the Great and Famous River Meschacebe or Missisipi*, London, 1722.
The Danverian History of the Affairs of Europe, For the Memorable Year 1731, London, 1732. (This work is attributed to Nicholas Amhurst, who wrote under the pseudonym "Caleb Danvers.")
Defense of [some] *Observations*, London, 1728.
Description of Georgia, London, 1741.
Description of Objects of Spanish War in West Indies, London, 1741.
England's Triumph, London, 1739.
Exact List of all those who Voted for and against the Late Convention, in the House of Commons, And of all who Voted for and against the Excise Tax in 1733, London, 1739.
Examination of King of Spain's Manifesto for not paying £95,000, London, 1739.
Experimental Discoverie of Spanish Practices, London, 1623.
The False Accusers Accused, London, 1741.
Full Reply to Lieut. Cadogen's Spanish Hireling, and Lieut. Mackay's Letter Concerning the Actions at Moosa, London, 1743.
Further Considerations on the Present State of Affairs, at Home and Abroad, as Affected by the Late Convention, London, 1739.
The Grand Question, Whether War, or no War, with Spain Impartially Considered, London, 1739. (This work is attributed to H. Walpole.)
Great Britain's Complaint against Spain, London, 1740.
His Catholic Majesty's Manifesto. . . , London, 1739.
Impartial Account of the Expedition against St. Augustine under General Oglethorpe, London, 1742.
Impartial Inquiry into the State and Utility of Georgia, London, 1741.
Jeffreys, T., *Florida, From the Latest Authorities*, London, 1763.
Jenkins, Captain Robert, *Spanish Insolence Corrected by English Bravery*, London, 1739.
Journal of the Expedition to Carthagena, London, 1744.
King of Spain's Declaration of War against Great Britain, London, 1739.
King of Spain's Reasons for not paying the £95,000. . . , London, 1739.
Knowles, Admiral Sir Charles, *An Account of the Expedition to Carthagena*, London, 1743.

Leslie, Charles, *A New and Exact Account of Jamaica. . .* , Edinburgh, 1739.
Letter from a Spaniard in London to his Friend at Madrid Setting Forth the Happy Consequences that Must Accrue to Spain, from the Late Conduct of Her Great Friends at the Court of England, London, 1739.
Letters and Memorials which Have Lately Passed between the Ministers of the Courts of Great Britain, France and Spain, London, 1727.
Letter on Danger Great Britain is in by Great Increase of Naval Power of Spain, London, 1718.
Letters, etc., on Treaty of Aix-la-Chapelle, London, 1748.
Lyttleton, George, *Considerations upon the present State of our Affairs, at Home and Abroad*, London, 1739.
Marchmont, Hugh Hume (Campbell), Third Earl of, *A State of the Rise and Progress of our Disputes with Spain, and our Ministers relating thereto*, London, 1739.
Martyn, Benjamin, *Reasons for establishing the Colony of Georgia*, London, 1733.
Memorials Presented by the Deputies of the Council of Trade in France, London, 1737.
Ministerial Prejudices in Favour of the Convention Examined and Answered, etc., London, 1739.
Ministerial Virtue, London, 1738.
The Mock Campaign, London, 1740.
Modest Inquiry into the Present State of Foreign Affairs, by a Lover of His Country, London, 1742.
Motives for a War against Spain, London, 1738.
Montgomery, Sir R., *Discourse for Establishing a colony South of Carolina*, London, 1717.
The National dispute or the history of the convention. . . , London, 1739.
New Voyage to Georgia, London, 1737.
Objections against Treaty of Seville Considered, London, 1730.
Observations on the Conduct of Great Britain with Regard to Negotiations and other Transactions Abroad, London, 1739.
Observations on Manifesto of Spain for not Paying £95,000, London, 1739.
Observations on the Present Convention with Spain, London, 1739.
Oglethorpe, J. E., *Account of the Establishment of the Colony of Georgia under General Oglethorpe*, Washington, 1835.
———, *A Full Reply to Lieut. Cadogan's Spanish Hireling. . .* , London, 1743.
———, *A New and Accurate Account of the Provinces of South-Carolina and Georgia*, London, 1733.
Old England forever, or Spanish Cruelty Displayed; Wherein the Spaniards' Right to America is Impartially Examined and Found Defective. . . , London, 1740.

Original Papers of an Honest Sailor, London, 1747.
Original Papers Relative to the Expedition to Carthagena, London, 1744.
Original Papers Relating to the Expedition to the Island of Cuba, London, 1744.
Original Papers Relating to the Expedition to Panama, London, 1744.
Paterson, William, *A Proposal to Plant a British Colony in Darien; to Protect the Indians against Spain; and to Open the Trade of South America to all Nations* (edited by S. Bannister), London, 1701.
Peace and No Peace: or an Enquiry Whether the Late Convention with Spain will be more Advantageous to Great Britain than the Treaty of Seville. . . ., London, 1739.
Political State of Great Britain (edited by Abel Boyer to October, 1729), X, *et seq.*, London, 1739.
Popular Prejudices against the Convention and Treaty with Spain, Examined and Answered, London, 1739.
Postlethwayt, Malachy, *Considerations on the Revival of the Royal-British Assiento. . .* , London, 1749.
———, *The National and Private Advantages of the African Trade Considered. . .* , Second edition, London, 1772.
Present State of Revenues and Forces by Sea and Land of Spain and France Compared to those of Great Britain, London, 1740.
Proposal for Humbling Spain, London, 1738.
A Proposition for Opening Spanish American Ports to All Nations: A Dissertation on the Present Conjuncture, Particularly with Regard to Trade, London, 1739.
Raisons justifications qy'a eues le roy d'Espagne de ne payer les 95,000 liv. . . , The Hague, 1739.
Reasons for a War against Spain, London, 1737.
Reply to a Pamphlet Entitled "Popular prejudice against the Convention and Treaty with Spain," Examined and Answered, London, 1739.
Report from the Committee of Secrecy, Appointed by Order of the House of Commons, to Examine Books and Papers, Relating to Late Negotiations of Peace and Commerce, etc., London, 1715.
Report of a Committee in South Carolina, to Enquire into the Causes of Disappointment, in the Expedition against St. Augustine under General Oglethorpe, London, 1743.
Pulteney, William, Earl of Bath, *A Review of all that Hath Passed between Great Britain and Spain*, London, 1739.
Review of the Short View; and of the Remarks on the Treaty with Spain, London, 1730.
A Series of Wisdom and Policy. . . , London, 1735.
Short View of the Encroachments of France in America, and of the British Commerce with Spain, London, 1758.
Some Observations on Damages done by the Spaniards, London, 1728.

Some Observations on the Assiento Trade as it has been exercised by the South Sea Company, London, 1728.
Spanish Merchant's Address to all Candid and Impartial Englishmen, London, 1739.
State of the Island of Jamaica, chiefly in relation to its commerce and the conduct of the Spaniards in the West Indies, London, 1726.
State of the Province of Georgia Attested upon Oath, in the Court of Savannah, Nov. 10, 1740, American Colonial Tracts, I.
"A Summary of the Title of the English to the Country of Florida," (Endorsed "Dr. Coxe's Paper, Rd. September 18, 1699," Fulham Road, S. W., London).
Tailfer, Patrick; Anderson, Hugh; and Douglas, D., *A True and Historical Narrative of the Colony of Georgia, in America*, Charles Town, 1741.
Thomas, Pascol, *True and Impartial Journal*, London, 1745.
Trade with France, Italy, Spain, and Portugal Considered, London, 1713.
Tratado definitivo de Paz, Madrid, 1749.
Treaty for the Composing of Differences, Restraining of Depredations, and Establishing of Peace in America, between the Crowns of Great Britain and Spain, Concluded at Madrid the 8/18 day of July, . . . 1670, London, 1670.
Treaty of Seville and Four Last Years' Measures Considered, London, 1730.
True Account of the Rise of the South Sea Company, London, 1728.
Vernon, Admiral E., *Specimens of Naked Truth from a British Sailor*, London, 1746.
———, *State of the British Navy*, London, 1744.
View of the Depredations and Ravages Committed by the Spaniards, London, 1731.
View of Political Transactions since Spanish Convention, London, 1739.
Walpole, H., *The Convention Vindicated from the Misrepresentations of the Enemies of Peace*, London, 1739.
———, see also *The Grand Question*. . . .
War Against Spain Declared, London, 1739.
Wilson, S., *Account of the Province of Carolina*, London, 1682.

2. Books

Acts of the Privy Council of England, Colonial Series, London, 1908-1912.
An Analytical Index to the Colonial Documents of New Jersey, in the State Paper Offices of England (vol. V, *Collections of the New Jersey Historical Society*), edited by Henry Stevens, New York, 1858.
Andrews, Charles Francis; Gay, Francis Edwin; Ford, Worthington C.; and Witmore, George Peabody, eds., *Commerce of Rhode*

Island, 1726-1774 (vol. IX, *Colonial Records of Rhode Island*), Providence, 1914.

Ames, Ellis, ed., "Participation of Massachusetts in the Expedition against Carthagena," *Massachusetts Historical Society Proceedings*, March, 1881.

Archives of Maryland, Published by Authority of the State, under the Direction of the Maryland Historical Society, edited by William Hand Browne and Bernard Christian Steiner, 42 vols., Baltimore, 1883-1923.

Bannister, Saxe, ed., *The Writings of William Paterson*, second edition, London, 1859.

[Barcía, A. G.], *Ensayo cronológico para la historia general de la Florida*, Madrid, 1723.

Barnwell, John, "Fort King George, Journal of Col. John Barnwell . . . ," edited by Joseph W. Barnwell, *South Carolina Historical and Genealogical Magazine*, XXVII (1926), 189-203.

Brock, R. A., ed., *The Official Letters of Alexander Spotswood, Lieutenant-Governor of the Colony of Virginia, 1710-1722*, 4 vols., Richmond, Va., 1882-1885.

Calendar of State Papers, Colonial Series, preserved in the Public Record Office, 27 vols., London, 1860-1927.

Calendar of Treasury Books and Papers, 17 vols., London, 1897-1931.

Cobbett, William, *Parliamentary History of England from the Norman Conquest in 1066 to 1803*, 23 vols., London, 1812 (continued from 1803 as *Parliamentary Debates*).

Collections of the Georgia Historical Society, 9 vols., Savannah, 1840-1842.

Colonial Laws of New York, from the year 1664 to the Revolution, compiled by the statutory revision commission, 5 vols., Albany, 1894.

Colonial Records of North Carolina, edited by William L. Saunders, 30 vols., Raleigh, 1886-1890.

The Colonial Records of the State of Georgia, edited by Allan D. Candler, 24 vols., Atlanta, 1904-1915.

Connecticut. See *Public Records of the Colony of Connecticut*.

Coram, Thomas, "The Letters of Thomas Coram," edited by Worthington C. Ford (vol. XVI, *Massachusetts Historical Society Proceedings*), Boston, 1923.

The Correspondence of the Colonial Governors of Rhode Island, 1723-1775, Boston and New York, 1902-1903.

Coxe, Daniel, *Memorial to the Board of Trade, 1719*, in Alvord, C. W. and Bidgood, Lee, *The First Explorations of the trans-Allegheny region by the Virginians*, Cleveland, 1920,

Coxe, William, *Memoirs of the Life and Administration of Sir Robert Walpole, Earl of Orford*, 3 vols., London, 1798.

Documents Relating to the Colonial History of the State of New Jersey, edited by William A. Whitehead, F. W. Ricardo and W. Nelson, 26 vols., Newark, 1880-1903.

Documents Relative to the Colonial History of the State of New York, edited by E. B. O'Callaghan, 15 vols., New York, 1856-1887.

Dumont, Jean, *Corps universal diplomatique du droit des gens, contenant un recueil des traités de paix, d'alliance. . . ,* 8 vols., Amsterdam, 1726, et. seq.

Egmont, Earl of, *Diary,* London, 1923.

Egmont, John Percival, *Manuscripts of the Earl of Egmont,* 3 vols., London, 1930-1923.

Entick, John , *A New Naval History,* London, 1757.

Feame, C., *Minutes of the Proceedings at the Trial of Admiral Sir Charles Knowles,* London, 1750.

Force, Peter (ed.), *Tracts and Other Papers, Relating Principally to the Origin, Settlement and Progress of the Colonies in North America, from the Discovery of the Country to the year 1776,* 4 vols., Washington, 1836, 1838, 1844, 1846.

Gentleman's Magazine, 253 vols., London, 1731-1883.

Georgia. See *Collections of the Georgia Historical Society, Colonial Records of the State of Georgia.*

Glover, Richard, *Memoirs (1742-1757),* London, 1814.

Grant, W. L.; Munro, James; Fitzroy, Sir Almeric W., eds., *Acts of the Privy Council,* vols. I-VI (1613-1783), Hereford, 1910.

Harris, John, *Navigantium atque Itinerantium Bibliotheca, or Complete Collection of Voyages and Travels,* 2 vols., London, 1744-1748.

Hening, William Waller, ed., *Statutes at Large, being a collection of all the laws of Virginia from the first session of the legislature in 1619,* 13 vols., Richmond, 1819-1823.

Hertslet, Lewis, ed., *A Complete Collection of Treaties and Conventions,* 22 vols., London, 1840-1905.

Hewatt, Alexander, *An Historical Account of the Rise and Progress of the Colonies of South Carolina and Georgia,* London, 1779.

Hill, Aaron, *The Works of the Late Aaron Hill,* 4 vols., London, 1753-1754.

Historical Collections of South Carolina, embracing many rare and valuable pamphlets and other documents, relating to the history of that state, from its first discovery to its independence in the year 1776, edited by B. R. Carroll, 2 vols., New York, 1836.

Jeffrys, Thomas, *A Description of the Spanish Islands and Settlements on the Coast of the West Indies,* London, 1774.

Journal of the Commissioners for Trade and Plantations, 1704-1763, 12 vols., London, 1920-1930.

Journal of the Governor and Council (in *Archives of the State of New Jersey*), edited by F. W. Ricardo and W. Nelson, 6 vols., Trenton, 1890-1893.

Journal of the House of Representatives of Massachusetts, edited by Henry Cabot Lodge, W. B. H. Dowse and C. H. Ford, 5 vols., Boston, 1919-1924.

Journals of the Commons House of Assembly, edited by A. S. Salley, 12 vols., Columbia, South Carolina, 1907-1915.

Journals of the Council of Colonial Virginia, edited by H. R. McIlwaine, 3 vols., Richmond, 1918-1919.

Journals of the House of Burgesses of Virginia, 1727-1734, 1727-1740, 1736-1749, edited by H. R. McIlwaine, Richmond, 1900.

Journals of the House of Burgesses of Virginia, 1741-1747, 1748-1749, edited by H. R. McIlwaine, Richmond, 1901.

La Harpe, Jean Francois de, *Abrige de l'Histoire générale des voyages*, 32 vols., Paris, 1780.

Lodge, Sir Richard, *Studies in Eighteenth Century Diplomacy, 1740-1748*, London, 1930.

———, ed., *Private Correspondence of Benjamin Keene*, Cambridge, 1933.

Long, Edward, *Jamaica, General Survey of the Ancient and Modern State of that Island*, London, 1774.

McCall, Captain Hugh, *The History of Georgia, containing Brief Sketches of the Most Remarkable Events up to the Present Day* (1784), Atlanta, 1909.

Marsden, Reginald Godfrey (ed.), *Documents Relating to Law and Custom of the Sea*, 2 vols., London, 1915-1916.

Maryland. See *Archives of Maryland*.

Massachusetts, General Court. *The Charters and General Laws of the Colony and Province of Massachusetts Bay. Carefully collected from the publick records and ancient printed books*, Boston, 1814.

Massachusetts. See also *Journal of the House of Representatives of Massachusetts*.

Minutes of the Common Council of the City of New York, edited by Herbert L. Osgood, 8 vols., New York, 1905.

Minutes of the Executive Council of the Province of New York, edited by Victor Hugo Paltsits, 2 vols., Albany, 1910.

Montiano, Don Manuel de, *Letters addressed to Don Juan Francisco de Güemez y Horcasitas, Governor General of Cuba*, translation in *Collections of the Georgia Historical Society*, VII, Part I, Savannah, 1909.

Nelson, William (ed.), *Documentary History of New York*, 7 vols., New York, 1850.

———, *Some Account of American Newspapers, particularly of the eighteenth century, and libraries in which they may be found*, 3 vols., Paterson, 1893-1897.

New Hampshire. See *Provincial and State Papers of New Hampshire.*
New Jersey. See *Analytical Index to the Colonial Documents of New Jersey, Documents Relating to the Colonial History of the State of New Jersey, Journal of the Governor and Council.*
New York (city). See *Minutes of the Common Council of the City of New York.*
New York (state). See *Colonial Laws of New York, Documents Relative to the Colonial History of the State of New York, Minutes of the Executive Council.*
North Carolina. See *Colonial Records of North Carolina, State Records of North Carolina.*
Norton, B., ed., "Journal of a Privateersman," *Atlantic Monthly*, VIII (1861), 353-59, 417-24.
Pennsylvania Archives, third series, edited by William Henry Egle, 30 vols., Philadelphia, 1896; fourth series, edited by George Edward Reed, 12 vols., Harrisburg, 1900-1902.
Pennsylvania Colonial Records, 1736-1745, edited by Samuel Hazard, 16 vols., Harrisburg, 1853.
Prevost, Antoine Francois, *Histoire générale des voyages ou Nouvelle collection de toutes les relations de voyages par mer et par terre*, 61 vols., Paris, 1746-1761.
Provincial and State Papers of New Hampshire, edited by A. S. Batchellor, N. Bouton, I. W. Hammond, and H. H. Metcalf, 33 vols., Manchester, 1867-1915.
The Public Records of the Colony of Connecticut, edited by J. H. Trumbull and C. J. Hoadly, 15 vols., Hartford, 1850-1890.
Records of the Colony of Rhode Island and Providence Plantations, in New England, edited by John Russell Bartlett, 10 vols., Providence, 1856-1865.
Rhode Island. See also *Correspondence of the Colonial Governors of Rhode Island.*
Salley, A. S., ed., *Journal of the Grand Council of South Carolina*, 2 vols., Columbia, 1907.
"Santiago and the Freeing of Spanish America," *American Historical Review*, IV (January, 1899), 323-38.
Serrano y Sanz, Manuel (ed.), *Documentos Históricos de la Florida y la Luisiana, siglos XVI al XVIII*, Biblioteca de los Americanistas, Madrid, 1912.
Shaw, William A., *Calendar of Treasury Books and Papers*, 6 vols., London, 1897-1906.
Smith, Caleb, *A Geographical Description of the Coasts, Harbours, and Sea Ports of the Spanish West Indies; particularly of Porto Bello, Carthagena, and the Island of Cuba*, London, 1740.
Smollett, Tobias, *Adventures of Roderick Random*, London, 1756.

Smollett, Tobias, *The History of England*, 6 vols., London, 1810, 1811.
South Carolina. See *Historical Collections of South Carolina, Journals of the Commons House of Assembly, Statutes at Large of South Carolina.*
State Records of North Carolina, edited by Walter Clark, 16 vols. (numbered XI-XXVI, following *Colonial Records of North Carolina*), Winston, Goldsboro, and Raleigh, 1895-1905.
The Statutes at Large of South Carolina, edited by Thomas Cooper, 9 vols., Columbia, 1836-1841.
Stephens, William, *A Journal of the Proceedings in Georgia, beginning October 20, 1737*, 3 vols., London, 1742.
Stevens, William Bacon, *A History of Georgia*, 2 vols., Philadelphia, 1859.
———, *A State of the Province of Georgia* (1740), London, 1742.
Thomson, James, *The Seasons*, London, 1730.
Transactions of the Royal Historical Society, fourth series, vols. I-XVI, London, 1918-1933.
Virginia. See *Journals of the Council of Colonial Virginia, Journals of the House of Burgesses of Virginia.*
Walpole, Horace, *Memoirs of the Reign of King George the Second*, London, 1846.
———, *Letters of H. Walpole, Fourth Earl of Orford*, edited by Mrs. Paget Toynbee, 16 vols., Oxford, 1903.
———, *Letters*, edited by C. D. Yonge, 2 vols., London, 1898.
Walpole, Robert, *A Short History of Ten Years' Negotiation, etc.*, 2 vols., London, 1913.
White, Robert, *The Case of the Agent to the Settlers on the Coast of Yucatan; and the Late Settlers on the Mosquito Shore*, London, 1793.
Whitehead, William A., ed., *The Papers of Lewis Morris, Governor of the Province of New Jersey, from 1738-1746* (Collections of the New Jersey Historical Society), New York, 1852.
Williams, A. F. B., *The Life of William Pitt, Earl of Chatham*, 2 vols., London, 1913.
Wood, William, *Occasional Papers on the Assiento and the Affairs of Jamaica*, London, 1716.
Zobáburu, F. de and Rayón, J. S., *Nueva colección de documentos inéditos para la historia de España y de sus Indias*, 6 tomos, Madrid, 1892-1896.

B. SECONDARY AUTHORITIES

Altamira y Crevea, Rafael, *Historia de España y de la civilización española*, 4 vols., Barcelona, 1906-1911.
Armstrong, Edward, *Elizabeth Farnese*, London, 1892.
Bancroft, Hubert Howe, *History of Central America*, 2 vols. (vols. VI-VII in *Works of Hubert Howe Bancroft*), San Francisco, 1883.

BIBLIOGRAPHY

Barrow, Sir John, *The Life of Lord George Anson*, London, 1839.
Baudrillart, Alfred, *Phillippe V et la cour de France*, 6 vols., Paris, 1898.
Becker, Jerónimo, *España é Inglaterra, sus Relaciones desde las Paces de Utrecht*, Madrid, 1906.
Bolton, Herbert E., ed., *Arredondo's Historical Proof of Spain's Title to Georgia*, Berkeley, 1925.
———, and Marshall, Thomas Maitland, *The Colonization of North America*, New York, 1920.
———, and Ross, Mary, *The Debatable Land: A Sketch of the Anglo-Spanish Contest for the Georgia Country*, Berkeley, California, 1925. (Also printed as the Introduction to *Arredondo's Historical Proof of Spain's Title to Georgia*.)
Boyd, W. K., Hamilton, J. G. and Others, *History of North Carolina*, 6 vols., New York, 1919.
Brewster, Dorothy, *Aaron Hill: Poet, Dramatist, Projector*, New York, 1913.
Brisco, Norris Arthur, *The Economic Policy of Robert Walpole*, New York, 1917.
Brooks, A. M., *The Unwritten History of Old St. Augustine, Copied from the Archives in Seville*, St. Augustine, 1909.
Bruce, Henry, *Life of General Oglethorpe*, New York, 1890.
Burdon, Sir John Alder, ed., *Archives of British Honduras*, London, 1931.
Callender, Geoffrey, *Bibliography of Naval History, the Historical Association Leaflet*, No. 61, Part II, London, 1925.
Clowes, Wm. Laird, and Others, *The Royal Navy, a History. . .*, 7 vols., London, 1897-1903.
Coggeshall, George, *History of the American Privateers*, New York, 1861.
Colin, J., *La Projet de débarquement en Angleterre de 1743-1744*, Paris, 1901.
Cooper, Harriet Cornelia, *James Oglethorpe, the Founder of Georgia*, New York, 1904.
Crane, Verner W., *The Southern Frontier*, Durham, 1928.
Deane, Charles, ed., "A Discourse of Virginia," in *American Antiquarian Society Archaeologia Americana*, IV (1860), 67-103.
Dewhurst, W. W., *The History of St. Augustine, Florida*, New York, 1881.
Esdaile, K. A., *Walpole and Chatham, 1714-1760*, London, 1912.
Ewald, A. C., *Representative Statesmen*, London, 1879.
Fairbanks, George R., *The History and Antiquities of the City of St. Augustine, Florida*, New York, 1868.
Forbes, A. W. H., *English History, George I, George II*, London, 1892.

Ford, Douglas, *Admiral Vernon and the Navy*, London, 1907.
Fortescue, Hon. John William, *A History of the British Army*, 11 vols., London, 1899-1923.
Greene, E. B., "The Anglican Outlook on the American Colonies in the Early Eighteenth Century," *American Historical Review*, XX (October, 1914), 64-85.
Guiteras, Dn. Pedro J., *Historia de la Isla de Cuba*, 2 vols., New York, 1865.
Hamilton, E. J., "The Mercantilism of Gerónimo de Uztáriz: A Reëxamination," *Essays in Honor of T. N. Carver*, Cambridge, 1935.
Haring, Clarence Henry, *Trade and Navigation between Spain and the Indies*, Cambridge, 1918.
Harris, Thomas Mason, *Memorials of Oglethorpe*, Boston, 1840.
Hart, A. B., and Channing, E., eds., *American History Leaflets*, nos. 1-32, New York, 1891—.
Hart, Francis Russell, *Admirals Caribbean*, New York, 1922.
———, "The Attacks upon the Spanish Main by Admiral Vernon," *Journal of American History*, II, New Haven, 1908.
———, "The Great Story of the Caribbean Sea," *Journal of American History*, II, New Haven, 1908.
Hassall, A., *Making of the British Empire A. D. 1714-1832*, London, 1896.
Hazeltine, Harold D., "Appeals from Colonial Courts to the King in Council." *Annual Reports of the American Historical Association for 1894* (Washington, 1895), pp. 299-350.
Hertz, G. B., *British Imperialism in the Eighteenth Century*, London, 1908.
Hodge, F. W., *Handbook of American Indians North of Mexico*, 2 vols., Washington, 1907, 1910.
Howland, Edward, *Annals of North America*, London, 1877.
Hunt, William and Poole, Reginald, eds., *The Political History of Great Britain*, 12 vols., London, 1906-1907.
Innes, A. D., *Britian and Her Rivals in the 18th Century, 1712-1789*, London, 1895.
Jameson, John Franklin, ed., *Privateering and Piracy in the Colonial Period*, New York, 1923.
Johnson, J. G., "The Spaniards in Northern Georgia during the Sixteenth Century," *Georgia Historical Quarterly*, IX (June, 1925), 159-68.
———, "The Spanish Period of Georgia and South Carolina History, 1566-1702," *Bulletin of the University of Georgia*, XXIII (1923).
Jones, Charles Colcock, *The English Colonization of Georgia, 1733-1752*, (vol. V, Justin, Winsor, *Narrative and Critical History of America*), Boston and New York, 1887.

———, *History of Georgia*, 2 vols., New York, 1883.
Labra, R. M. de, *La Reforma colonial en las Antilles*, Madrid, 1896.
Lanning, John Tate, "The American Colonies in the Preliminaries of the War of Jenkins' Ear," *The Georgia Historical Quarterly*, XI (June, 1927), 129-55.
———, "American Participation in the War of Jenkins' Ear," *The Georgia Historical Quarterly*, XI (September, 1927), 191-215.
———, "A Descriptive Catalogue of Some Legajos on Georgia in the Spanish Archives," *The Georgia Historical Quarterly*, XIII (December, 1924), 410-21.
———, "Don Miguel Wall and the Spanish Attempt against the Existence of Carolina and Georgia," *North Carolina Historical Review*, X (July, 1933), 186-213.
Laughton, J. K., "Jenkins' Ear," *English Historical Review*, vol. IV, pt. 2 (October, 1889), pp. 741-49.
Lawrence, William Beson, *Visitation and Search*, Boston, 1858.
Lecky, W. E. H., *History of England in the Eighteenth Century*, 7 vols., London, 1892.
Lee, Francis Bagley, *New Jersey as a Colony and as a State*, New York, 1903.
Lodge, Sir Richard, "Sir Benjamin Keene, K. B. : A Study of Anglo-Spanish Relations in the Earlier Part of the Eighteenth Century." *Royal Historical Society Transactions*, 4th ser., XV, 1-43.
McCarthy, J., *A History of the Four Georges and of William IV*, 4 vols., London, 1884-1901.
McCrady, E., *The History of South Carolina under the Royal Government, 1719-1776*, New York, 1899.
Maclay, Edgar Stanton, *A History of American Privateers*, New York, 1899.
Macpherson, David, *Annals of Commerce, Fisheries and Navigation, with Brief Notices of the Arts and Sciences Connected with Them*, London, 1805.
Mahan, A. T., *The Influence of Sea Power upon History, 1660-1783*, Boston, 1893.
Marfil García, M., *Relaciones entre España y la Gran Bretaña desde las paces de Utrecht*, Madrid, 1907.
Marshall, J., *Royal Naval Biography*, 12 vols., London, 1823-1835.
Mereness, N. D., ed., *Travels in the American Colonies*, New York, 1916.
Morley, John, *Walpole*, London, 1909.
Nulle, Stebelton H., *Thomas Pelham-Holles, Duke of Newcastle, His Early Political Career, 1693-1724*, Philadelphia, 1931.
Osgood, Herbert L., *The American Colonies in the Eighteenth Century*, 3 vols., New York, 1924.

Peabody, William B. O., "Life of James Oglethorpe, the Founder of Georgia," (vol. XII, Jared Sparks, ed., *The Library of American Biography*), 1848.

Penson, L. M., "The West Indies and the Spanish-American Trade," *Cambridge History of the British Empire* (7 vols. to date, Cambridge, 1929——), I, 330-45.

Pezuela y Lobo, Jacobo de la, *Historia de la Isla de Cuba*, 4 vols., Madrid, 1868.

Pope, Alexander, *Poetical Works*, 2 vols., Boston, 1851.

Ramsay, David, *History of South Carolina*, 2 vols., Charleston, 1809.

Richmond, Admiral H. W., *The Navy in the War of 1739-1748*, Greenwich, 1920.

Riera y Sanz, P., *España y sus colonias*, Barcelona, 1891.

Rivers, W. J., *A Sketch of the History of South Carolina to the Close of the Proprietary Government by the Revolution of 1719*, Charleston, 1856.

Root, J. W., *Spain and Its Colonies*, London, 1898.

Roscher, Wilhelm Georg Friedrich, *The Spanish Colonial System*, New York, 1904.

Russell, Elmer Beecher, *The Review of American Colonial Legislation by the King in Council*, New York, 1915.

Scharf, J. Thomas, *History of Maryland*, 3 vols., Baltimore, 1879.

Scheidnagel, M., *Colonización española*, Madrid, 1893.

Seeley, J. R., *The Expansion of England*, London, 1883.

Sharpless, Isaac, *A Quaker Experiment in Government*, 2 vols., Philadelphia, 1898-1899.

Sinclair, John, *The History of the Public Revenue of the British Empire*, London, 1785.

Stover, Malcom, "Vernon Medals," *Massachusetts Historical Society Proceedings*, vol. LII (1918-1919), Boston, 1924.

Tejada, M. Lerdo de, *Commercio Esterior de México*, 1853.

Temperley, H. W. V., "The Relations of England with Spanish America," 1720-1744, *Annual Report of the American Historical Association for 1911* (Washington, 1913), I, 229-37.

———, "Causes of the War of Jenkins' Ear," *Royal Historical Society Transactions*, 3rd ser. (London, 1909), III, 197-236.

Tiverton, Hardenge Goulburn Gifford, *The Principles and Practice of Prize Law*, London, 1914.

Tyerman, Luke, *The Life and Times of Rev. John Wesley*, 3 vols., New York, 1872.

Vattel, Emmerich de, *The Law of Nations, or Principles of the Law of Nature, Applied to the Conduct and Affairs of Nations and Sovereigns*, Philadelphia, 1817.

Vaucher, P., *Robert Walpole et la Politique de Fleury, 1731-1742*, Paris, 1924.

Vernon, William Frederick, *Memorial of Admiral Vernon*, London, 1861.
Villa, Rodríguez, *Patiño y Campillo, reseña histórica biográfica de estos dos ministros de Felipe V, formada con documentos y papeles inéditos y desconocidos en su mayor parte*, Madrid, 1882.
"A Voyage to Georgia," *Collections of the Georgia Historical Society*, I, 80-152.
Washburne, George Adrian, *Imperial Control of the Administration of Justice in the Thirteen American Colonies, 1684-1776*, New York, 1923.
Wood, G. A., *William Shirley, 1741-1756*, New York, 1920.
Wright, Irene A., "Spanish Policy towards Virginia," *American Historical Review*, XXV (April, 1920), 448-79.
Wright, Robert, *A Memoir of General James Oglethorpe, one of the earliest reformers of prison discipline in England, and the founder of Georgia, in America*, London, 1867.

INDEX

Abaria, Don Estéban, 173. *See also* Habaria
Aberdeen, merchants' petitions from against the Convention of Pardo, 156
Admiralty, Court of, 132
Alabamas, members of Creek Confederacy, 85, 106
Albany Congress of 1754, 10
Altamaha, 4, 7, 11, 13, 14, 16, 17, 19, 26, 29, 30, 32, 34, 93, 160; occupation of the mouth of, 10; fortified, 10; navigation of, 17; fort on, 23; Spaniards refuse to relinquish, 36; Scotch settlement on, 37; erection of forts inside of urged by Trustees, 85; English title to, 231
Amelia Island, 40; highlanders killed on, 222; fortifications on strengthened, 222
America, interlopers of sacrificed, 177; potentialities of mainland colonies of, 182
American regiment, 213, 217; inadequate commissions for, 196; illness in, 212
American Revolution, 191
American Treaty of 1670, 2, 19, 110, 119, 149-50, 165, 172; marks adoption of principle of effective occupation, 19; English possessions at the time of, 26; historical meaning of perverted, 29; Spanish delegates required to negotiate on basis of in 1730, 30; alleged infraction of, 103; no concrete basis for adjustment, 116; defied by Jamaicans, 128; Spanish representatives revert to, 169
American troops, 207, 208; suspected, 193; sail for Jamaica, 200; sail from Capes of Virginia, 204; regimented under Gooch, 204; take to cover at Cartagena, 209; reputation of defended, 210; called Banditti, 210; held up to opprobrium, 215; proposed settlement in Cuba, 216
Anastasia Island, 224, 225
Anglo-French rivalry, 9
Anglo-Spanish rivalry, 9; diplomacy, 17
Antin, Marquis d', French fleet under called to protect Spanish flota, 166
Apalache, 23

Apalachicola, 24; English plan to build a fort in, 30
Aranjuez, 145
Archer, Henry, Georgia Trustee, 151, 152, 153; labors to defend Georgia, 150; refuses to support Walpole before the Convention of Pardo, 150
Armada de Barlovento, use of in projected attack on Georgia, 64; commander of, 76
Arredondo, Don Antonio de, engineer, 51, 52; attacks "Observations," 18; abruptly sent to St. Augustine by the governor of Havana, 45; writes letter to Oglethorpe, 46; calls upon Oglethorpe to evacuate coast to St. Helena Sound, 46; draws up Treaty of 1736, 47; renders lengthy account of his stewardship, 48; mentioned by Don Miguel Wall, 77
Arredondo-Oglethorpe agreement, 52. *See also* Oglethorpe-Moral Sánchez Treaty
Arundel, Earl of, patents and grants of, 4
Asao, Spain demands restoration of, 149
Asiento Contract, 130, 139, 218, 233; meaning of, 128; signed, 128; losses involved in, 129; provisions of, 129; La Quadra insists upon Spanish right to suspend, 147; suspended, 178
Asiento de Negros, 147
Atlantic coast, Spanish right to, 85
Augusta, 222
Augusta River, Wentworth's camp on, 214
Austria, 28, 231
Ayola y Escobar, Don Juan de, 27
Azilia, Margravate of, 7-9; fantastic project for a buffer colony, 7; becomes bubble, 9

Bahama Channel, 14, 100, 183; trade, 220
Bahamas, 28, 127, 170, 200
Baradera fascine battery, 205
Barba, Captain Antonio, 227
Barbados, 127
Barcía, Andrés González de, 6, 75, 163
Barnard, Sir John, 157

Barnwell, Colonel John, 7, 10, 11, 12, 19, 32; advocates and defends southern march, 9; influences border policy, 10; designs and undertakings of, 30
Bath, Earl of. *See* William Pulteney
Bathhurst, Earl of, 160
Battery de Chamba, 206
Bayard, Captain, near Santiago, Cape Verde Islands, 190
Bedford, Duke of, 231; takes Newcastle's place, 231
Benavides y Bazán, Governor Antonio de, 13, 14, 20; faces problem of English encroachments, 7; complains against English excesses, 11; sends Spanish officer to reconnoitre Fort King George, 14; demands return of Spanish Indians held as slaves, 15; complains against excesses of Indians of English allegiance, 23; takes depositions for diplomatic comedy of 1725, 24
Bermuda, 99
Bermudas, 127
Biscayans, fishing rights of in Newfoundland, 131
Bizarrón y Eguiarreta, Juan de, Viceroy of Mexico, defaults in Miguel Wall campaign, 76
Bladen, Colonel Martin, 16, 153, 164; labors to defend Georgia, 150; writes best defense of English title to Georgia, 164-65
Blakeney, Colonel William, 191, 194, 198, 199, 200, 204; named Adjutant General, 193; brings supplies for Americans, 193-94
Bland, Colonel Humphrey (?), regiment of, 207
Bloody Marsh, 227, 228
Board of Trade, 9, 10, 17, 19, 29, 30, 32, 129, 233; considers Carolina expansion, 16; takes vigorous stand, 19; investigates English title, 28; prepares to defend southern rivers, 34; petitioned to appoint a governor for the Bay of Campeachy, 128; designated to receive claims of British subjects, 132
Boca Chica Castle, 206, 207
Bolingbroke, Henry St. John Viscount, attempts to ruin the Convention of Pardo by a *coup de théatre*, 156-57
Bonitta, convoys troops to Ruatan, 217
Boston, defense of, 186; fits out vessels, 187; troops collected at, 200
Boston Post Boy, characterizes capture of Porto Bello, 204
Boston Weekly News-Letter, 187, 211
Boundaries. *See* Limits

Boyne, 216
Bray, Dr. Thomas, philanthropy of, 32
Brest, French fleet forced to return to, 205
Breton's Point, 188
Brims, Creek Indian, 30; takes neutral stand, 30; political acumen of commended, 31; policy of duplicity of, 31; plied with presents, 31
Bristol, merchants' petitions from against the Convention of Pardo, 156
Bristowe, agent, 139
British Honduras, basis of, 217
British Merchant, 127
Broughton, Thomas, Governor of South Carolina, 75; begins furious correspondence in fear of Wall expedition, 64; informs the Duke of Newcastle of Spanish designs, 66; signifies to Trustees his intention to coöperate in thwarting the Spanish design, 66
Budon, Stephen, affidavit from, 226
Bull, Governor William of South Carolina, 226; called upon to aid Oglethorpe, 221; two letters from, 226
Burrell, agent, 139

Cabot, Sebastian, 3
Cádiz, 76, 78, 82, 96, 97; consul at to keep Wall under surveillance, 58, 59; consul at refuses to harbor Wall, 78; ships move from under utmost secrecy, 123
Caledonia Indians, 216
Calumet, smoked by Oglethorpe, 221
Campeachy, logwood cutting along the bays of, 127, 177
Campeche, 28. *See also* Campeachy
Canada, 186, 192; intelligences of the French and Indian expedition from, 221
Canadees, possible French use of, 183
Canzo, Governor Gonzalo Méndez, discloses English designs on the coast, 2
Cape Fear, defenses of increased, 187; troops delayed at, 199; petition for a man-of-war on, 202
Capes of Virginia, 200, 204; rendezvous of Americans at, 197, 199
Cardross, Henry Erskine Lord, 8, 9
Carribbean Sea, 127, 181, 182, 188, 218; important economic center of, 174
Carolana, 4; permanent foundations of, 5
Carolina, 53, 76, 98, 100, 140, 183, 186, 220, 230, 234; proprietors of, 5, 8, 31, 63; English possession of, 93; Spanish claim to dropped, 102; claimed by Spaniards to 33° 30'

north latitude, 120; Spanish claim to, 136; limits of, 151, 177; charters of a basis of English title to Georgia, 155
Carolinians, 15; anti-Spanish feeling of, 32
Cartagena, 127, 192, 201, 205, 208, 209, 211, 218; campaign against, 83; fiasco at, 181; battle at, 207; discipline vanishes at, 211
Carteret, John Lord, 15, 16, 17, 18, 19; sends restraining orders to South Carolina, 12; "No search" speech of, 138
Carvajal, 233
Castle Hill, 188
Castres, Abraham, 165, 168, 173, 176; consul-general in Spain, 146; serves with Keene as English plenipotentiary, 146; supplies the Spanish with English pretensions, 170
Cathcart, Charles Lord, 191, 192, 193, 196, 216; expedition against Spanish West Indies under, 191, 192; instructions to, 192; death of reported, 204
Caufield, Major, 217; desires to have Americans sent away, 217
Causton, Thomas, machinating bailiff of Savannah, 64
Cavendish, fighting men of, 207
Cayley, Consul William, 82; reports on Wall, 59; receives Don Miguel Wall, 76; reports Spaniards sending storeship and four hundred men, 96; reports negotiations of 1739 broken up, 166
Chagres, smuggling at, 127
Champeaux, M., French ambassador in Madrid, 122
Chancery Lane, war celebrations at, 179
Charing Cross, war celebrations at, 179
Charles I, King of England, 4
Charles II, King of England, 4, 5, 20, 119, 121, 126, 164; donates St. Augustine, 34
Charles II, King of Spain, 2, 5
Charles Town, 15, 19, 20, 26, 27, 31, 35, 159, 165, 227; assembly at prepares to defend the Altamaha, 11; Spanish claim to, 18; diplomatic mission to, 25; attacked by La Fibaer, 27; inhabitants of to be denied belligerent status by the Spaniards, 53; lawless trader of arouses Indians, 92; built before the Treaty of 1670, 106
Cherokees, 31, 222, 231; runners dispatched to, 64; complain of epidemic of smallpox, 222; hastily invade Florida, 223-24

Chetwynd, Walter, 16.
Chickasaws, 230, 231; threaten English plantations, 185; complain of an epidemic of smallpox, 222; burn Fort Picolata, 223
Chicken, Colonel George, 31
Choctaws, 231; possible French use of, 183; in amity with the French, 220
Cider House, 101
Claims, 133, 139, 233. *See also* Pardo, Convention of, and South Sea Company
Clarendon, Edward Earl of, 164, 165
Clark, Lieutenant Governor George, 198, 202; responds to Oglethorpe's request for aid, 60; called upon to aid Oglethorpe, 221
Cocke, Leonard, Royal Asiento Factor at Santiago, reports Wall's arrival to Digby Dent, 62
Colbert, Jean Baptiste, mercantilism of, 131; ideas of exploited by Uztáriz, 131
Colonization, English, 2
Coltrain, family, in War of Jenkins' Ear, 195
Commissaries, 115; question of limits referred to by Treaty of Seville, 96
Connecticut, 188, 199, 202; enlistment in, 187; offers bounties for enlistment, 195; troops from collect, 200; troops of in War of Jenkins' Ear, 206
Convention of The Hague, 15
Coram, Thomas, of religious-minded faction of Trustees, 33
Corsica, 142
Council at Boston, 187
Council of the Indies, 14, 16, 20, 24, 75, 146; reviews English position on Georgia, 112-13; *consultas* of, 116
Coweta, the rivalry for control of, 30; three hundred English display their standards at, 89; English trader in, 106; dramatic visit of Oglethorpe to, 221
Coxe, Dr. Daniel, 29; patents and grants of, 4
Crane, Verner W., cited, 7
Creek-Cherokee feud, 31
Creeks, 30, 31, 222, 231; dependence of on Spain, 26; policy of, 26; vital problem of, 33; runners dispatched to, 64; support the English, 222; burn Fort Picolata, 223; hastily invade Florida, 223-24
Cromwell, Oliver, 192
Crookshanks, John, secretary to commissaries of 1730, 132
Cuba, 127; Anglo-American plan to seize, 182; in jeopardy, 188; collapse of English Expedition in, 215; British

subjects in, 234
Cumberland Harbor, 213; abandoned by the English, 214
Cumberland Island, 40
Cumberland Sound, Spanish fleet enters, 227
Cupar, merchants' petitions from against the Convention of Pardo, 156
Curaçao, smuggling center, 128; Dutch depot of Caribbean, 144

D'Arcy, Don Manuel, 41, 45
Darien, 34, 44
Darién, experiment at, 127
Darkins, John, prisoner of a Spanish *guarda costa*, 65; depositions of concerning Miguel Wall, 65
De Brahm, John Gerrar William, *Survey of America*, 235
Defense, sloop, 188
De Foe, Daniel, lends pen to opposition polemics, 28; recommends war with Spain, 127
De León, Juan Ponce, 3
Dempsey, Charles, 36, 39, 40, 45, 48; mission to St. Augustine, 36-37; civil reception of in St. Augustine, 37; suavity of, 37, 41, 42; handsomely supported by the Trustees, 42; draws up Treaty of 1736, 47; arrangement of approved by the Trustees, 47; berates Walpole, 163
Dent, Digby, 64, 95; receives Leonard Cocke's tidings of Wall, 62; reports a considerable Spanish force preparing to attack Georgia, 65
Depredations, 88, 95, 135, 137-38, 175, 179; the Elizabethan tradition of "beyond the line," 2; protests against Spanish, 113; of the *guarda costas*, 114; begin to figure in Anglo-Spanish affairs, 131; laid at feet of Elizabeth Farnese, 134; alleged priority of, 170
Desertion, in Northern Colonies, 198-99
De Soto, Hernando, 3
Dieppe, Don Miguel Wall lands at, 55
Docminique, Paul, 16
Dinwiddie, Robert, reports American resources, 181
Doña María Bay, Vernon anchors at, 205
Drake, Sir Francis, raid of, 4, 20, 93, 188, 214; raid of the title of England to St. Augustine, 47
Dunbar, Lieutenant George, 227; accompanies Oglethorpe to Coweta, 221; attacks Fort St. Francis de Popa, 223; attacks Fort Picolata, 223; holds Fort Diego, 224; captain at Fort William, rebuffs Spanish fleet, 227
Dundee, merchants' petitions from against the Convention of Pardo, 156
Dutch, 121; seek English coöperation, 113; move of La Quadra to prevent making common cause with English, 122
Duxburg, family, in War of Jenkins' Ear, 195

Edinburgh, merchants' petitions from against the Convention of Pardo, 156
Effective Occupation, theory of, 19, 29, 119, 136-37, 165; triumph of theory of, 235
Egmont, Earl of, 152, 160, 163; *Diary* of, 92; labors to defend Georgia, 150; asks that question of Georgia be separated from all other questions, 154
Elibank, Lord, 191; pays his respect to the colonial troops, 208
Elizabeth Farnese, 124; baleful influence of, 28; conniving of, 134; accused of promoting depredations, 134; reviews *pacte de famille*, 230
El Pardo, 118. *See also* Pardo, Convention of
England, logwood cutters from, 127; irreconcilable position of, 166, 167, 170; king of demands war, 178
English, shirking-and-delaying tactics of, 19-25, 91, 94; ecclesiastical imperialism of, 32; excesses of in the Georgia country, 71
Enlistments. *See* Recruiting
Escamacu, Spain demands restoration of, 149
Escorial, agreement of, 144
Escudero, Friar Joseph Ramón, 34
Española, 100
Excise Bill, excitement in House occasioned by compared to that of the Convention of Pardo, 157
Eyre, Cadet, accompanies Oglethorpe to Coweta, 221

Fairfax, Anne, marries Lawrence Washington, 219
Falmouth, Wall lands at, 79, 80, 81
Fandino, Juan de León, Spanish captain, credited with Jenkins' Ear, 145; mutilates Jenkins, 176
Faskey, Oglethorpe drinks, 221
Ferdinand VI, 230, 231
Fiesta religiosa, 169
Fitch, Tobias, incites Creeks, 31
Fleury, Cardinal, 146; in a good dispo-

sition for a rupture between Spain and England, 144
Florida, 30, 35, 36, 100, 103, 111, 140, 146, 170, 200; "Continent of,'" 3; extent of settlements in, 4; Carolinian mistrust of, 16; in the Georgia grant, 34; border of threatened by a Creek Indian attack, 38; defense of, 48; governor of to attack Florida, 60; limits of, 80, 90, 115, 151; strengthened, 87; abandoned by Spain, 235
Floridas, provinces of ceded to Great Britain, 234
Fort Diego, repossessed by Oglethorpe, 223; premature attacks on, 224
Fort Frederica, 34, 44, 163, 225, 227, 228; building of, 32; attack upon planned, 39; erection of proposed by Trustees, 86; auspiciously located to watch the galleons, 86
Fort King George, 9-17, 19, 21, 24, 25, 26, 28, 34, 35, 41, 89, 92, 121; uncertainty of, 4; foreshadows buffer colony, 9; abandonment of, 11, 32; erection of, 13; hardships at, 13; Spanish officer calls at, 15; function of, 16; proposed demolition of, 21-22; Grimaldo presses case against, 23; rebuilding provided for, 27; burning of investigated, 27
Fort Mansanilla, 207
Fort Moosa. *See* Moosa
Fort Picolata. *See* Picolata
Fort St. Andrews, 44, 163
Fort St. Francis de Popa (Pupo), 51, 121; attacked by Dunbar, 223; repossessed by Oglethorpe, 223; invested, 223; premature attacks on, 224
Fort St. George, 120, 184; bitter Spanish memorials against, 46; agreement to abandon, 47; Arredondo looks with alarm upon, 52; crux of the Spanish grievance, 119
Fort St. Joseph, 206
Fort San Felipe, 206
Fort San Lázaro, 208
Fort San Luis, 206
Fort San Marcos, 23, 89, 91, 106
Fort Santiago, 206
Fort William, 227; attacked, 228
France, 185
French, 35; encircling movement of, 9, 10
French Guinea Company, 128
French-Indian diplomacy, 31
"Friend No. 101," a spy of Keene, 125, 161
Fury, Peregrine, agent of province of Georgia, 65

Gascoigne, Captain John (?), of the *Hawk*, 41
George I, King, 11, 34
Georgia, 35, 36, 48, 53, 63, 71, 86, 97, 101, 102, 110, 111, 113, 117, 118, 137-38, 146, 147, 151, 153, 155, 160, 161, 183, 184, 187, 222, 230, 232, 234; propaganda of, 8; first English settlement in, 13; English title to, 19; limits of, 20, 21, 112, 146, 177; between Fort King George and Florida, 26; confines of, 34; naming of, 34; charter of, 34; defense of, 48, 49, 65; political strength of faction of, 50; regiment to be sent to, 50; charter of, 53, 86; colony of a menace to Florida, 55; attack against discovered, 62; report of preparations for attack on, 65; committee of assembly of appeals to agent of the province, 65; strength of, 65; possible loss of, 65; limits of, 70, 80; political pressure of Trustees of, 74; fever of anxiety in, 75; Spanish intention of attacking leaks out, 80; flat-bottomed boats for attack upon, 82; threat to Spain, 85; inhabitants of build fort at mouth of "River St. Simon," 88; Trustees of answer Geraldino's memorial in accordance with their own predilections, 90, 91; English possession of, 93; forts in, 93; a Parliamentary project, 94; memorials contesting the right to, 95; faction of runs over the ministry, 100; settlement of by English subjects, 102; forts in disagreeable to Spaniards, 103; suspension of demanded, 103; ports of command homeward passage from the Indies, 105; British title to, 109; to receive a battalion from Gibraltar, 110; Spain's reasons for opposing, 111; Spanish request evacuation of and the demolition of the forts prior to the conferences, 115-21; English right to, 114, 119; "usurped by the English nation," 136; Spanish claim to, 136, 162; not to be abandoned prior to discussions, 137; forts in, 140; matters in to remain *in statu quo*, 142; reports and papers relating to the English right to, 148; as a political pawn, 150; considered a debit, 150; rumor of surrender of, 150, 151, 152, 153, 154-55; subsidy to, 151; defended in pamphlets, 158; negotiations about, 168; defense propaganda of, 183-84; levies in not

permitted during War of Jenkins' Ear, 194; baffles the Spaniards for four years, 220; the debatable land in dangerous proximity of to St. Augustine and Havana, 220; troops of defend home base, 220; a regiment ordered to, 221; precarious situation in, 223; menaced, 226; invasion of, 226; bemoanings of, 226; imperiled at St. Simons, 226; left *in statu quo*, 235. *See also* Trustees, Board of Georgia Grant Company, 5

Georgians, gain fresh ground below the Altamaha, 116; fever of, 173

Geraldino, Don Tomás, Spanish minister, 6, 53, 70, 74, 75, 80, 81, 87, 88, 90, 94, 97, 99, 100, 101, 108, 112, 115, 117, 118, 136, 137, 139, 140, 141, 142, 144, 151, 159, 160, 161; blustering nature of his remonstrances, 35; "blustering memorials" of, 50, 101; depends upon adroit manipulation of opposition politics, 50; recommends expulsion of South Sea Company factors, 63; learns English had discovered the Spanish aims, 63; offices of go unanswered, 67; memorial of, 68; activities of in London, 69; urges bellicose attitude towards England, 71; ordered to deny reports of impending attack on Georgia, 71; reports English ministry hostile to Georgia, 71; laments success of the military efforts of Oglethorpe, 73; discovers Walpole's plan to support Oglethorpe, 73; diligence of, 79; investigates landing of Wall at Falmouth, 80; lays complaints of his government before English ministry in 1736, 85; friendship with Newcastle and Walpole, 88; succeeds Montijo as minister plenipotentiary in London, 88; pro-British leanings of, 88; attempts orally to undermine Oglethorpe, 90; memorial of shock to Newcastle, 90; complaisant disposition of, 90; displays his inquietude to Newcastle, 91; interviews Walpole, 94; becomes Spanish minister to England, 96-97; hopes to force a wedge between the Trustees and the English ministry, 98; receives instructions for a second memorial, 101; second memorial of, 102-4; drops claim to Carolina, 102; threatens force, 103, 107, 111; convinced of the justice of the Spanish cause in Georgia, 105; mentions abandonment of Fort King George, 106; presses the right of Spain to all Georgia, 106; overt threat, 107; memorials of mentioned in the papers, 108; "very extraordinary memorial" of, 108; the vigorous memorial his idea, 109; reasonably satisfied with the reply to his memorial, 110; office of creates amazed uncertainty, 111; supplies La Quadra with English reply to his overture, 112; papers relating to memorial of, 114; new polemic instructions sent to, 116; disobedience of investigated, 117; reports London rumors of a Spanish attack on Georgia, 140; gives out that his court would on no account acquiesce in the English possession of Georgia, 160; peremptorily ordered to return home, 179; disgraced in Spain, 179; compared to Gundemar, 179; makes absolute claim to 33° 50', 232

Germany, 232

Gibraltar, surrender of rumored, 16; battalion ordered sent from, 110; English unwilling to surrender, 231

Gibraltar, convoys languid and infirm back to mainland colonies, 219

Glasgow, merchants' petitions from against the Convention of Pardo, 156

Glen, Governor James of South Carolina, 233; decries anti-Spanish alarms, 233

Glover, Charlesworth, 31

Goddard, John, commissioner in 1730 for settling Carolina boundary question, 29, 132

Goldolphin, Sir William, signs American Treaty, 165

Gómara, Francisco López de, name of exploited to uphold English claims, 3

Gooch, Colonel William, 191, 199, 201, 204; returns of regiment of, 191, 217; takes Spotswood's place, 199; sails to Jamaica ahead of Colonel Blakeney, 200; succeeds Spotswood, 201

Gough, Señor Hen., 163

Grant, Colonel, grenadiers of, 207; death of, 209; philippic of, 209

Great Britain, takes strong stand to hold lands, 139

Greene, Captain Daniel, daughter of marries Don Miguel Wall, 55

Grimaldo, Marqués de, 14, 16, 19, 23; begins diplomatic defense of Spanish Georgia, 12

Guadalquina, Spain demands restoration of, 149

Guale, 20; claim of the English to, 30; Spain demands restoration of, 149

Guarda Costas, 130, 131, 175; depredations of the, 114; Spanish governors connive with, 133; increasing vigi_

lance of, 134; English attempt to curb, 149
Güemez y Horcasitas, Juan Fernando de, governor of Havana, 48, 50, 59, 61, 75; thanks Oglethorpe for reception of Arredondo, 52; lays bold plan of surprise attack against Georgia before Torrenueva, 52; supervises projected attack on Georgia, 59; judges Wall unworthy of trust, 61; gives orders for Georgia-Carolina expedition, 75; receives orders to stay Wall expedition, 82; dispatches fleet and eight thousand men to Florida, 227
Guipuscoans, fishing rights of in Newfoundland, 131
Guise, Brigadier John, 212
Gulf of Mexico, 9, 59, 164
Gundemar, compared to Geraldino, 179

Habaria, Don Estéban de, 167; Spanish plenipotentiary after the Convention of Pardo, 148; instructed to negotiate on basis of American Treaty, 149
Haddock, Admiral Sir Nicholas, 139, 162; fleet of ordered to Mediterranean, 138; withdrawn from Mediterranean, 162; 162; ordered back to Mediterranean, 162; presence of menaces negotiations, 166; recall of, 171; ordered to Spain's back door, 178
Hague, The, 113
Hague Gazette, reports anti-Spanish agitation of the Trustees, 232
Halberdiers, major of aids Miguel Wall, 55, 56
Hales, Dr. Stephen, 101
Hampton Court, Geraldino at, 112
Harley, Robert, 128
Harrington, William Stanhope Earl of, Secretary of War, 139, 142; receives Geraldino's second memorial, 102
Hastings, Theophilus, 30
Havana, 63, 66, 68, 76, 98, 103, 110, 192, 213, 218, 220; preparations in to re-annex Georgia, 50; Spanish designs at, 53; military preparations in, 56; English factors in, 61; presidial soldiers suggested to attack Georgia, 64; naval preparations reported in, 65; Spanish vessels at, 65; governor of, 82; campaign against, 83; governor of called upon to aid in defense of St. Augustine, 87; garrison at, 97; preparations at, 134; original object of the invading expedition, 205;
boom chain thrown across the mouth of the harbor at, 205; expedition against, 212; Spanish squadron delayed at, 220; Spanish strength at, 221; St. Augustine galleys at, 223; exchanged for Floridas, 234
Hawkins, Sir John, 214
Heath, Sir Robert, 29; patents and grants of, 4, 5, 164
Heathcote, George, 160; wishes to be rid of Georgia, 150
Heathcote, Sir William, 101, 152
Henry VII, King, 3
Hermsdorf, Captain, 39
Heron, Major, reënforces Oglethorpe, 229
Herreda, Don Alonzo Fernández de, sends dragoons to expel English, 234
Herrera y Tordesillas, Antonio de, name of exploited to uphold English claims, 3
Hill, Aaron, 9; Azilia projector, 8
Hispanic America, strategic ports of, 126
Hispaniola, 127, 215; Anglo-American plan to seize, 182
Hodgson, Captain, 216
Holton, family, in War of Jenkins' Ear, 195
Honduras, vessels from menaced, 61; logwood cutting along the bays of, 127
Hopkins, Captain, 215
Horton, Major William, 38, 40, 41, 227; arrested by Spaniards, 39; returns to Frederica, 39; examined by Moral Sánchez, 40
Hosier, Vice-Admiral Francis, memorable expedition of, 132; holds instructions to capture Spanish fleet, 132
House of Commons, 69, 155, 156; inundated with petitions against Spanish maritime onslaughts, 131; stirring resolutions of, 131; bellicose resolutions of, 138
House of Lords, debates on the convention, 155
Hucks, Robert, 160; wishes to be rid of Georgia, 150
Hyllispilli, Chief, 43; seeks revenge against Spaniards, 43

Indentured servants, enlistment of, 197; in War of Jenkins' Ear, 204
Indians, 16, 35, 66, 85, 188, 220; excesses of, 13, 18, 22; Newcastle urges alliance with, 66; summoned at Coweta to demolish Fort San Marcos, 106; used by English to make

doubtful case, 121
Innes, family, in War of Jenkins' Ear, 195
Iras Bay, Vernon anchors at, 205
Irish Catholics, 208; as Papists unfit to fight, 193
Irish servants, 202
Isla de Providencia, Spain demands restoration of, 149

Jacobites, movement of in England, 156
Jamaica, 76, 98, 99, 188, 192, 204, 212, 214, 215; proposed attack on, 58; vessels from menaced, 61; war vessels at, 71; English intention of sending six hundred men from to join Oglethorpe's command, 111; subjected to Negro insurrections, 111; smuggling of sloops of, 127; value of sloop trade of, 127; logwood cutters from, 127; governors of charged with raising 500 Negroes, 192; English officers resolve to return to, 212; trade of, 213; British return to, 215
Jamaicans, in War of Jenkins' Ear, 206; in attack on Fort San Lázaro, 208
Jamestown, 7, 34, 35
Jekyl, Sir Joseph, forward in affairs of Georgia, 104
Jekyl Island, plantation on destroyed, 228
Jekyl Sound, 40
Jenkins, Robert, in Parliament, 144; ear of, 145, 174; psychological influence of, 145; mutilated, 176-77; influence of incident of, 177
John, 190
Johnson, Governor Robert, 32; granted £2,000 to rebuild Fort King George, 27
Johnston, Governor Gabriel, of North Carolina, 195, 202; warns against Indian attack, 185; delays N. C. troops at the Cape Fear, 199
Journal, of the Earl of Egmont, 151
Journal of the Sloop Revenge, 187

Keene, Benjamin, English minister, 28, 50, 58, 66, 70, 71, 79, 83, 94, 96, 99, 101, 110, 112, 113, 114, 115, 116, 117, 118, 119, 130, 131, 135, 136, 138, 141, 142, 144, 145, 149, 162, 165, 166, 168, 173, 175, 176, 177, 230, 233, 234; commissioner in 1730 for settling Carolina boundary question, 29, 132; reveals English knowledge of Wall to La Quadra, 67; relies on La Quadra's probity, regards Spanish as unable to support an expensive campaign in 1737, 68; agent of South Sea Company in Madrid, 69; unable to run down rumors of on Georgia, 71; reports greater moderation in Spanish counsels, 72; marvels at liberties of Don Miguel Wall, 77; renders account of the Wall affair, 82; presents bundles of claims for ships, 84; urges appointment of Geraldino, 96; sounds La Quadra on an American expedition, 107; reports newspaper accounts of Geraldino's memorial, 108; says Spanish claims were without foundation, 109; strikes note of mildness, 109; suggests settlement of boundaries by commissioners, 109; reports that Spain was never in worse condition for attacking the English, 114; thinks Spain unprepared to fight, 116; appraises Torrenueva, 124; fat, good-natured, agreeable, resolute and adroit, 125; official title of, 125; signs Treaty of Seville, 125; Minister Plenipotentiary, 125; agent of South Sea Company, 125-26; consul general at Madrid, 125; goes to Portugal, 125; exalted to the rank of ambassador, 125; tardiness of government in conferring Order of Bath, 125; his most important diplomatic undertaking, the Convention of Pardo, 125; serves in Parliament for Maldon in Essex and Looe in Cornwall, 125; the most important English ambassador in Spain during eighteenth century, dies in Madrid, 125; reproached by Spanish government, 142; attempts to restrict subjects for discussion, 143; English plenipotentiary, 146; contemptuous reference to, 157; pays his respects to the Spanish officials, 162; supplies the Spanish with English pretensions, 170; ordered to return home; ambassador to Portugal given credentials as ambassador extraordinary, 230; thrust anew into Spanish diplomacy, 231; refused the Order of Bath, 234
Kettleby, Amos, Azilia projector, 8
Kinghorn, merchants' petitions from against the Convention of Pardo, 156
Kingston, smuggling at, 127
King William's War, American participation in, 192
Knowles, Admiral Sir Charles, 191, 200

La Fibaer, attacks Charles Town, 27
La Marck, Louis Pierre Engilbert

INDEX 265

Comte de, French ambassador, 147; warns the English of the heat of the Spaniards, 172
Lamberto Rotinello, Don Pedro, 37, 41, 43; humorously suggests Santa Helena River as Florida boundary, 45
La Mina, Marques de, Spanish ambassador in France, 122, 144, 145, 146
Lancaster, merchants' petitions from against the Convention of Pardo, 156
La Popa Hill, advantage of overlooked by Wentworth, 209
La Quadra, Don Sebastián de, 63, 70, 71, 72, 74, 75, 82, 96, 97, 101, 107, 108, 109, 110, 113, 114, 116, 118, 122, 130, 134, 136, 139, 141, 142, 143, 144, 149, 163, 171, 177; pretends ignorance of reports of armaments, 67; vehemently denies projected Wall attack, 67; disapproves Oglethorpe-Moral Sánchez Treaty, 67; regards Georgia as a private grant to a company of adventurers, 67; coaches Torrenueva on Georgia, 68; denies preparations at Havana, 68; denies knowledge of Wall, 72; requests answer to Geraldino's memorial, 72; removes suspicion of Spanish attack, 73; orders study of Georgia question, 75; denies Spanish attack on any part of his Britannic Majesty's possessions, 97; denies preparations against Georgia, 105, 106, 108, 110; interviewed by Keene, 109; remits English reply to Geraldino's memorial to Count Montijo, 112; decides to suspend expedition preparing under the governor of Havana, 113; pacific disposition of ministry of, 113; uncertainty of, 114; declares himself unable to report his Catholic Majesty's sentiments on Georgia, 117; divides territory held by English into three categories, 118; demands abandonment of Oglethorpe's recent advances prior to the commission, 119; strategic move of to keep the Dutch from making common cause with England, 122; uncomplimentary appraisal of, 124; shifts the onus of responsibility onto Torrenueva, 124; emphasizes pacific intentions of his government, 139; awakes from a lethargy, 141; takes exception to inclusion of Georgia "in South Carolina," 143, 148, 149, 158; insists upon Spanish right to suspend the *asiento* contract, 147; falls under influence of Uztáriz, 148; points to the beam in the English eye, 162

Lauder, merchants' petitions from against the Convention of Pardo, 153
Laurie, Captain Thomas of Pennsylvania, 195
Layssequilla, Don Joseph de, 6, 75, 163
Leeward Islands, in War of Jenkins' Ear, 192
Leman, Ensign, accompanies Oglethorpe to Coweta, 221
Leso, Don Blas, fortifies Cartagena, 205
Limerick, Lord, 154
Limits, 143, 169, 231, 235; disputes concerning referred to Europe, 47; armistice on of Georgia-Florida, 54; delineation of, 96; of Georgia, 112; of Florida, 115, 170; ideas of a convention to settle, 135; Carolina-Florida dispute over, 141; alleged priority of, 170
Linch, Thomas, reports naval preparations in Havana, 65; depositions of concerning Miguel Wall, 65
Lisbon, 78
Litchfield, convoys troops to Ruatan, 217
Logwood, trade in, 216
Logwood cutting, 175; along the bays of Campeachy and Honduras, 127-28, 177
London, 140, 153, 201; efforts on foot in, 51; rumors in, 66; merchants in ridicule government, 104; government at considers nomination of military commander for mainland colonies, 111; agitation in, 141; merchants' petitions from against the Convention of Pardo, 156; arms bought in, 202; Geraldino's feverish activity in, 230
London Gazette, Board of Trade advertisements in, 132
Lords Commissioners for Trade and Plantations, 181
Lords of Trade, 9
Lords Proprietors, 164
Louis XIV, mercantilism of, 131
Louisiana, in the Georgia grant, 34
Lovel, Lord, 160
Lower Creeks, 30
Lowther, Lieutenant George, 215; ex-buccaneer, advises the English, 213; reports on Mosquito coast, 216
Ludlow Castle, 215

McCulloch, Captain, commander of a sloop in the *asiento* service, detained in Havana by Güemez y Horcasitas, 63
Mackay, Hugh, 42
Madre la Popa, Convent of, colonial troops scale, 207

Madrid, 109; denies authority of Moral Sánchez to make treaty, 48; suggested seat of the conference on limits, 115

Manijo. 163

Mare clausum, 171

Marque and reprisal, letters of, 175; colonial governors directed to grant commissions of, 188; granted by Oglethorpe, 222

Marqués, Don Francisco Menéndez, heads a diplomatic mission to Carolina, 14

Martha, 83

Martyr, Peter, name of exploited to uphold English claims, 3.

Maryland, 185, 186, 196, 198-99, 201; illicit commerce from, 128; offers bounties for enlistment, 195; troops of, 199; troops of in War of Jenkins' Ear, 206; governor of thanks Oglethorpe, 228

Massachusetts, 189, 198, 228; military reviews in, 187; offers bounties for enlistment, 195; troops of collect at Boston, 200

Massey, Captain Edward, investigates burning of Fort King George, 27

Massward, Captain, 190

Matanzas River, 225

Mediterranean Sea, Haddock in, 138, 139, 141; Haddock withdrawn from, 162

Meer, Van der, office of conciliation in Madrid, 171; encourages Spain, 171

Merchant Adventurers, 156

Mexico, troops from to aid in crushing Georgia, 63; viceroy of called upon to aid in defense of St. Augustine, 87; mines of prospective booty, 191; trade with, 216

Middleton, Arthur, president of South Carolina Council, 22, 26

Mississippi, 164; Spaniards and French on the, 184

Mobile Bay, 234, 235

Monteleón, Marqués de, Spanish ambassador in London, 35

Montgomery, Sir Robert, 9; Azilia projector, 8; *Discourse* of, 8; designs and undertakings of, 30

Montiano, Governor Manuel de, 51, 188, 225, 227, 229; judges Oglethorpe will be "exceedingly troublesome," 49; deceived by Oglethorpe, 228

Montijo, Cristóbal Gregorio Portocarrero Count of, 6, 75, 113, 148, 163; ambassador at London, 87; death of, 96; "a double in cases that embarrassed him," 114; informs Keene that Spanish officials had not instructed Geraldino, 114; keen discernment of, 114; investigates Geraldino's conduct, 117; reasonable disposition of, 124; sums up both sides, 133; expresses willingness to submit the question of depredations, to commissaries, 135; points to the beam in the English eye, 162; president of the Council of the Indies, 177

Montijo, Countess of, 88

Montrose, merchants' petitions from against the Convention of Pardo, 156

Moore, Robert, 160; wishes to be rid of Georgia, 150

Moosa, garrison of, 224, 225

Moral Sánchez, Governor Don Francisco, 37, 48, 87, 88, 120; suspects Dempsey, 37; buys arms for the Florida Indians, 38; hopes to desolate St. Simons, 38; examines Major Richards, 40; reported hanged for being duped by Dempsey and Oglethorpe, 48; frequently reports English inroads, 86

Morgan, Sir Henry, 188, 214, 216

Morris, Governor Lewis, of New Jersey, 189, 198, 202; complains of contemptuous British attitude towards Americans, 215

Morro, Castle, 65

Mosquito coast, Lowther's report of, 216

Mosquito Indians, 215; British attempt to incite insurrection of, 216; alliance with, 217

Mount Vernon, erected by Lawrence Washington, 219

Murray, Captain James, spikes Baradera fascine battery, 206

Murray, William Earl of Mansfield, sums up depredations of Spain on behalf of the merchants, 155-56

Musgrove, Captain John, 30

Nairne, Captain Thomas, 10; map of, 28

Nassau, depositions made out at Nassau, 65

Navigation, 137-38, 143; 170, 172; security of, 83; freedom of, 133, 146, 171

Navigation Acts, 131

Negroes, 202, 208, 214, 215; proposed use of in Wall attack's on Georgia, 62; in War of Jenkins' Ear, 192, 204; use of at Cartagena, 206; disposition of to scamper off, 206; of South Carolina rebel, 222

New Brunswick, troops collect at, 200

Newcastle, Duke of, 20, 21, 22, 25, 28, 29, 30, 36, 59, 66, 69, 70, 71, 72, 74, 88, 90, 91, 96, 98, 99, 100, 117, 119, 120, 121, 137, 139, 142, 156, 165, 178, 190, 193, 198, 199, 217, 231, 234; makes non-committal reply about Fort King George, 23; informed of Don Miguel Wall's movements, 58; informed of Spanish designs on Georgia, 66; hopes to countermand Wall expedition through instances of Keene, 66; urges that Indians be kept in alliance, 66; orders Keene to make strong representations to Spain against Wall expedition, 66; temperate course of memorial of, 68; repugnance of for Georgia, 74; shows less readiness to preserve harmony, 74; "manifest neglect of," 86; urges appointment of Geraldino, 96; declares Oglethorpe's orders will protect Spain, 99; realizes ministry cannot back down on Georgia, 105; at times virtual prime minister during Walpole era, 105; influence carries fourteen extreme royalist members of Parliament, 105; shows more firmness and more unequivocal assurance than had been his wont, 105; denies mention of limits in American Treaty and Treaty of Utrecht, 106; deems English possession of Georgia notorious, 107; shocked by Geraldino, 107; his answer to Geraldino, 109; suggests settlement of boundaries by commissioners, 109; joins Horace Walpole against amicable settlement, 114; requires all British merchants forthwith to withdraw ships and effects from the ports of Spain, 122; an efficient and well-balanced official, 125; influence and preponderance of, 125; control of the extreme royalists by, 125; designates the Board of Trade to receive claims of the British subjects, 132; laments *guarda costas* and accuses Spanish governors, 133; analyzes Anglo-Spanish trade relations, 135; demands punishment for Spanish officials, 135; issues peremptory demands, 135; memorials of, 136; regards the Spanish administration as incomprehensible, 136; calls a halt on the southern frontier, 166; instructs Keene and Castres, 166; asks Keene to determine the number and whereabouts of Spanish troops and ships, 171; suspends conferences in Madrid, 172; offers share in booty for enlistments, 177; goes into the war faction, 179; doubts of about Georgia, 184; directs governors to grant commissions of marque and reprisal, 188; secretary of Southern Department calls upon the governors of the northern colonies to prepare for war, 193; attempts additional recruiting in America, 215

New England, 186, 187, 190, 202; logwood cutters from, 127; illicit commerce from, 128; coast of menaced, 187; troops in War of Jenkins' Ear, 206

Newfoundland, codfishing rights around, 130

New Granada, smuggling in, 175; English supply viceroyalty of, 218

New Hampshire, offers bounties for enlistment, 195

New Haven, 200

New Jersey, 196, 198, 202; defenses of increased, 187; impossibility of negotiating bills of exchange in, 198; troops of collect, 200; troops of in War of Jenkins' Ear, 206; governor of thanks Oglethorpe, 228

New London, Connecticut, 188

New Providence, naval preparations reported in, 65

New Spain, 127; viceroy of, 75, 82

New Treaty of Vienna, 147

New York, 196, 199, 200; illicit commerce from, 128; defense of, 186; military reviews in, 187; coast of menaced, 187; fits out vessels, 187; offers bounties for enlistment, 195; troops of in War of Jenkins' Ear, 206; governor of thanks Oglethorpe, 228

New York City, 200

Nicholson, Governor Francis, 6, 10, 12, 13, 14, 15, 16, 22, 25, 27, 32; fails to adjust dispute over Fort King George, 14; delays compliance with Spanish demands, 21; prepares to defend southern rivers, 34

Nicholson, South Sea Company factor, 81; expulsion recommended by Geraldino, 63

North America, 100; loyalty of, 194; forces raised in, 206; death of soldiers from, 211

North Carolina, 186, 199, 200, 201; defenses of increased, 187; impossibility of negotiating bills of exchange in, 198; emission of bills frustrated by the imperial government in North Carolina, 202; troops of in War of Jenkins' Ear, 206; governor of thanks Oglethorpe, 228

Northern Colonies, 184, 188, 215; their vital part in the War of Jenkins' Ear,

191; governors of called upon to prepare for war, 193; recruiting in, 195; problem of desertion in, 198-99; troops from in English command, 206
Nova Colonia, 70
Nova Scotia, 192; levies in not permitted during War of Jenkins' Ear, 194

"Observations," formulation of English arguments, 18, 22, 29, 155
Ochee Town, 221
Ogle, Sir Chaloner, 216
Ogle, Governor Samuel, 199, 208, 212; recommends appropriations for the purchase of arms, 186
Oglethorpe, James, 11, 17, 31-33, 39, 41, 43, 46, 48, 50, 51, 52, 60, 69, 70, 73, 74, 86, 90, 94, 96, 99, 101, 103, 118, 119, 140, 189, 221, 223, 226, 234, 235; arguments for English title, 4; designs and undertakings of, 30; Indian diplomacy of, 31; chairman of the "Goals" committee of the House of Commons, 32; personality and early career of, 32-33; a member of the Society for the Propagation of the Gospel in Foreign Parts, 33; deputy-governor of the Royal African Company, 33; wordly aims of, 33; imperialistic nature of, 34; interest in Georgia, 36; buccaneering spirit of, 36; determines to colonize to the Altamaha, 36; determines to fortify islands beyond St. Simon, 36; insists on St. Johns as Georgia boundary, 36; writes conciliatory letter to Moral Sánchez, 37; encroachments of irritate Spaniards, 38; backs his claim to the St. Johns with arms, 38; sends a piragua to St. Johns, 38; presses Fort St. George to completion, 38; cunningly exaggerates his strength, 41; confuses the Spaniards with luxuries and kindness, 42; puts his case to the Trustees, 44; draws up treaty of 1736, 47; voted thanks of the Trustees, 48; activities become a thorn in the flesh of Walpole ministry, 49; "Commander of the English Colonies," shirking-and-delaying tactics of, 49; to be made commander-in-chief of the southern forces, 50; agrees to evacuate Fort St. George, 52; instructions of, 53; dissimulation in plan of, 54; buccaneering spirit of, 54; makes anxious overtures to the mainland colonies seeking reinforcements, 60; reports made to, 64; return of to England, 67; delays answer to Geraldino's memorial, 68; in London a thorn in the side of the Spanish ambassador, 73; exploits rumors about Spanish expedition against Georgia, 73; commands king's forces in Georgia and South Carolina, 74; proposed commission of, 80; promises to take St. Augustine or "leave his bones before its walls," 85; spends money for border defense, 86; lays claim to the St. Johns, 86; voted twenty-six thousand pounds, 87; departure of for Carolina, 88; return of to England in 1737, 94; appears before the Trustees and announces good correspondence established with governor at St. Augustine, 94; arrival of embarrasses representatives of Spain, 97; causes anxiety to the ministry, 98; ingratiates himself with Parliament and secures an appropriation of ten thousand pounds, 98; consummate craftiness of, 99; solicits a regiment, 100; exploits Savy-Patiño menace, 100; appointed commander-in-chief of the troops of Carolina and Georgia, 100; complained of, 103; has sharp words with Walpole, 103-4; forces a crisis by demanding £30,000, 104; tires of being Don Quixote for Georgia, 104; proposes general colonial militia and is named General of the Forces of South Carolina and Georgia, 104; keeps vigil over the Cabinet Council, 104; a connecting link between the government and Trustees, 105; crown assumes a tone of righteousness for, 107; voyage of, 109, 111, 115; appointment of not to be taken as a cause for alarm, 112; admits his intentions of making the St. Johns River the southern boundary of his march colony, 119; names the forts built in Georgia, 119; undertakes without success to convince the Spaniards that Fort St. George was on the Altamaha, 120; confuses Fort King George with Fort St. George, 120; departure of dark prospect for the opposition, 123; theory of effective occupation, 136-37, 173; accused by Geraldino of falsifying, 140; instructed to do "nothing contrary to the treaties," 141; regiment of ordered to Georgia, 178; orders Indians to annoy the Spanish, 188; projected trip of to Coweta, 188; advised to hold himself in readiness to join Cathcart, 193-94; wins against odds, 220; goes to Coweta, 221; smokes Calu-

met, 221; drinks Faskey, 221; lies sick with fever at Augusta, 222; perplexed by privateering commission of Rhode Island, 222; grants letters of marque and reprisal, 222; visits Charles Town, 223; appeals to home government, 223; besieges St. Augustine, 225; erects batteries on Anastasia Island, 225; retreats from St. Augustine, 225; returns to Frederica from siege of St. Augustine, 225; strengthens fortifications on St. Simons Island, 226; death of falsely reported, 227; heralded as savior of the mainland colonies, 228; attempts to provoke the Spaniards, 229; reinforced by men from Virginia, 229; retires to Westminster, 230; success of his shirking-and-delaying tactics, 235

Oglethorpe-Moral Sánchez Treaty, 97-98, 105, 119-20, 135; Spanish disapproval of, 70; disavowed, 99

"Oglethorpians," 33; among Trustees, 123

Ohio, 234

"Old Grog." *See* Vernon

Order of Bath, tardiness of the government in conferring upon Keene, 125

Ossabaw, Spain demands restoration of, 149

Oviedo y Valdés, Gonzalo Fernández de, name of exploited to uphold English claims, 3

Oxford, Robert Harley Earl of, signs *asiento* contract, 128

P*acte de famille*, 122, 146, 171, 175, 229; attempted exploitation of by Spain, 123; casts gloomy shadow, 144; renewed by Elizabeth Farnese, 230

Palmer, Captain John, raid of restores English prestige, 32

Pamphleteering, 178, 180, 181, *passim*

Panama, 192, 212; campaign of, 215

Pardo, El, Convention of, 33, 75, 84, 123, 128, 141, 146, 149, 150, 154, 156, 167, 176, 184, 222, 233; signed, 142; second article of, 147, 155; ratification of, 147; debated in Parliament, 150; political nature of treatment of, 155; vehement attacks upon, 156; pamphleteering about, 158; passed by the Lords, carried into the House of Commons, 161; mobbish clamor against, 162; doomed, 172; concluded, 177

Parliament, 69, 86, 100, 110, 144, 153, 154, 155, 181, 182; opposition of in dispute over Georgia, 121; vehement resolution of against depredations, 138; votes £3,750,000 for combating injuries, 144; debate on Convention of Pardo, 150, 154; Georgia and opposition politics in, 152; agitation against Spain in, 177

Parma, problem of complicates negotiations, 26

Paterson, William, Darién scheme of, 9; adventurous speculator, 126

Patiño, Don Joseph, Secretary of State for Marine and Indies, 55, 56, 81, 87, 90, 95, 109, 110, 119, 159; calls upon Wall to come to Madrid, 56; assured of Don Miguel's grasp of Georgia affairs, 57; supported by the English, 70; death of, 71, 75; project of suspended, 76; respite resulting from the death of, 76; original plan of, 82; death of halts hostile plans, 82; attempt of against the existence of Georgia, 84; especially militant nature of, 87; instructs Geraldino to protest against Oglethorpe's expansion of Georgia, 88; project of opportunely comes into the hands of the English government, 95; plans revealed from all quarters, 98, 99; his plan to proceed *a des voyes de fait*, 108

Paulo, Diego, 40

Paz, Marqués de la, 27

Peace of Aix-la-Chapelle, 230. *See also* Treaty of Aix-la-Chapelle

Peace of 1721, 130

Peace of Utrecht, 128, 130. *See also* Treaty of Utrecht

Pelham, Henry, forward in affairs of Georgia, 104

Pelham-Holles, Thomas, 16. *See also* Newcastle, Duke of

Pembroke, Henry Earl of, forward in affairs of Georgia, 104

Peña, Lieutenant Don Diego, heads diplomatic mission to Coweta, 30

Penn, Sir William, lesson of, 191-92; Cromwell's instructions to, 192

Pennsylvania, 197, 198, 201, 202; illicit commerce from, 128; war preparations in, 186; dominated by the Quakers, 197; troops in War of Jenkins' Ear, 206; governor of thanks Oglethorpe, 228

Pensacola, 234; fortified, 10

Perth Amboy, troops collect at, 200

Peterborow, Lord, Queen Anne's instructions to, 192

Peyton, Captain Sir Yelverton, 224; ordered to convoy Oglethorpe's regiment to Georgia, 178; no longer

willing to hazard his fleet, 225
Philadelphia, 199, 201, 202; burning of, 190
Philip II, King of Spain, 180
Philip III, King of Spain, takes Jamestown lightly, 7
Philip V, King of Spain, 230; seized with new sense of dignity, 130
Picolata, 87, 223; fortress at, 51; attacked by Dunbar, 223
Pitt, William, bitterly attacks the Convention of Pardo, 156, 184; assails the Convention of Pardo, 177; leads attack on Walpole, 181
Placentia, problem of, 26
Playa Grande, Vernon anchors at, 205
Pohoia, king of the Floridas, 43; threatened, 43
Point Judith, 188
Point Quartel, 225
Pope, Alexander, cited, 178
Popple, Henry, map of, 164
Porto Bello, 212; attacked, 28, 127; victory at, 181; capture of, 204; project to land at, 215
Port Mahon, surrender of rumored, 16
Porto Rico, 127; Anglo-American plan to seize, 182
Port Royal, 192, 204; smuggling at, 127
Port Royal Harbor, 4
Portsmouth, England, English fleet at, 97
Portsmouth, N. H., 188
Portugal, Keene departs from, 231
Potosí, 177
Pozobueno, Don Jacinto Marqués de, 6, 12, 14, 17, 18, 19, 20, 22, 35; passes vigorous memorial on Carolina expansion, 12; vigorous office of, 16
Pretender, feared, 156
Primo de Rivera, José, 24; erects post to maintain prestige of Spain among Lower Creeks, 30
Prince Frederick, South Sea Company ship, seized, 129
Prince of Wales, 179; sides with war faction and Trustees, 103; opponent of the government, 104
Privateers, 190, 191; ships seized by, 188
Privy Council, considers the proposition of the Trustees of Georgia that a regiment of infantry be formed immediately for the defense of Georgia, 99; decides "not to give way to the menaces of Spain," 103-4
Proprietors, 9
Providence, island of, 170; vessels from menaced, 61; possession of debated, 170
Providence, Rhode Island, troops collect at, 200
Province House, at Charles Town, 31
Pulteney, William, attempts to ruin the Convention of Pardo by a *coup de théatre*, 156-57; leads attack on Walpole, 181. *See also* Bath, Earl of
Pupo. *See* Fort St. Francis de Popa
"Purple friend," Keene's leading spy, 97
Purry, Jean Pierre, designs and undertakings of, 30

Quadra, La. *See* La Quadra
Quakers, 185; obstructions in War of Jenkins' Ear, 186
Queen Anne's War, American participation in, 192
Quintana, Don Joseph de la, 6, 75, 163, 167; uncomplimentary appraisal of, 124; Spanish plenipotentiary after the Convention of Pardo, 148; instructed to negotiate on basis of American Treaty, 149; succeeds Torrenueva as Secretary of State for the Indies and Marine, 161

Ramusio, Giovanni Battista, name of exploited to uphold English claims, 3
Rebecca, 144, 176
Recruiting, 195-98, 211; enlistment of indentured servants, 197
Regalia, Marqués de la, 6, 75
Represalia, 139
Revenge, sloop, 189; *Journal of*, 187
Rhode Island, 190, 199, 202; military reviews in, 187; offers bounties for enlistment, 195; recruiting in, 195-96; troops from collect at Providence, 200; troops of in War of Jenkins' Ear, 206
Richards, Major William (?), of Purrysburgh, 37, 38, 41; takes Charles Dempsey, 36; carried to St. Augustine, 38; arrested by Spaniards, 39; examined by Moral Sánchez, 40
Right of discovery, 3
Río de la Cacha, 127
Roderick Random, 203
Rosso, Don Ignacio, alarmed at the martial appearance of the golden isles, 40
Royal African Company, Oglethorpe deputy-governor of, 33
Royal Exchange, war celebrations at, 179
Ruatan (Roatan), in the Bay of Hon-

duras, 217; proposed settlement of Americans in, 216

S**achmast Point, 188
St. Augustine,** 3, 4, 14, 20, 24, 29, 38, 50, 51, 59, 66, 82, 94, 164, 165, 185, 188, 220, 223, 224, 226, 227, French menace to, 10; within English grant, 4-5, 18, 19-20; Council of War in, 48; increase of garrison at, 49; Spanish designs at, 53; people of agog over pending arrival of a man-of-war with five hundred soldiers, 60; presidial soldiers suggested to attack Georgia, 64; stories in newspapers concerning the nine hundred men sent to, 80; defenseless condition of, 87; fortress near attacked, 88; continual incursions from Georgia, 89; Anglo-American plan to seize, 182; Spanish strength at, 221; designs on, 223; Castle of, 224; defenses of, 224; beseiged, 225
St. George Island, 51; fort on, 36; default of the English at, 52. *See also* San Juan
St. Gil, Marqués de, 140
St. Helena Sound, Spanish forts at, 46; Arredondo asks withdrawal of English to, 52
St. Helen's, English sail from, 216
St. James's, 234; Oglethorpe presents himself at, 49; war celebrations at, 179
St. Johns Island. *See* St. George Island
St. Johns River, 5, 40, 46, 52, 53, 54, 164, 184, 223, 224; insisted upon as southern boundary of Georgia, 36; English have no knowledge of at first sight, 86; southern boundary of Georgia, 86; English agree to vacate the fort on, 98; Fort St. George stands athwart the navigation of, 119; legality of the English title to, 120; northern limit of Florida in Oglethorpe's eyes, 120; Oglethorpe sweeps down to, 223
St. John the Baptist, Feast of, postpones conferences in 1739, 169
St. Marys River, 28, 235
St. Rupert's Bay, 204
St. Simons Island, 11, 32, 34, 38, 226, 227; Oglethorpe's title to called into question, 44; Arredondo-Oglethorpe conference at, 51; Spaniards assail harbor of in battle formation, 227
St. Simons Sound, inhabitants of to be denied belligerent status by the Spaniards, 53
St. Thomas, smuggling depot, 128

Salgrado, Don Antonio, retakes Fort Moosa, 225
Salsburg, Archbishop of, 56
Salzburgers, abandonment of decried, 159
Salter, John, depositions of concerning Miguel Wall, 65
Sánchez, Governor. *See* Moral Sánchez
San Felipe, Spain demands restoration of, 149
San Francisco de Popa. *See* Fort St. Francis de Popa and Pupo
San Juan, island of, 52; Spain demands restoration of, 149
San Luis, 76, 80; ordered to return Wall to Spain, 64
San Luis, castle of in Cartagena, 205
San Marcos de Apalache, 51, 59
Santa Catalina (Catarina), Spain demands restoration of, 149
Santa Elena, 20, 24, 165
Santa Helena, Spain demands restoration of, 149
Santa María, Spain demands restoration of, 149
Santa Teresa, case of, 139
Santiago de Cuba, 212, 213, 214, 218; English expedition near, 213; English march on, 214
Santo Domingo, mission of, 11
Sarah, 189
Sardinia, 231
Savannah, 10, 34
Savannah River, 26, 30, 34, 221, 232
Savy, John, 221; alias Don Miguel Wall, 55, 58. *See also* Wall, Don Miguel
Searching, 134, 135, 138, 171, 182; Spaniards agree to abandon, 153
Seashore, 214
Seepeycoffee, Creek Indian, 31; visits St. Augustine, 30
Seven Years' War, 234
Seville, conferences at, 118; commissaries at on April 24, 1732, 167
Shaftesbury, Anthony Ashley Cooper Earl of, 154
Shannon, Henry Boyle Lord, Queen Anne's instructions to, 192
Shelton, Richard, secretary to Carolina proprietors, 28
Shoreham, 226; convoys languid and infirm back to mainland colonies, 219
Sir Walter Raleigh, replayed, 179
Six Nations, growing menace of the, 185
Smollett, Tobias, Cartagena campaign in *Roderick Random*, 203
Smuggling, 126, 127, 130, 175; Spanish governors issue instructions against, 131

Society for the Propagation of the Gospel in Foreign Parts, Oglethorpe a member of, 33
South Carolina, 17, 21, 103, 147, 226, 232; Scotch settlers in, 8; Council of, 22, 24; strength of, 65; possible Negro riots in, 66; increases presents to Indians, 66; precautionary measures of approved, 66; fever of anxiety in, 75; levies in not permitted during War of Jenkins' Ear, 194; troops of defend home base, 220; memorial deploring defenseless condition of, 220; precarious situation in, 223; invasion of, 226; imperiled at St. Simons, 226
South Sea Bubble, excitement occasioned by compared to that of the Convention of Pardo, 157
South Sea Company, 95, 126, 128, 129, 148, 171, 218; ship of, 79; factors of report Spanish plans, 80; holds *asiento de negros*, 129; claims of against Spain, 129; resorts to a ruse for smuggling, 130; connection of English officials with, 130; voluminous papers of, 133; debt of £68,000, 139; affairs of complicate negotiations, 150; growing discontent of, 174; disproportionate returns of, 174-75; defended, 177; counter claim of £68,000 against, 178; renews *asiento* contract, 233; awarded £100,000, 233
South Sea Stock, collapse of, 9
Sovereignty, determination of in America, 3
Spain, 24, 171; Royal Council of convenes to consider Oglethorpe's arrival at the St. Johns, 98; king of would be contented with the southern side of the river Altamaha, 160; urged by France "no longer to have patience" with the English, 162; refuses to pay £95,000, 166; threatens to suspend *asiento*, 166; irreconcilable position of, 166, 167, 170; withholds payment of £95,000, 178; loss in ships, 211; Indians disparage the claims of, 222; domestic situation in, 230
Spaniards, 29, 35; their principle of *mare clausum*, 3, 4, 5, 171; give sanctuary to slaves, 26; rendered desperate by extreme aggressiveness of English in Georgia, 35; caution their plenipotentiaries against the English method of "measuring ground by the sky," 35; ardently desire to secure this amicable settlement, 115; declare absolute compliance with treaties the only acceptable basis of negotiations, 117; bungle their efforts to exploit English partisan intrigue, 137; agree to abandon searching, 153; raids of feared, 187; panic among, 188; try to debauch the friendly Indians, 220; intend to attack Savannah, 220; repelled by Oglethorpe, 227; ambushed, 227
Spanish America, proposed liberation of, 192
Spanish Empire, priority of, 1
Spanish Main, Jamaican smuggling on, 127-29
Spence, dispatched with the Spanish admiral's flag, 207
Spotswood, Governor Alexander, 9, 10, 191, 194, 199; named Quartermaster-General, 193; succeeded by Gooch, 201
Sprague, family, in War of Jenkins' Ear, 195
Squirrel, sloop, 189
Stanhope, Colonel James, envoy to Spain begins to speak in bulk of English claims, 131
Stanhope, William, English ambassador at Madrid, 12
Stert, Arthur, commissioner in 1730 for settling Carolina boundary question, 29, 132; begins conversations with Geraldino, 139; acceptance of the plan proposed by, 141
Stirling, merchants' petitions from against the Convention of Pardo, 156
Stone, Andrew, secretary to the Duke of Newcastle, 93
Strafford, 213
Success, case of, 139
Survey of America, by De Brahm, 235
Symond, Oglethorpe returns to America in, 36

Talaje, Lugar de, Spain demands restoration of, 149
Talapooses, 85, 87
Tartar, sloop, 188
Tasker, Benjamin, chairman of Maryland assembly, 202
Tassel, agent of the South Sea Company, 81; expulsion recommended by Geraldino, 63
Texas, in the Georgia grant, 34
Thomas, Benjamin F., 195
Thomas, Governor George of Pennsylvania, 201; defensive measures of, 185; sanctions the Duke of Newcastle's instructions, 197
Thomas, family, in War of Jenkins' Ear, 195
Thomson, Captain William, convoys Don Miguel Wall to Europe, 55

Tiberon Bay, Vernon anchors at, 205
Tilbury, 213
Tolomato, mission of, 11
Tolson, Lieutenant, falsely reports death of Oglethorpe, 227
Tomochichi, travels with Oglethorpe to London, 43; temporizing influence of, 43
Torrenueva, Matheo Pablo Marqués de, 52, 69, 70, 81, 82, 97, 113, 114, 120, 136, 137; disapproves Oglethorpe-Moral Sánchez Treaty, 67; president of the Council of the Indies, 68; coached on Georgia by La Quadra, 68; denies preparations at Havana, 68; gives orders for watching Don Miguel Wall, 78; characterized, 97; takes over responsibility for American affairs, 113; informs Geraldino of the willingness of the Spanish government to settle limits by commissaries, 115; effusive in his professions to avoid coolness or interruption, 115; demands evacuation and demolition of forts built by Oglethorpe, 116; orders of disobeyed by Geraldino, 117; baffled, 118; receives responsibility from La Quadra, 124; appraised by Keene, 124
Torres, Don Rodrigo de, 212; fleet of, 213; menace of at Havana, 214
Tortuga, 175
Towers, Henry, 152; labors to defend Georgia, 150
Townsend, Lord, 191
Tracy, Robert, trustee, 160
Trade, 126, 134, 182
Treaty of Aix-la-Chapelle, 173, 230, 234; provides restoration of all conquests, 233
Treaty of Aranjuez, 233
Treaty of Münster, 1
Treaty of Paris, 7
Treaty of Peace and Commerce, 1
Treaty of 1715, cancels four-year renewal of the *asiento* contract, 233
Treaty of Seville, 28, 29, 33, 70, 96
Treaty of 1667, 134
Treaty of 1670, precludes mutual trading in America, 134
Treaty of Utrecht, 2, 5, 90, 93, 103, 115; defied by Jamaicans, 128
Trelawney, Governor Edward of Jamaica, 192, 212, 213, 216, 217, 226; admits frustration, 216
Treviño, Don Fernando, secretary to Spanish embassy, 55, 56, 57; reports Wall ready to go to Madrid, 56
Trevor, Captain, upbraided by Vernon, 212
Trustees, Board of, 47, 48, 49, 66, 74, 79, 85, 90, 96, 98, 101, 104, 110, 120, 150, 151, 152, 153, 154, 155, 161, 165, 178, 183, 222, 232, 233; opposition members, 34; treaties of peace laid before, 48; delay answer to Geraldino's memorial, 68; alarmed, 69; uneasy, 71; addressed by Don Miguel Wall, 76-78; use Wall's information to strengthen their pretensions and to claim the support of the government, 81; power of, 86; fails to pay for forts in Spanish territory, 86; soon assert forts were "in Carolina," 86; selfish whims of, 91; defend sites of forts, 91-93; deny ordering construction of forts, 93; militant activity of, 98; petition Walpole, 100; decide to present a memorial supplicating forces, 105; letter from makes good impression at the council meeting, 105; virtually frame answer to Geraldino, 112; "Oglethorpians" among, 123; resolve to ruin the Convention of Pardo, 150; sell their support of the Convention of Pardo, 151; petition for £20,000, 152; attempt to prevent the surrender of any part of Georgia, 153; endeavor to filibuster in board meeting, 155; try to exempt Georgia from discussion by plenipotentiaries, 155; considered mere tools of the ministry, 156; petition of to Parliament, 160; bind England not to relinquish territory, 160; seek to win the Indians, 220; lay their case before the Duke of Bedford, 231. *See also* Georgia, Trustees of
Tuscany, Duchy of, 142; problem of, 26; English refusal to aid in seizure of, 134
Two Brothers, brigantine, 55
Tyrawly, James O'Hara Lord, sends Savy to England as prisoner, 79
Tyry, agent of the South Sea Company, takes place of Geraldino as agent for the affairs of the South Sea Company, 97

"Uchees and Talapoosees," English fort reported among, 85
Utrecht Gazette, reports anti-Spanish agitation of the Trustees, 232
Uztáriz, Don Casimiro, economist and First Commissioner of the War Office, 124; gains influence over La Quadra, 148
Uztáriz, Gerónimo, 130; his attempt at the rejuvenation of a nationalistic

commercial policy, 130-31; appropriates mercantilism of Colbert, 131

Vanderdussen, Alexander, 225; South Carolina regiment under, 223
Varas y Valdés, Governor Francisco de, charged with guarding Don Miguel Wall, 78, 79; charged with case of Wall, 79
Venables, Robert, lesson of, 191-92; Cromwell's instructions to, 192
Vera Cruz, 63, 82, 192, 218
Vernon, Admiral Edward, 181, 188, 192, 203, 205, 208, 212, 213, 214, 218, 226; arrests Don Miguel Wall, 83; expedition against Spanish West Indies under, 191, 192; engages in debate with Wentworth, 203; trusts only a part of the Americans, 208; American regiment presents a memorial to, 210; drops anchor in Walthenam Bay, July 18, 1741, 213; decides to quit Cumberland Harbor, 214; attempts additional recruiting in America, 215; builds huts for the suffering, 215; arrives at Porto Bello, 216; ordered to return to England, 216; seizes Spanish quicksilver ships, 218; conducts trade negotiations with Vera Cruz, 218; fights and trades with the Spaniards simultaneously, 218; delays the Spaniards in the West Indies, 223; issues instructions to Captain Roderick of the *Shoreham*, 226
Vernon, James, 101
Villarias, Marqués de, 163, 172. *See also* La Quadra
Virginia, 100, 199; Council of stands ready to aid Oglethorpe on Marshes of Glyn, 61; military reviews in, 187; Capes of rendezvous of Americans, 197; grants £5,000, 202; troops of in War of Jenkins' Ear, 206; governor of thanks Oglethorpe, 228
Virgin Islands, in War of Jenkins' Ear, 192

Wade, General George, 160
Wager, Sir Charles, 139; first Lord of the Admiralty, 189
Waldegrave, James Earl, British ambassador at Paris, 122, 161; steps of in Paris, 122
Wall, Don Miguel, 55-84, 110, 159; allowed to return to Spain, 53; flees debts and murder charge in South Carolina, 55; marries daughter of Captain Greene, 55; alleges religious dispute with Oglethorpe, 55; offers to reduce English settlements to limits of the Treaty of Utrecht, 56; exhibits his half-tattooed body, 56; native of Ireland, goes with dignity to Madrid, 57; early life and connections of, 57; designs of reported by French officer in Madrid, 58; sent to Cuba, 59; knowledge of coasts of South Carolina, Georgia, and Florida, 59; plan of his attack, 60; arrives at El Puerto Príncipe and Santiago de Cuba, 61; reception of at Havana, 61; plan of not feasible, 61; judged incapable and unworthy, 61, 63; drunk under table in Santiago, 62; passes for Peter Jac de Tombe, 62; suspicion falls on, 63; ordered back to Spain, 64; treated with respect and followed with suspicion, 64; known as Savy in the Bailey in South Carolina, 65; threatened with incarceration in the Castle Morro, 65; Indian trader in South Carolina, 65; his bustling activity and plotting at Havana, 65; holds blank commissions, 65; admits suspension of his project, 70; blustering, talkative disposition of, 71, 76-78; ordered to Spain, 75; addresses Trustees, 76; reviews his career, 77; escapes from Cádiz to Lisbon, 78, 79; offers to tell Trustees of Georgia how to take St. Augustine, 79; addresses long letter to the Duke of Newcastle, 79; proposes to disclose Spanish plans, 80; ordered to return to Spain, 80; offers to reproduce papers signed by Patiño, 81; mysterious proceedings of, 82; facility afforded to make his escape, 82; international adventurer, treachery of, 83; made a captain lieutenant of American troops, 83; under sentence of death in South Carolina, 83; arrested by Admiral Vernon, 83; attempt of against the existence of Georgia, 84
Walpole, Horace, 156; warns against *pacte de famille*, 33; called upon to aid in frustrating Oglethorpe, 100; regards Georgia question as settled, 113; probably emboldened by the Dutch, 114; moves for address of thanks for the king's negotiations, 156
Walpole, Robert, 34, 53, 120; ministry of, 49, 59, 73, 81, 82, 85, 88, 90, 101, 111, 112, 117, 133, 139, 142, 144, 150, 151, 152, 160, 161, 163; susceptibility of ministry to parliamentary necessity, 51; ministry of reported hostile to Georgia, 69; plia-

bility of, 79; interviewed by Spaniards on activities of Trustees, 81; regards Georgia as of no advantage, 86; looks upon Georgia as a sample of American independence, 86; supine disposition of government of, 88; pretends to support limits of the treaties, 91; informs Geraldino Georgia is a Parliamentary project, 94; refuses to receive Geraldino's memorial, 102; terrified by apprehensions of the Spaniards falling out with England, 103; backwardness in affairs of Georgia, 104; natural timidity of, 104-5; ministry of its temporizing and subserviency to the Trustees of Georgia, 111; ministry of favors an amicable arrangement through commissaries, 112; pacifism of ministry of, 117; easy, good-natured, and desirous of peace, 124-25; standards of political corruption in age of, 125; relentless political machine of, 125; a master of groups, 125; desires the fruits but not the costs of war, 132; willingness to appoint commissaries, 140; calls Gentlemen of Georgia his Enemies, 151; agrees to sanction Georgia appropriation, 152; swears the Spanish shall not have Georgia, 153; his political approach to Georgia, 154; accused of deceiving the people, 159; berated by Captain Dempsey, 163; caught in the anti-Spanish agitation, 175; enemies of in Parliament, 176; engulfed, 178; gives Vernon instructions to sail against Spanish America, 179; pathetic figure of in 1739-1742, 180; resignation of, 181

Walthenam Bay, 213

War of Austrian Succession, 123, 173, 181, 230

War of Hanover, 28

War of Jenkins' Ear, 84, 123, 174, 190; beginning of, 173; Anglo-Spanish affairs on the eve of, 174; North American participation in, 181; vital part of Northern Colonies in, 191; American officers in, 194; legislation of the English colonies in, 201-3; significance of, 229

War of Spanish Succession, 128

Warren, Captain, ordered to land sailors on Anastasia Island, 224

Washington, family of Virginia, in War of Jenkins' Ear, 195

Washington, Captain Lawrence, 214; spikes Baradera fascine battery, 206; decorated with Vernon Porto Bello medal, 219; returns to Virginia, 219; marries Anne Fairfax, 219; erects Mt. Vernon, 219

Watch Hill, 188

Welles, Sir William, 4

Wentworth, Thomas, 83, 192, 203, 207, 212, 214, 216, 217, 226; defeat of, 201; engages in debate with Vernon, 203; commander after the death of Lord Cathcart at St. Rupert's Bay, 204; returns of, 205; pauses at Cartagena, 208; persuaded to advance, 208; betrayed by a renegade Genoese, 209; defeated, orders Wolfe's marines to cover the retreat, 209; American regiment presents a memorial to, 210; criticized for not furnishing infirmaries, 212; makes charges against the colonials, 214; attempts additional recruiting in America, 215; ordered to return to England, 216

West Indies, 171, 186, 201; Yankee skippers and interlopers in, 182

Westminister, Oglethorpe retires to, 230

White, John, 160; wishes to be rid of Georgia, 150

Whitefield, George, 184

Whiteford, Hugh, 204

Whitehall Evening Post, reports anti-Spanish agitation of the Trustees, 232

William, King, 127

Wilson, James, depositions of concerning Miguel Wall, 65

Windham, Captain, calls upon Virginia ships to repair to southern coasts, 64

Winslow, Captain, 215

Wolfe, Colonel, marines of, 208

Wood Street, war celebrations at, 179

Woolball, capture of, 26; seizure of, 129

Wyatt, Captain, brings ominous information from Havana, 60

Wyndham, Sir William, probably not a party to Bolinbroke's and Pulteney's scheme, 157

Wynyard, Colonel, repulsed at San Lázaro, 209; tragedy of, 209

Yamacraw Bluff, 34

Yamasees, 31; combine against the English, 27

Yamasee War, 7, 22

Yuchis, 85, 87, 106; English reported building a fort among, 89

Zacatecas, 177

Zápala, Spain demands restoration of, 149

Zúñiga, Don Pedro de, warns against Virginia, 7

www.ingramcontent.com/pod-product-compliance
Lightning Source LLC
Chambersburg PA
CBHW021356290426
44108CB00010B/264